Praise for
The Personality Self-Portrait

"One of the leading figures in developing our modern understanding of personality disorders has turned his attention to the universal personality styles that shape our lives. *The Personality Self-Portrait* makes the best thinking of modern psychiatry available to a wide audience."
—Robert Michels, M.D.,
Professor of Psychiatry and Dean,
Cornell University Medical College

"Eminently readable . . . It tracks the range from personality style to personality disorder and offers well-aimed tips on dealing with each personality type."
—Kenneth Altshuler, M.D.,
Stanton Sharp Professor and Chairman,
Department of Psychiatry, University of Texas
Southwestern Medical Center

"As entertaining as it is well informed and useful. Anyone who reads the book and answers the questionnaire will be fascinated by the complexity of his or her personality."
—Ethel S. Person, M.D., author of
Dreams of Love and Fateful Encounters

"This book is a most welcome departure from the superficiality of much of modern pop-psychology literature. . . . The descriptions are clear, and the advice is solid, practical, and nonpatronizing. Highly recommended."
—Stanley Turecki, M.D.,
author of *The Difficult Child*

The New Personality Self-Portrait

*Why You Think, Work, Love,
and Act the Way You Do*

John M. Oldham, M.D.,
and
Lois B. Morris

BANTAM BOOKS
NEW YORK · TORONTO · LONDON · SYDNEY · AUCKLAND

THE NEW PERSONALITY SELF-PORTRAIT

A Bantam Book / September 1995

Grateful acknowledgment is made for permission to reprint excerpts from the following copyrighted works: *Diagnostic and Statistical Manual of Mental Disorders, Fourth Edition.* By permission of the American Psychiatric Association; © 1994. "Of Weirdoes and Eccentrics" by Pico Iyer. Reprinted by permission; copyright © 1988 Time, Inc. "Richard Harris." Reprinted by permission; © 1987 The New Yorker Magazine, Inc. All rights reserved. "Back in the High Life" by Ron Rosenbaum. Used by permission of the author, copyright © 1988. *Abnormalities of Personality; Within and Beyond the Realm of Treatment* by Michael H. Stone. By permission of W. W. Norton & Company, Inc. Copyright © 1993 by Michael H. Stone.

Book design by MM Design 2000, Inc.

Library of Congress Cataloging-in-Publication Data
Oldham, John M.
    The new personality self-portrait : why you think, work, love, and
act the way you do / John M. Oldham and Lois B. Morris.
        p.   cm.
Rev. ed. of: The personality self-portrait. 1990.
Includes bibliographical references and index.
ISBN 0-553-37393-5
1. Typology (Psychology) 2. Personality disorders. I. Morris,
Lois B. II. Oldham, John M. Personality self-portrait. III. Title.
BF698.3043   1995
155.2′64—dc20   95-12233
                                                                          CIP

Published simultaneously in the United States and Canada

Bantam Books are published by Bantam Books, a division of Bantam Doubleday Dell Publishing Group, Inc. Its trademark, consisting of the words "Bantam Books" and the portrayal of a rooster, is Registered in U.S. Patent and Trademark Office and in other countries. Marca Registrada. Bantam Books, 1540 Broadway, New York, New York 10036.

PRINTED IN THE UNITED STATES OF AMERICA

30 29 28 27 26 25 24 23

For Karen
and
For Susan and Gene

Acknowledgments

Grateful thanks to all our test subjects. By volunteering their time and allowing us to peer into their personalities, they helped us to develop the test that serves as the basis for this book. To Michael First, M.D., and Peggy Gallaher, Ph.D., we offer heartfelt appreciation for their assistance in gathering and interpreting the data that helped us to refine the test and thus to proceed with this new edition.

Contents

Preface to the Second Edition

In 1984, it first occurred to us to devise a system of—and test for—normal personality styles based on the new system for classifying personality disorders that had recently been developed by the American Psychiatric Association, which had never been attempted. We believed then, as now, that the disorders of personality that psychiatrists have identified can be seen as extremes along a continuum of normal, adaptive, individual personality differences. Thus we set out to identify and describe these normal personality styles. Six years later, in 1990, *The Personality Self-Portrait* was published. Little did we imagine how well it would be received and how eagerly it would be applied by researchers, clinicians, human resources departments, teachers, students, individuals wishing to know more about themselves, and even dating services!

We have prepared this new edition of both the book and the test for two principal reasons. For one, the system upon which we had based our first edition has changed. The personality styles represented in our first edition corresponded to the categories of personality disorder published in the American Psychiatric Association's DSM-III-R: the *Diagnostic and Statistical Manual of Mental Disorders* (Third Edition-Revised). The 1994 publication of the fourth edition of the manual, the DSM-IV, brought with it some changes to the personality disorder classifications and diagnostic criteria, which we have reflected in our own schema and revised test in *The New Personality Self-Portrait*.

Changes in this edition also reflect the data we have collected since the original publication. The earlier test was devised primarily as a descriptive tool. Its almost immediate adoption into formal settings necessitated information as to its scientific validity, which was begun at several sites. This new test incorporates results of that initial work, and the process of data collection continues. In addition, we have received valuable feedback from researchers, readers, and mental health professionals throughout the world, to whom we are extremely grateful.

We encourage continued involvement of and reactions from those who wish to use this system. Although the test that appears in this book is intended only for personal use and may not be copied, additional test booklets and software, plus research permission, is available from: Multi-Health Systems, Inc., telephone toll-free 1-800-456-3003 (U.S.) or 1-800-268-6011 (Canada).

JOHN M. OLDHAM, M.D.
LOIS B. MORRIS

The New
Personality Self-Portrait

The Newest Personality System

In this book we present a system for defining your personality style and understanding the particular ways it affects six key domains of your life: your relationships and love life; your work; your self-image; your emotional life; your self-control, impulses, and appetites; and your sense of reality and of spirituality.

The fourteen normal personality-style categories that we present, and the test to determine your individual personality pattern, are derived from the important—some say revolutionary—classification system of personality *disorders* published by the American Psychiatric Association most recently in 1994. This classification system is presented in the "bible" of American psychiatry: the *Diagnostic and Statistical Manual of Mental Disorders, Fourth Edition,* popularly known as the DSM-IV. I have been privileged to play a role in this new classification process. Although Lois Morris and I speak in a mutual voice throughout the following chapters, I'll briefly discuss what the DSM-IV is and how it came about, so that you can better understand the origins of *The New Personality Self-Portrait.*

DIAGNOSTIC LANGUAGES

In the 1994 DSM-IV and its recent predecessors, the DSM-III and DSM-III-R (published in 1980 and 1987, respectively), many of the most prominent clinical and research psychiatrists, psychologists, and epidemiologists in the United States established a more systematic way to diagnose most of the disorders treated by psychiatrists and other mental health professionals. Standard sets of criteria were developed to make possible greater uniformity among clinicians and researchers in their diagnostic terminology.

Prior to 1980, clinicians and researchers spoke a variety of diagnostic languages. For example, a clinician might refer to a patient as depressed, but researchers might disagree with that diagnosis if the patient didn't meet all of the "research diagnostic criteria" that they used for diagnosing depression. Therefore, two research projects on the same condition often yielded conflicting or confusing results because the disorder was defined differently by each research team. Particularly when it came to the fixed patterns of personality that cause lifelong dissatisfaction to so many people, prior to DSM-III there were no criteria agreed upon by either clinicians or the research community. While an individual practitioner might be able to help a patient, he or she might not be able to share information effectively with other clinicians or with clinical researchers.

Although mental health diagnoses were based on extensive clinical wisdom and experience, there was little consistency among professionals in the field. Ironically, with each breakthrough in brain research and the development of psychoactive drugs, the problem became even more complicated. We had a wealth of tantalizing new data, but since we had no unified system to define the mental disorders, we had great difficulty performing reliable research into the causes of the many forms of mental suffering, determining how many people suffered from them, and assessing whether any of the existing treatments worked.

No one could deny that mental suffering existed, or that some individuals could be helped by clinicians using various forms of treatment. By the 1970s, however, psychiatry and the mental health field in general were under increasing pressure from the scientific and research communities to develop a systematic method that would more efficiently and consistently identify and classify the sufferings of hundreds of thousands of individuals who required help.

AT LAST, A COMMON LANGUAGE

The research and development for DSM-III began in 1974. The enormous project was overseen by a task force of psychiatrists and psychologists expert in diagnosis and epidemiology. Reporting to the task force were fourteen advisory committees consisting of clinicians and researchers specializing in all the key areas of psychiatry. Liaison committees with other professional mental health organizations—such as the American Psychological Association and the American College Health Association—worked with the task force to clarify issues, to try to resolve differences in points of view, and to arrive at a consensus about the types of mental and emotional suffering to which people are subject.

During and following the development period, the new classifications were extensively field-tested, after which the categories were modified and refined. An important aspect of these studies consisted of evaluating diagnostic reliability among clinicians. The question was: Using the new criteria, would different clinicians arrive at the same diagnosis of the same patient, or would they offer conflicting opinions, as before? These studies, in which the National Institute of Mental Health played an active role, showed that the DSM-III diagnostic categories were far more reliable than any system used before. Using the new manual, mental health practitioners could independently assess a patient and much more often reach the same diagnosis—a giant step forward.

The new system was approved in 1979 and went into use in 1980. It met with even greater than anticipated success. Although intended for use in the United States, the manual now has been translated into many languages and is consulted worldwide. Continued research, using the new criteria, began quickly to test and further refine this classification system. It was clear from the start that the new system improved our ability to study the causes, preventions, and treatments of the mental ills that afflict so many people.

THE NEW PERSONALITY DISORDERS

Once the new system was in operation, we began to receive feedback on the clinical and research usefulness of the new categories. In 1983, I was asked to serve on the advisory committee to revise the personality disorder diagnoses for the DSM-III-R; after its publication I became a consultant to the work group revising these diagnoses for DSM-IV. Identifying the personality disorders that afflict people and pinpointing the symptomatic traits and behaviors that distinguish the categories proved among the more challenging undertakings for the framers of the manual. Specific psychiatric illnesses (which the DSM-IV calls Axis I disorders), such as major depression, are disordered internal states that come and go; with the new, ultrasophisticated research technology, these disorders are beginning to yield their biological secrets. However, since personality disorders reflect a troubled way of being in the world, it is more difficult (but, as you will see throughout this book, increasingly possible) for "hard science" to come to terms with them. Thus, the personality disorder categories (so-called Axis II disorders) were somewhat more controversial and the clinical and research feedback more mixed than for the affective (mood) disorders.

In 1987, we changed or clarified some of the personality disorder criteria, reduced overlap among categories and inconsistencies within them, and added new categories of disorders that clinicians found common in their practices but had not been represented in the prior manual. Altogether, there were thirteen personality disorders in the DSM-III-R, two of them appearing only in the Appendix of that edition for purposes of further study.

The DSM-IV, published in 1994, made additional refinements and changes based on research resulting from the DSM-III-R. It retained ten of the eleven Axis II personality disorders that had been present in the body of the previous edition, modifying some of the criteria used to diagnose them. At the Axis II work group's recommendation, one disorder (Passive-Aggressive) was moved to the Appendix, because some experts felt that more evidence was needed to justify continuing to use it as an "official" diagnosis.

Meanwhile, a new tentative diagnosis, Depressive personality disorder, made its appearance in the Appendix as well. Surveys of practicing clinicians revealed that they were seeing significant numbers of patients with this condition. But the two personality disorders from the DSM-III-R Appendix—Self-Defeating and Sadistic—were dropped from the manual altogether. As we explain at greater length in Chapters 15 and 16, these two diagnoses were controversial to begin with. Nonetheless, the decision to delete them from DSM-IV had more to do with concern about their inappropriate use in forensic settings than with a strong consensus that these are not "real" disorders. In fact, as psychologist Thomas Widiger, a key DSM-IV consultant, has pointed out, a majority of psychiatrists surveyed in a large study reported seeing patients with Self-Defeating behavior as their primary diagnosis, and a majority of forensic psychiatrists responding in a separate survey reported experience with patients meeting the criteria of Sadistic personality disorder.

In this book we have chosen to include all of the Axis II personality disorder diagnoses included in the Appendix of the DSM-III-R and the Appendix of the DSM-IV, since there remain many experienced clinicians who report seeing patients with each of these disorders. We prefer an over-inclusive stance, which we believe corresponds with the wide range of human behavior and with the broad diversity of personality styles that makes each of us unique.

The process of identifying and refining the categories of mental suffering continues. It is a relief for those of us in the field at last to have a systematic way to identify the disorders that is more objective and free from the theoretical bias that in the past distorted mental health diagnostic systems. Now we hope to learn how many people suffer from these disorders, predict who is likely to do so, study the causes from many theoretical perspectives, pinpoint effective treatments, and comprehend the vastly accumulating body of genetic and biologic data.

TESTING FOR PERSONALITY DISORDERS

Much of the feedback about the personality disorders and their constellations of traits and behaviors results from applying the tests that have been developed to assess them. I participated in the development of one such test, the Personality Disorder Examination (PDE). Much as laboratory tests verify medical diagnoses, the PDE reliably establishes personality disorder diagnoses. The PDE is called a "semi-structured interview." It must be administered and scored by a trained clinician, using his or her professional judgment to evaluate the responses. The PDE is used in many research studies throughout the world, including a large World Health Organization multinational study of personality disorders.

DERIVING ORDER FROM DISORDER

The principles inherent in the DSM-III, DSM-III-R, DSM-IV, and the PDE form the foundation for the personality-style system and the Personality Self-Portrait test that we present in this book. The fourteen personality styles that we identify are the common, utterly human, *non*pathological versions of the extreme, disordered constellations identified in the DSM-III-R and DSM-IV (including those from the Appendix of each edition). To put it another way, much as high blood pressure represents too much of a good thing, the personality disorders are but extremes of normal human patterns, the stuff of which all our personalities are made. Whereas the DSM-III-R and DSM-IV identify categories of disorder, we describe here equivalent categories of orderly human functioning.

Unlike the PDE, our Personality Self-Portrait test is not a tool for the diagnosis of personality disorders. Rather, we have developed it to help you delineate the constituent parts of your personality "order," by which we mean your personality style. Use it to understand who you are and why you behave as you do, and to learn how to strengthen or readjust your pattern. Use it especially to appreciate—and accept—the identifiable differences among us all.

John M. Oldham, M.D.

CHAPTER 1

Who Am I?

UNDERSTANDING INDIVIDUAL DIFFERENCES

How can people who are so alike be so different?

Four cousins went to their grandfather's eighty-fifth birthday celebration, held at the New Mexico community where their grandparents had retired. Carolyn, Alexander, Jonathan, and Katy had grown up in the same large northeastern city and had spent many holidays and summers together at their grandparents' New Hampshire lake cabin. Theirs had been a close-knit family, and their parents had raised them to be ambitious, determined, and to feel entitled. Ranging in age now from their late twenties to early forties, the four cousins, seated at the same restaurant table, began catching up on what had happened to them since they'd gone their separate ways so many years before.

After some polite chitchat, they began to let down their guard and confide what was really going on in their lives. Katy called it "karma" that they should come together after all these years to share what turned out to be a major crisis for each of them.

CAROLYN'S CAREER CRISIS

In her early forties, Carolyn was the oldest of the cousins. To be the most powerful woman at a major corporation had been her life's dream. She had thought of little else as she spent twenty years climbing the ladder at a major multinational corporation, forcing her way through power barriers that had long impeded women's progress in the business world. Then, just as she was about to be named senior vice president, a corporate takeover intervened. Management changed hands, and Carolyn was out on the street. In the nine months since, she had received many job offers, but none of them offered the power and prestige she had worked so hard to achieve. Her momentum was gone. It had been shattering to her, Carolyn revealed complacently, without expression or emotion.

"Jeez, that's awful," gushed her younger cousin Katy. "And you never even got married!"

KATY'S LOVE LIFE

Carolyn shot Katy an icy look. Katy told Alexander later, as they were dancing, "God, I really put my foot in it. Carolyn's always thought I was a real airhead, because I was into boys and dressing up and going out, when she was always trying to talk me into getting *serious* about things."

Katy, the youngest of the cousins, was in fact not married, and this was at the bottom, she felt, of her current misery. She was a talented junior copywriter at a major New York ad agency. Initially she had been quite successful at her work, but this year she'd been passed over for the raise she had hoped for. "I guess my star's slipping a little," she admitted as she danced with Alexander, to whom she'd always liked to talk. "I suppose Carolyn would say I wasn't *applying* myself."

When Katy was young, her mother would tell her how smart her older cousin Carolyn was, how successful, how Katy should go to business school like Carolyn, should think of her as a role model. But business wasn't Katy's thing. "Too dry," she'd told both her mother and Carolyn. Katy was colorful, flamboyant, creative, and imaginative. The advertising agency was just the place for her talents—but mostly Katy was looking forward to the day when she would get married. A rich and gorgeous husband, an elegant home, and children were what she wanted out of life. Maybe when the kids were in school, she fantasized, she'd try her hand at writing—romantic novels, best-sellers, no doubt.

Attractive, sexy Katy never lacked for dates. Yet somehow she always got involved with the wrong guys. Just a few weeks ago she'd learned that the man she'd fallen head over heels for was married.

"Can you believe it?" Katy wailed later, as she told her cousins her tale of woe. "He was practically living with me, but the couple of nights a week I didn't see him he'd go back home to her and his kids. It was humiliating!" Katy's eyes filled with tears. "For a while I didn't think I could live through it. I mean," she said, looking down at the napkin she was twisting in her hands, "I seriously considered killing myself."

Alexander, ever the kind heart, handed her his handkerchief. He reassured her that she was a terrific, worthwhile, beautiful, and gifted woman. Someday soon she would meet a wonderful man who'd really appreciate her and want to marry her. They'd have a fine marriage, Alexander told her, and at that Katy looked up and grinned.

ALEXANDER'S MIDLIFE CRISIS

As far as the world could see, Alexander had it made. He was living with a woman he loved and probably would get married soon. In addition, his father was turning the reins of the family accounting firm over to him. So why wasn't he happy?

He blamed it all on age. He was about to turn forty and thought he was having a midlife crisis. Everything he'd worked for in his relationship and in his career was coming to fruition. But he'd lost a sense of meaning in his life, especially in his work.

"After all these years of trying to get somewhere, when you finally do, isn't it supposed to mean something to you? Aren't you supposed to feel fulfilled and happy?" He looked at Carolyn and said, "If you'd made it through the glass ceiling the way you'd planned to, you'd be on cloud nine. I'm stepping into the prime of my life, and all I can think is, Is this all there is?"

Carolyn admitted that she could not comprehend his feelings. She couldn't imagine being without a meaning or a purpose, a structure to her days, to her life. True, she'd had a rough go the first couple of months after she'd lost her job. She hadn't known what to do with her days. So she joined a health club and gave herself a daily workout schedule. That was enough to get her back to being organized again, she said.

"It's all in setting goals," she told Alexander firmly. "I set my daily goals for my job hunting and for my personal schedule. I have short-term goals and long-term goals. I have a schedule for myself every day. I work out every morning from six to seven. Then I shower and dress and start making phone calls to headhunters and calling around for job leads. I'm on boards and committees and I'm using those contacts. I'm meeting with my lawyer next week to talk about starting my own consulting firm.

"I want to be in the corporate world, and maybe I'll get back there," Carolyn said with her typical determination, as if she were not experiencing an emotional crisis. "Maybe I won't. It matters to me, but what matters most is that I'm working, doing, staying organized. *Taking responsibility,* that's what life is to me. Yes, I wish there were a man in my life," she said directly to Katy, "but work is where it's at for me. I'm sorry, Alexander, I don't understand your experience. If I were you, I'd tough it out by keeping track of your goals and by throwing yourself into your work even more seriously."

JONATHAN'S NEED TO BE FREE

"Work work work," cousin Jonathan commented dourly. "You remind me of my wife."

"Uh-oh," said Katy. "Trouble in paradise?"

Jonathan ignored the question. "Who says it's so great to work? I mean, it's okay for you, Carolyn—but maybe Alexander would like to give up the game. Alex has been the good little boy all his life, the pride and joy of his parents," he said, nodding toward the table where Alexander's parents and grandparents were sitting. "Maybe now he wants to run off to Tahiti and paint naked ladies."

"Well, I don't know if I want to *paint* naked ladies." Alexander laughed. "You know," he added seriously, "I'm kind of surprised to see you here, Jonathan. Coming all the way out here to a family function isn't exactly your style."

"That's for sure," Jonathan agreed. "To tell you the truth, I wasn't going to come. But when Mara decided that we should paint the whole inside of the house during spring vacation, suddenly a trip to Santa Fe seemed like a great idea. Tomorrow I'm going to do some hiking and maybe stick around a few more days. By that time she'll probably have the place painted and everything will be neat and clean."

Jonathan and his wife, Mara, were high school teachers. Jonathan had chosen teaching because he liked having so much vacation time. He liked to garden, to read, to "do his thing." Mara, as Jonathan had just commented, was more Carolyn's type—a worker, a doer. "She likes the feeling of exhaustion that comes from really pushing herself. She needs the tension of always going herself one better. Me," Jonathan said, shrugging, "I like to feel loose, relaxed, at peace. When I sit home reading a book, she says I don't do enough. I say she does too much.

"You know," Jonathan continued, "I love Mara a lot. I think she does her *job* of being a wife just great. She takes great care of the house, of me, of her kid from her first marriage. But I just wish she'd stop insisting I be the person she is. I work, I do a lot of stuff around the house, I keep the garden—I just don't have the same values she has in life. I like to kick back, watch sports on TV. She calls me a couch potato. I say that it's very fashionable to be a couch potato. 'It used to be,' she says, as she marches outside, slams the door, and rakes the leaves."

Katy said, "Yeah, you were always good at getting out of doing things when we were kids. Do you remember up at the lake that summer when Grandma decided that we kids had to clear the table and do the dinner dishes every night? I was really little, but I remember the first night when you were clearing the table, Jonathan, you dropped Grandma's big serving bowl and broke it in a million pieces. The second night you spilled coffee all over the tablecloth. The third night something else happened, until Grandma excused you from dishes duty. Do you remember that?" she asked the others. They all laughed, while Jonathan protested that that wasn't fair, he had helped out a lot.

"Is your marriage really in trouble, Jonathan?" Alexander asked. Jonathan nodded.

"What will you do?"

Jonathan shrugged. "A person's gotta do what he's gotta do. I'm not going to sign on for more years if I can't be free in my own home with my own wife. I mean, I really do love Mara, but I don't like my life with her. There's too much stress. Tension isn't for me. I am who I am. I can't be who she wants me to be. The quality of life is too important to me. You guys can be into success," he said, gesturing to Carolyn and Alexander. "I'm into enjoying my life the only way I know how." A waiter came around with champagne then, and Jonathan lifted his glass for a refill.

Katy said, "It's amazing you're so laid back about it. There you are calmly watching your marriage fall apart. If it were me and my marriage were breaking up, I'd be writing suicide notes and preparing to jump off the Empire State Building."

"Yeah, and if it were me, I'd stay in bed for three months feeling sorry for myself," said Alexander. "And Carolyn, she'd be putting on that stiff upper lip and getting up at dawn to rewrite her life goals."

"I'M A LEO"

That's when Alexander made the comment, "How can people who are so alike be so different? Here we are, four peas from the same pod. We grew up together in the same extended family. We were well taken care of—no hunger, no major traumas, good schools. But look at how different we all are. We're all trying to tough out something difficult in our lives right now, and we're each handling it completely differently. In terms of our emotional reactions, our loves and hates, our likes and dislikes, our ambitions for ourselves, our relationships, we couldn't be less alike. How do you figure it?"

Nobody had an answer to that except Katy. "That's easy," she said. "I'm a Leo."

COMING TO TERMS WITH
THOSE CONFOUNDED DIFFERENCES

Astrology is one of the oldest ways of accounting for the differences in our individual personality styles. The questions of why we are different and what is the nature of those differences have intrigued some of the best minds throughout recorded time. In the third century B.C., for example, Theophrastus, a student of Aristotle, posed much the same question as Alexander asked at the birthday party: "Why is it that while all Greece lies under the same sky and all Greeks are educated alike, nevertheless we are all different with respect to personality?"

From astrological signs to bodily fluids or humors, to body types and biological styles, to philosophy, psychology, and medicine, we have been trying to come to terms with the predictable variations in behavior, values, motivations, and mind-sets that characterize human personality types. Throughout history, thinkers and healers have also felt the need to determine which personality types are "better" or "worse," "normal" or "abnormal," "healthy" or "maladaptive," which ones will "fit in," which will need "help." The practice continues today. For example, applying for a job or going for career counseling may bring a battery of assessment tests and inventories—such as the Minnesota Multiphasic Personality Inventory, the Myers-Briggs Type Indicator, and our own Personality Self-Portrait (see chapter 3)—to determine whether you have the "right" personality for your workplace or to find your appropriate niche.

We seem historically to be more comfortable with others who are similar to us rather than different—same language and nationality, same skin color, same religion, same politics, and so on. We usually strive to be like, to be with, or to work with some perceived ideal personality type. The ideal personality type of our times, for example, might be someone who is emotionally open, giving, understanding, hardworking, moderate in all things, and interested in self-improvement.

Yet, no matter how we may work to be like others and to seek others like ourselves, we bump into one another's differences every way we turn—in bed, at the breakfast table, at school, in the boardroom, on the assembly line, on the freeway, and at Grandpa's birthday party. The four cousins here are all the same religion, the same race, the same generation, and have the same city of birth and even the same eye color. But they differ in striking and predictable ways with respect to the people they love, the way they love them, their emotional range, their sources of stress and typical coping mechanisms, their way of resolving conflicts, their susceptibility to certain illnesses, their imagination, their self-esteem, their appetites, plus their career interests, work styles, and motivations, among other identifiable differences.

WHAT'S WRONG WITH YOU?
(WHAT'S WRONG WITH ME?)

Despite genuine family fondness for one another, these cousins, like most people, misunderstand and judge one another's differences. Carolyn does indeed think that Katy is an "airhead" and that she should be settling down and working harder rather than always being involved in her "silly" romantic dreams. Carolyn's idea of hell, in fact, is having to spend eternity around somebody with Katy's—or Jonathan's—approach to life. Carolyn thinks that her cousin Jonathan is lazy and selfish. If she were his wife, Mara, she would have thrown him out long ago.

Katy thinks Carolyn is dull and that the only reason she works so hard is that she can't find a man and probably is too old to have children. Jonathan thinks that Carolyn makes a religion of her work and is afraid to let her hair down and have a good time. Her tendency to lecture everyone about what he or she should do drives him crazy. He believes that Katy would be okay if she weren't so emotional about everything. He thinks Alexander is a mama's boy.

Although Alexander is perceptive about people and understands that Carolyn is more vulnerable than she seems, he is both frightened and envious of her strength. He feels he never measures up to her idea of what a man should be. Alexander recognizes ways in which his personality is different from others', but to him "different" means "inadequate." Measuring his own traits along an ideal yardstick, Alexander asks himself (or his therapist): "What's wrong with me?" Alexander has told his therapist that because he's not taking charge of his career right now, he's a "wimp." Although she does not betray her emotions, Carolyn too is deeply ashamed that she has not lived up to her career goals and feels she's worthless. Katy believes she is not a normal woman because she has not found a husband. Jonathan is an exception; he thinks he's just fine—he wishes everybody else would get off his back.

In other words, although we embrace our similarities to others, with respect to our differences from one another and from an ideal personality type, we do not always accept ourselves, and we often misunderstand or outright condemn the other guy.

LEARNING THE LANGUAGE(S)

In this book we show that the seemingly mysterious differences among people are relatively easy to understand and deal with once you learn to "decode" the constellation of attitudes and traits that comprise each of the fourteen personality styles. None of the styles is "good" or "bad." Although some are more common than others, all are normal. All have their strengths as well as their potential trouble spots. Each has its own "language"—and learning the different grammars of the fourteen personality styles will make it substantially easier to deal with, resolve, or avoid conflicts with everyone you encounter, including yourself.

Cousin Carolyn, for example, is strongly a Conscientious type, with a streak of the Self-Confident style. She speaks the Self-Confident language of stardom ("I'm going to be the top woman at my company") and the Conscientious language of "shoulds" ("I should be successful"; "You should have goals"). She measures herself against strong moral principles and feels guilty unless she works to meet these stringent external standards. No wonder she's so hard on herself and on everybody else. Will Carolyn find the job she wants? Will she ever find a man who is strong enough to meet her standards? See chapter 6.

Jonathan's personality style is Leisurely. His wife is Conscientious, like Carolyn—not a great match, for Jonathan's language is that of comfort, relaxation, and pleasure, and he is utterly resistant to ambition and to guilt. Will he and Mara split? See chapter 10.

Katy speaks the language of love. She is Dramatic to an extreme. She needs to be appreciated, pampered, adored. She is deaf to the language of goals, planning, detail, and discipline, but she wouldn't mind if somebody (Prince Charming, for instance) came along to take care of the necessary details of her life. Will Katy survive her heartbreak and find a man who treats her right? See chapter 7.

Alexander is Devoted, along with two other strong styles, plus a touch of the Serious, in his personality pattern. His key phrase is: "Whatever makes you happy." But ask him what makes him happy and he'll draw a blank. That's one reason why taking charge is so hard for him right now. See how he works it out in chapter 6.

NORMAL FOR YOU

Learn to speak the language of each of the fourteen personality styles and you'll find you can get through to others much more easily, perhaps even develop compassion for those you never thought you could tolerate (see "The Mother-in-Law Project," p. 103).

But first, learn to understand *your* style. Listen to your personality speak, find the key words that unlock your pattern—learn what's normal for you. You will find, once you determine your Personality Self-Portrait, that your personality imposes its own definite order on your past, present, and future—on all your hopes and dreams, on what you feel, and what you accomplish in life.

CHAPTER 2

Your Unique Life Pattern

STYLES, DISORDERS, AND DOMAINS

Your personality style is your organizing principle. It propels you on your life path. It represents the orderly arrangement of all your attributes, thoughts, feelings, attitudes, behaviors, and coping mechanisms. It is the distinctive pattern of your psychological functioning—the way you think, feel, and behave—that makes you *definitely* you.

Your personality style is what causes—after you have gained thirty pounds, started to turn gray, and begun wearing glasses—your classmates at your twenty-fifth high school reunion to exclaim, "Why, you haven't changed a bit!"

What has stayed the same and is so easily recognizable is the way you react to others, your emotional style, your way of reasoning and expressing yourself, your body language—the outward effects of the core traits that have consistently marked your style since your earliest years.

THE POSSIBILITIES FOR YOU

Scientific exploration of human personality is on the cutting edge of modern psychiatry. In the fields of neuropsychiatry and behavioral genetics we are beginning to prove that the foundations of personality are inherited—in other words, biologically determined. To psychiatrists, the inborn biological, genetic aspect of your personality is called your temperament. Your natural activity level (Are you "speedy" or easygoing and slow?), your characteristic mood ranges (Definitely moody? cheerful? even-keeled?), and your reaction ranges (Does change throw you?) are among the many features of your temperament or biological style, with which you emerged "preprogrammed" from the womb. As we will show in chapter 18, research is even beginning to match the traits and behaviors that mark each personality style with the underlying biochemical communication patterns among brain cells.

GENES AND EXPERIENCE

As with a number of physical traits, such as height, genes confer a range of personality predispositions. Environment and life experience—parents, family, life events, culture, peers—then sculpt the final "you" from the possibilities. Adverse experience can alter the possibilities for the worse. For example, you may have grown taller were it not for poor nutrition or illness during your childhood. By the same token, had your parents abused instead of appreciated you and responded sufficiently to your needs, your powerful aggressiveness might have landed you in jail instead of fueling your brilliant legal maneuvers in the courtroom.

THE CARD GAME

Personality is like a deck of cards. You are dealt a hand at conception, and life experiences determine which genetic cards will be turned up and therefore what the nature of your normal experience will be. Your hand—your personality style—will be fairly set by the end of childhood, and you will be playing the "game of life" in your distinctive way for the remainder of your years.

While no psychiatrist or psychologist has invented a crystal ball that can predict what "move" you or anyone else will make in response to any single situation, research shows that we can indeed count on people playing the game true to their personalities more times than not, well into old age.

STYLE VERSUS DISORDER

You do, of course, grow and change throughout your lifetime, but you do so in your consistent, characteristic manner. Your personality style is your way of being, of becoming, and of meeting life's challenges. Most people's styles have a built-in flexibility factor that allows them to deal with the hurdles thrown in their path. They can adapt to change, which makes a variety of experiences possible. Other people, however, find themselves up against the same old walls. They are locked into rigid, inflexible personality patterns—personality disorders—that cause them to have the same troubled, bored, empty, lonely, or disruptive experiences repeatedly throughout their lives.

THE CASE OF GARY G.

A man goes to a psychiatrist because his wife has threatened to leave him: "If you don't get your act together, Gary—I mean it this time—I'll take the kids and go to Mother's."

Gary is forty-four years old and has just been put on three months' probation at his job because he mistakenly erased from the computer and somehow managed to destroy the backup copies of the key documentation for a project. His department consequently failed to meet an extremely important deadline and the company nearly lost a major contract.

Gary is an industrial engineer at an auto parts manufacturing company. He's lost three jobs in the last ten years. He says to the psychiatrist that there's nothing wrong with him. He's had a run of bad luck with rotten bosses. It's not his fault if it's the losers who get promoted and then ask you to do the impossible, says he. Gary concedes that all his "bad" bosses accused him of being forgetful, slow, stubborn, and uncooperative—the same complaints, he admits when pressed, that his wife has against him. She's always on his back to help around the house, which he refuses to do. She also annoys him by complaining about his constant grouchiness and his drinking, which Gary is sure he has under control. Gary says that his wife doesn't understand him. *That's* his problem, he tells the psychiatrist.

Nearly everybody delays and procrastinates and passively resists authority once in a while. And some people simply are more relaxed and easygoing than others about deadlines and assignments; they put them off while they attend to other, more interesting things, but they do them eventually. These folks, like cousin Jonathan in chapter 1, have a strong streak of the Leisurely personality style. They get along fine in life as long as they steer clear of rush-deadline, high-demand careers and don't pair up with perfectionists. They'll reward you with love and appreciation if you accept them as they are and take good care of them.

But Gary has more than a healthy share of these traits. For him, passive resistance to the demands of authority has become his only way of life. At home he avoids everything his wife or teenage kids expect of him. At work he continually sabotages his efforts, to the point of jeopardizing his livelihood and his family's welfare. He's been this way at least since adolescence, when, although intellectually gifted, he flunked out of two colleges before finally receiving his degree. Now he's about to lose his marriage and his job.

Gary misses his second appointment with the therapist—"I forgot," he explains—but by the end of their next visit, the psychiatrist believes he has heard enough to make a preliminary diagnosis. Gary has a personality disorder. His personality style has become rigid and inflexible. Instead of providing a way of coping and adapting to the demands of life, his personality pattern has thrown him into one vicious cycle after another. He doesn't recognize that his repetitive patterns of behavior have made his life miserable. All he knows how to do is blame and envy others and say no—so nothing good ever happens to Gary anymore. Gary needs help.

Specifically, Gary is suffering from Passive-Aggressive personality disorder, as defined by the DSM-IV.

DIFFICULT PEOPLE

The DSM-IV distinguishes between personality disorders (Axis II disorders) and acute, painfully symptomatic conditions, such as depression, schizophrenia, eating disorders, sexual disorders, and panic disorders. These latter (Axis I disorders) are considered "clinical symptom syndromes." Their dramatic symptoms tend to flare up periodically. Often they have a powerful biological component and can be treated with medication.

Personality disorders, on the other hand, are long-term patterns of inflexible and maladaptive behavior that are manifest from adolescence. (See "General Diagnostic Criteria" below.) Without treatment they last a lifetime, although they may lessen in intensity in middle and older age. This does not mean that people with problems stemming from their personalities do not also get depressed or develop sexual problems, have panic attacks, become addicted to drugs, or suffer severe mental anguish. Very often, as you'll see in the chapters that follow, certain personality disorders create vulnerability to specific clinical-symptom syndromes. The acute conditions erupt under particular kinds of stress (e.g., the breakup of a relationship).

GENERAL DIAGNOSTIC CRITERIA
FOR A DSM-IV PERSONALITY DISORDER

A. An enduring pattern of inner experience and behavior that deviates markedly from the expectations of the individual's culture. This pattern is manifested in two (or more) of the following areas:

(1) cognition (i.e., ways of perceiving and interpreting self, other people, and events)
(2) affectivity (i.e., the range, intensity, lability, and appropriateness of emotional response)
(3) interpersonal functioning
(4) impulse control

B. The enduring pattern is inflexible and pervasive across a broad range of personal and social situations.

C. The enduring pattern leads to clinically significant distress or impairment in social, occupational, or other important areas of functioning.

D. The pattern is stable and of long duration and its onset can be traced back at least to adolescence or early adulthood.

E. The enduring pattern is not better accounted for as a manifestation or consequence of another mental disorder.

F. The enduring pattern is not due to the direct physiological effects of a substance (e.g., a drug of abuse, a medication) or a general medical condition (e.g., head trauma).

According to the few studies that have been conducted, personality disorders afflict between 10 and 14 percent of the total population; future studies, conducted with better methodology, will likely reveal a substantially higher percentage. The incidence is higher in urban than in rural areas, and among lower socioeconomic groups. Men and women are affected in relatively equal numbers, although some of the specific disorders, as we will see, favor one sex over the other.

When earlier versions of the DSM were field-tested prior to publication, more than 50 percent of psychiatric patients were found to suffer from full-blown personality disorders. Most of the people who consult mental health professionals have difficulties that can be traced, at least in part, to aspects of their enduring personality patterns. As in Gary's case, something about the way they are and the way they behave is damaging their lives and/or making them, and likely the people around them, miserable.

Many people with disordered personality patterns do not realize that there is anything amiss with them. Others see it, though. Individuals with personality disorders are frequently in conflict with family members, employers, colleagues, and subordinates. These problems are quite difficult to resolve, because these individuals usually do not recognize that it is their own repetitive patterns of behavior that so greatly contribute to their troubles.

Chances are, when you read about the fourteen personality disorders in the following chapters, you will recognize the people in your life who are the most frustrating to deal with. For Gary's wife, that person was her husband. He wasn't a bad person, and she loved him, but she couldn't make him understand that his behavior was destroying their family. Gary did not volunteer to go for help—his wife had to threaten him. In his therapy, for a long time he didn't understand that he was doing anything inappropriate. He believed his problems were everyone else's fault.

TOO MUCH OF A GOOD THING

The DSM-IV follows medical tradition in distinguishing between normal and abnormal and in recognizing discrete categories of disturbance for mental health professionals to diagnose, study, and treat. The personality disorders that the DSM-IV formulates represent the state of the art in the diagnosis of personality malfunctioning. (As mentioned in the introduction, the DSM-IV includes twelve personality disorders, two of which are "unofficial." The fourteen personality disorders we discuss here encompass these as well as two that were included for study purposes in the DSM's previous edition.)

Yet, the difference between personality functioning and malfunctioning—between style and disorder—is often only one of degree. "Only when *personality traits* [or styles] are inflexible and maladaptive and cause significant functional impairment or subjective distress do they constitute Personality Disorders," states the DSM-IV. The fourteen personality disorders are exaggerations of the fourteen personality styles that are present to varying degrees within every individual. It is the *quantity* of each personality style along a continuum, not its quality, that tends to spell problems in life.

Take Gary. He scores at the top of the Leisurely–Passive-Aggressive continuum. The disorder dominates his work life and personal existence, making him rigid and incapable of coping and adapting. When anyone wants anything from him, he automatically digs in his heels. Now that he is about to lose his job and his marriage, he is pulling his head even tighter into his turtlelike shell, refusing to recognize how he contributes to the mess he is in. He vacillates between feeling angry and contrite, but he doesn't see that he needs to change. Neither does he think that his life will ever get any better. When he finally does agree to go for help—"because my wife doesn't understand me"—he "forgets" his appointments. Gary's personality style has become so exaggerated that it leaves little room in his personality for balancing tendencies to flourish.

PERSONALITY STYLE: THE GOOD THING

Psychiatry concerns itself with disorder. Our primary concern in this book is to delineate the normal, adaptive personality styles that the disorders take to an extreme. (See the style–disorder chart on p. 23.) We will return to Passive-Aggressive Gary in chapter 10. There, in addition to Leisurely cousin Jonathan, we will also find Anton Z., an artist for whom the Leisurely style makes for an often intriguing, highly creative life. He can be stubborn and resist his wife's demands, but not under every circumstance. He'll feel guilty about his behavior, and eventually he'll end up doing something about it, although perhaps not right away. Fortunately, Anton's second wife, unlike his first, knows how to deal with him.

THE FLEXIBILITY/VARIETY/ADAPTABILITY STANDARD

Although no one can say exactly where style ends and disorder begins, the differences between Gary and someone like Anton, who is leading a productive and satisfying life, involve flexibility, variety, and adaptability. Establishing a diagnosis is the responsibility of a mental health professional, but you can think about your behavior and life experiences or your level of frustration with another person in terms of these standards:

1. *Flexibility and inflexibility.* Gary is stuck with one principal way of behaving in reaction to the demanding people and situations in his life. Anton has a larger repertoire of behaviors. For instance, he will negotiate with his wife if he sees that a particular issue is extremely important to her.

2. *Variety and repetition.* Gary lives a life of repetitions: he is always in trouble at work; his marriage is often in crisis. He has few rewarding experiences, and he makes no progress. His life is the same old story,

THE PERSONALITY STYLE–PERSONALITY DISORDER CONTINUUM

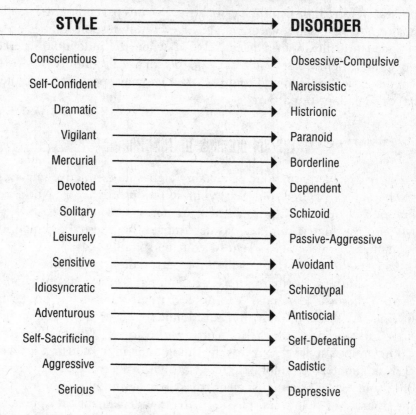

STYLE	→	DISORDER
Conscientious	→	Obsessive-Compulsive
Self-Confident	→	Narcissistic
Dramatic	→	Histrionic
Vigilant	→	Paranoid
Mercurial	→	Borderline
Devoted	→	Dependent
Solitary	→	Schizoid
Leisurely	→	Passive-Aggressive
Sensitive	→	Avoidant
Idiosyncratic	→	Schizotypal
Adventurous	→	Antisocial
Self-Sacrificing	→	Self-Defeating
Aggressive	→	Sadistic
Serious	→	Depressive

day after day. Anton, however, even though he is a creature of habit, has spontaneous fun with his family, has creative inspirations, and has been known to go in daring new artistic directions.

3. *Adaptability and incapacity to cope with stress.* Anton, as we will see, has a tendency to withdraw and to become obstinate when faced with stressful demands from other people and from the art market. But he usually rallies and deals with it, often with profound results. For example, through some long hard years when his work wasn't selling, he stuck with his highly original painting style, which deepened and matured. Gary, on the other hand, cannot master the slightest stress. When he was under the pressure of a departmental deadline, instead of tolerating the extra demands on him and demonstrating the ability he possessed, he unconsciously erased from the computer months of painstaking work.

"When an individual displays an ability to cope with the environment in a flexible manner, and when his or her typical perceptions and behaviors foster . . . personal satisfaction, then the person may be said to possess a normal or healthy personality," writes psychologist Theodore Millon. "Conversely, when average or everyday responsibilities are responded to inflexibly or defectively, or when the individual's perceptions and behaviors result in . . . personal discomfort or curtail opportunities to learn and to grow, then we may speak of a pathological or maladaptive pattern."

THE SIX DOMAINS OF FUNCTIONING

Flexibly or otherwise, your personality etches its distinctive imprint on six key areas of life: your Self; your Relationships; your Work; your Emotions; your Self-Control; and your notions about the Real World. Modern psychiatric thinking has determined that these six domains are fundamental to the assessment of your personality pattern.

As we will demonstrate, each of the personality styles betrays a characteristic, utterly normal pattern of thinking, feeling, and behaving in each of these six domains. Also, for each personality style one or two (in one case three) of these domains dominate the entire style and determine functioning in all the domains. For example, Work is key to the Conscientious style; clearly it is the ruling domain for cousin Carolyn. It even dominates her emotional life; Carolyn is miserable if her life isn't on a solid work-accomplishment track. For Leisurely cousin Jonathan, the domain of Self rules. His need to be independent and pursue his own meaning in life is essential to him—more important than his relationships, should he be forced to choose.

SELF

This domain includes your sense of self, your self-esteem, your self-image—the way you see, think, and feel about yourself, your place in the universe, and your place in other people's estimation. Self-Confident types, for example, have a sense of entitlement and a real feeling of personal destiny. For them, the Self domain is key, which helps to explain their sureness of purpose, their drive, and their ability to succeed despite obstacles. Idiosyncratic types are sustained by the rich inner worlds of their Selves; they may or may not be successful by other people's standards or fit comfortably into the social order, but no matter what others say or convention dictates, they continue to march to their own drummer. For those with Dramatic style (cousin Katy, for example), the Self shines brightest when others appreciate their qualities; they rise to the occasion when all eyes are on them.

Your style of functioning in the Self domain influences many important aspects of your behavior—for instance, how you perform at a job interview. Adventurous types may have such power in the Self domain that they can talk people into giving them jobs for which they are not really qualified. Those with Self-Sacrificing style, who, as the name of the style suggests, come into their own when they are giving of themselves to others, commonly will play down their very real capabilities rather than appear to be boastful.

How do you think and feel about yourself? What do you think about your body? Where do you place yourself in the universe and in other people's estimation? Who comes first, you or them? What do you dream for yourself? Questions such as these reveal what is normal for you in the Self domain.

RELATIONSHIPS

This domain is a dominant factor in more than half of all personality styles. It defines how important other people are to us and how we lead our lives. Besides being individuals, we are members of families, couples, friendships, school classes, communities, business organizations, even crowds of strangers. The nature and style of our reactions and involvements with these other people reveal a great deal.

Solitary people, for example, need to keep others at a distance; they can connect with others as long as they can then step away. Dramatic men and women often function poorly when they are alone; they need to be surrounded, admired, applauded. Vigilant types are very cautious of others. They take their time getting to know you before they move close; they're at their best with people when they feel in control in their relationships. For Devoted types, other people are their reason for being; they feel incomplete unless they are committed to or even merged with someone. Sensitive people flourish in the company of a small group of friends or within their families, but they are uneasy and definitely "not themselves" in large groups or among strangers. Aggressive types have to be one step ahead in all their relationships.

WORK

This domain encompasses your style of "doing," and—through play, school, career, housework, child care, chores, and hobbies—you've

KEY DOMAINS

STYLE	WORK	SELF	EMOTIONS	RELATIONSHIPS	SELF-CONTROL	REAL WORLD
Conscientious						
Self-Confident						
Dramatic						
Vigilant						
Mercurial						
Devoted						
Solitary						
Leisurely						
Sensitive						
Idiosyncratic						
Adventurous						
Self-Sacrificing						
Aggressive						
Serious						

been spending your day working at something virtually all your life. Your personality style reveals itself in how you complete tasks, take and/or give orders, make decisions, plan, handle external and internal demands, take or give criticism, obey rules, take and delegate responsibility, and cooperate with other people.

For the Conscientious-style person, Work is the ruling domain. People like cousin Carolyn are always busy doing something even in their leisure time; it's their work and how well they do it that defines them and makes them comfortable in life. Work is a key domain for the Aggressive style too; political success at work is essential for this take-charge, top-dog style. Work also directs the Serious-style person; life is Work and Work is life for this sober, no-nonsense individual.

Although for Conscientious and Aggressive styles, work and fun are often synonymous, Leisurely types usually think otherwise; they do what is required of them and no more, so that they can escape their labors and relax and have a good time. Adventurous types are notoriously unresponsive to authority. They love a challenge, though, and as long as their work (meaning also sports and hobbies) includes conquering some risk, they'll stick with it.

What you choose to do in your life, how you choose it, and how you deal with Work-domain difficulties (including being out of work or having to work two jobs to make ends meet) are also revealing of your personality style. Devoted-style Alexander went into the family business because it was expected of him. It never occurred to him to ask himself what he'd rather do; when he felt empty and dissatisfied, his personality style led him to assume that he'd just have to stick it out.

EMOTIONS

The Emotions or feelings domain includes your usual moods and emotional states, such as happiness, sadness, sexual feelings, anger, irritability, fear, anxiety, and sensitivity to praise and to criticism. What weight does this domain play in your personality pattern? People with Dramatic style are ruled by their feelings; they judge an experience not by what they think about it but how they *feel* about it. They are sensuous, seductive, sexy. Their emotional style can serve them well in their work, if they choose careers or environments in which they are encouraged to be intuitive, impressionistic, and creative. Conscientious-style individuals, on the other hand, give little weight to their feelings. To them, logic counts. They have strong feelings, but they prefer to submerge them under a cool, controlled veneer.

Level of emotional intensity—from hot and high-pitched to cool and imperturbable—is a feature of this domain as well. The Mercurial style is emotionally "hot"; these individuals experience the widest range of moods and feelings with deepest intensity, anger included. Their intense and changeable moods may facilitate creative experiences and accomplishments, but they will be less of an asset in the corporate boardroom. Solitary types tend to be cool, calm, and relatively unmoved by others' opinions of them. They often make gifted rational observers of other people and of the natural world, but when others insist that they experience and express feelings, they feel a great deal of anxiety. Serious types dwell in a solemn emotional world. Not given to levity in the best of times, they prove better able to handle sobering experiences than are those with most other personality styles.

Sensitive types have very tender feelings. They are easily made anxious and self-conscious—so they build their personal and career lives around people they know well and situations with which they are familiar. As a result, they tend to form deeply meaningful relationships and become expert at what they do.

SELF-CONTROL

Do you have an "executive director" in your head who considers each temptation and determines whether you should indulge your appetites and passions, to what degree, and for how long? Or does nothing intervene between desire and surrender? This domain—your control or your impulsiveness—rules your level of spontaneity and ability to act on impulse, your risk-taking behavior, your ability to forestall rewards and fulfillment, your planning skill, your self-discipline, your frustration tolerance, and your ability to stop and think before you act.

Issues of Self-Control are key for the Adventurous and the Mercurial styles. Adventurous types love to act on the moment—they couldn't live any other way. They do not plan for the future or spend much time worrying about the consequences of their actions. Their personalities thrive on excitement, thrills, gambles, and risks. Their spontaneity gives their lives meaning and fuels their daring accomplishments. Mercurial men and women are similarly spontaneous, often in creative fields. When a passion comes upon them, they give in to it completely. They are thoroughly responsive to pleasure and sensation, hungry for sensuous experience. They are remarkable lovers.

On the other side of the Self-Control continuum are the Aggressive, Conscientious, Vigilant, and Sensitive styles. In varying ways and for differing reasons, these personality styles emphasize control. They are all plan-ahead, goal-directed types who are focused either on future rewards or present safety. Aggressive and Self-Confident types are masters of the calculated risk. Serious-style people seek predictable regularity.

In this as in all other of the six domains, there is no "right" or "wrong" way of behaving, unless the style of functioning brings harm to oneself or others. Nonetheless, in this era of eating disorders, sexually transmitted diseases, drug and alcohol abuse, violent crimes and suicide, controversy over abortion, our culture demonstrates strongly mixed feelings about how a person "should" function in the domain of Self-Control. Culture influences the expression of personality traits and styles, and as the pendulum has shifted from the radical, let-it-all-hang-out sixties through the conservative get-control-of-yourself eighties, into the shifting moderate/conservative get-control-of-others nineties, people whose personalities are dominated by the impulsive side of the Self-Control domain may feel pressured to bridle their natural passions.

REAL WORLD

Do you live in a world of concrete objects such as people and buildings, where things are pretty much what they seem? Or, when you walk through a forest, are you listening for the spiritual beings that inhabit the trees? Philosophers have disagreed about the nature of reality since earliest times. In personality assessment, psychiatrists are less interested in what's "true" than in the degree to which your ideas vary from the prevailing standard and how these notions influence your behavior.

What's your reality? Your spirituality? If you are an Idiosyncratic type (the only style in which this domain is key), the conventional explanations, religions, institutions, and scientific understandings do not hold great weight with you. If you believe in ESP, it exists; you are not swayed by doubters. Your mind might be open to the existence of ghosts, extraterrestrials, or past lives. On the other side of the spectrum, Conscientious individuals are perhaps the most accepting and respecting of conventional, shared realities, be they scientific, religious, political, or philosophic.

In chapters 4 through 17, we'll discuss how each personality style shapes a person's approach to his or her self-styled reality in a more metaphoric sense, as well. For example, Sensitive types perceive the Real World to be full of danger; therefore, they create safe harbors for themselves, they stick close to family, they embrace the known. Vigilant types may approach the Real World as if they are the only sane ones in a sea of madmen. Self-Confident folks strut around their planet as if it belongs to them personally, whereas Devoted types may react to a Real

World in which they perceive themselves to be less important or to carry less weight than other, more important people.

A CHANGEABLE FATE

By ordering your experiences and reactions in a systematic way throughout all the domains of functioning, your personality style directs your life and becomes a kind of fate. But it is a changeable fate. Even for those with personality disorders, the potential for change always exists. Intense life pressures and experiences—from the horrors of war to the birth of a child to the rigors of psychotherapy—can exert tremendous force on the personality. To adapt, your personality restructures itself. You can also learn to make certain small changes and adjustments, first by understanding how your personality is structured, and then by knowing how to enter the system and fine-tune it.

This capacity for change, like the foundations of personality, is an inborn biological reality. Researchers in neuropsychiatric laboratories are daring to speculate that learning and significant experience can trigger previously unexpressed potentials that have been encoded in our genes from the start. The elegant work of neuroscientist Eric Kandel, M.D., implies that no matter how rigid or how limited your personality, biologically your fate is never really sealed. Through experience, learning, or psychotherapy, you can turn up long-covered cards and expand your hand at any age.

In the last two chapters of this book we'll look more closely at where your personality style comes from, how it develops, and how to change it. For the most part, however, we'll devote these pages to the discovery of your "hand"—the nature of your normal personal order. We will show you what your unique personality style means in the full context of how your life plays out.

CHAPTER 3

The Personality Self-Portrait

TAKING AND INTERPRETING THE TEST
AND READING THE BOOK

Your personality style is your own, utterly individual amalgam of fourteen separate, identifiable styles. It can be pictured on a graph. Fill in the questionnaire that begins on p. 36, score it, transfer your scores to the Self-Portrait graph, connect the points, and you will see the unique outline of your Personality Self-Portrait. No one else has the identical configuration of styles that compose your Personality Self-Portrait.

The fourteen chapters that follow explore each of the personality styles individually. You need not take the test in order to discover the pieces of your personality style within these chapters. All readers, with or without completing the test, will discover aspects of themselves and of others (parents, children, relatives, friends, teachers, spouses, lovers, bosses, employees) scattered throughout each of the style chapters. By completing your Personality Self-Portrait, however, you will be able to visualize both the structure of your whole personality and the complex relationships among its parts.

All fourteen styles are normal and universal. While each one brings its share of strengths and problem areas, there is nothing "wrong" with any of them, and there's nothing "abnormal" about having a predominance of one or a lack of another. The styles and the infinite variety of patterns that the Personality Self-Portrait can capture are but manifestations of the rich and wonderful differences among us all.

THE FOURTEEN STYLES AND THE SIX DOMAINS

Each chapter includes, first, a list of the key characteristics of each style. Then we go on to cover in great detail each style's characteristic influence on functioning in the six domains that we discussed in chapter 2: Relationships, Work, Self, Emotions, Self-Control, and the Real World.

You will see that each style is "ruled" by a different domain or a different combination of key domains. In addition to the many facets of each domain that we will cover (including, to name a few, the best and worst love matches, parenting style, best career choices, and management style), we will discuss the characteristic sources of stress and coping styles for each personality style. We offer extensive tips on dealing with people with each personality style. We also offer a number of exercises designed to help you make the most of your personality style.

THE FOURTEEN DISORDERS

At the close of each of the style chapters, we present the personality disorder that corresponds to that style. We discuss how individuals with these disorders feel and behave, how psychiatrists diagnose and treat them, and some reasons (including genetic predispositions and early life experiences) why an individual will develop a particular disorder. It is important to note again that *the Personality Self-Portrait does not diagnose personality disorders*. In other words, if you score high in the Vigilant personality style, it means only that you are highly Vigilant—it does *not* mean that you are suffering from Paranoid personality disorder. A high degree of any of the fourteen styles will bring its share of pluses and minuses, but it does not mean you are "mentally disturbed." Only a qualified psychiatrist or other mental health professional can diagnose a personality disorder. If the description of any disorder in these chapters leads you to think that you or someone close to you may be suffering from a personality disorder, seek a professional opinion (we'll have more to say about this in the final chapter).

SUGGESTIONS FOR USING THIS BOOK

There are many ways to approach the personality-style chapters. You may choose to read about individual styles in the order of their importance on your Personality Self-Portrait, or you may decide to read the chapters consecutively, from Conscientious all the way through Serious. We recommend that you read all the chapters, in whatever order, for at least two reasons. First, you will encounter many characters you have come across in your life and you will learn ways of dealing with them—or why you were unable to get along with them before.

Second, you can learn a lot about yourself and your relationships from understanding not only the styles that are prominent in your makeup but also the styles that are least prominent or absent. For example, Duncan L. and his wife, Sharon, are having a stressful time. They're fighting a lot, mainly over money. Sharon cries, "You're so uptight! You just don't like to spend money and have a good time. I can't stand it! You're always worrying. For God's sake, Duncan, lighten up!"

Duncan completes the Personality Self-Portrait and finds out not only that the Conscientious style is prominent in his personality but that the Dramatic style is relatively low. Having so much Conscientious style implies that he is orderly, organized, a saver, detail-oriented, a thinker. Having so little Dramatic style means he tends not to consider the emotional and social issues that are all-important to his wife. Duncan realizes, in his intellectual way, that he and Sharon use different communication techniques. He talks with his head, she with her heart. Maybe their problems have less to do with money than with the need to find a way to "translate" each other's personality styles into a mutually understandable language.

THE PERSONALITY SELF-PORTRAIT FOR COUPLES

Any self-test is necessarily one-sided. While you are the best judge of how you feel and what you think, the people who are closest to you may add perspective on how you behave. To arrive at the most accurate diagnoses, psychiatrists often seek information about patients' behavior from their spouses or family members.

Couples may wish to consider drawing each other's Personality Self-Portrait as an exercise in mutual understanding. To do this, take the test for your partner, answering the questions in a way you believe reflects his or her attitudes and behavior. Then compare these results with each other's self-tests. Your version of your partner's Self-Portrait will show only how he or she comes across to *you*—but that can be very useful information if you treat it with interest and respect.

Sometimes this exercise can reveal each other's blind spots—and we all have them. Some Leisurely-style people, for instance, become so involved in their personal activities that they may not realize that they often come across as uncooperative. They may feel that they do everything that anyone asks them to do. Present your results saying, "This is how I see you"—then talk about your differing perceptions. Next, let your partner answer the questions for you, and face some of your own blind spots.

Whether or not couples dare to take the test for each other, you'll find it interesting and revealing to chart both your styles on one graph, using different colors or types of lines. This will give you a vivid view of how your individual styles compare—how alike and how different you are in fourteen separate ways. Later in this chapter we'll talk more about interpreting the results, for individuals, couples, and groups.

CASE HISTORIES, VIGNETTES, REAL PEOPLE, AND "TYPES"

To illustrate the personality styles and their various combinations, we use examples of some 150 real people. For each chapter we have chosen individuals whose personalities strongly demonstrate that particular style (and sometimes disorder). Thus, in chapter 5 we introduce Sargent, a powerfully Self-Confident theatrical producer, and we show how his personality style has shaped his relationships, including his two former marriages and his present live-in affair with a well-known dancer-turned-choreographer. For the sake of convenience and illustration, we refer to Sargent as a Self-Confident "type"—even though there is no such thing as a pure personality type or style. No one has but a single personality style, as you will see from your own Self-Portrait; everybody, Sargent included, reveals a pattern of styles, with one or a few dominating the picture. When we refer to a particular personality "type," we mean someone who has a strong predominance of that particular style.

In your own Personality Self-Portrait, perhaps no one style will stand out as vividly as in the examples we use throughout the following chapters. See the section near the end of this chapter for suggestions on how to interpret your results. Should you decide to skip the test for now and go on to read the following chapters, you'll find yourself identifying to varying extents with the living examples of each of the styles. The degree to which you say, "That's me!" will give you some idea of the relative strength of a particular style in your overall pattern.

As for Sargent and the many other individuals named in the following chapters, each of the case histories and vignettes is based on a story from real life. To protect the privacy of these individuals and to respect the confidentiality of clinical material, we have changed their names and taken great care to "fictionalize" all the details of their actual identities and their highly personal tales.

TAKING THE TEST

Set aside a half hour to an hour to complete your Personality Self-Portrait. With all due respect to those who design quick-and-easy personality tests, capturing the many layers of individual personality is necessarily a complex process. We have made the Personality Self-Portrait as easy as possible for you to take (we've even tested the instructions on children). It is not difficult, but it is somewhat time-consuming. Take time to think about and answer the 107 questions as accurately and as honestly as possible. Your Self-Portrait is only as valid as your answers to the questions.

The questions are very personal, so take the test in private and consider keeping your answers confidential. Do not discuss the questions and answers with anyone while you are taking the test (although you may find the questions interesting to discuss with your confidants at a later time). To promote privacy, we have designed an answer sheet that is separate from the questionnaire itself. (For information on where to obtain copies or a computerized version for such purposes, see p. 61.)

Don't hesitate to show your Personality Self-Portrait to others and even to compare results. Although you may not wish to share the private details on the questionnaire, your Personality Self-Portrait is something to be proud of. It is unique, it is individual, it is you.

The Personality Self-Portrait Questionnaire

Test Instructions

I. Complete all 107 questions on the questionnaire.

Even if you do not think the question applies to you or to your life circumstances, answer how you think you would respond if it did apply to you.

Circle *one:*

Y (**Yes,** I agree)
Choose this option if the entire statement is *completely true* for you most of the time.

M (**Maybe** I agree)
Choose this option if the entire statement is *sometimes or somewhat true for you.*
Choose this option also for multiple-part statements when you *agree with one part but disagree with another part.*

N (**No,** I don't agree)
Choose this option if the statement is *completely false* for you.

---

1. I tend to spend more time on my work than do some of Y M N
    my colleagues or coworkers, since I'm a perfectionist
    and like things to be done right.

2. I am a very organized person. I like to follow a schedule Y M N
    and make lists of things I have to do. Sometimes I have
    more lists than I know what to do with!

3. I've sometimes been called a "workaholic." It's true Y M N
    that I work very hard even when I have enough money
    and the bills are all paid. I suppose if I wanted to I
    could knock off and relax, at least for a little while.

4.   I like my usual routines for doing things and I can be   Y M N
quite stubborn if people try to get me to change them.

5.   I hate routine and I'm not very good at obligations, so I   Y M N
put things off as long as I can or I just never get around
to doing them.

6.   Whenever I succeed at something, I find that either I   Y M N
don't really enjoy it much or something goes wrong
somewhere else in my life.

7.   I have a lot of abilities I can't seem to take advantage   Y M N
of. When I'm good at something, I can help other peo-
ple with it, but I can't seem to put my ability to work
for myself.

8.   I have a fairly good sense of myself. I know what kind   Y M N
of work I want to do, what kind of friends I like to be
with, and overall what sorts of things are important to
me.

9.   I feel like I'm just an outer shell with nothing inside. I   Y M N
can feel pretty aimless.

10.   I like to daydream. I imagine myself rich or powerful or   Y M N
famous—maybe being applauded for winning the
Nobel Prize, or idolized by crowds of fans for my talent
or beauty.

11.   Even though I'm not sure I should be, I find myself   Y M N
fascinated by violence, weapons, and the martial arts. I
like films and TV shows with a lot of action and violence in them.

12.   People say that I express myself in an odd way—that I   Y M N
say things that are too deep for them, or that I don't
explain what I mean.

13. I've been called arrogant, but so what!   Y M N

14. I like to be admired, and I have a habit of fishing for   Y M N
    compliments when I'm being ignored.

15. My appearance is very important to me. I spend a great   Y M N
    deal of time making sure I look attractive.

16. People sometimes think I'm eccentric because I dress   Y M N
    my own way and because I seem a little "spaced out" to
    them. It's true that I live sort of in my own little world.

17. Even though I think I understand people, they're always   Y M N
    telling me I don't have a clue about how they feel.

18. When it comes to standing in line or being seated in a   Y M N
    crowded restaurant, I usually try to get to the front and
    get waited on right away—or at least I feel that's how I
    should be treated.

19. I don't believe in feeling guilty about what I've done.   Y M N

20. I'm a cut above most people. The people I associate   Y M N
    with and the organizations I belong to are all influential
    and important.

21. Perhaps some people think I'm uptight or rigid, but I   Y M N
    believe strongly that there's never an excuse for im-
    moral or unethical behavior.

22. I prefer to get other people's input or advice before   Y M N
    making decisions, even everyday ones.

23. I just can't seem to throw things out, even if they're   Y M N
    useless or meaningless to me.

24. Maybe I do exaggerate my own importance, but frankly I think I'm worth it.   Y M N

25. I judge myself much too harshly: I'm always blaming myself for everything that goes wrong or doesn't work out.   Y M N

26. I wouldn't call myself a light-hearted person. Things weigh more heavily on me than on most people and I tend to be pretty somber most of the time.   Y M N

27. Sometimes I think that Guilt is my middle name, since I'm always feeling guilty and remorseful or like I've done something wrong.   Y M N

28. I don't have much confidence in myself. Sometimes I feel I'm just worthless.   Y M N

29. Even though I don't hesitate to tell others about my problems, I'm very uncomfortable letting them help me with them.   Y M N

30. People may think I talk too much about my misfortunes, but they don't understand how bad things really are for me.   Y M N

31. I sometimes find myself laughing at other people's misfortunes, even though I'm not very proud of that reaction. Maybe it's just a way of saying, "There but for the grace of God go I."   Y M N

32. I find it hard being around people who are better off than I am, since I often feel jealous of their good fortune.   Y M N

33. I sometimes find it difficult to let go and have fun. When opportunities to enjoy myself come up, for some reason I have a hard time taking advantage of them.   Y M N

34. When it comes to relationships, sometimes I think I am   Y M N
my own worst enemy. I keep getting involved with people who end up treating me badly or disappointing me.
I can't believe I'm so bad at sizing up others—I must be
naive.

35. I can be difficult to be with lots of times, and, when I   Y M N
think about it, my own expectations of others can be
pretty unreasonable. But I still get upset when they get
mad at me.

36. When someone really cares about me or treats me with   Y M N
a lot of kindness or tenderness, I often feel uninterested.
Somehow it just seems boring to me unless there's a real
challenge in the relationship.

37. I think sometimes I do too much for other people.   Y M N

38. I usually leave the big decisions to the important people   Y M N
in my life.

39. I'm not what you would call a self-starter. I'm a much   Y M N
better follower than a leader, but I can be a very loyal
team player.

40. I like to express agreement with other people. When I   Y M N
disagree, I usually keep it to myself.

41. I'll go out of my way to do things for other people—   Y M N
sometimes even unpleasant things—to get them to like
me.

42. I do much better when I'm in a relationship, because I   Y M N
feel pretty helpless when I'm on my own.

43. When a relationship ends, I get kind of panicky and   Y M N
start searching right away for a new one.

44. Probably I worry too much that I won't be able to take care of myself if I lose the important person in my life.   Y M N

45. Sometimes I worry so much that people will leave me that I get sort of frantic and call them up to get them to reassure me, which must get pretty annoying.   Y M N

46. I love being the center of attention—it's exhilarating. I'm much more comfortable in the middle of the action than at the sidelines.   Y M N

47. I like to flirt, and I like for people to think I'm sexually appealing.   Y M N

48. People describe me as very entertaining. I can tell about things that happen in a very enjoyable and colorful way, without having to get all the facts straight all the time.   Y M N

49. I'm rather suggestible. I have to watch out that I'm not too easily swayed by other people.   Y M N

50. All too often I assume there's more to a relationship than there really is. This causes me a lot of heartache.   Y M N

51. I typically get into very intense relationships, and I usually find my feelings about the person change from one extreme to another. Sometimes I almost worship, and other times I can't stand, the person I'm with.   Y M N

52. For me, envy is a fact of life. Either I'm envying somebody else, or someone else is probably envying me.   Y M N

53. I am not a very trusting person, even though I would like to be. I just can't help worrying that other people might take advantage of me unless I'm careful.   Y M N

54. Sometimes I think that my friends or colleagues are not really as loyal as I would like them to be. Y M N

55. I don't really have any close friends, except maybe some members of my immediate family. Y M N

56. I'm the jealous type. In my relationships I find myself worrying whether my partner is being faithful. Y M N

57. I am a fairly private person and I generally keep things to myself, since you never know who will use personal information to their own advantage. Y M N

58. I tend to be a loner, which is fine with me. I don't really enjoy being around other people that much, even my family. Y M N

59. When I have a choice, I prefer to do things by myself. Y M N

60. I don't have a very strong drive to have sex with anyone. Y M N

61. It's hard for me to be myself in intimate relationships. I'm afraid I'll seem ridiculous, so I hold back. Y M N

62. I'm shy around new people. Y M N

63. I often find social situations unbearable, even with people I know. I can't stand the feeling that the others are looking at me and sort of sizing me up, not always in a flattering way. Y M N

64. I usually wait to get involved with people until I'm sure they like me. Y M N

65. I feel more comfortable in work settings that do not involve a lot of people, because I can't help worrying that my coworkers will be critical of me. Y M N

66. Socially I am a very confident person. I talk comfortably and am not awfully self-conscious or anxious that I'll say something stupid or appear uninformed. Y M N

67. People don't really appreciate or understand me. Y M N

68. I can be rather critical of my boss or of other people in authority. Maybe I don't appreciate what it's like to be in their shoes, but it seems to me I sure could do a better job much of the time. Y M N

69. When somebody asks me to do something I don't want to do, I can be a real pain—I'll sometimes argue or sulk or get very grouchy. Y M N

70. If somebody nags me, I can get really stubborn and obnoxious, but later I might feel guilty and try to make up. Y M N

71. I wish I weren't always so down on other people. No matter what they do, I seem to find something wrong with them. Y M N

72. Some people say that I insist on doing too much myself, but I'd rather do the work myself than have someone else do it wrong or incompletely. And I'll risk being called "bossy" if that's what it takes to get people to do things in what I believe is the correct way. Y M N

73. I think strict discipline is extremely important. Although I don't necessarily believe in physical punishment, I do believe in the principle behind the saying "Spare the rod and spoil the child." Y M N

74. My family members sometimes complain that I don't   Y M N
    allow them enough independence or freedom. I guess I
    do run a pretty tight ship.

75. People have told me that I put them down in front of   Y M N
    others. They shouldn't be so thin-skinned—words
    aren't going to hurt anybody. And if they really think
    I'm being too critical, they should be able to stand up to
    me.

76. I suppose I can be fairly intimidating. Some people have   Y M N
    told me that they do what I want because they're afraid
    of me.

77. I prefer to be in the dominant position in my relation-   Y M N
    ships. As a result I can sometimes seem mean or cruel
    without realizing it.

78. I believe there are situations in which you have to step   Y M N
    on someone's toes to get where you're going.

79. I find that certain people do little things to tease, annoy,   Y M N
    or even insult me, just to get my goat.

80. If somebody doesn't treat me right, I'll probably hold a   Y M N
    grudge for a long time.

81. I don't necessarily tell the truth.   Y M N

82. Occasionally I make up stories or distort the truth, just   Y M N
    to see how other people will react. These are just jokes,
    though—no reason for anybody to get angry.

83. People sometimes tell me I act like I have a chip on my   Y M N
    shoulder. It's true that I'll fight or argue with anybody
    who gets on my bad side.

84. I have a keen sense for when I'm being criticized, even when it's veiled, and I can tell you that I don't let anybody get away with it.   Y M N

85. I have a terrible temper, but there's nothing I can do about it.   Y M N

86. People sometimes tell me that they can't be sure when to take my feelings seriously.   Y M N

87. I express my feelings in a vivid and dramatic way.   Y M N

88. I go my own way emotionally. For example, something sad may strike me as funny and I'll laugh.   Y M N

89. I'm very reactive mood-wise. Little things can set me off. In a matter of a few hours I can experience a wide range of feelings, from happy to sad, annoyed, or anxious. But the bad moods never last long.   Y M N

90. I tend to brood and worry a lot.   Y M N

91. I wish I didn't worry so much about what other people think of me in social situations.   Y M N

92. I hate trying new things or taking risks, because I'm afraid I'll make a fool of myself.   Y M N

93. There's not all that much that I really enjoy doing.   Y M N

94. You can call me "poker-faced," since I'm generally very unemotional.   Y M N

95. I'm not the type to reveal any reaction when others criticize me or even compliment me.　Y M N

96. I guess I'm on a different wavelength from most other people. Sometimes I can feel strange things that are very real to me, even though I can't prove them, such as being outside of my own body or in the presence of a family member who has died.　Y M N

97. I am fascinated by things like magic, ESP, and the supernatural. I have a sort of "sixth sense" and have sometimes had eerie experiences where I knew something was going to happen before it did.　Y M N

98. I tend to see the glass as half empty rather than half full.　Y M N

99. I do not spend money easily. Even though some people think I'm stingy, I believe that money belongs in the bank, in case something terrible happens.　Y M N

100. I like to act on impulse when the spirit moves me. For instance, I'll get drunk or stoned if I'm in the mood, I may indulge in food, maybe I'll drive too fast or enjoy a big shopping spree. Acting this way makes life a lot more interesting, although of course it backfires sometimes.　Y M N

101. I can be very dramatic when I'm upset. I have been known to threaten to harm myself, but I don't really mean it.　Y M N

102. I am intrigued by an underground kind of life where you can break the rules and get away with it.　Y M N

103. I just don't have the patience to stick with a job for long or worry about finances or paying my bills, so some people think I'm irresponsible.　Y M N

104. I'm not the kind of person who always takes the careful   Y M N
route. I may take risks—like driving over the speed
limit or driving when I've had something to drink—but
I know what I'm doing and I get where I'm going.

105. I like to do things spontaneously, without planning   Y M N
ahead.

106. When I was a kid I was something of a hell-raiser and   Y M N
was always getting into trouble. Some of these things
applied to me: I skipped school; I ran away from home;
I got into fights; I fooled around sexually; I told lies; I
stole; I bullied people; I messed up people's property.

107. When I'm under a lot of stress I can get unreasonably   Y M N
suspicious, or else I just tune everything out and pretend it isn't happening.

II. *Now transfer your answers to the score sheet.*

1. Note that the score sheet (pp. 48–52) is divided into fourteen columns, lettered A to N. Each of these columns in turn is subdivided
into three columns, lettered a, b, and c, in which you circle your
answer.

2. For each of the 107 questions, circle the appropriate letter *where it
appears* in the row. For example, your answer for Question 1 must
be entered in the J column.

Note that for questions 53, 55, and 57, you must enter the answer *in
two columns rather than one*.

question number	A			B			C			D			E			F			G			H			I			J			K			L			M			N		
	a	b	c	a	b	c	a	b	c	a	b	c	a	b	c	a	b	c	a	b	c	a	b	c	a	b	c	a	b	c	a	b	c	a	b	c	a	b	c	a	b	c
																									Y M N																	
													N M Y																													
													Y M N																	Y M N											
2							Y M N												Y M N																						
3																																					Y M N					
4																			Y M N																		Y M N					
5							Y M N									Y M N			Y M N																							
6																			Y M N																							
7																			Y M N											Y M N											
8																			Y M N											Y M N											
9										Y M N									Y M N																							
0																			Y M N			Y M N																			
1																																										
2																																										
3																																										
4																			Y M N																							

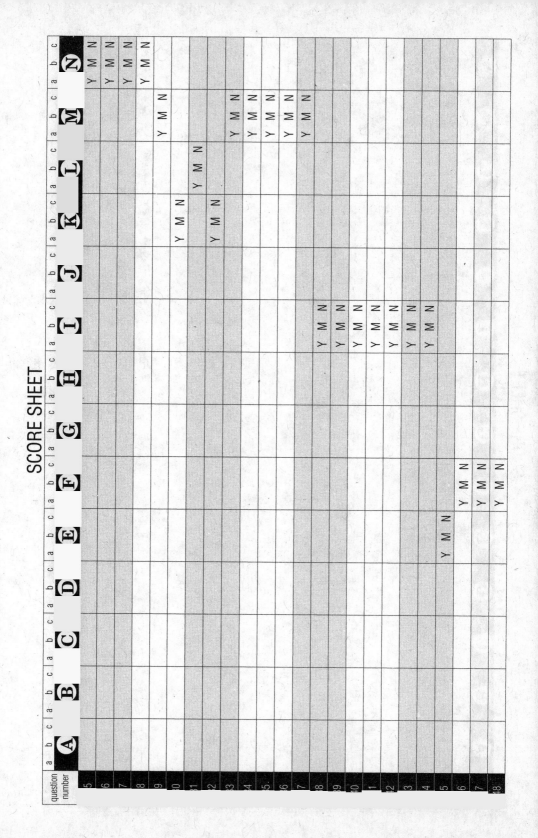

SCORE SHEET

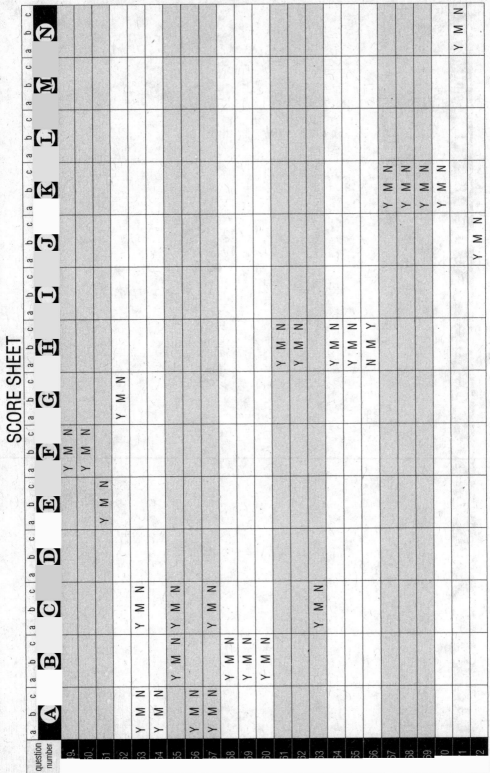

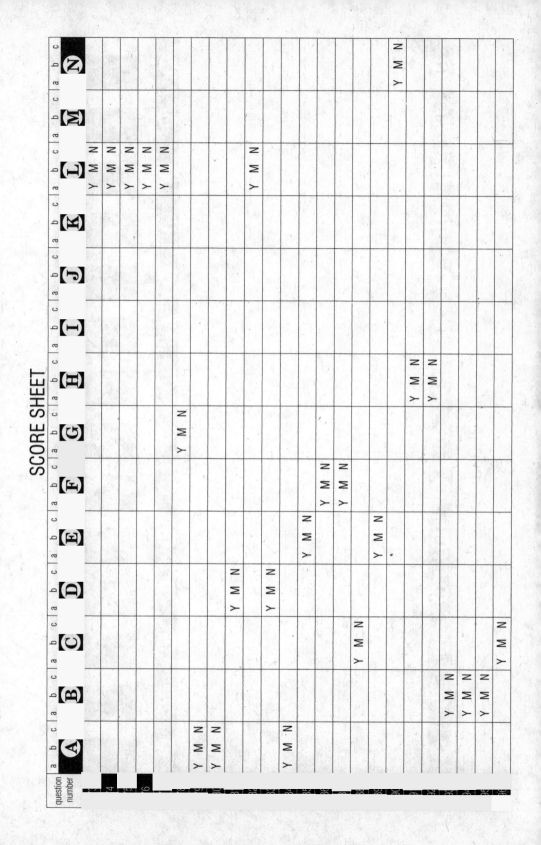

SCORE SHEET

SCORE SHEET

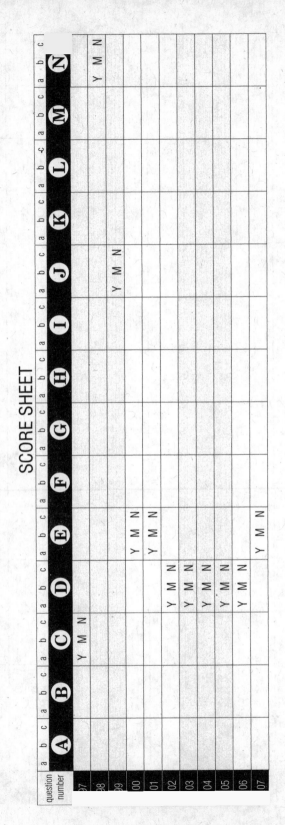

TOTALS SHEET

III. *Calculate your total score as follows:*

1. In column A, count the number of circled items that appear in the *left hand* of the three answer columns (subcolumn a). Enter this number in the appropriate box on the totals sheet.

   You will then multiply this number by 2. (For example, if you circled 3 items in the left-hand column of column A, your score will be $3 \times 2 = 6$.)

2. In column A, count the number of circled items (M) that appear in the *center* of the three answer columns (subcolumn b). Enter this number in the appropriate totals box. (For example, if you circled 4 items in the center column of column A, your score will be 4.)

3. To complete your total score for column A, add the scores from subcolumn a $\times 2$ and subcolumn b. (For example, if subcolumn a $\times 2$ is 6 and subcolumn b is 4, your total score for column A is 10.)

4. Repeat these steps for columns B through N.

Note: The score for the right-hand column (subcolumn c) is not calculated and will not be used in your graph.

EXAMPLE:

TOTALS	**A**		
col. a	3	x2=	6
col. b		+	4
add for total		=	10

IV. Draw your Personality Self-Portrait on the graph as follows:

1. For each of the fourteen personality styles listed on the graph, enter your score from the totals sheet in the appropriate column of the graph by circling the number. (For example, if your total score in column A on the score sheet is 7, circle 7 in the A—"Vigilant"—column of the graph.)

2. After entering all fourteen personality-style scores on the graph, draw a line connecting each circled score in the next column. The resulting pattern is your Personality Self-Portrait. (Examples of completed graphs appear in the Appendix.)

PERSONALITY SELF-PORTRAIT GRAPH

Letter	Category	Scale (top to bottom)
A	VIGILANT	14 13 12 11 10 9 8 7 6 5 4 3 2 1 0
B	SOLITARY	14 13 12 11 10 9 8 7 6 5 4 3 2 1 0
C	IDIOSYNCRATIC	18 17 16 15 14 13 12 11 10 9 8 7 6 5 4 3 2 1 0
D	ADVENTUROUS	16 15 14 13 12 11 10 9 8 7 6 5 4 3 2 1 0
E	MERCURIAL	18 17 16 15 14 13 12 11 10 9 8 7 6 5 4 3 2 1 0
F	DRAMATIC	16 15 14 13 12 11 10 9 8 7 6 5 4 3 2 1 0
G	SELF-CONFIDENT	18 17 16 15 14 13 12 11 10 9 8 7 6 5 4 3 2 1 0
H	SENSITIVE	14 13 12 11 10 9 8 7 6 5 4 3 2 1 0
I	DEVOTED	16 15 14 13 12 11 10 9 8 7 6 5 4 3 2 1 0
J	CONSCIENTIOUS	16 15 14 13 12 11 10 9 8 7 6 5 4 3 2 1 0
K	LEISURELY	14 13 12 11 10 9 8 7 6 5 4 3 2 1 0
L	AGGRESSIVE	16 15 14 13 12 11 10 9 8 7 6 5 4 3 2 1 0
M	SELF-SACRIFICING	16 15 14 13 12 11 10 9 8 7 6 5 4 3 2 1 0
N	SERIOUS	14 13 12 11 10 9 8 7 6 5 4 3 2 1 0

INTERPRETING YOUR PERSONALITY SELF-PORTRAIT

Your Personality Self-Portrait consists of a graph of the structure of your personality pattern. Each of the fourteen individual styles contributes to this pattern in some way, perhaps in its very absence. All the styles work together to determine the personality style that is unique to you. Use this graph as a key to finding yourself within the fourteen personality-style chapters.

WHAT TO LOOK FOR

You will learn most about yourself if you concentrate first on the styles that are the strongest (that is, they score highest) in your pattern and then on the relative order of importance of all the styles. The complexity of your personality is revealed in the relationship of the styles to one another, not just the degree of any one particular style. The individual chapters that discuss each style in depth will reveal how the styles enhance, offset, or even contradict one another.

WHAT THE NUMBERS MEAN

Your specific numerical score on any individual style is not itself significant. The numbers are used simply to plot the graph. It is meaningless to say that you are a "ten" in Devoted style or a "four" in Serious.

Should you be nearly off the chart in a particular column, you are clearly influenced very strongly by that style. Some people will have high scores overall. These people will likely have very definite, intense personalities when compared with those who score lower overall. This does not make them either better or worse than anyone else.

Similarly, a low score in any style does not indicate a deficiency in your personality. For instance, scoring low on Sensitive style does not mean that you are an insensitive person, and scoring low in Self-Confident does not mean that you lack self-esteem. A low score on Adventurous relative to your other styles does not signify that you have no sense of adventure (it does mean, though, that you don't enjoy risk for its own sake). Most people can expect to score low in one or even many columns.

The difference between people who score high on most styles and those who score low may boil down only to the low-scorer's hesitation to answer an unqualified Yes on questions he or she agrees with.

Your Highest Scores

The highest peaks on your Self-Portrait graph are your dominant, leading styles; these shape the character of your personality most strongly. If you choose to read the chapters that correspond to your leading styles first, you will gather the information that applies most strongly to you. To discover how you come across to others, why you worry about the things you do, how to recognize your strengths and take advantage of them, among much else, these chapters are the place to begin. You can then refer to the chapters in order of their diminishing importance on your graph.

Understanding How the Styles Blend Together

As we have said, there is no "pure" style. As the two chart interpretations in the Appendix show, all the contributing styles in a personality pattern will express themselves in some way.

For example, we have mentioned that people who are dominated by the Dramatic style are very emotional, fun-loving, and outgoing, and that people who are ruled by the Conscientious keep their feelings to themselves and are more circumspect and controlled. But many people are strongly influenced by both of these styles. If your Personality Self-Portrait is most strongly Conscientious, with Dramatic inching up close behind, you may find that you experience very intense feelings but seldom reveal them. If, on the other hand, you are primarily Dramatic, with Conscientious coming second, you will tend to be emotional and give great weight to your feelings, but you may be able to put your feelings aside and be very determined and goal-directed in your work.

As you learn about the various styles, you'll find many others that seem almost opposite from one another—as if they couldn't exist in the same person. Seeing how your personality exhibits such apparently opposing styles may provide insight into some of your recurring inner conflicts. For example, if Dramatic is among your dominant styles, you're very social and love parties. But if you are highly Sensitive also, you feel uneasy in social situations. The coexistence of these two styles could explain your self-consciousness among strangers or your struggle to shake off inhibitions and be your lively self on some social occasions.

Reflecting on opposing styles of similar strength in your pattern could also help you recognize a side to yourself you keep trying to hide or deny. If you are, say, chiefly Conscientious (highly responsible and proper) with a strong streak of Adventurous (a challenger who thrives on risk), you may have spent enormous energy trying to bury your "escapist" fantasy of leaving your job and sailing around the world for a year or two. But the urge to be a free spirit will not go away. Face it, it's part of you. Instead of feeling you should (Conscientious types are full of "shoulds") map out a career in a job bores you, accept that you will never be content unless you find a way to embrace rather than punish the risk-loving adventurer in you.

Your Lowest Scores

The styles that are least characteristic of you can also explain a lot about your personality and your life course. Thus, a predominantly Idiosyncratic person marches to his or her own drummer; highly spiritual, this person has difficulty operating according to conventional beliefs and rules. An Idiosyncratic person with little or none of the Conscientious style in his or her personality should not consider a job or a relationship, no matter how attractive, in which toeing the conventional line in personal beliefs, interests, or lifestyle is all-important.

As another example, someone who is highly Mercurial loves spontaneity. Although Vigilant people are always second-guessing the motives of other people, an absence of this style in a strongly Mercurial person could indicate a person who would benefit by thinking about what companions have in mind before going off for a good time.

Finding Hidden Strengths

Study your chart to discover personality assets that you may not have realized you had. The styles that are most dominant in your personality make themselves known to yourself and others. But some of those that are only moderate in relation to your principal styles may harbor hidden strengths. If you are highly Leisurely, you probably already know just how much you resist getting to work or meeting deadlines. Discovering that you have a moderate amount of Self-Confident style could alert you to your inherent ambition and frustration-tolerance, strengths to get on with your direction in life. Often extremely Conscientious people come off as emotionally ungiving. Commonly their mates grow frustrated over not hearing those three little words: I love you. But a Conscientious person who finds he or she has at least a moderate degree of one of the emotional styles (perhaps Dramatic or Sensitive) will discover a reservoir of hidden emotionality that perhaps can be put to use.

Key Domains

Other useful information can be garnered by considering your styles' collective key domains, which are explained in the previous chapter (see also the chart on p. 26) and detailed within each style chapter. Notice the extent to which your strongest personality styles overlap in their ruling domains. If you're a predominantly Dramatic, Sensitive, and Devoted person, for instance, you'll notice that Relationships is key for each. You may not realize the extent to which you rely on other people's opinion of you. Knowing this, you may be encouraged to focus more on what *you* think. On the other hand, someone with a preponderance of Solitary, Idiosyncratic, and Leisurely styles, for which Self is the key domain, may want to work on looking at things from the other person's point of view.

INTERPRETING CHARTS FOR COUPLES AND GROUPS

Those who wish to understand and strengthen their relationships to one another—couples, families, therapy groups, colleagues, and coworkers—can compare charts in a number of ways.

By looking at each participant's dominant styles, you'll reveal perhaps striking differences as well as similarities in how you each function in the six fundamental domains of life. As mentioned in chapter 1, it's all too human to value similarities over differences and to blame the other person for going about things the "wrong" way. Comparing charts is one way to picture individual differences as a function of normal, predictable variations. Consulting the appropriate style chapters will then provide specific information about how each style operates in each life domain and about predictable conflicts that arise among people with various styles.

For example, as already alluded to, the contrasts between Dramatic and Conscientious people are the source of obvious problems. Tidy and logical and detail-oriented to the point of being perfectionists, Conscientious types clash with the Dramatic's colorful, emotional, creative, disorganized nature. At home, the Dramatic person often feels hurt and rejected because the Conscientious partner doesn't show emotion. Meanwhile, the Conscientious person fumes over the Dramatic mate's dislike of balancing the checkbook or saving tax-deduction receipts and grows highly irritated by his or her moods. At work, problems surface because the Conscientious person needs to be in control and to have everything done his or her often overly detailed way. Here the Dramatic person functions best when allowed to trust hunches rather than logic and to be excused from detailed follow-through.

Each style chapter offers specific advice on dealing with people of that particular style. Underlying all the suggestions is the basic principle that if you can accept that everybody's different and pinpoint your similarities and dissimilarities along dimensions of style, you can find a way to cooperate, compromise, and coexist.

Much as you can look at your own personality as a system consisting of different, sometimes contradictory styles, you can also approach the personalities of those in couples or groups as complex personality-style systems. The information will guide you in identifying ways to make the system function better. Often the source of the conflict points the way to the solution. Using the same example of a highly Conscientious person paired with a very Dramatic one—an extremely common match —although they're miles apart in style on so many domains of life, when they accept their fundamental differences, they end up creating a functioning, well-balanced unit. The dry, logical Conscientious person can learn to appreciate that he or she lives vicariously through the Dramatic individual's rich emotional experience. The Dramatic partner can recognize the value of the order and security that the Conscientious person provides, in which they both can thrive.

Remember that the Self-Portraits reveal all test-takers as they are— not what's "wrong" with them or how they should change in order to become acceptable. The object of interpreting the charts in relation to couples and groups is not to change anyone's personality or to force someone to come around to your way of approaching life. Rather, use the Personality Self-Portrait to recognize what you all are like, to problem-solve using this information, and to improve communication for the benefit of all.

TRACKING GROWTH AND CHANGE

Your Personality Self-Portrait is not etched in stone. It is as alive as you are. Nothing organic stays precisely the same from day to day. Although your overall pattern will likely stay the same at least over the short term, the degrees of each style within that pattern may vary somewhat, depending on what's going on in your life at the moment. If you've broken up with the love of your life, or if you've just fallen in love, your mood today may color your answers to some of the questions and alter the degree of one or more styles.

Powerful life experiences may also change your personality more drastically. The birth of a child, for example, may bring the Devoted personality style to the fore while reducing a Solitary influence substantially. Intense psychotherapy can also restructure your personality pattern.

Draw your Personality Self-Portrait again from time to time. Track how your personality "breathes," grows, changes, and in every way keeps up with the path that you have taken in your life.

———————————

Note: For information about how to obtain "The Personality Self-Portrait" test for your computer, or if you wish separate test booklets, call Multi-Health Systems, Inc., toll-free, at: 1-800-456-3003 (U.S.) or 1-800-268-6011 (Canada).

CHAPTER 4

Conscientious Style

"THE RIGHT STUFF"

Call them the backbone of America. Conscientious-style people are the men and women of strong moral principle and absolute certainty, and they won't rest until the job is done and done right. They are loyal to their families, their causes, and their superiors. Hard work is a hallmark of this personality style; Conscientious types *achieve*. No accomplished doctor, lawyer, scientist, or business executive could get far without a substantial amount of Conscientious style in his or her personality pattern. Neither could a computer whiz, an efficient housekeeper, an accountant, a straight-A student, a good secretary—or anyone else who works hard to do well.

The Conscientious personality style flourishes within cultures such as ours in which the work ethic thrives. Conscientious traits—hard work, prudence, conventionality—may even confer a longevity advantage. We address this style first among the fourteen because the Conscientious style is adaptable, common, and thus likely to be a principal component of many diverse personality profiles. Indeed, within our society so wide a range of Conscientious behaviors is considered normal, even admirable, that it may be hard to draw the line between the Conscientious personality style and the Obsessive-Compulsive personality disorder (p. 77) that marks its extreme. What are we to say about the man or woman who always takes a briefcase filled with work along on vacation? Is he or she a workaholic who can't relax and is headed for an early heart attack? Or is this a person who loves to work, thrives on challenge, and is bound for great things in his or her career? That depends on whether the style enriches the six domains of this person's life or controls and distorts them. Read on.

THE EIGHT CHARACTERISTICS

The following eight traits and behaviors are clues to the presence of the Conscientious style. A person who has a strong Conscientious tendency will demonstrate more of these behaviors more intensely than someone who has less of this style.

1. *Hard work.* The Conscientious person is dedicated to work, works very hard, and is capable of intense, single-minded effort.

2. *The right thing.* To be Conscientious is to be a person of conscience. These are men and women of strong moral principles and values. Opinions and beliefs on any subject are rarely held lightly. Conscientious individuals want to do the right thing.

3. *The right way.* Everything must be done "right," and the Conscientious person has a clear understanding of what that means, from the correct way to balance the checkbook, to the best strategy to achieve the boss's objectives, to how to fit every single dirty dish into the dishwasher.

4. *Perfectionism.* The Conscientious person likes all tasks and projects to be complete to the final detail, without even minor flaws.

5. *Perseverance.* They stick to their convictions and opinions. Opposition only serves to strengthen their dogged determination.

6. *Order and detail.* Conscientious people like the appearance of orderliness and tidiness. They are good organizers, catalogers, and list makers. No detail is too small for Conscientious consideration.

7. *Prudence.* Thrifty, careful, and cautious in all areas of their lives, Conscientious individuals do not give in to reckless abandon or wild excess.

8. *Accumulation.* A "pack rat," the Conscientious person saves and collects things, reluctant to discard anything that has, formerly had, or someday may have value for him or her.

THE SIX DOMAINS OF
CONSCIENTIOUS FUNCTIONING

WORK: THE KEY DOMAIN

Most of the key behaviors that identify the Conscientious style occur in the area of work. And work—be it housework, career, or leisure-time projects—is where this style shines. Work is the key domain of functioning for the Conscientious style, and it dominates all others.

Conscientious individuals are competent, organized, good with detail, perfectionistic, thorough, determined, and loyal—the employee whom every boss dreams of finding, the student who makes a teacher's year worthwhile, the housekeeper who keeps the family functioning like clockwork. They're doers, and "doing" extends to all hours of the day. Even during their leisure time, Conscientious people are busy with projects and activities. Conscientious is the man who retires, finally, at age seventy-five and is delighted to spend all day at his workbench. Conscientious is the executive who spends lunch hours at her health club doing sit-ups. Conscientious is the person who takes up gardening as a hobby and, with only evenings and weekends to devote to it, in just one season manages to create a gorgeous bed of annuals and perennials, all fertilized, mulched, staked, and weed-free. Conscientious are all those people who work the daily crossword puzzles until every square is complete.

Conscientious people enjoy intense, focused, detailed activity. They try hard at everything they do—elbow grease is their stock in trade—and they'd rather try hard than have it easy. The effort is part of what makes the undertaking worthwhile.

Don't feel sorry that the Conscientious person has to work so hard. He or she needs the challenge of working to perfection and thrives on sheer drive toward accomplishment. It doesn't matter how much time it takes. Diana W. asked Ken C., her extremely Conscientious assistant, to run her all-important 175-page document through the copying machine. Ken chose to stay late to hand-feed every page, checking to make sure the printing was uniformly dark and centered perfectly on each page, and discarding pages that were even slightly unacceptable. If she'd had to do it herself, Diana would have run the document off automatically and then spent the evening at the theater. But that's the difference between Diana and Ken. She'd settle for good enough; to a Conscientious person like Ken, no task is worth doing if it isn't done just right.

Ken's typically Conscientious perseverance is both a plus and a minus at his job, though. Self-Confident Diana is delighted to have an assistant who devotes himself to the details that she has no patience for, and who doesn't demand special treatment for investing extra time in the pursuit of perfection—that's why she hired him. But when Diana wants Ken to go on to something else before he feels he has completed a job to his personal standards, or to do something a different way, she grows frustrated and impatient with his inflexibility. Ken in all his Conscientiousness cannot change course midway or defer to someone else's methodology. He cannot eliminate steps in a process or skip by details. Indeed, reports he writes for Diana are, to her mind, drowning in minutiae. But Diana's Self-Confident style makes her good at delegating. Most of the time she accepts that he simply can't "cut to the chase," but since she can, she edits his reports down to essentials.

The Conscientious Manager

Because they are willing to devote so much time and hard work, people with a substantial amount of Conscientious style tend to move toward the top of many professions. While people with personality styles such as Self-Confident and Aggressive can rise through the ranks through sheer political acumen and/or manipulation of power, Conscientious individuals become successful through good old-fashioned hard work. They're loyal, they respect authority, and they often do their best work when they're accountable to someone for it. For these reasons, a Conscientious man or woman will often make an extraordinary second in command—the behind-the-scenes individual whom you can count on to implement your policy and projects.

The top managerial positions, however, may require skills that go against the Conscientious grain, such as making quick decisions, setting priorities, and delegating responsibility. Conscientious types set a high standard for themselves. Some need to be so thorough, to check and recheck every detail before coming to any conclusion, that they can be exasperatingly slow to make up their minds, even on minor matters (see "Decisions, Decisions," p. 69).

Conscientious individuals tend to expect the same above-and-beyond-the-call-of-duty thoroughness, devotion, and accomplishment from others, which may not always be appropriate. Successful management requires greater flexibility in standards, ability to set priorities, and respect for differing work styles in other people than the "unadulterated" Conscientious personality style may permit (a streak of Self-Confident or Aggressive style could contribute these qualities; see chapters 5 and 16). Still, even extremely Conscientious people tend to rise fairly high. If you work for someone who has more than his or her share of this personality style, see the survival tips on p. 73.

Careers for the Conscientious

The Conscientious personality style goes hand in hand with a mind for facts, categories, and technical detail. Thus, Conscientious types tend to gravitate toward work in science, medicine, research, mathematics, business, accounting, law, engineering, computers and data processing, and many skilled crafts, or to the technical, organizing side of any profession. The Conscientious style brings with it a greater appreciation for and ability to deal with the fine points than the big picture. Individuals with this personality style can often function well as right-hand assistants for leaders or supervisors who have strong conceptual skills and good hunches but who need someone to research the background and fill in the details.

SELF: THE HARDWORKING CONSCIENCE

The Conscientious person is quick to ask, "What do you do?" A person's occupation is the most important information a Conscientious person can seek, for to a Conscientious person, Self *is* Work: "I am a psychiatrist." "I am a writer." Conscientious individuals who do not have (or believe they do not have) important-enough work by which to define themselves may squirm at the what-do-you-do question—like some modern-day homemakers who (although they may be extraordinarily competent at that multiskilled job and put in ceaseless overtime) may believe that they should be out in the workplace as well. Conscientious men and women set a high standard of responsibility for themselves. They believe that they must produce to the best of their abilities in socially or culturally approved ways at all times. They must never underperform and they must never have it easy.

The Case of the Guilty Multimillionaire

At age fifty, Michael B. is a millionaire several times over. He is an M.D. who was at the helm of his family's drug company until the family decided to sell. Now, for the first time, Michael is free to pursue his many beloved activities—travel, yacht racing, scuba diving, art collecting, and photography. Yet, Michael feels awkward when anyone says, "Nice to meet you, Michael. What do you do?" He can't simply say he's retired, and he doesn't feel right saying he's a doctor, because he isn't using those skills. So, instead he runs through a list of his activities: "Well, I race my yacht, I collect post-Impressionist art, I travel in the Far East . . ."

It's difficult for Michael to enjoy his retirement because, like all other Conscientious types, he has a powerful conscience and a huge sense of responsibility. He believes he *should* be working, and he will assure you, if you ask him what he does, that all his activities require a great deal of effort and that he is always busy. In fact, Michael, whose personality has a moderate streak of Self-Sacrificing style, is a very active philanthropist and spends considerable time helping out at a home for kids whose parents are in prison. But, typical of Conscientious and Self-Sacrificing styles, he has a similarly strong sense of propriety and doesn't think it's right to brag about helping others.

Conscientious people measure themselves and their behavior along the strict yardstick of a strong, demanding inner authority. When you listen to a Conscientious person speak, count how many times he or she says, "I should . . ." or, "You should . . ." (Conscientious types do like to give advice). Because of this very developed conscience, Conscientious people often contribute greatly to our society. They demand perfection in their own moral behavior and often expect it from everyone else. They may become heroes in popular or unpopular wars because they believe they should support their cause and/or their country.

Michael believes strongly that he should share his wealth with persons less fortunate than himself. But the same sense of *I should,* the same pressure for moral perfection, can be personally tormenting. Self-acceptance may come hard for Conscientious people. They often have a deep feeling that they fall short of the mark. Michael thinks that to be a truly upstanding member of society and a respectable human being, he should resume his professional career—he should have a "real" job. He can't accept that he's doing good, and being good, just as he is.

EMOTIONS, SELF-CONTROL, AND REAL WORLD: THE VOICE OF REASON

The voice of authority, inner or outer, that the Conscientious person heeds provides the basis for excellent self-discipline. Self-discipline is the *sine qua non* of success. Bobby D. made it to the major leagues by following a daily baseball training schedule for seven years in the minors and by refusing even to consider trying the recreational and supposedly performance-enhancing drugs that some of his teammates were using. Conscientious young musicians practice their instruments while other kids take off on their skateboards. Conscientious adults stay within their credit-card limits. When they finally decide to go to Weight Watchers, they can follow the regimen without veering into the ice cream store.

Conscientious individuals are ruled by their heads. Emotions, urges, whims, or hungers do not often get the best of them. You could call them "left-brained"—and there is some physiological evidence that people with Conscientious personality styles *are* dominated by the left hemisphere of their brains, which is associated with reason and analytic thinking style.

You won't catch Conscientious Connie staying in bed late to make love again with Norman the first time he stays over. Connie enjoys making love, but there's a time and place for everything, she'll tell you. Connie isn't made of iron, however, and had Norman been more amorous she might have given in—but then she would have felt guilty about being late for work. The stronger the Conscientious bent, the harder it is to forgive oneself for ordinary human lapses. When one's behavior does not measure up to high self-expectations (the "shoulds"), guilt results. Thus, guilt and worry are frequent companions to the Conscientious personality style.

Reserve generally marks the emotional behavior of the Conscientious style. If this is your dominant style, you're not sentimental or gushy; you play your feelings close to the vest. You prefer to act on reason and to react coolly. Conscientious men and women generally do not operate at their best in the "emotional mode." They do not express feelings easily or comfortably and often come across as dry, formal, and intellectual. Although they find it easier to express anger when they're with people whom they consider subordinate, in response to a conflict with someone in authority they prefer to reason their way back into the boss's good graces. Early in her career, Carolyn, the corporate executive we met in chapter 1, was so horrified with herself for bursting into tears while being criticized by her boss that she sought an immediate consultation with a psychotherapist. (She later canceled the appointment.) Situations that produce strong feelings and lead to their spontaneous expression can be among the greatest sources of stress for individuals who, like Carolyn, are dominated by this personality style.

This rational focus can sometimes turn the Real World of the Conscientious individual into a place devoid of nuance. The music of a Conscientious virtuoso pianist may be a technical tour de force that, to those with an ear for it, lacks feeling. Failing to perceive the world's subtle, emotional grays, Conscientious individuals tend to perceive everything as clearly black and white. Fanatics, religious or otherwise, often are Conscientious to an extreme. They know that they and their followers are right—and that everyone else is wrong. To exceedingly Conscientious and Obsessive-Compulsive people, the world may consist of two extremes, with no question marks in between.

Decisions, Decisions

Individuals dominated by this Conscientious rational/intellectual orientation may easily discern the differences between good and bad, right and wrong. Where they may run into trouble is in deciding between two good or right things. For instance, Martha D. is trying to figure out what's the best activity for her family for the summer. She has used her Conscientious abilities to put together a list of possibilities that are all interesting and appealing: (1) they could spend a month on a working farm; (2) Martha and her husband could stay in town and have some time to themselves while the children go away to ice-hockey camp; (3) they could all stay in town for the summer and plan different outings every weekend; (4) they could rent a house at the beach.

It's now mid-May and Martha isn't close to a decision. Martha's husband says anything's fine with him, the kids change their minds from week to week—and Martha's beginning to wake up at four in the morning agonizing over which activity to choose.

Well, Martha, what do you really *want* to do? "I want to do what's best for my family," she answers Conscientiously. She's searching for the perfect activity, as if there were such a thing, and "head"-oriented as she is, she can't trust her feelings to help her decide. Conscientious people can't operate comfortably on hunches, inspiration, or emotion. This protects them from acting on ill-considered impulses—but it also keeps them stuck weighing and reweighing all sides of the issue(s).

In fact, down deep Martha dreams of plopping herself and her family at the beach for the summer and having a loose, free, spontaneous, good time—which makes her feel guilty. She worries (how Conscientious people can worry!) that this desire to take it easy conflicts with her duty to provide appropriate, constructive learning experiences for her family.

In part because she waited so long that some of the options became unavailable (which is one way to make a decision), they ended up going to the beach. Martha needn't have worried. Her family did not grow lazy, fat, or ineffectual in the sand. With Martha's unfailing focus and direction, they were assured of having projects and activities to occupy them throughout the summer. Neither did they get sunburned; Martha had them all slathered with just the *right* degree of sunblock.

Stress!

Conscientious is a high-stress personality style—prone to Type A health risks when the style becomes extreme (see p. 83). For all their enviable self-control and direction, many Conscientious people find it difficult to relax, let stress drift away, calm their thoughts and worries, and experience pleasure.

To a Conscientious person, unstructured free time can be more stressful than a briefcase full of work. So the Conscientious individual will bring work home or take it along on vacation, and plan structured activities to occupy leisure time. When Carolyn lost her job following the corporate takeover, she plummeted briefly into panic and despair because she had *time* on her hands. It didn't take her long, however, to master her crisis using the typical Conscientious coping mechanism: Roll up your sleeves and get to work at something! To some non-Conscientious individuals, a work-work-work world like Carolyn's may seem an endless treadmill. But to Carolyn and her many comrades in style, even running in circles beats sitting around.

Stuff!

Walk into a Conscientious person's basement or attic and take a look at the piles of things stored there that may never be used again—although you'll never convince him or her of that.

Conscientious types are the prototypical pack rats. They save and collect anything and everything—string, books and magazines, tools, cosmetics, records and tapes, stationery supplies, antiques and just plain junk, all the letters they ever received, pictures they ever took (even the lousy or duplicate shots), and clothes they ever wore. This stuff may be a major source of stress to their spouses, but Conscientious people want to know it's all there where they can find it.

RELATIONSHIPS: STEADINESS AND DISTANCE

Conscientious people can make great husbands or wives and good and lasting friends. These folks value their relationships and families and are not quick to give them up. They're loyal, faithful, responsible, and will take extremely good care of their mates—but they're unemotional and unromantic about it. You may not get silk lingerie from your Conscientious husband, or a dozen roses on your anniversary, but your house will have the most efficient new furnace on the block. The bills will be paid, and the life insurance policy will have all the provisions you could ever need. The Conscientious homemaker will take pains to have her husband's meals on the table, his shirts ironed, and the house cleaned spick-and-span, even if she works outside the home.

But intimacy is hard for a Conscientious person. For all their certainty about who they are and what they do, they are less secure with the emotional part of life. Conscientious people like to be around people, but they keep their emotional distance. Because they are task oriented, Conscientious individuals are most at ease with people when they are doing something together—say, fishing, playing tennis, or visiting a museum. They can discuss computers, cars, recipes, gardening tools, and baseball statistics with great enthusiasm, and they can tell you what they think about politics and world events. But please don't ask them to share their feelings.

This does not mean that Conscientious people have no feelings or emotional needs. They simply find it anxiety-provoking to express their feelings, or even, sometimes, to recognize them. A common source of stress in their love relationships is that Conscientious men and women can't, don't, and won't say "I love you" or otherwise emotionally reassure their mates, to whom they may nonetheless be deeply attached.

Other relationship difficulties arise from the Conscientious person's stubbornness and need for perfection. Conscientious men and women may have a hard time letting others do things their own way. Problem solving may be difficult, because Conscientious people may need to be "right" and to "win." To the person with a lot of Conscientious style in his or her personality pattern, to compromise means to "give in."

Conscientious people can appear stingy, overcautious, and ungenerous, but beneath these habits is often a devoted, emotionally steady person who can be relied and depended upon, who is a good provider, and who will always come through for the people who stay close to him or her. During times of stress, Conscientious people may bury all suggestion of emotion as they dive deep into their work, but they won't run away from you unless you push them. A healthy degree of Conscientious personality style in either partner is good glue for lasting relationships.

The Good Conscientious Parent

Conscientious parents teach their kids strong moral values and instill an appreciation for hard work and ambition. Their families are very important to them and they take care of them well. As with their subordinates and coworkers, Conscientious mates tend to demand an across-the-board high level of competence from the members of their families.

They must take care, though, not to take all the fun out of learning experiences by turning them into strict lessons in how things should be done. They must beware, too, of subjecting their kids to the pressure of always having to achieve extraordinary results to measure up to their parents' expectations. Sometimes children of very Conscientious parents grow up to feel that they were never appreciated with, or for, all their human frailties. They may be fearful of making mistakes and have an inner sense that they're not and never will be good enough. The Conscientious parent may in fact be very proud of his or her offspring but may be unable to express the approval or just plain affection that the child craves. If there is a non-Conscientious parent in the family, however, he or she may be able to provide enough sentiment, reassurance, hugs, and kisses to make up for the other parent's apparent distance and stiffness.

Good/Bad Matches

Although Conscientious people tend not to share their feelings, they are not against feelings, nor do they mind other people expressing theirs, as long as there is no demand for reciprocity. For all their emotional reserve, Conscientious people often pair up with people strong on the Dramatic personality style—which is among the most emotionally effusive of the fourteen styles. Through their emotionally expressive mates, they vicariously gain the emotional freedom they lack. And the Dramatic spouse gains the emotional cool and rational competence that better grounds him or her in life. This match can be very workable—if the Conscientious person can squeak out a couple of "I love you's" and the Dramatic spouse can manage with a little less display of affection at times. Consider the Conscientious-Dramatic duo formed by Ralph and Alice Cramden of the old *Honeymooners* television series. Good, accommodating, loyal, thoughtful, dedicated, reasonable, hardworking Alice is the Conscientious partner, whereas emotional, excitable, life-of-the-party, vain, often exasperating Ralph is Dramatic to a tee. They stick it out through thick and thin, night after night, rerun after rerun.

Similarly, Conscientious people often appreciate risk-taking Adventurous others, as long as that style is at a moderate level. Moderate-level Serious and Sensitive styles may also be appealing. Relationships with Devoted and Self-Sacrificing types can be very solid. Conscientious-Conscientious relationships are quite common and mutually respectful but are prone to power struggles.

The strongly Conscientious personality style does not usually coexist well with predominantly Self-Confident, Aggressive, or Vigilant styles in others. The need of these three personality styles to have things their own way and/or their inflexibility rubs abrasively against similar traits in the Conscientious person. Strongly Leisurely people, with their lack of time urgency or drive to achieve at work can drive Conscientious partners to distraction. Nonetheless, because Conscientious types are good at taking care of the details of life, and because they feel so strongly about doing such tasks their own way, they often end up pairing up with Leisurely people, who are only too willing to be relieved of responsibility.

TIPS ON DEALING WITH THE CONSCIENTIOUS PERSON IN YOUR LIFE

1. Be humorously tolerant. Let the Conscientious person have his or her habits. Instead of shrieking, "For God's sake, come to bed! It's three A.M.! You can work out the computer glitch in the morning!" smile and say to yourself, "That's my Ernie. He can't relax until he's figured it out."

2. Stay flexible. Just because Ernie stays up all night tinkering with the computer doesn't mean you have to lose sleep. Go to bed. And during all those waking hours in which your Conscientious mate is working, develop your own interests and activities.

3. Don't wait for the Conscientious person to change. Bring your strengths to the relationship and use them. For example, your Conscientious mate may be reluctant to experiment sexually and your sex life may become a boring routine. If you are a little looser, why don't *you* try something new with your mate?

4. Don't expect compliments or easy expressions of affection; these are not a barometer of how a Conscientious person feels about you. Your Conscientious husband may fail to say a word about your appearance after you've spent half the day dressing for the dinner-dance. Rest assured that he sees how fabulous you look and is beaming inwardly.

5. Avoid arguments and power struggles at all costs. Conscientious people must win—it's their nature. Conscientious men and women are consummate arguers and may nitpick and split hairs until you walk out or give in. You can often prevent an escalation of hostility simply by listening to what the person has to say, no matter how

provocative, and responding, "I understand what you're saying," or a similarly neutral comment.

6. Appreciate and enjoy the security and stability that the Conscientious person brings to the relationship. Be reassured that he or she takes care of the details of your life so well. Tell the person how much you appreciate and depend on him or her. Conscientious people like to be needed. While you're at it, tell your Conscientious husband, wife, father, or mother how much you care for him or her. We all need to hear that, even if some of us aren't so good at saying it.

If the Conscientious person in your life is your boss, see the tips on pp. 79–80.

MAKING THE MOST OF YOUR CONSCIENTIOUS STYLE

Great organizers and list makers, Conscientious individuals can harness these skills in particular to overcome some of the pitfalls of their personality style. The potential stress-related health risks of this style (see p. 83) make an urgent priority of broadening one's personal life and learning to relax.

Exercise 1

Make a list of ten relaxing, nonwork activities that will enhance your leisure time. Consider possibilities such as noncompetitive sports, yoga, meditation classes, a family picnic, going to a movie or concert, taking a walk in the park or along the beach, and so forth. Consult your family or partner for suggestions. Next, choose one of the activities to pursue this coming weekend. If you can't make that decision, read on.

Exercise 2

Consult your list of possible leisure-time activities. Number them from 1 to 10 in order of priority. You must use all ten numbers, and no two items can receive the same number. Now plan *only* the first-priority activity for this coming weekend. If you begin to worry whether your choice was the best one, ignore your doubts. Just smile and say to yourself, "There I go again—worrying and doubting my decisions. I mustn't take myself so seriously all the time." Make a list and establish priorities each time you have trouble choosing among various options, in any area of your life.

Exercise 3

When you have difficulty making a decision, always keep in mind that it often makes no difference which decision you make as long as you do *something*. If you have to choose between two apparently equal alternatives, consider simply flipping a coin. You can always try the other alternative later. This exercise will also help tackle the common tendency of Conscientious people to do nothing—i.e., procrastinate—until the "perfect" solution presents itself to you.

Exercise 4

Is your boss or your spouse on your back because you spend too much time on your tasks? To manage your time more efficiently, aim for results that are *good enough,* not perfect. If your boss asks you to prepare a quick report, find out precisely what he or she wishes included in it and cover those points only. In all your efforts, determine what the job requires and do *only* that. Resist your tendency to include additional material or to do extra work. Instead of concentrating on the minor flaws, pay attention to how pleased other people are with you for getting the job done. Tell yourself, "Good enough is just right!" Sometimes, of course, "good enough" will require a 100 percent effort. If you practice this exercise consistently, you will find that you have the necessary energy and enthusiasm to do thorough and brilliant work— and to get it done on time.

Exercise 5

Is your Conscientious head spinning with so many possibilities that you can't think anymore, much less come to a decision? Take time out— turn off your brain. Imagine that your mind is a calm, blank screen. Or visualize a peaceful, deeply pleasing scene, such as the seashore or a snowy mountain slope. Gently discourage all thoughts and worries from creeping back in. Learning meditation techniques will make this exercise relatively easy. Practice it every time your mind goes into overload from agonizing over decisions or worries. Calming your overbusy brain will help it work more efficiently once you turn it back on again.

Exercise 6

To recognize the pressures you put on yourself, keep track of how many times you begin a sentence or a thought with "I should." Try rephrasing each statement with "I want" or "I don't want" instead of "I should." For example, if you say or think, "I should visit Great-aunt Lulu," say instead, "I want to visit Great-aunt Lulu. I haven't seen her in almost two months, which really is too long, so let me call her and plan a visit right now." Or, "I don't really want to visit Great-aunt Lulu, but I haven't been to see her in two months and I feel guilty; maybe I'll give her a call to let her know I haven't forgotten about her." The point of this exercise is both to ease up on yourself and to help you to act appropriately. When you recognize what you really feel—not what you think you *should* do or feel or believe—in any given situation you will find that you may be able to solve some thorny moral dilemmas with less continuous stress on your self-esteem.

Exercise 7

Every time you catch yourself making a mistake, say to yourself, "Aha! I'm human!" Odd as this may sound, you need to appreciate that nobody's perfect, including you, and that you berate yourself too much for human errors. Try a variation of this exercise when you catch people you're hard on having an occasional lapse: "Aha! She/he is human!"

Exercise 8

Since the people who are close to you may not understand that you care for them, practice sharing your feelings with your loved one(s). Tonight, for example, tell your mate or child, "I love you," or, "You look good in those colors," or something similar. If you prefer, make a list of the things that you could say; think about saying them now or later. And while you're at it, why not also tell your subordinates at work how much you appreciate the job they are doing? Don't worry that you may sound stiff or unnatural when you give compliments and express your feelings about people. You'll get better with practice—and anyway, the others will be so happy to hear your praise that they won't be concerned with its delivery.

Some of the exercises for Aggressive style (chapter 16) may also improve your relationships with other people. Try Aggressive Exercises 2 (Give people a chance to make their own mistakes), 3 (Learn to compromise and even to give in), and 4 (Practice doing things someone else's way) (p. 360).

OBSESSIVE-COMPULSIVE PERSONALITY DISORDER

The difference between Conscientious style and Obsessive-Compulsive personality disorder—indeed, between any of the styles and its accompanying disorder—is one of degree and of consequence. Individuals suffering from the disorder are so *exceedingly* Conscientious that they can no longer adapt to the demands of reality or meet their personal and professional goals, and to others they may seem exasperating, even impossible, to deal with.

DIAGNOSTIC CRITERIA

The DSM-IV describes Obsessive-Compulsive personality disorder as:

A pervasive pattern of preoccupation with orderliness, perfectionism, and mental and interpersonal control, at the expense of flexibility, openness, and efficiency, beginning by early adulthood and present in a variety of contexts, as indicated by four (or more) of the following:

1. is preoccupied with details, rules, lists, order, organization, or schedules to the extent that the major point of the activity is lost

2. shows perfectionism that interferes with task completion (e.g., is unable to complete a project because own overly strict standards are not met)

3. is excessively devoted to work and productivity to the exclusion of leisure activities and friendships (not accounted for by obvious economic necessity)

4. is overconscientious, scrupulous, and inflexible about matters of morality, ethics, or values (not accounted for by cultural or religious identification)

5. is unable to discard worn-out or worthless objects even when they have no sentimental value

6. is reluctant to delegate tasks or to work with others unless they submit to exactly his or her way of doing things

7. adopts a miserly spending style toward both self and others; money is viewed as something to be hoarded for future catastrophes

8. shows rigidity and stubbornness

WORK AND WORRY

Conscientious-style people like to do things just right. Individuals suffering from Obsessive-Compulsive personality disorder, however, *must* do things *perfectly*. Since perfection can never be attained, this perpetually losing battle destroys their ability to act freely or to gain fulfillment. As with the Conscientious personality style, the disorder ranges from mild (where it can be difficult to distinguish from Conscientious style) to incapacitating. Although you'll find many Obsessive-Compulsive persons in high positions in the world of work, the disorder can nonetheless be particularly destructive in the Work domain.

Work is the key domain for this disorder as it is for the style, but now the need to attain perfection results in never finishing a project because the finished product never seems good enough or because the person must continually check and recheck for errors. An Obsessive-Compulsive writer will write and rewrite each sentence because perhaps there's a better way to say it. The Obsessive-Compulsive person is drowning in never-ending possibilities and details that can never be completed, doubts that cannot be stilled, and decisions that cannot be made. He or she can't see the forest for the trees. An Obsessive-Compulsive housekeeper cannot recognize that the kitchen is clean, because he or she keeps spotting minor imperfections—a tiny spot on the ceiling, a speck of dust behind the curtain. These individuals become so obsessed with the tiniest details that they often leave the most important tasks to the end, when time has run out. They lose all sense of priorities. They may spend more energy keeping lists than in completing the jobs or steps so carefully listed. Or, to cite an example from the DSM-IV, "such a person, having misplaced a list of things to be done, will spend an inordinate amount of time looking for the list rather than spending a few moments re-creating it from memory and proceeding to accomplish the tasks."

Men and women whose lives are made miserable by this disorder avoid opportunities to relax. They invest all their energy in work but they lose all enthusiasm for it. Unlike Conscientious individuals, who thrive on their work, Obsessive-Compulsives are tense, strained, anxious, and overwhelmed by the amount of work they have to do, whether it involves their job or profession or their hobby.

Walter P., a twenty-nine-year-old physicist who finally sought help for his difficulties, had existed on a joyless treadmill of work and worry. "I work too hard. I always have," he said. "I don't know why I do it. I feel a real need to be working, to be striving for something. If I'm not working, then I don't know what to fill the time with. It was a problem for me in college. I would read everything about everything. I couldn't discriminate. I remember a classmate I envied. I'd talk to him about his studies and his eyes would light up. He was interested, excited in what he was doing. This guy would walk into the library and say, 'Wow, look at all the exciting things there are to know!' I'd walk into the library and say, 'How depressing—look at all I have to know but don't know.' "

HOW TO SURVIVE AN OBSESSIVE-COMPULSIVE (OR VERY CONSCIENTIOUS) BOSS

Obsessive-Compulsive/very Conscientious bosses can be overly critical, demanding, and even tyrannical when you make just a small mistake. They will demand more attention to neatness, small details, perfection in general, and procedure than will people with personalities dominated by other disorders or styles. They equate overtime with devotion to your job; often they think that if you go home on time, you're going home early. Never let this type of boss know that you think the workday ordinarily ought to end at 5:00 P.M. Put in a little overtime every once in a while, and always make sure the boss knows about it. But don't come in late the next day or take an extra-long lunch to compensate for that extra time; these bosses are very mindful of rules and regulations, especially those concerning timeliness.

But keep in mind that when the going gets rough, your Obsessive-Compulsive or very Conscientious boss achieved his or her position through sheer ability. Your boss may be rigid and lack some interpersonal skills, but he or she is (or used to be) extremely competent. Under this person's tutelage, you can learn a great deal. If you treat such bosses the same way they treat those in authority over them with loyalty, deference, and respect—in time they will begin to trust you and delegate more substantial work. In general, however, don't be discouraged if your Obsessive-Compulsive/very Conscientious boss does not encourage you to find creative or innovative approaches to your work. Learn to do the job the boss's extremely thorough way; you'll have a solid grounding from which to experiment when you move on later.

Know, too, that the Obsessive-Compulsive/very Conscientious boss deeply appreciates a job well done, even if he or she can't comfortably show it. Once you prove yourself, the boss will be loyal to you too, which can be very reassuring. He or she will prove a staunch ally and will go to bat for you, if necessary, with the powers that be. But if you get on his or her bad side, you may stay there long past your due, for once an idea gets into this person's mind, it's hard to get rid of; Obsessive-Compulsive/very Conscientious individuals hold grudges.

THE TYRANNY OF THE SHOULD

The person with Obsessive-Compulsive personality disorder is a virtual prisoner of his or her stern, unrelenting conscience, which the late psychoanalyst Karen Horney called "the tyranny of the should." This person can't make decisions or complete tasks or realistically evaluate his or her own (or anyone else's) behavior, because the yardstick of absolute perfection is always the measure. This may be true to a lesser extent of Conscientious types too, but they can recognize their perfectionism if you point it out to them. A Conscientious person may also understand that it's one thing to ask a lot of yourself, another to expect, even insist, that you *always* meet these high goals. A person beset by the personality disorder, however, cannot recognize that these impossible demands of oneself are a function of his or her personal psychology—"life," he or she thinks, imposes these strict rules.

Obsessive-Compulsive Arnold believes that unless he wins *all* the lawsuits he becomes involved in, he's not a good lawyer. He believes he is working to meet professional standards—not to live up to unrealistic standards that he inflicts upon himself. Like most people with this personality disorder, Arnold does not recognize that these demands cannot humanly be met.

It is very painful to live by such "shoulds." To have Obsessive-Compulsive personality disorder is to be tormented by worries and fears of failure and to be unable to stop brooding about them. Unfortunately, the sufferers usually do not recognize that they are experiencing a psychological disorder that is causing them anxiety, tension, and anguish.

As painful as it can be to have this personality disorder, it can be equally uncomfortable having to deal with someone else who has it. Conscientious individuals can be exasperating, but Obsessive-Compulsive people can be impossible. Ernie Conscientiously totes his briefcase on vacation. When his wife challenges, "Ernie, are you married to your work or are you married to me?" he'll look abashed, put down his briefcase, take his wife in his arms, and say, "You're right, you're right. I hang on to this thing like a security blanket." He may still do some work on the vacation, but he can moderate his behavior, and he can recognize when his behavior or reactions are inappropriate. Conrad, who suffers from Obsessive-Compulsive disorder, and who is now divorced, possesses no such self-observing capacity. When his ex-wife used to become upset with him for staying late at the office every night, he would defend and justify his behavior and berate her for her criticism, until she gave up and cried herself to sleep. Finally she gave up on him altogether. Individuals with Obsessive-Compulsive personality disorder cannot and will not admit to being wrong.

Since Obsessive-Compulsive people expect that the same "rules" apply to everyone, they can be exceedingly judgmental. To mention another example from the DSM-IV, someone with this disorder may "not lend a quarter to a friend who needs one to make a telephone call, because 'neither a borrower or lender be' or because it would be 'bad' for the person's character." In the service of doing things "right," this person will have little feeling for others or compassion for the human problems that can cause any individual to behave imperfectly. Obsessive-Compulsive Abigail had no sympathy for her cousin Linda, whose dog was hit by a car, suffered a broken spine, and had to be put to sleep. Linda was grief-stricken, but Abigail refused to console her. The way she saw it, Linda got what was coming to her. "Anyone who lets a dog run loose deserves to watch it die a horrible death!" declared Abigail with typically rigid Obsessive-Compulsive self-righteousness.

COPING WITH OBSESSIVE-COMPULSIVE PEOPLE

To deal with a spouse, parent, or friend who has these personality difficulties, some of the tips on coping with the Conscientious person in your life (see p. 73) may come in handy, particularly if the personality disorder is not too severe. Try to encourage the person in your life who is beset by these problems to seek help, but remember that an Obsessive-Compulsive person is extremely rigid in his or her point of view, and change is tantamount to catastrophe. As the DSM-IV points out,

"Even when individuals with Obsessive-Compulsive Personality Disorder recognize that it may be in their interest to compromise, they may stubbornly refuse to do so, arguing that it is 'the principle of the thing.'"

HELP!

Mental health professionals have long been familiar with this personality disorder. In 1908 Freud described the "anal character" as a person who was orderly, parsimonious, and obstinate. Since then, many psychoanalysts have elaborated on our understanding of this personality disorder and its treatment. However, individuals with the disorder will not necessarily come for help. Obsessive-Compulsive people need to believe that they are in total control of their lives, and they might prefer to inundate themselves with work and drive themselves to near-burnout rather than deal with what they may see as any "weakness" or "failure" in themselves.

Those who do seek help—perhaps because their relationships are falling apart or they are failing at work, or because they come to realize that life doesn't have to be so driven and unfulfilling—traditionally have been helped most with psychodynamic types of psychotherapy. Cognitive treatment tackles maladaptive thinking patterns of a person with this personality disorder, such as: "To make a mistake is to have failed," and "I must be perfectly in control of my environment as well as myself." (See chapter 19 for a description of treatment approaches.) The experienced therapist will be able to stay clear of power struggles with Obsessive-Compulsive men and women, while helping them to loosen up. Slowly, they may be able to recognize their rigidity, their perfectionism, their fear of weakness in themselves and in others, and their need for control, especially control over their emotions. These individuals must learn to feel rather than to intellectualize all their problems.

Those individuals who must perform certain rituals—such as hand washing or checking and rechecking that the oven is off before they can leave the house—can be helped by behavioral techniques to overcome these repetitive habits. Some types of medication may also be helpful for patients with certain psychiatric symptoms, such as depression, anxiety, and obsessions and compulsions (clomipramine, which affects the serotonin system in the brain, is one relatively new antidepressant that shows promise in this category).

TYPE A AND OTHER RISKS

Obsessive-Compulsive personality disorder equals high stress. The constant pressure to live up to some ideal standard, as well as some other typical Obsessive-Compulsive personality traits—including overconcern with time and punctuality, impatience, hostility, and competitiveness are prominent among the Type A characteristics that are associated with the vulnerability to heart disease. Another Obsessive-Compulsive personality characteristic, the tendency to deny or to suppress feelings, has also been linked with cardiovascular risk, especially in people with a family history of essential hypertension. Extremely Obsessive-Compulsive persons can feel very cut off from others, and at least one study has linked the combination of suppressed emotionality and loneliness to the development of cancer later in life (discussed in more detail in chapter 13, p. 280).

Obsessive-Compulsive persons are also vulnerable to depression, panic disorder, hypochondria, paranoia, and to obsessive-compulsive anxiety disorder. This last is an Axis I acute condition (see chapter 2, p. 19) marked by persistent thoughts, impulses, or images (such as intrusive thoughts of hurting a loved family member) as well as irresistible repetitive behaviors (such as the continual need to wash one's hands).

PREDISPOSITIONS AND INCIDENCE

People with this personality disorder may be genetically predisposed. Studies suggest that some babies who are born with a temperament that makes them very sensitive to change (see chapter 18) may be especially vulnerable to developing this disorder, especially if their family environment causes them certain kinds of early developmental stresses. Very often, people who develop the disorder by adulthood have had parents who are rigid, overbearing, and faultfinding. The parents put pressure on these children to get control of themselves and to behave like little adults (or even like good little robots) rather than as independent, individual human beings. In order to be good and to gain their parents' approval, the vulnerable children become trapped in an internal struggle to get control of their own "bad" or "dangerous" impulses, desires, and feelings. They develop into adults who are inwardly, perhaps unconsciously, angry, and outwardly very driven to achieve respect and approval.

In any case, the disorder does seem to run in families. In the past, clinicians have reported that Obsessive-Compulsive personality disorder occurs most often among firstborn children, which one recent study confirms. It is a common personality disorder, occurring among roughly 1 percent of the general population and in up to 10 percent of people seeking help from mental health practitioners. Historically it has been diagnosed most frequently among men, and presently it is diagnosed twice as often among men. Because culture influences personality style, possibly more women will be "earning" this diagnosis as expectations of women's roles change in our families and throughout our society.

CHAPTER 5

Self-Confident Style

"STAR QUALITY"

Self-Confident individuals stand out. They're the leaders, the shining lights, the attention-getters in their public or private spheres. Theirs is a star quality born of self-regard, self-respect, self-certainty—all those *self* words that denote a faith in oneself and a commitment to one's self-styled purpose. Combined with the ambition that marks this style, that magical self-regard can transform idle dreams into real accomplishment.

The Self-Confident personality style is one of the two most goal-directed of all fourteen (the other is the Aggressive style). Self-Confident men and women know what they want, and they get it. Many of them have the charisma to attract plenty of others to their goals. They are extroverted and intensely political. They know how to work the crowd, how to motivate it, and how to lead it. Hitch on to their bandwagons, and you'll be well rewarded.

The Self-Confident style adds go-getting power to other personality styles. For example, it counteracts the Conscientious person's tendency to get sidetracked by details, and it fuels the Adventurous person's great feats of daring. It propels any personality pattern into the realm of success. Indeed, the Self-Confident style confers an ability to be successful more than any but the Aggressive personality style.

THE NINE CHARACTERISTICS

The following nine traits and behaviors are clues to the presence of the Self-Confident style. A person who reveals a strong Self-Confident tendency will demonstrate more of these behaviors more intensely than someone who has less of this style.

1. *Self-regard*. Self-Confident individuals believe in themselves and in their abilities. They have no doubt that they are unique and special and that there is a reason for their being on this planet.

2. *The red carpet*. They expect others to treat them well at all times.

3. *Ambition*. Self-Confident people are unabashedly open about their aspirations and possibilities.

4. *Politics*. They are able to take advantage of the strengths and abilities of other people in order to achieve their goals, and they are shrewd in their dealings with others.

5. *Competition*. They are able competitors, they love getting to the top, and they enjoy staying there.

6. *Stature*. They identify with people of high rank and status.

7. *Dreams*. Self-Confident individuals are able to visualize themselves as the hero, the star, the best in their role, or the most accomplished in their field.

8. *Self-awareness*. These individuals have a keen awareness of their thoughts and feelings and their overall inner state of being.

9. *Poise*. People with the Self-Confident personality style accept compliments, praise, and admiration gracefully and with self-possession.

THE SIX DOMAINS OF
SELF-CONFIDENT FUNCTIONING

SELF: THE JOY OF BEING ME

The Self is the reigning domain of the Self-Confident style. It gives this style its special character and power, and all the other domains fall under its sway. It provides purpose, structure, and meaning to the life of the Self-Confident individual, for whom, in short, *the world is me.*

It is impossible to describe this personality style without recourse to words that reflect back on the Self: self-made, self-possessed, self-respect, self-propelled, self-reliance, self-fulfillment, self-enrichment, self-asserting, self-love, self-esteem, self-starter, and so on. As this style becomes extreme, other *self-* words increasingly come into play, including: self-aggrandizing, self-preoccupation, selfish, and indeed self-destructive. Here, as with all of the fourteen personality styles, the key domains can achieve too much control of the proud possessors' lives. *Looking out for number one,* perhaps the catch phrase of this style, can reap a life harvest for Self-Confident individuals, their families, and their devotees, whereas for Narcissistic individuals it may threaten to destroy them and those around them, as we will see later in this chapter.

Charmed Lives

Self-Confident people believe in themselves. They are prepared to work hard, to plan, and to endure hardship if necessary in order to get what they feel they deserve. Other, perhaps equally qualified people may be assailed by self-doubt and thus led astray by setbacks. A strong Self-Confident personality style protects against these demons. From the moment he got his first electric guitar, rock star J. believed he'd be a great in the rock-and-roll pantheon—a dream that was shared by untold numbers of other young people. J. was more than thirty years old before he cut a hit record. He'd formed band after band, made demos, courted producers, cut singles that went nowhere, played obscure clubs; but after a decade in the business he still refused to give up. He believed in himself so much that others ended up believing in him too. He found backers for the demo tapes and promoters who would donate their time. Now you see the way he occupies the center of the stage in concert, you hear that sureness in his voice, and you know he was made for this life. He is exactly where he belongs.

So too Lana, in her own way. From her childhood she saw her future as a wife and mother with all the trappings of the good life. To her this meant fine houses, servants, cars, jewels, and "name" schools for her children. Lana has never been embarrassed by or defensive about her ambitions.

Lana, whose personality shows a strong streak also of the Conscientious style, did not come from a family of means. She put herself through school and then worked hard and well as a secretary to support herself and her widowed mother, while waiting for her expected prince to appear. He came in the form of Joey, her last boss. Joey, a salesman-promoter type, showed a lot of ambition and promise. He gave her everything she wanted: the house in the suburbs, the cottage in the country, the housekeeper, the diamonds, and the free time to shop and to linger at the club. After their children were in school, he even bought her a small fashion boutique to run because she'd always said she had better taste than any of the exclusive clothing stores in their town.

For Lana's part, in addition to running her store, she took good care of Joey and their two children, and she put up with her husband when many people couldn't. As long as he treated her with respect and deference, Lana dealt with his tantrums, his sometimes boorish and bullying behavior toward his associates, his employees, and some of their friends, and his cheating in business.

Lana had no illusions about Joey; she often said, to him and to others, that she would leave him in a second if he treated her one-tenth as badly as he treated other people. Then Joey began to suffer reverses in his business. He blamed his losses on his associates and his employees. Night after night he came home angry, looking to Lana for solace from the abuses he felt he suffered at the hands of others. But the great strain on their finances made Lana short-tempered and less accepting of Joey. She found she could not tolerate his constant complaining. She began to let the saleswoman who worked for her have more responsibility, so she could spend more time at the club, in the company of a rich, retired widower who had always shown her much consideration. They were not sleeping together, but Joey wouldn't believe that. He became possessed with jealous rage. During one of their now-frequent fights, Joey lost control and struck Lana. That night she took the kids and moved to a hotel suite. She never went back to Joey (whom we will meet again later in this chapter). In the divorce settlement she received both houses, the new Mercedes, and considerable child support. She sold the suburban house and the boutique when she decided to marry her widower friend. Now Lana and her children can be found at one of the best addresses in her city, where she lives the good life that she has always felt she deserves.

Status, Image, and Power

Self-Confident individuals believe that they were "born under a lucky star," and their lives seem to bear it out. Usually what they want involves status and image and/or power. They want to be department heads at the very best universities, to belong to the best clubs, to live in the classiest neighborhoods, and to send their kids to the most renowned schools. If they are Hollywood types, they'll have gorgeous bodies and wear fabulous clothes. If they are intellectuals, academics, or politicians, they'll sit on the most powerful and prestigious committees. Their image-consciousness is genuine; they seek to be and succeed in becoming what they believe they are to begin with: important, deserving people.

Tender Spot

Self-Confident men and women are at most times cognizant of and comfortable with their strengths. They are not, as a rule, so keenly aware of or so comfortable with their shortcomings. To those who have a lot of this personality style, even the most constructive criticism feels barbed.

Professor H. criticized Tanya's political science term paper. He told her that her research was weak and that she depended too much on her interesting but unsupported opinions. She was a good student, and he generously allowed her the opportunity to rewrite the paper before he graded it. Tanya had always held Professor H. in high esteem. But she considered his criticism insulting and now began to think of his seminar as a waste of time. Nonetheless, she remained cooperative. She reworked the paper as the professor suggested—not because she fully understood his point, but because she wanted a good grade. Had Tanya been open to her teacher's instructive remarks, she might have saved herself embarrassment in later years. Two years after graduate school, Tanya lost a job as a political speech writer for much the same reason—overconfidence in her opinions without the backup or hard information that the candidate needed. Fortunately, when Tanya went into politics a few years later, she found someone else to research her own speeches. She had the Self-Confident ability to delegate important tasks that she really didn't want to do. Today she makes an excellent political party chairperson for her state.

WORK: LEADERSHIP AND SUCCESS

Men and women with a strong Self-Confident personality style are outgoing, high-energy, competitive people who are able to absorb data easily, to see the big picture, to make decisions, to plan, to set priorities and goals, and to delegate. This is the person whom you, as chairman of the board, want to put your new corporation on the map.

At work as well as in every other aspect of their lives, Self-Confident individuals are instinctively political. They're naturals at understanding the power structure of any organization and at establishing effective political alliances. They can be jealous of those in power and, like their Aggressive brethren, they're not squeamish about attempting to unseat them. They'll "play politics" to get ahead, whereas work-hard-to-go-places Conscientious types will keep their noses so close to the grind-stone that they'll miss out on the power plays that could carry them to the top.

Outgoing and political as they are, Self-Confident men and women work very comfortably and effectively with others. For this personality style, people are a means to a successful end. To those in authority and/ or from whom there is something to gain, they will be deferential and cooperative. To their own staffs, in exchange for their loyalty, Self-Confident men and women will be very generous with money, "perks," and support. People against whom they compete can also serve as a measure of their own importance.

The Self-Confident Manager

Self-Confident individuals are genuine, often gifted leaders. They are happy to delegate to members of their staffs not only the dirty work but responsible undertakings. Unlike highly Conscientious types, they often allow their subordinates autonomy and leeway, as long as the job gets done. They are quite skilled at building an effective, highly motivated team—of which they must be the absolute center. As long as everybody acknowledges who's boss, Self-Confident managers do not insist on the strict hierarchical structure that the Aggressive manager needs to func-tion effectively. But the team must work to achieve the goals of the Self-Confident leader, not those of the individual team members. Start to compete with or criticize the goals of the Self-Confident supervisor or boss, or insist on sharing the credit and/or glory, and you'll be off that team, or at the bottom of the heap, before you realize what you did to deserve it.

Innately competitive, Self-Confident individuals are like racehorses: they run all the faster when anyone edges up on them. They thrive on the competition, and they love staying one step ahead at all times. They respect the same inclination in others (as long as they are not in direct competition), and can make excellent mentors and pull strings on your behalf should you get on their good side.

Tips on Working for Self-Confident People

1. Be absolutely loyal. Don't criticize or compete with them. Don't expect to share the limelight or to take credit. Be content to aspire to the number-two position.

2. Don't expect your Self-Confident boss to provide direction. Likely he or she will expect you to know what to do, so be sure you are clear about the objectives before you undertake any task. Don't hesitate to ask.

3. You may be an important member of the boss's team, but don't expect your Self-Confident boss to be attentive to you as an individual. Don't take it personally.

4. Self-Confident bosses expect your interest in them, however. They may be susceptible to flattery, so if you're working on a raise or a promotion or are trying to sell your point of view, a bit of buttering up may smooth the way.

Careers for the Self-Confident

If this is your dominant style, follow ambitions that lead toward leadership and the limelight. Many performers, broadcasters, and politicians have a predominance of this personality style. In all cases, choose careers in which you work with or influence others; Self-Confident folks need other people around them.

RELATIONSHIPS: GOOD AT BEING LOVED

Self-Confident men and women are popular and attractive. Their sense of themselves and their certainty in their projects draw others to them. And they are very good at being loved. They are not shy, not in the least embarrassed by the attentions paid by a person who loves them.

Self-Confident people need to be needed, and they will work hard to gain and maintain a person's loving admiration. They know what to do to get your attention and how to win you over.

Sargent Woos Thalia

When Self-Confident Sargent, a twice-divorced, fifty-year-old theatrical producer, fell head over heels for Thalia, she was slow to warm up. A ballerina-turned-choreographer, she had recently endured a painful divorce and was not eager to begin another involvement. But Sargent began to spin his web of endearments: he cooked elaborate dinners for the beautiful Thalia, he sent her flowers, he brought munchies for her miniature terrier, he found her a new housekeeper when hers quit. Very slowly Thalia's heart opened to this wonderfully attentive man. Increasingly they were seen in each other's company. But forty-one-year-old Thalia still wished to keep her independence. At last, after nearly a year, she invited Sargent to live with her in her waterside mansion. Sargent installed himself that day.

Some of Sargent's oldest friends, who had lived through his two marriages, wondered cynically whether it would all fall apart now that Thalia would have him. These friends had witnessed Sargent when he was in love and charming a woman. They had also watched him turn his back on the women he had won over. Would he stop his impressive attentions to Thalia?

The answer is no—because Thalia continued to impress and challenge him, intellectually and sexually. He had enormous respect for this accomplished woman, who was always just a little removed emotionally. Sargent was never sure that he possessed her body and soul. This uncertainty kept him continually on his toes.

And Thalia did not need from Sargent the kind of love she had sought when she was married as a young ballerina. Back then, her dancer husband had understood Thalia and treasured her for her inner beauty. Now she wanted Sargent's respect and acceptance, but she no longer needed a man to truly *know* her. For this she relied on her old friends and longtime colleagues. She found Sargent a stimulating and exciting companion, and she enjoyed the merger of their two artistic worlds. She admired his self-certain style. It was a match among equals, she felt. Thalia understood Sargent; she understood better than he did that he would never deeply love her.

People like Sargent, whose personality patterns are unmistakably dominated by the Self-Confident style, are so strongly ruled by the Self domain that they do not gain sufficient distance from their own thoughts and feelings to provide unstinting, selfless love. Often they believe that the people close to them feel what they feel or think what they think. Although they thrive on the love that others provide, and they appreciate what others do for them, they may find it difficult to comprehend that the people who are important to them may have separate, individual needs. They get so wrapped up in their ambitions, they just don't notice. This is why they are often shocked to discover, for instance, that their spouses have been unhappy for many years. By contrast, a Devoted person, exquisitely sensitive to a loved one's feelings, would have picked up the signs of discontent early, perhaps even before the unhappy spouse became fully aware of his or her own distress. A Self-Confident spouse assumes that his or her own happiness spells a contented relationship for them both.

Sargent's Two Ex-Wives (And How He Coped with the Stress of Losing Them)

Resolution of conflict in their relationships may be difficult for Self-Confident people; without sensitivity to others, they can find little reason to change their position or to sacrifice important needs. Sargent's first wife was his college sweetheart, a beauty from a well-to-do family whom he pursued with fervor. They married as soon as he completed college. Her family supported them in his early days in the theater, while she finished school. Then she went to work for her father in order to supplement her husband's still meager income.

Two years later Sargent's young wife became pregnant and stopped working. Over the next ten years they had three children. Sargent produced several plays that drew attention, although they earned only enough money to make ends meet. Then his wife said one night that she wanted to go to law school and that her father had agreed to provide the tuition. All she needed from Sargent was greater participation in child care. Would he at least be there when the children came home from school? She felt his work schedule would allow that flexibility. Sargent could not comprehend how she could suggest such a thing. How could he sacrifice his work time? Hadn't they always understood that his success in his career was the most important goal for the family? He took a long hard look at his wife and noticed that she was no longer beautiful. He began to believe that she wasn't the kind of wife he wanted. Their marriage unraveled quickly.

Sargent took the divorce hard, though. Despite his contributions to it, Sargent felt rejected, an often-devastating stress for Self-Confident people, worse even than being severely criticized. Sargent coped in a typical Self-Confident manner: he kept his misery to himself while putting on a charming face and surrounding himself with admirers. Soon he became entranced with an actress, whom he wined and dined and married. They were the happiest couple in town, or so he thought, until he discovered a few years later that she was having an affair with one of her Broadway costars. He sought and won an immediate divorce. What his wife did not know, and what he himself did not consider relevant, was that Sargent had had many affairs. The marriage had been brief, but it took Sargent almost eight years to get over the collapse of his two marriages and start something really serious, with Thalia.

Good/Bad Matches

As Sargent demonstrates in his relationship with Thalia, the Self-Confident individual can make a good and devoted mate. The partner will need strong self-esteem and not require frequent assurances and understanding from the Self-Confident partner, however.

Personality styles that match up well with the Self-Confident style are those that find happiness in fulfilling the needs of others, such as the Devoted and the Self-Sacrificing, as long as these styles do not become too extreme and rob the spouse of definition and individuality. Sensitive people need strong, outgoing mates, and Self-Confident people need to be needed, so these two will often be complementary. The life-of-the-party, other-directed Dramatic personality style may make for an exciting, mutually flattering match, if the Dramatic need for reassurance is small. When two Self-Confident individuals powerfully attract each other, they may be headed for Self-to-Self combat. The combination worked for Thalia and Sargent, though. A little Conscientious style helps any union, and Thalia's style was a mature, balanced mix of Self-Confident, Conscientious, and Dramatic.

Personality styles in others that tend particularly to clash with the Self-Confident include Vigilant, Leisurely, Adventurous, and Aggressive; individuals with these styles cannot subordinate their needs to another's. Mercurial individuals, although they become involved in deep relationships, are usually too emotionally demanding for the Self-Confident patience. Although a somewhat Serious person would bring necessary steadiness to the relationship, usually the pessimistic outlook of this style throws too much cold water on the Self-Confident inherent optimism.

The Self-Confident Parent

Self-Confident parents can confer a star quality on their children, too. They teach them to aim high and to expect the best for themselves. They offer a model of self-esteem, ambition, drive, self-discipline, and social success. Strongly Self-Confident parents, however, may not recognize or credit their children's individual differences or needs, because they tend to assume that the kids are all chips off the old block. And it may not occur to them to step out of the spotlight long enough to let the children know what it feels like to be the center of the universe on their own merits. Some children of extremely Self-Confident parents grow up to be good at giving love but to feel unworthy of receiving it.

The non-Self-Confident parent may be able to remind his or her moderately Self-Confident spouse to look at things from the child's point of view. And strength in some of the other-directed styles (including Conscientious, Devoted, Self-Sacrificing, and Dramatic) may protect a moderately Self-Confident parent from this style's predisposition to insensitivity to others' emotional needs.

EMOTIONS, SELF-CONTROL, AND THE REAL WORLD

Self-Confident individuals have a temper, and when they're crossed or slighted, they'll show it. In addition, they can be envious of others whom they perceive as more successful than themselves. But their strong sense of self, their success orientation, and their political savvy usually protect them from letting their less "admirable" feelings get the best of them, at least in public.

As we have seen, individuals with this personality style, depending on the degree to which they are dominated by it, will have some or much difficulty experiencing love. They can and do feel powerful attractions and emotional and sexual fulfillment, however. Their moods are characteristically optimistic, energetic, even "hyper." When the style crosses over to the Narcissistic personality disorder, however, depression becomes a great risk.

In general, Self-Control is strong in Self-Confident types. Their strength in achieving their goals reflects their self-discipline and ability to keep conflicting impulses at bay. When they slip, it's more from grandiosity than from problems with impulse control. Individuals whose personalities are heavily dominated by this style may see the Real World unrealistically as their own personal stage. As with the politician who makes no attempt to conceal his philandering and whose career is shattered when the truth is revealed, some overly Self-Confident individuals lose sight of their faults, their vulnerabilities, and their relative places in the scheme of things—and they fall from grace. We'll explore this further when we discuss the Narcissistic personality disorder. (See also "Aggressive Versus Self-Confident," in chapter 16, p. 356.)

TIPS ON DEALING WITH THE
SELF-CONFIDENT PERSON IN YOUR LIFE

1. Self-Confident individuals need to be number one. To love a Self-Confident person requires that you accept, admire, and respect this aspect of his or her character. Appreciate the considerable gifts and

the strengths this person brings to the relationship. Enjoy the fruits of your partner's success and the interesting life he or she may provide.

2. To hold this person's attention, pay a lot of attention. Your love and loyalty are very important to the Self-Confident person in your life. You bring to the relationship the ability to love, and your mate counts on it. Accept that you may be more capable of selfless love than is your Self-Confident partner. Give your love without keeping track of who's giving more. If you need to be loved more intensely and equally, however, accept that this person is not for you.

3. Be careful not to tie your self-esteem to the amount of love and attention the Self-Confident person in your life spontaneously shows you, or by the extent to which he or she really understands you. Love yourself no matter what. This "message" is especially important for children of highly Self-Confident parents.

4. Many Self-Confident types will alternately move emotionally close and then apparently lose interest in you, especially after a relationship has become established. Be aware of this back-and-forth pattern, try to wait it out while maintaining your own emotional balance, and do *not* jump to the conclusion that your Self-Confident partner no longer has feelings for you. More likely, he or she has become preoccupied with other concerns. Remind the Self-Confident person that you exist and that you continue to care for him or her.

5. When you need to confront your Self-Confident partner, simply state how you feel or what you observe without judging him or her. Remember that for all their self-esteem, Self-Confident people have difficulty dealing with criticism. Be sure at the same time to express your admiration and praise. Keep in mind that although the Self-Confident individual may not admit that you have a point, he or she will try to deal with it. Self-Confident individuals *can* step back from themselves and correct their behavior, even if they're not so good in the you're-right/I'm-wrong department.

6. Continually make your feelings known, even about apparently obvious matters; don't count on a Self-Confident individual to sense or keep track of them. Keeping your partner informed about your feelings and attitudes will enable him or her to understand you better and avoid conflict later.

MAKING THE MOST OF YOUR SELF-CONFIDENT STYLE

Your ability to be successful and your nerve to go after it (some people call it *chutzpah*) set you apart from all other personality styles. You can call upon these singular advantages in order to smooth out some of the problem areas that may plague you.

You are probably aware of your capabilities. To strengthen your personality and help it work to best advantage for you, you may need to develop a more realistic sense of your own shortcomings.

Exercise 1

Make a list in answer to this question: *What's not totally great about me?* One item may be: "I'm not as responsive to others/not as interested in them as I like them to be in me."

Exercise 2

Try to see yourself as others see you. Again, concentrate on your weak areas. Ask yourself, *What would (my mother, my father, my husband or wife, my best friend, my teachers, my colleagues, etc.) say is not totally great about me?*

Exercise 3

Observe your reactions to criticism. Do you feel hurt or humiliated or attacked when people say negative things about you or your work? Try to live with these feelings instead of lashing out at, distancing yourself from, or beginning to dislike the people who offer criticism. The more you watch your reactions, the easier they will be to bear.

Exercise 4

This exercise takes advantage of your ability to concentrate in order to improve your relationships. During any conversation or interchange, especially with people whom you deal with frequently, ask yourself, "Who *is* this person?" Collect data. Concentrate on each person's way of talking, facial expressions, characteristic body postures, tones of voice, mannerisms, emotions, clothing styles, jewelry, eye color, hair, teeth, and so on. In this way you will paint an increasingly detailed, interesting, rich portrait of the people with whom you come in contact.

Exercise 5

Once a day ask each member of your household, or your lover or best friend, a question about him- or herself. Ask, perhaps, "What is it that you like about that book?" A question that elicits an opinion about you —such as "What did you think about my speech today?"—doesn't count. You might also try Exercise 5 for the Aggressive style: At least once a week, ask the people who are closest to you in your personal life what you can do for them (see p. 360).

▇ NARCISSISTIC PERSONALITY DISORDER ▇

In Greek mythology, Narcissus was a young man who loved no one. He was made to fall in love with his own reflection in a pool of water. He could not embrace this watery image, and he pined away. Eventually he was transformed into a flower. In American psychiatry, Narcissistic personality disorder defines a pathological condition characterized by self-centeredness and self-interest, grandiosity, lack of empathy, and manipulativeness. While individuals with this condition often achieve high positions, their lives are not satisfying. If they are in public life, they may create scandals that humiliate and undo them. Persons with this disorder cannot ultimately find happiness or fulfillment in their accomplishments or their relationships. Yet, as is true of persons who suffer any of the disorders, they may not realize that the way they think, feel, and behave distorts their lives.

▇ DIAGNOSTIC CRITERIA ▇

The DSM-IV describes Narcissistic Personality Disorder as:

A pervasive pattern of grandiosity (in fantasy or behavior), need for admiration, and lack of empathy beginning by early adulthood and present in a variety of contexts, as indicated by at least *five* or more of the following:

(1) has a grandiose sense of self-importance (e.g., exaggerates achievements and talents, expects to be recognized as superior without commensurate achievements)

(2) is preoccupied with fantasies of unlimited success, power, brilliance, beauty, or ideal love

(3) believes that he or she is "special" and unique and can be understood only by, or should associate with, other special or high-status people (or institutions)

(4) requires excessive admiration

(5) has a sense of entitlement, i.e., unreasonable expectations of especially favorable treatment or automatic compliance with his or her expectations

(6) is interpersonally exploitative, i.e., takes advantage of others to achieve his or her own ends

(7) lacks empathy: is unwilling to recognize or identify with the feelings and needs of others

(8) is often envious of others or believes that others are envious of him or her

(9) shows arrogant, haughty behaviors or attitudes

THE ALL-CONSUMING SELF

Narcissism is a disorder of self-esteem. Although they don't realize it, the men and women who suffer from it have so little genuine self-esteem that they create a huge Self in order to survive. Many of them behave (or imagine in their fantasies) as if they are the most important people in their own or the larger world, and that everyone should recognize their special place.

While Self-Confident individuals are able to use their faith in themselves to fuel their willingness to work hard and prove their mettle, some Narcissistic people show little evidence of any real ability outside of their fantasy lives. Those who have the natural ingredients for success often lose sight of their objectives. Their goal becomes success for its own sake. Narcissistic Neva, for example, might have had an important career as an opera singer, but she couldn't pass up any major role in order to allow her voice and ability to grow and mature. Her manager cautioned her to proceed carefully; she turned on him viciously, accused him of being too "small time" for an artist of her caliber, and fired him. She found other managers who would go along for the quick buck, and she destroyed her voice within five years of her attention-getting debut. She went on screeching in smaller and smaller opera houses throughout the world, deluding herself into believing that she was an unrecognized genius.

People with this disorder often self-destruct, because their grandiosity and self-preoccupation blind their judgment and perspective. Thus, a statesman who believes he is so important that laws or public morals do not apply to him will tape-record himself in the act of wrongdoing and create the evidence that will bring him down.

Some people with this disorder may at times feel as unimportant as they feel important at other times. Psychiatrist Michael H. Stone writes about a Narcissistic man named Nelson, age 31, who was an academic scientist who dreamed of receiving great honors for his research. "Each year," Stone reports, "when the Nobel prizes were awarded, he would read the announcements tense-jawed and with bitterness, as though the medals had been stolen out of his pocket and given to others."

SELF-IMPORTANCE AT WORK AND WITH OTHER PEOPLE

With Narcissistic personality disorder, one can be very successful, particularly in worlds of power and form, such as politics and the corporation. Sufferers are often smooth and charming, with manic energy, able to talk their way in the door and convince people of their special abilities. Those who can prove they have these abilities often are tolerated as talented but difficult people. They exploit others to get ahead, and they expect and demand special treatment. Stanley F., a lawyer who headed a department subdivision at a major law school, continually undermined his own effectiveness by battling arrogantly with the department chairman and becoming bitterly enraged when his way was rejected. Someone with Self-Confident style would be loath to commit such political errors. But Stanley's personality disorder distorted his ability to size up a situation and to perceive the larger complexities. He believed that he alone could take on the chairman, because, as he assumed everyone in the department recognized, he was better than them all, including the boss. Fortunately, therapy saved him from quickly destroying a promising career.

Narcissistic individuals cannot bear criticism. Some react inwardly with devastating hurt and shame that far outweigh the actual remark. Others react with inappropriate rage, even tantrums, and in the process manipulate others to accede to their demands. Obsessive-Compulsive individuals may be crushed when they are criticized, but they will work hard to get back in the criticizer's good graces. Narcissistic individuals, on the other hand, attempt to destroy the attacker.

We spoke about Self-Confident Lana earlier in this chapter. Her ex-husband, Joey, who suffered from a mixed Narcissistic, Histrionic, and Antisocial personality disorder, with Paranoid features, threw violent tantrums whenever he was crossed. In his business, he often hired young free-lance commercial designers and artists, whom he frequently neglected to pay. He expected them to understand his "special" circumstances (he had used the funds to pay his kids' tuition, or mortgage payments, or his wife's credit card bills) and to agree to wait until the financial pressure eased. These young people were hardly in a financial position themselves to do without even a day's pay, but when they would press him, often growing heated and criticizing his ethics, Joey would fly into a rage, attack the quality of their work, insult them, and threaten to ruin them. Most of these talented men and women would have loved to walk away from Joey, but they were new in the business, they lacked confidence, and Joey had convinced them that they would go nowhere without him. So they continued to work for Joey, who when things were going right could be very seductive, flattering, and encouraging.

All Narcissistic individuals share the inability to empathize; they cannot recognize or experience how other people feel. To cite the DSM-IV: "These individuals may be oblivious to the hurt their remarks may inflict (e.g., exuberantly telling a former lover that 'I am now in the relationship of a lifetime!'; boasting of health in front of someone who is sick)." Individuals with this disorder may be sexually very active, and they are the types who seduce and abandon. They form few genuine emotional commitments. Needless to say, relationships with persons suffering from this disorder are very hard on the partner, whose worth in the relationship may depend only on how well he or she can bolster the Narcissistic partner's self-esteem.

Narcissistic individuals must at all times be admired. They manipulate others to this end, they work to achieve admirable successes yet they are consumed with feelings of envy and rage and disdain for others; they grow depressed and find little satisfaction or contentment from their work or from the people in their lives.

HELP!

Some people with very mild forms of this disorder may function relatively well, although they feel empty or bored, are driven by ambition, have an overwhelming need for approval, and experience shallow, uncommitted relationships. Severe forms of Narcissistic personality disorder can be very disabling; the characteristic grandiosity may prevent afflicted individuals from working effectively and realistically in any area of their lives.

A person suffering from this personality disorder will not usually seek help until a part of his or her life (a marriage, a career) begins to unravel. Often when Narcissistic people reach middle age they begin to succumb to deep depression as youth and its hopes and dreams begin to pass them by. Then they realize that their lives have come to nothing, that they are lonely, and that they are terrified of dying. Now their neediness may make them reach out and possibly open up to a psychotherapist who can show them the empathy that they themselves lack.

Psychoanalysis and psychodynamic psychotherapy are the most often employed treatments for Narcissistic individuals. Cognitive therapists have also begun to offer treatment, aiming at changing their maladaptive beliefs and thinking patterns. "Alternative beliefs" that cognitive therapists such as Aaron T. Beck and Arthur Freeman hope to inculcate include, for example, "Be ordinary. Ordinary things can be very pleasurable." Or "I can go for long-term respect from others instead of short-term admiration."

In therapy, individuals tend to demean or at times overvalue the therapist, withhold their "weaker" feelings, and consistently demand special treatment. The well-trained, experienced therapist will be able to deal with his or her own frustration while remaining sympathetic to the plight of the person who seeks help. Medication may be useful for severe depression.

RISKS, PREDISPOSITIONS, INCIDENCE, AND THE ME GENERATION

Men and women who suffer from Narcissistic personality disorder frequently exhibit features of Histrionic, Borderline, Antisocial, and Paranoid personality disorders. Depression is common, as are hypochondria, preoccupation with health, anorexia, and substance abuse problems, particularly with cocaine, which enhances grandiosity.

The disorder appears to occur equally among men and women, although some studies show that it is diagnosed more commonly in men. The familial pattern is not yet known, and researchers have no information as yet on the genetic and temperamental factors that might predispose an individual to develop this personality disorder. Psychoanalysts have observed that some Narcissistic adults were spoiled and overindulged in their childhoods, treated as if they could do no wrong. Others were emotionally or physically neglected or abused and sought psychological "shelter" in inflated self-importance.

Clinicians report that Narcissistic personality disorder is on the rise, although no studies have been conducted to substantiate this. The late social historian Christopher Lasch, in his 1978 cultural history, *The*

Culture of Narcissism, believed that the reported increase of Narcissistic personality disorder is related to the ascendancy within our culture of "Me Generation" values (which in this book we associate with the Self-Confident personality style). "On the principle that pathology represents a heightened version of normality," wrote Lasch, "the 'pathological narcissism' found in character disorders of this type should tell us something about narcissism [the style] as a social phenomenon."

Lasch subtitled his popular work: "American Life in an Age of Diminishing Expectations." He believed that "narcissism appears realistically to represent the best way of coping [me! now!] with the tensions and anxieties of modern life. The prevailing social conditions therefore tend to bring out narcissistic traits that are present, in varying degrees, in everyone. These conditions have also transformed the family, which in turn shapes the underlying structure of personality," wrote Lasch.

Regarding the influence of society on personality disorders, eminent psychoanalyst Otto Kernberg, M.D., has commented, "It is possible that, at times of rapid social change and breakdown of traditional social structures, the more severe types of personality disorders [including the Narcissistic] emerge because of the loss of the compensating functions of social structure."

COPING WITH THE NARCISSISTS IN YOUR LIFE

Manipulative, demanding, and emotionally ungiving as they are, Narcissistic men and women are among the most trying people to deal with. Some of the advice on dealing with Self-Confident individuals may help with mildly Narcissistic types. You will find additional suggestions within the following case history, which shows how one family at last came to terms with the Narcissistic personality disorder of one of its members. As you read this case, note that stress and conflict can trigger the worst behaviors in anyone, especially a Narcissist, who may have difficulty getting along with people under the best of circumstances. Because, presumably, you have your behavior under better control, it may be up to *you* to step away from your areas of conflict with the personality-disordered individual and change your own responses, in order to encourage better behavior on his or her part.

The Mother-in-Law Project:
The Case of Maryann and Mabel; Mike, Too

In every life a little rain must fall, and the cloud over Maryann's life invariably was her mother-in-law. From their first meeting, every interaction with Mike's mom brought Maryann frustration or pain. Ten years ago, Mike brought his future bride home to Atlanta to meet Mabel, his widowed mother. Mabel threw them a large engagement party at a restaurant and advised Maryann to dress simply. Maryann pulled from her suitcase a bright summer sundress. "That will be fine, dear," said Mabel. When Mike and Maryann showed up at the restaurant, there was Mabel in an elegant black-sequined evening gown.

Maryann felt like a farmhand. "You look great," Mike tried to reassure her. "My mother's doing one of her numbers. Don't let it get to you."

That summed up Mike's attitude as the years went by and Mabel would one-up, manipulate, or undermine Maryann. Mike didn't want to talk about his mother. He wanted as little to do with her as possible. But he didn't want to break with her, either, so it fell to Maryann to deal with Mabel. And no matter how strong Maryann felt, Mabel always managed to do her in.

Maryann and Mike lived in Memphis. Mabel called from Atlanta at least four times a week. She would talk for hours no matter what time it was—at midnight or early on a Sunday morning—without the slightest embarrassment. When Maryann would suggest tactfully that it was an inconvenient time to speak, Mabel would lash out at her for being selfish and inconsiderate. She never asked about Maryann when she called; she just gabbed about herself and how unhappy she was over this or that. She always sounded as if her miseries were special and unique—no one had ever suffered the way she had.

Maryann kept trying to help. "I'll find you the name of a good gastroenterologist in Atlanta," she would say. Or, "Why don't you try a hot-water bottle?" Her offers were brushed aside. Once Maryann suggested that perhaps Mabel had too much time on her hands and would be happier donating some of her time to helping other people. Mabel reacted with frightening rage, shouting over the telephone, "How can I expect anyone like you to understand me? Look at what you've done to my son!"

Maryann reported this to Mike, who said it was typical garbage. End of subject. Maryann thought he was probably right, but for several weeks she worried that maybe Mike wasn't as happy in the marriage as he seemed. Otherwise, why would his mother have said such a thing?

For a while after their twin boys were born, Mabel was on good behavior. She came bearing gifts, expensive showy things, like a near life-size stuffed pony. She came to stay with them more often, ostensibly to see the boys. But after she delighted the twins with their presents, she never really wanted to be alone with them or truly get to know them. If Mike and Maryann wanted to go out for a long-awaited evening alone, Mabel would refuse to be responsible for the children. Maryann began to believe that Mabel didn't like her or the twins. She voiced her thoughts to Mike.

"You'll never get it, will you?" he said, exasperated with his wife. "It's not that she doesn't like you or the kids. It's that she can't stand taking the attention off herself." Mike wouldn't elaborate further, and Maryann let it drop.

Maryann frequently thanked heaven that her own mother was loving and straightforward, and that the children had at least one healthy relationship with a grandparent. Maryann and her mother had grown closer after Maryann's father had died a few years before. Maryann increasingly valued their mature friendship and her mother's sensible advice.

Maryann was devastated when her mother called from her home in Little Rock to say she had lung cancer. When Mabel telephoned later that night, Maryann told her the news and shared how upset she was. "Did you hear"—Mabel interrupted her daughter-in-law—"that Mike's old baseball coach broke his neck in a car crash?"

Maryann hung on while Mabel chattered on. She heard nothing. She was in a kind of shock. "Dear God," she prayed, "spare my mother. Take this monster instead." Afterward, she felt guilty for the thought, but she began to find excuses not to speak to Mabel when she called. Mabel's response was to call before breakfast, at three-thirty when the twins got home from school, or even at one o'clock in the morning.

This went on for more than a month. Maryann felt as if she were being driven mad. While visiting her own mother in the hospital, she blurted, "If that woman doesn't change, I'll go out of my mind!"

Her mother lay quietly. Finally she said, "Maryann, honey, I think you've got that backwards. I think that if you don't change, you'll let that woman drive you out of your mind."

Her mother was right. Mabel was the most difficult but certainly not the only confusing person in Maryann's life. Maryann had to stand back and stop taking such behavior at face value. She had to learn what made these people tick, and find out how to apply this knowledge to her own behavior in relation to them.

Mabel required constant attention, as Mike had pointed out. Now the therapist whom Maryann consulted explained that her mother-in-law appeared to be suffering from Narcissistic personality disorder—and that the disorder rendered Mabel unable to pay attention to anyone but herself. All her energy went to feeding her overblown sense of importance. To that end she would use other people, especially Maryann.

Making sure that Maryann dressed "like a farmhand" for the engagement party ensured that Mabel would remain the glittering star. As her behavior repeatedly proved, Mabel had to feel unique, favored, admired, and always "better than" her daughter-in-law. She gave the impression that she expected Maryann to envy her. And when she was criticized, she reacted with rage—typical of people with this disorder.

Mabel's overreactions were a key to the quality of her inner life. Criticism hurt her so much because deep down she felt worthless, vulnerable, threatened, and excruciatingly envious of other people. She had to keep the attention always on herself because her own sense of self was too weak to stand on its own, explained the therapist.

Mabel's behavior existed for a reason—to allow her to feel like somebody, because inside she was extremely insecure. Stepping back from her mother-in-law's hurtful behavior helped Maryann finally to stop taking it so personally. Mabel wasn't trying to hurt her so much as she was trying to protect herself.

Establishing her own emotional distance was Maryann's first step in learning how to deal with her mother-in-law. Step two was to stop trying to change her. Maryann's frequent attempts to "help" Mabel actually brought on her worst overreactions, such as the time Maryann had innocently suggested that Mabel turn her time and attention to other people—that is, take the spotlight off herself.

Step three was to accept Mabel's behavior as predictable; not to expect it to change. Maryann was always being wounded by her mother-in-law because Mabel's behavior was consistently bad. Why not accept that Mabel was not going to baby-sit the kids under any circumstances, and avoid being shocked and upset each time she refused? Similarly, once Maryann recognized that Mabel never respected her feelings, she could decide whether she wished to reveal her vulnerability.

Step four was to let Mabel have what she needed. Mabel needed so much attention because inside she felt weak. There were many ways to provide her with comfort and prevent a struggle. For example, Maryann found that when Mabel telephoned, she could simply let her rattle on about herself without becoming intensely involved in the conversation. Maryann could cook or crochet with the phone to her ear, uttering an occasional sound to let Mabel know she was still listening. She and Mike could tell Mabel how nice she looked when she arrived at the house so that she would not fish for her quota of compliments throughout her stay.

Learning to deal with Mabel after a decade of hurts was an enormous challenge. The hardest part for Maryann was to stop overreacting to Mabel's overreactions. Maryann had her own personality style, after all, and her Devoted tendencies made her easily hurt by criticism and disapproval. Step five for Maryann was to untangle her personality pattern from Mabel's, and to recognize where her own style contributed to the problem.

Her Mother-in-Law Project, as Maryann came to call it, produced gratifying results. Maryann gave up hope that her mother-in-law would change, and she resisted being hurt by her. The tension that had existed between them began to recede. Much to both Maryann and Mike's astonishment, once the pressure was off Mabel to behave like a decent human being, a better side occasionally emerged. At times she seemed calmer, more cooperative, less prone to erupt and attack. She even tried to act unselfishly. A few times Mabel inquired about Maryann's mother's health and did not interrupt or change the subject. Maryann recognized the effort it took for Mabel not to feel envious of Maryann's love for her mother. She chose to change the subject herself before Mabel's success gave way. And instead of feeling regret that she could not speak at length about a subject so important to her, Maryann felt pleased to have had her mother-in-law's attention for that time.

The project yielded other unexpected bonuses. In this more comfortable environment, Mike felt more responsive to his mother—and to his wife. Their need for approval and their sensitivity to criticism had sent Mike into emotional hiding. Now he could venture back without being burned, and be the better for it.

CHAPTER 6

Devoted Style

"THE GOOD MATE"

Devoted types *care*, and that's what makes their lives worth living. You won't find anyone more loving, more solicitous of you, more concerned for your needs and feelings or for those of the group as a whole. At their best, individuals with this style are the loyal, considerate, ever-so-helpful players on the team—whether it is the couple, the family, the assembly line, the department, the religious or charitable organization, or the military unit. Their needs are those of the group or of its leader, and their happiness comes from the fulfillment of the others' directives and goals. Devoted people are the ones who tell you, "I'm happy if you're happy"—and mean it.

The Devoted style is common in our society, and it occurs among both men and women. Traditionally this helping and giving personality style has been particularly encouraged and approved among women. The customary view of the good wife has been that of a tender-hearted Devoted woman who lives through her husband and relies on him to make the worldly decisions for her, while she dedicates herself to providing a fulfilling home life for the family. As views of women's roles change in this society, some women with this personality style may have mixed feelings about expressing it. Because of today's cultural pressures on women to step out of the shadows of other people, both in and out of the home, they may feel that wanting to make someone else happy is something to be ashamed of. While these women struggle to come to terms with all sides of their personality patterns, more men are feeling freer to enjoy their own domestic, nurturing Devoted tendencies. In any case, as we will see throughout this chapter, the Devoted personality plays itself out in many ways in the personality profiles of males as well as females, traditional and otherwise.

THE SEVEN CHARACTERISTICS

The following seven traits and behaviors are clues to the presence of the Devoted style. A person who reveals a strong Devoted tendency will demonstrate more of these behaviors more intensely than someone who has less of this style.

1. *Commitment.* Individuals with the Devoted personality style are thoroughly dedicated to the relationships in their lives. They place the highest value on sustained relationships, they respect the institution of marriage as well as unofficial avowals of commitment, and they work hard to keep their relationships together.

2. *Togetherness.* They prefer the company of one or more people to being alone.

3. *Teamwork.* People with this personality style would rather follow than lead. They are cooperative and respectful of authority and institutions. They easily rely on others and take direction well.

4. *Deference.* When making decisions, they are happy to seek out others' opinions and to follow their advice.

5. *Harmony.* Devoted individuals are careful to promote good feelings between themselves and the important people in their lives. To promote harmony, they tend to be polite, agreeable, and tactful.

6. *Consideration.* They are thoughtful of others and good at pleasing them. Devoted people will endure personal discomfort to do a good turn for the key people in their lives.

7. *Attachment.* Relationships provide life's meaning for this personality style. Even after a painful loss of someone around whom their life was centered, they are able to form new meaningful bonds.

THE SIX DOMAINS OF
DEVOTED FUNCTIONING

RELATIONSHIPS: MY WORLD IS YOU

For Devoted men and women, the domain of Relationships is key. Other people are their reason for being, lending purpose to their lives and fulfillment to their dreams. Their attachments center them in the universe and make them feel complete.

People with the Devoted style prominent in their personalities form relationships easily, and they devote themselves to pleasing the principal people in their lives. They remember your birthday. They bring a hot meal when you're sick. They think about you; they listen to you; they keep up with what's going on in your life. They are gifted hosts and hostesses, careful that their guests match up well, that the food is catered to everyone's tastes, and that conversation never lags. Because they pay so much attention to you they always seem to anticipate your needs. The phone rings; it's your Devoted friend or family member, who somehow knows you need someone to talk to.

It feels good to have such considerate, undivided attention. And if you feel good, so does the Devoted person. An individual with this personality style will often endure discomfort or hardship to make sure those close to them do not. Harriet's husband, Sidney, comes late to the party and there's no food left at the buffet. Devoted Harriet offers him her plate of food. Sidney feels guilty taking Harriet's food—but Devoted Harriet would feel worse if Sidney went hungry.

Keepers of the Flame

People with a predominance of this style will do more of the work and make more of the sacrifices involved with keeping a relationship going—without keeping score or complaining about the apparent inequality of things. Take Maggie. She and Lyle have been married for fourteen years. Her talent as a photographer of cityscapes began to be recognized before she and Lyle met. She met Lyle when he was studying music composition at a midwestern conservatory. They married when he finished his graduate studies. At that time, while Maggie was just on the threshold of making a name for herself, Lyle's compositions had yet to be heard, much less recognized. For income he gave piano and violin lessons. But Lyle was not a patient music instructor. He longed to be free to compose, away from the hassles of the city and its expenses and obligations. Maggie encouraged him in his dream. Soon Lyle learned of a composer-in-residence program at a small private school on an island off the coast of Maine that would allow him ample time for composing in return for minimal teaching duties. The day the letter of acceptance arrived, Lyle swung Maggie in his arms and cried with joy.

When Maggie told a good friend where she and Lyle would be moving, the friend, an artist, was appalled. If Maggie abandoned the art scene now, the friend pointed out, she would lose her momentum. And it was her unique perspective on the city that had won her attention—she couldn't just drop it all when people were beginning to comprehend her particular vision.

Maggie did not disagree with her friend. She knew that the sacrifice was enormous, and it had cost her much private anguish (she hadn't shared this with Lyle). But she would go wherever Lyle needed to go. He was her man. "Can't he at least stick it out here a few more years until you're more established?" asked the friend. Maggie shrugged. "I don't know," she said. "I never asked him."

The composer-in-residence position ended after a year. Because Lyle had been so happy on the island and so productive, they decided to stay on. He secured a teaching position at the school that required few hours of his time. The pay, of course, was low. So Maggie got a job as reporter and photographer for the weekly community newspaper. She's held this job for almost ten years now, taking off three months when she gave birth to each of their two children. Child care is mostly her responsibility, although Lyle helps out when she asks him. Twice Maggie has exhibited her photographs of island life at the small art gallery that opens during the summer for the tourist trade. Her work is unquestionably good, but she is no longer a serious contender in the art world. It's hard to know what she feels in her most private moments about the road not taken. She doesn't talk much about herself. Her letters to her old friends are filled with Lyle-this and the-children-that. Unquestionably Lyle is the center of her universe. He may never achieve serious acclaim as a composer. But Maggie believes in him. No matter what her old friends may think about his influence on her, organizing their married life around him is what she wants to do.

The Balance of Power

Lyle is by no means an ogre. He loves his wife deeply and has dedicated much of his music to her. Often he stops to thank the heavens for gracing him with such a woman. He consults Maggie in everything, and if ever she said, "No, I can't go along with that," he'd have second thoughts about proceeding. However, with Devoted types there is a risk that they will hook up with overbearing, control-hungry mates. This is because within their relationships Devoted types like Maggie automatically assume the less dominant, more passive, caretaking role. They prefer to rely on the judgment of the central person in their lives to make the major life decisions. Thus, relationships that Devoted individuals form are mercifully free of power struggles. Trust is paramount, the lines of family authority are clear, and so decision making often boils down to "Whatever you say, dear." That can work well as long as the Devoted person does not sacrifice his or her best interests (as happens particularly with people who also have substantial Self-Sacrificing style in their patterns) and the mate is responsible, has no major personality problems, and does not take advantage.

A Husband for Carolyn

While we are familiar with women in this role of the more passive, less powerful, Devoted partner, couples in which the Devoted mate is male can work well under this unequal balance of power. Indeed, women with very powerful personality styles—such as Carolyn, the corporate executive whom we first met in chapter 1—may have much to gain by hooking up with men who have Devoted tendencies.

Despite setbacks, Carolyn had always achieved great success in the working world. Not so in her private life. One reason was that her Conscientious personality style kept her focused mostly on her work. Another reason was that in her moderately Self-Confident way, she had always been attracted to supersuccessful, powerful men, with whom relationships often deteriorated into competitive who's-in-charge-here battles with no winners. Even when a relationship was more peaceful, Carolyn ran herself ragged fulfilling the traditionally female roles as meal and social planner and keeper of the house, in addition to her business responsibilities. Carolyn needed someone to think about *her* needs. "Fat chance," she used to think.

Since we last met Carolyn in these pages, she had joined an import-export firm. Now she has become the firm's president and, at age forty-four, married Devoted Jerry, much to the surprise of her family and friends. Everybody knew she'd be president of something someday, but nobody (least of all Carolyn) ever thought she'd get married.

She met Jerry at a ski resort. They had a week-long affair. He proved to be a most considerate lover and companion, willing to do anything to make her happy. Handsome and personable though he was, Jerry was hardly Carolyn's type. He earned a modest living as a computer consultant, but he was more into cooking and carpentry and athletics than making money and gaining power. Carolyn assumed she had seen the last of him when her brief vacation ended.

Much to her discomfort, Jerry continued to pursue her. Finally she accepted a date, thinking she would get rid of him that evening. But he gave her the best back rub she'd ever had, and the lovemaking was unbelievable. She continued to go out with him, beginning to grow accustomed to Jerry's warm, relaxing, thoughtful, undemanding presence, but she was embarrassed to tell her friends or family about him. She worried that they would accuse her of "wearing the pants in the family" or "settling for less," since she took the lead in the relationship, made most of the decisions, and paid for almost everything. Jerry took care of the details, from getting the car serviced to cooking meals to adding a deck onto the house and overseeing the housekeeping.

But she was happy, as she had never been before in a relationship. She returned to the therapist she had consulted from time to time throughout the years, hoping that she would help her break from this most "inappropriate" match. Instead, the therapist helped Carolyn to accept her newfound, well-deserved happiness.

Still, it cost her much anxiety before she could agree to marry Jerry. Carolyn had one last fling, with a high-powered banker. They fought, the sex wasn't great, and no one had dinner waiting on the table when she got home from work. She missed Jerry—who was deeply upset by her unfaithfulness—and she realized she didn't want to lose him.

Jerry was immensely relieved. He feels blessed that he's the one who can make this active, exciting, important, powerful woman happy. He knows that he and Carolyn have a good marriage—better than many couples. He hopes she'll always see it that way, but he continues to worry that Carolyn will be tempted away from him sooner or later by "some heavy-duty guy." He can't imagine losing interest in her, even though Carolyn is eleven years older than he is.

Step Up on the Pedestal

Devoted men and women rarely tire of their mates. They idealize them and place them (along with most other people in their lives) on pedestals. The Devoted partners make sure that their spouses remain on their thrones. They need it this way; their own place in the world becomes secure and comfortable. They like to involve them in all aspects of their lives, and they ask their opinions about any old thing: "How do you like this dress?" "Do you think I ought to sell stocks and buy bonds?" "I have to pick out new wallpaper for this room. Can you come over and tell me what you think?"

Often this Devoted idealization of the mate is more subtle, especially in people who have more mixed personality patterns than do Jerry or Maggie. Alan, for example, runs a small trucking company. In business he's used to making decisions and having other people rely on him. But at home he demonstrates more of his Devoted traits. He goes along with his wife, Joan, on many family issues, including going to church. He has no particular faith and he'd rather play golf, but he wouldn't think of crossing Joan on this or other matters that are important to her.

Stress!

Trouble in a relationship is a severe source of stress for the Devoted person, second only to a breakup itself. Individuals with this personality style take criticism hard and feel personally responsible for things that go wrong in the relationship. They may spend more energy than other people worrying about the short- or long-term fidelity of their spouses. And when they are worried about the relationship they may need excessive affection and reassurance in order to forestall periods of anxiety or depression. They cope with these stresses by taking it upon themselves to make things better: they aim to please. Unfortunately, this coping style often compounds their problems. The mates of overly Devoted individuals may already have become exasperated with their compliance and lack of initiative. What they may need to see now is a show of strength from their Devoted mates. But when the Devoted person is feeling threatened, he or she may become more extreme. In response to a question such as, "Where would you like to eat?" all the stressed Devoted partner can answer is, "Wherever you want is okay with me."

The end of a relationship, by breakup or through death of a spouse, may feel like the end of the world to a Devoted person. Devoted types do not do well alone, when depression becomes a real risk. The actual extent of the Devoted style may not become apparent in an individual until this dreadful occurrence. Often the spouses of Devoted people are happy to be the responsible ones in the family. But when the spouse is no longer present, the overprotected Devoted partner may discover for the first time that he or she is unprepared to make the decisions and show the initiative required for life on his or her own.

Devoted men and women cope with loss by filling the void as soon as possible. Some Devoted people go from relationship to relationship rather than be alone with themselves even for a few months. This tendency to rebound immediately is a strong clue to the presence of the Devoted style in a person's personality profile. Nonetheless, that they are able to create new relationships is to their credit. Some people, such as those with Vigilant or Sensitive personality styles, cope with the pain of loss by steering clear of opportunities to love again.

The Devoted Parent

Few others are more nurturing than Devoted parents, especially when their children are babies. Devoted individuals are exquisitely sensitive to the needs and feelings of their infants, and they take care of them without discomfort or complaint. Indeed, they're so good at understanding and fulfilling the dependency needs of their young ones that they must take care not to overprotect them and keep them dependent when they begin to take steps toward autonomy. Devoted parents should at all times be sure to work on helping their kids test and appreciate the rewards of independence. Single Devoted parents may have some problems making important decisions for themselves and their children. By and large, however, moderately Devoted parents will give easily and happily to their children and will be remembered with great love.

Good/Bad Matches

Men and women with Devoted personalities are not fussy and are capable of gaining favor with virtually any personality style. They have the knack for finding out what a person needs and then filling those needs. All their matches are not made in heaven, however. Since Devoted individuals prefer, to varying extents, to be compliant and to let the other person be in charge, they must beware of mates with personality disorders such as the Sadistic or the Antisocial, who may take advantage of and possibly hurt them.

The best match for a Devoted person may well be with a Conscientious person, who likes to take control and to do the right thing; this is the match that worked so well for Carolyn and Jerry. Someone with a moderate amount of Vigilant style will also prefer to be in control and will appreciate the Devoted person's deference; Vigilant individuals require a great show of loyalty first, but this is no problem for someone with Devoted traits. Aggressive-Devoted matches are common and often workable, as long as neither style is extreme and the Aggressive partner holds back on taking advantage of the Devoted's compliance.

Relationships with Serious people are also workable. Serious mates are steady and predictable, if critical, but Devoted people are used to criticism and will often work harder at the relationship as a result. And Serious types are at their best with mates who fuss over them. Highly Serious people are prone to depression, however, as are Devoted men and women when their relationships are in trouble; the outlook of the Devoted mate could be overly influenced by the Serious partner's tendency to pessimism.

Self-Confident types are quite happy to receive the you-come-first attentions of a Devoted mate. However, these matches can be problematic for someone whose personality style is very strongly Devoted, because the Self-Confident partner cannot provide the reassurances the Devoted person needs. An Adventurous person may be attracted to a Devoted person, but Adventurers tend to stray, which is too stressful for the Devoted person. Leisurely and Devoted men and women are naturally reluctant to take charge, which leads to an unstable relationship. Dramatic individuals will require too much reassurance themselves to provide the necessary emotional security the Devoted style requires; the Sensitive style is even more similar and cannot provide the strength for the Devoted person to lean on. Mercurial individuals, while they provide many needs for the Devoted person to fill, prove too changeable for them to deal with.

Finally, while it might seem obvious that two Devoted people could not rely on each other, mutually Devoted matches are in fact common. When neither partner is predominantly Devoted, each relies on the other for different things, perhaps one inside the home and one outside. Or the personality pattern of one of the partners will also have strength in a decisive, assertive style.

EMOTIONS, SELF-CONTROL, AND THE REAL WORLD: THE ATTACHED SELF

Since Devoted people find contentment via attachment, their sense of themselves may be weak. They don't necessarily appear unconfident or fragile; many people with moderately Devoted traits lead active, productive lives, as long as they are within a successful, caring, mutually respectful relationship. With a great deal of this style, however, individuals often feel that they don't measure up to the idealized partner. And they may be hesitant to voice their opinions, or, as the style becomes extreme, they may change them to suit others, even going so far as to assume the opinions of their partners. When men and women with this style are not involved in a relationship, they may feel that there's something wrong with them.

Frequently, Devoted people think of themselves and their mates as one. Thus, the Devoted wife who says, "We don't think we're going to the toy-manufacturer's convention," means that her husband, who always attends alone, has decided not to go to the convention this year. A veterinarian's Devoted wife who serves as his receptionist confused a caller who asked for her husband when she responded, "We're in surgery now."

Emotionally, people with this personality style can be steady and open, if they're attached. If they're not involved in a relationship, or if they're having troubles as a couple, they may become depressed, anxious, and worried.

They can express and accept love—this is their gift. They may have difficulty showing strong negative feelings, including anger, if these feelings put them in conflict with the people they care for. When they are angry, they are more likely to brood and become resentful than to express it directly.

Self-control is not usually a problem for people with this personality style, at least when their relationships are proceeding well. When they're worried about their relationships, they may need an excessive amount of reassurance, and after a loss they may seek symbolic substitutes, such as food. As soon as they find a new number-one, they snap out of it.

The Real World for the Devoted person is one in which other people loom rather large. Or, in other words, it is a world in which the Devoted person can, without fully realizing it, feel a bit small and needy, like a child, carrying less weight compared with idealized, apparently more substantial others.

WORK: IN THE SERVICE OF OTHERS

Devoted men and women can be good, hard workers who do whatever is required to please the boss. They take orders well, cooperate with their coworkers, and have little need to put their own imprint on the work or to share the credit or glory. When their work life is functioning smoothly, they do need frequent expressions of appreciation. They work well with Conscientious bosses, who prefer to be in direct control of their employees' work. While Self-Confident bosses appreciate the loyal, noncompetitive nature of Devoted people, they may expect their subordinates to show more initiative and independence than is characteristic of someone with this personality style.

People whose personalities are dominated by the Devoted style are generally content to steer clear of the "fast lane": they tend not to be avid competitors or eager decision makers. However, because they are often so cooperative and competent at doing what they're asked, they may be promoted into positions that require some non-Devoted, creative decision making. Unfortunately, these management-level jobs may prove their undoing.

Management Style

A person who is ruled by the Devoted style generally avoids becoming a manager. Since this style is common in mixed personality patterns, however, many men and women in management positions possess their fair share of Devoted traits. Such moderately Devoted managers will prove to be sensitive, friendly, encouraging, and caring toward their staffs. Often they will go out of their way to make the work situation pleasant and rewarding. They are quick to express their gratitude for a job well done. They may rely on key staff members to make or contribute to important decisions. But they may worry too much about what subordinates think of them and will thus have difficulty asserting their authority during conflict. Assertiveness training can help here.

Careers for the Devoted

Men and women with the Devoted personality style thrive in jobs or careers in which they take direct orders and/or fulfill the needs of others—from secretarial work to a secure position in the family business to line work or middle management in the corporation. Service careers such as nursing, working with children, and social work are naturals for this personality style. A streak of Devoted style, balanced among other personality styles, can benefit psychotherapists. Devoted volunteers are godsends for service agencies, where there is no end of need for people who can give so much of themselves to others.

If this is the dominant style in your personality, steer clear of any work that does not involve other people and/or that requires you to spend most of your time making, implementing, and being responsible for decisions.

TIPS ON DEALING WITH THE
DEVOTED PERSON IN YOUR LIFE

1. The Devoted person in your life likes to help and to please. Don't fight it, and don't feel guilty for accepting it. Enjoy.

2. Don't take the attentions of this person for granted. The Devoted person in your life may be so good at anticipating your desires and putting you first that you may not recognize that he or she has unfulfilled, unexpressed needs and longings. Devoted types often seem more confident and assertive than they actually are. When they want something from you, they may not ask. Indeed, they may wait for you to anticipate their needs the way they anticipate yours. Foremost among their needs is reassurance. Devoted people are extremely sensitive to your feelings about them; express your love and appreciation frequently and honestly. If the Devoted person in your life is your employee, express your appreciation for the good work and stop and consider whether you owe this person a raise. Devoted types may be reluctant to request one or to remind you that it's time. They may assume that if they deserved it, you'd provide it.

3. Keep in mind that criticizing this individual, or blowing your top, will likely lead to Devoted self-doubt and self-blame—not particularly constructive reactions. When you need to resolve a conflict with a Devoted person, or deal with unpleasant personal business, contribute as much reassurance as you can. Resist the temptation to allow the Devoted person to shoulder the blame for everything that goes wrong between the two of you, which he or she may be all too willing to do. At the same time, don't provide so much reassurance that you neglect to work out a solution to your conflict.

4. Take the stated opinions of this person with a grain of salt. The more Devoted a person is, the more that person will express an opinion that he or she thinks you want to hear. Underneath it all, this Devoted person may have an altogether different opinion. If you say, "What do you think about going on a camping vacation for a change?" your mate, hearing the enthusiasm in your voice, may say, "Oh sure." In reality he or she may prefer to go on a cruise. Unless you make sure that this person's opinion is a true one, you may be stuck in the woods with a less-than-cheerful partner.

MAKING THE MOST OF YOUR DEVOTED STYLE

You know how to love and how to give. You are keenly aware of other people's needs and feelings. Now turn your attention to yourself and see what you can do on your own behalf, and let other people know who you are and what they can do for you.

You are diplomatic and you like to promote harmony. To this end you may tend to agree with the people who are important to you, perhaps stifling your own opinions. By this you run the risk of appearing less interesting to the people whose opinions you care about most.

Exercise 1

Whenever someone asks you for your opinion, say what you honestly think. For example, if your date or mate asks you what you would like to do tonight, *don't* answer, "I don't care. Whatever you want is fine with me." Instead, think of an answer. If you can't come up with one, say, "I don't know right now, but I'll think about it."

Your Devoted personality style may make it difficult for you to express your anger in addition to your opinions, for fear that you'll rock the relationship boat. However, trying to suppress your feelings when you are angry may lead you to express your anger sideways, such as by pouting, by getting a headache, or by becoming uncooperative. These expressions of anger tend to be destructive to a relationship.

Exercise 2

Get it off your chest. Express your anger directly. Tell people what you are angry about and why, instead of allowing it to distort your behavior. If you can't get yourself to do that, start by making a list of all the things you are angry about. Then, when you are alone, pretend the person you are angry at is in the room and that you are telling him or her what you are angry about.

Devoted people like you prefer to rely on other people and to let them make their decisions for them. As in the case of Alexander A., which follows shortly, going along with the wishes of others may lead to dissatisfaction with the results of those decisions, now or years from now. Also, decision making is an essential survival skill, necessary to avoid becoming helpless and dependent should you lose the person or people you rely upon most.

Exercise 3

Practice decision making. Each time you are about to seek someone else's opinion or advice in making a decision, stop and think whether you can make up your own mind or come up with the answer yourself. If you have a big problem with decisions, concentrate on minor decisions first (such as what to wear today or which movie to see or where to go to dinner); when you get better at these, start practicing on the more important ones (such as whether to look for another job).

Conscientious people often have problems with decisions too; see Exercises 2 and 3 in chapter 4 (pp. 74–75). Also, notice how Alexander A. began to deal with his reluctance to make decisions. And while we're borrowing exercises from other personality styles, try the Sensitive style's Exercise 7: Every time someone criticizes you, stand back from yourself and observe how you (over)react (p. 195).

Exercise 4

Your total devotion to your family or your mate is admirable. Make sure you do not give up all your other interests, though.

Develop or rekindle your own activities. Go bowling once a week, join a charitable organization or the volunteer fire department, volunteer at your local hospital, sign up for a class—whatever you think you would like to do. In order to remain balanced and to avoid overdependence on your spouse, you need other connections to the world.

Remember that most people no longer have the extended family network to fall back on when they grow old or face aloneness. In this day and age, the better you learn how to take care of yourself, the more independent dignity you will have in later life.

Exercise 5

Develop the life skills you lack. For example, learn to do the banking and pay bills, or shop for food and cook a meal; find out how to buy a car, how to claim insurance benefits, how to make travel reservations, and how to plan social activities, in the event that your spouse takes care of these tasks for you. These responsibilities may all fall to you sooner or later, should your mate die or fall ill. Life will go on more easily if you learn what to do.

Exercise 6

If you're used to throwing yourself blindly into a new relationship after one ends, try to resist it, no matter how powerfully attracted to this person you may feel. Take it slowly. Experience yourself as a capable, independent person. If being on your own makes you anxious, experience these feelings as growing pains. Consult the Sensitive style's Exercises 2 through 9 (pp. 193–95) for anxiety-management techniques.

"IS THIS ALL THERE IS?"
THE CASE OF ALEXANDER A.

Alexander A. (whom we first met in chapter 1) is deep in the throes of a midlife crisis. His personality pattern is a mixture of primarily Devoted, Conscientious, Leisurely, and Serious influences; notice in particular how his Devoted tendencies have contributed to his current dilemma.

It started soon after his thirty-ninth birthday. Alexander A., accountant, MBA, CPA, woke up and asked himself, "Is this all there is?"

He lay in bed weighted by an indefinable something-or-other. He got up and, while shaving, scrutinized his face in the mirror. He liked what he saw. It was just the face he would have wanted for himself at age thirty-nine—the strong, prominent brows and deep, sensitive eyes. He even liked the suggestion of gray at his temples. That, plus his neatly trimmed mustache, made him look wise.

He sighed. Alexander expected more, somehow. Being thirty-nine meant he was supposed to be coming into his prime. To him, a man at this stage of life was supposed to feel powerful, fulfilled, satisfied. But as the days went on, Alexander felt more and more uncomfortable with his life. He couldn't say why.

It wasn't that he hadn't done well. He was about to take over the helm of a thriving family business. He had a good relationship with Arlene, who had moved in with him six years ago. Living together had been her idea, but that was okay with him. Lately she'd been saying they should get married. Arlene was thirty-five and wanted to have children. Probably Alexander would go along with her—he didn't mind the idea of having children. If his business continued to grow, he would be able to provide well for his family. Yet he thought of this supposedly rosy future with a shudder. "Is this all there is?"

Alexander began to call it his midlife crisis. He told Arlene that he felt bored and dissatisfied, especially at work. Frankly, he confided, he was beginning to hate being in the office. They talked about it; both agreed that Alexander was going through a "phase" that people have to endure as they reach forty. After you work for ten or fifteen years to establish a career, you can't expect the same excitement. But you go on, and you get used to it, they decided.

And there were definitely good aspects to his work, he acknowledged as he attempted to shore up his mood. He loved to be around people, especially his clients. Some of them were like members of the family. Tax time, rushed and harried though it was, meant months of listening to his clients relate the personal ups and downs of their year. They liked to confide in Alex. They appreciated his advice about their kids, their relationships, and their work. They trusted him. He was a good listener and he took them seriously.

One of his clients had even taken to calling him "my accountant-analyst." Unfortunately, he'd said it in front of Alexander's father, who'd had a fit. This aspect of Alexander's service to his customers had always irritated his father, who felt that Alexander paid more attention to his clients' emotional needs than to their tax forms. Alexander disagreed that his work suffered for his interest in his clients. He was continually disappointed that his father wished to deprive him of the most fulfilling aspect of his work.

But no life, no career, is perfect, Alexander and Arlene agreed. He had found his path in life and would follow it.

Alexander's malaise did not improve. He perceived the rest of his life as a long hall with one grim doorway at the end. He steeled himself to endure the long walk with dignity. And in his heart of hearts he nursed fantasies of escape from the deadly daily drudgery. But he was ashamed of his unmanly attitude. Alexander felt terrible.

He consulted a psychiatrist.

Alexander went into therapy assuming that there must be something wrong with him—why else would he be so unhappy, when things appeared to be going so well for him? His personality assessment revealed no personality disorder. But Alexander did possess a personality-style pattern that years earlier had set the stage for his current life crisis. Specifically, the Devoted style dominated his personality, with the Conscientious following and the Leisurely and Serious trailing right behind. The Devoted style revealed itself, for example, in his leaving the important life decisions to his parents and to Arlene, in giving his personal attentions to his clients, and in his fear of being on his own as the head of the family firm, among many other traits and behaviors. Typical of his Conscientious style were his tendency to worry a lot about being good and his black-and-white thinking style. His tendency to find other things to do when faced with his clients' tax forms was one of the behaviors that suggested the Leisurely style. His fundamental pessimism and shaky self-esteem were characteristic of Serious style.

As intuitive as he was about his clients' inner lives, Alexander lacked awareness of his own personality. He knew that his problems manifested themselves mostly in the Work domain of his life. But he had no notion, until he and the psychiatrist had worked together for many weeks, that the career he had chosen was wrong for him. No wonder he felt unfulfilled and disappointed.

Rather, the career he had *not* chosen for himself was wrong for him. Since childhood, Alexander had allowed his parents to make the important decisions for him. He had become an accountant because he felt it was the right thing to do. His father had founded the firm. From the time Alexander had been a small boy, his father had said proudly, "Someday it will be yours, my boy." Alexander pursued this course of life because it was there waiting for him and because he wanted to please his parents, but also because he never believed that the future held anything spectacular for him. After college he went to graduate business school; his father had decided it would be good preparation. Although Alexander's favorite courses were management relations and psychology, he was good enough with figures and detail to specialize in accountancy and eventually to earn his degree and to become a CPA.

Alexander worked hard and enjoyed the financial rewards and the overall approval of his parents and of Arlene. Arlene was the daughter of his parents' best friends. They'd been going together off and on since high school. When she married someone else right after she finished college, Alexander was shattered. He rebounded immediately into a relationship with another woman that lasted nearly nine years. They were going to get married, finally, but his parents were dead against it because she was of a different religion. Alexander couldn't stand the pressure and broke off the relationship, although he felt terrible for being such a coward. But not too long after that Arlene got divorced, moved back to the city, and called him. Getting back with her was just fine with him.

Both sets of parents hated the fact that Alexander and Arlene chose to live together instead of getting married. Alexander preferred marriage, but Arlene made it clear that she wasn't about to get married again, at least not for a long time. Now she was changing her tune. Besides wanting to have a child, she thought that it would be appropriate to be man and wife now that his father was about to retire and Alexander was going to replace him as president of the firm. Arlene liked the idea of Alexander becoming "top banana," which she began calling him. "Good morning, Top Banana." "What do you want for dinner, Top Banana?"

Alexander wished he could like it too. It wasn't just that he was afraid of being on his own professionally for the first time in his life. Alexander had progressed quickly in his therapy. He knew now that someone with such a strong streak of the Devoted style would panic at being in a position where there was no one to tell him what to do. But it went deeper than that, he now saw. Going along with everybody his whole life meant that he had created a niche for himself in which he had "made everybody happy except me. I never really *wanted* to be in the family business," he admitted ruefully.

At first Alexander reacted to the truth about his predicament with even greater misery. "I should have been a shrink," he moaned. "I've always been good with people's problems." The psychiatrist suggested that Alexander might consider the possibility of becoming a psychotherapist. But Alexander couldn't see how. Now when he looked in the mirror he saw a man trapped by the practical realities of life. He was too old to throw it all over. He had too many responsibilities to turn away from a good living. He wanted to start a family, not give up everything he had to invest in "a pipe dream."

Although he could help other people solve their problems, Alexander reacted to his new dilemma by intensifying the down side of his personality styles. For a while he sought only all-or-nothing, black-and-white answers, such as either quit his job and go back to school or stay and be miserable (Conscientious). He began neglecting his therapy appointments (Leisurely). He felt guilty for being such a worthless person (Serious). But most of all, he wanted someone else to make his decisions (Devoted).

"What should I do?" Alexander asked his psychiatrist Devotedly.

To begin to change, Alexander needed to imagine less extreme alternatives. "What would you suggest to someone who came to you with this problem?" asked the psychiatrist.

Alexander brightened. "Lists!" he said.

Alexander, Conscientious as he was, proved a master at making lists. One afternoon he sat down to perform what he called a "mind exercise": he would list all the things that he could possibly do to refocus his work without walking out on his business. He knew that he wanted to work more with people, to help them in some way, but how to do that and continue to work left him painfully blank. Finally, after several unsuccessful attempts, it occurred to him that he could teach. He might teach a night course in client-accountant relations at a business school.

That possibility gave birth to many others. Maybe he could take night courses himself, to see if he really wanted to be a psychotherapist. If he went to social work school part-time, he might be able to receive a degree in only a few years. Or maybe he could simply do volunteer work on weekends in a local halfway house for troubled kids.

Alexander was on a roll. He'd never had so many ideas for his own sake. He came to his therapy appointments excited and talkative. Not long ago he reported a very creative idea: once the business was officially his, he could restructure it to suit his own needs and abilities. He might hire someone to whom he could delegate the responsibilities he tended to put off, while he pursued teaching or course work or eventually new professional responsibilities outside the accounting firm. Alexander was thrilled with this vision of a new autonomy.

Although Alexander has made no firm decisions, already, after only six months, he seems different. He is resisting the urge to let everyone else determine his future. He suffered a setback, though, when he told his father what he was contemplating. "Dad got so upset that I thought he was having a stroke—I really thought I was killing my father," Alexander reported. He was so shaken by his father's reaction that for a few weeks he agreed with his dad that he was behaving like an "ungrateful child." His work on his personality style enabled him to recognize and cut short this Devoted overreaction to criticism, and soon Alexander bounced back. He was ready to start a new project. He wanted to figure out how he might go about restructuring the company. Usually the subject made him too anxious to think, so this time he came up with a new tactic. He pretended that his father had asked him to draw up these plans, and the ideas began to pour out of him.

Life is becoming more exciting for Alexander A., and not only in the Work domain. Things in the Relationship domain are becoming much more interesting. Arlene has been supportive and encouraging (now that Alexander has reassured her that he isn't planning to walk out on the firm). She likes his new assertiveness, especially in the bedroom. She calls him "my sexy Banana."

"Is this all there is?" she teases in her little-girl voice.

"There's a lot more where that came from," he whispers in her ear. "Just you wait and see."

DEPENDENT PERSONALITY DISORDER

People suffering from Dependent personality disorder, the pathological extreme of the Devoted style, have the misfortune to experience themselves as helpless, weak, empty, and inferior. By attaching themselves to another person they gain the strength and self-esteem to survive. Yet they live in fear of losing the person that is so necessary to them. They can't bear the very thought of being alone.

DIAGNOSTIC CRITERIA

The DSM-IV describes Dependent personality disorder as:

A pervasive and excessive need to be taken care of that leads to submissive and clinging behavior and fears of separation, beginning by early adulthood and present in a variety of contexts, as indicated by five (or more) of the following:

(1) has difficulty making everyday decisions without an excessive amount of advice and reassurance from others

(2) needs others to assume responsibility for most major areas of his or her life

(3) has difficulty expressing disagreement with others because of fear of loss of support or approval. Note: Do not include realistic fears of retribution

(4) has difficulty initiating projects or doing things on his or her own (because of a lack of self-confidence in judgment or abilities rather than a lack of motivation or energy)

(5) goes to excessive lengths to obtain nurturance and support from others, to the point of volunteering to do things that are unpleasant

(6) feels uncomfortable or helpless when alone because of exaggerated fears of being unable to care for himself or herself

(7) urgently seeks another relationship as a source of care and support when a close relationship ends

(8) is unrealistically preoccupied with fears of being left to take care of himself or herself

---

THE OVERWHELMING NEED
FOR ANOTHER

Dependent people—sometimes referred to popularly as "codependent"—lead their lives determined not to disturb or offend the people who become the entire focus of their lives. They yield up their individuality and autonomy at the doorstep, becoming placating, submissive, self-deprecating, undemanding, and apologetic, without self-assertion or ambition. (Note the tentative way they walk and speak.) They attach themselves uncritically and may run the risk of being victimized by partners who take advantage of their passivity. If the relationship becomes unsteady, Dependent individuals will appear helpless and clinging. But if they form a solid relationship, with a partner who will provide the reassurance, strength, and protection they need, these Dependent individuals seem content and comfortable. To others they appear kind, gentle, generous, and humble.

Their tendency to depreciate themselves before others—"You are so smart; you'll understand that book so much better than I did"—can seem a genteel and thoughtful manner of complimenting you on your intelligence. It is not, however. Despite all apparent evidence to the contrary, they honestly believe that they are inadequate in everything from looks to abilities to mental capacity. Underneath the smiling face of a Dependent person lurks someone who has little or no confidence, coupled with a huge need for reassurance. This man or woman reaches out to gain self-esteem from other people. If you say, "Nonsense, you're extremely smart," your Dependent friend may be able to believe it, but only for a moment. Primarily, Dependent people acquire the self-esteem they lack through their attachments to other people.

Dependent individuals tend to reveal a cheerful demeanor to the world. This sunny expression may mask great internal suffering. People with Dependent personality disorder may be very reluctant to confide their darker feelings to anyone, lest these truths burden or upset others or otherwise undermine their relationships. Even a mate of many years may be unaware of the Dependent partner's inner life. Indeed, Dependent individuals are very often unaware themselves of the extent of their depression and dejection, as well as their need to be dependent.

Instead, many of them prefer to pretend that the world is a storybook place with happy endings everywhere.

Others may mask their psychological helplessness by feeling physically frail and therefore requiring other people (including medical personnel) to take charge and pay attention.

HELP!

The end of a relationship, or an ongoing insecure one, destroys a Dependent person's equilibrium and often propels him or her to the therapist's office in a state of depression and/or terror. Very often these individuals themselves unintentionally doom their relationships by their excessive compliance and anxious, clinging eagerness to please. Their reluctance to make any independent decisions or to state their opinions can be exasperating to those people who prefer to love someone for his or her interesting individuality. Also, the Dependent person's nagging fear of abandonment may prove self-fulfilling. The partner grows so tired of hearing, "Tell me you love me! Say you'll never leave me!" that one day he or she can't stand it anymore and leaves. Notes psychiatrist Michael H. Stone: "The lesson [that if someone loves you, he will stay if you give him breathing space, but flee if you confine him], though absolutely crucial to the amelioration of Dependent personality disorder, goes contrary to a lifetime of thought on the part of the patient."

That dependence will be transferred to the psychotherapist. This can be very constructive in psychodynamic types of psychotherapy when the therapist is able to help the Dependent person understand these deep needs and to achieve autonomy by working them through. (If the therapist does not address these needs, however, the patient may remain in therapy interminably.) Some psychiatrists prescribe antidepressants and tranquilizers when anxiety, phobias, panic (see below), and depression are acute and disruptive. Behavioral types of therapy may be able to help people with this disorder to deal with the anxiety they encounter when trying to behave more independently. Cognitive treatments tackle typical beliefs, such as "If I were independent, I'd be isolated and alone," or "I'm much too stupid and weak."

RISKS, INCIDENCE, AND PREDISPOSITIONS

Individuals suffering from Dependent personality disorder are highly vulnerable to Axis I depressive disorders (see chapter 2, p. 19), particularly in response to loss, and to phobic, anxiety, and panic disorders.

Some researchers have found that they are at increased vulnerability of physical illnesses. Others report that a person with this disorder is at high risk of alcoholism and drug abuse and obesity. Frequently it occurs along with Borderline, Avoidant, and Histrionic personality disorders.

The disorder is one of the most common in mental health treatment settings and is diagnosed most frequently in women, although there is increasing evidence that it strikes men and women equally. (See our discussion of "women's personality disorders" in chapter 7, p. 152.)

Submissive behavior may be a genetically determined trait, predisposing some children to develop this personality disorder if they encounter certain kinds of stresses. Parents with Dependent personality disorder tend to overprotect their children, which may lay the groundwork for the vulnerable offspring to develop the same disorder. Clinicians have found that many Dependent individuals come from families in which parents were very intrusive and discouraged the child's attempts to be independent and autonomous. Chronic illness in children and adolescents may also predispose an individual to develop this personality disorder in adulthood. Some psychiatrists believe that children who suffer from extreme separation anxiety may later develop Dependent personality disorder.

COPING WITH DEPENDENT PEOPLE

Refer back to the section "Tips on Dealing with the Devoted Person in Your Life," which can come in handy. Resist the urge to take over the lives of these needy persons, whom you may love dearly. Remember that they are not helpless; they only think they are. Instead of making their decisions for them, help them to make them on their own. Lovingly discourage their attempts to go too far out of their way to please you. Keep in mind that it's difficult not to take advantage of people who are very passive. Encourage them to seek help. You may wish to seek counseling together if your relationship is foundering.

CHAPTER 7

Dramatic Style

"THE LIFE OF THE PARTY"

Dramatic types are all heart. They have been granted the gift of feeling, with which they color the lives of everyone around them. When possessed of great talent, Dramatic men and women can transform human emotion into the highest art form. Even in their daily lives, their wit, their laughter, their sense of beauty, their flamboyance, and their sensuality can lift the spirits of a roomful of strangers. All the world's a stage for individuals with this very common personality style. Life is never dull or boring for them and certainly not for those who share it with them. Dramatic people fill their world with excitement; things *happen* in their lives.

THE SEVEN CHARACTERISTICS

The following seven traits and behaviors are clues to the presence of the Dramatic style. A person who reveals a strong Dramatic tendency will demonstrate more of these behaviors more intensely than someone who has less of this style.

1. *Feelings.* Dramatic men and women live in an emotional world. They are sensation oriented, emotionally demonstrative, and physically affectionate. They react emotionally to events and can shift quickly from mood to mood.

2. *Color.* They experience life vividly and expansively. They have rich imaginations, they tell entertaining stories, and they are drawn to romance and melodrama.

3. *Attention*. Dramatic people like to be seen and noticed. They are often the center of attention, and they rise to the occasion when all eyes are on them.

4. *Appearance*. They pay a lot of attention to grooming, and they enjoy clothes, style, and fashion.

5. *Sexual attraction*. In appearance and behavior, Dramatic individuals enjoy their sexuality. They are seductive, engaging, charming tempters and temptresses.

6. *Engagement*. Easily putting their trust in others, they are able to become quickly involved in relationships.

7. *The spirit is willing*. People with Dramatic personality style eagerly respond to new ideas and suggestions from others.

THE SIX DOMAINS OF DRAMATIC FUNCTIONING

The rich, complex lives of Dramatic men and women are governed simultaneously by two key domains: Emotions and Relationships.

EMOTIONS: THE HEART SPEAKS

The men and women who possess this personality style know the world through their emotions; how they feel about someone or something gives them all the information they need. The Conscientious person—the voice of reason—sees a movie and offers a thoughtful critique of the performances, the direction, the cinematography, the sound track, the costumes, and the script. The Dramatic person may sum it up in one word: "Wow!" It's the impact of life that counts and which they seek.

They dwell in a world of flamboyant color, and they extract passion from every experience. Their lives often seem so much more eventful than other people's. They're full of exciting tales. They transform the ordinary happenings of life into real theater.

Listen to how Valerie explains to her friend why she was late meeting her for lunch at a restaurant. Note how one of the tedious daily frustrations of life in New York—finding a parking space—turns into a lively afternoon adventure:

"I was halfway to the subway when I realized I hadn't moved my car. The spot I was in was only good for another half hour. *God!* I raced back into my building to get the key—but the elevator was stuck, so I ran up a million stairs, found my key, flew down again, ran out to my car. Would you believe, a parking space materialized before my very eyes? My fairy godmother was with me today! So I'm backing into the space, and suddenly I hear this *vroom-vroom*—this total-leather guy on a motorcycle has pulled in behind me. I get out of my car, he gets off his bike—and I tell you, I've never seen a human being so big. He just glowers down at me, and I think the guy must be a Hell's Angel—if I open my mouth he'll kill me. But this teeny-weeny little voice comes out of me and squeaks, 'Excuse me, Large Leather Person, but I was here first.' There's this long pause, which I'm convinced is my last moment on earth—and then The Leather Hulk says, 'Okay, lady.' He grins— what a set of teeth! Then he swings his leg back over his Harley and *vrooms* away. Would you believe it? I taught a Hell's Angel how to be a good American!" Valerie lapsed into delighted laughter. Her friend, who had sat waiting nearly a half hour, forgot her annoyance, charmed by the colorful tale and Valerie's talent for turning a potentially distressing experience into an enjoyable one.

Expression and Impression

Dramatic men and women generally display their emotions freely and openly. If they possess no competing, more emotionally reticent styles (see "Dramatic on the Inside," p. 144), their emotions are there for everyone to see—no stiff upper lips for them. They are good-natured, sentimental, and effusive, they enjoy melodrama, intrigue, and gossip, and they are easily moved. They react powerfully and often immediately to events.

Because they are so reactive, their feelings can change very quickly— for example, from joy to fury to misery to despair, depending on the day's experiences. Predominantly Dramatic people tend to express their moods with whatever degree of passion they feel—if a very Dramatic person is mad at you, watch out!—but they don't hold grudges, and they expect other people not to.

They seek emotional experience in life, and they may have little appreciation for life's drier side. The Dramatic style tends to bring with it impatience and/or anxiety with details, routines, organizing, planning, and finances. Highly Dramatic individuals will often steer clear of weighty conversation, preferring gossip and intrigue. When they read a newspaper, they may skim the headlines, skip the politics and the finance, and concentrate on the murders, the human interest and lifestyle stories, entertainment, and/or the sports sections. The Conscientious person prefers to read the whole paper straight through, word for word. A person with a mixed Dramatic-Conscientious style (a very common pattern) may read the "good stuff" first, then return to the beginning of the paper and dutifully read what he or she "should."

When you listen to a Dramatic person tell a tale, note the absence of factual description. Like Impressionist painters, they create a picture without relying on realistic detail. "He's so big!" Valerie says of the man on the motorcycle. How big? As big as the impression of the man on the motorcycle that forms in the mind of the listener. She says, "I ran up a million stairs," instead of mentioning the number of stories. In this way Dramatic people may distort factual reality, but they do convey the emotional impact of their experiences.

Overall, they live their lives intensely. To plumb the emotional heights and depths of any experience, all aspects of their lives—their work, their relationships, their imaginations, their leisure-time activities —are infused with stimulating, extroverted energy. With little tolerance for boredom, Dramatic men and women usually do not wait for life to happen to them. They don a dashing costume, they go out on the town, they laugh until everyone else laughs with them—they actively provoke experience by stirring the passions of other people.

RELATIONSHIPS:
STIRRING THE PASSIONS

Dramatic men and women are highly social. Like fish in water, they are in their element when surrounded by others. The central focus of their lives is to win friends and influence people. Dramatic men and women rouse others, energize them, charm them until they drop their reserve and open their hearts. Dramatic individuals are the life of the party, happiest when the atmosphere is highly charged and all eyes are on them.

Dramatic men and women genuinely like other people and are very attentive to what pleases them and makes them comfortable. Many are gifted with profound intuition about other people's feelings, and they are extremely skilled at reading people by their gestures, their tones of voice, their body language. These social gifts ensure their places on everybody's party lists. Dolly V. always invites her friend Lucie L. to dinner when her husband, Don, brings home some of his straitlaced out-of-town clients. Lucie gets them all talking and relaxed before the soup's on. All woman, she dresses with an eye-catching flair, she smells wonderful, her eyes are wide with enraptured interest as she listens to these businessmen and women answer her questions about what they do and where they come from. She draws out what makes these out-oftowners feel important and good about themselves. She wants to know about them. And she intrigues everyone at the table. "It's like living a kind of romance when Lucie's around," Dolly says. "There's a feeling of excitement and possibility. Everything's so striking, so interesting, so vivid. She weaves a spell. Don's clients have a wonderful time—we all do."

The Seduction

Dramatic individuals are particularly effective in the early stages of a relationship. They know how to draw people to them, using their own natural sensuality and flirtatiousness to stir others' passions, and making the person they're focusing on feel like the center of the universe. They are open with compliments, flattery, and appreciation. Like Devoted people, they seem to have an uncanny sense of a person's desires and needs. They watch and listen with attention to what you like, want, and need, and they'll go to great lengths to provide it for you.

When the object of the Dramatic individual's attentions responds with admiration and desire, the relationship ignites and passions are set aflame. In emotional connection with someone, the Dramatic person experiences profound infatuation. She or he is fully open to the new love, trusting, accepting. While in the best of situations, solid relationships can spring from such emotional heat, the Dramatic person's feelings can create a vulnerability to passionately wishful thinking. This individual wants so much for the ardor to continue that he or she may well misread important cues. Rob S., an up-and-coming actor and singer with Hollywood good looks and Broadway talent, had little difficulty meeting attractive, intelligent women. The women he'd really fall for were usually very glamorous and even more successful than he was. In his infatuation, he would suddenly begin to see their every gesture, word, glance as a confirmation of their equally profound feelings for him. But he wouldn't necessarily be taking in all the relevant information and acting appropriately. Kimberly, the last woman to break his heart, was a cosmetics industry executive whose career was on the front burner of her life when Rob began taking her out. She was much taken with Rob, which was obvious to all. What was equally obvious to everyone except Rob was that Kimberly's attention was not about to be diverted from the fast track she was on right at the time. Rob was so sure that he was dead center of her universe that when she told him she didn't have room in her life now for the encompassing commitment he wanted from her, he felt like he'd been hit with a bolt of lightning on a sunny day—where could it have come from? But Kimberly had never been trying to lead him down a garden path. What Rob had done in his Dramatic way was read only the "good" signs—that she loved and cared for him. But he selectively ignored information that would round out the story—that her soul was in her work right now and that if he wanted a deep relationship to develop, he'd have to give her space.

Vigilant and Sensitive people also misread other people frequently, but in an opposite way from Dramatic types. Vigilant and Sensitive look to others for signs of questionable motives or criticism; Dramatic people overinterpret the come-hither side. Faced with someone's ambivalence, Vigilant and Sensitive will see only the negative reaction, while the Dramatic person will react to only the good vibes. In such ways, all three styles end up charting an inaccurate course with people, based on incomplete information. Vigilant and Sensitive people hold back from others or even push them away, when these people might be well disposed to them if they only let down their guard. Dramatic individuals assume an involvement that may not have had time to develop, so they sometimes scare away the people who count most.

Related to the Dramatic openness to people is an easy willingness to respond to others' ideas, suggestions, and activities—a very likable trait. Highly Dramatic people will need to ask themselves from time to time, however, whether they really do want to go along with an activity, or whether they are so bedazzled by the attentions of people they like, or so taken with a fad, that they are sometimes too easily swayed.

Keeping the Fire Lit

A Dramatic individual requires a high degree of excitement, so when the ardor tempers, as usually happens after the infatuation phase, this person may become bored. People whose personalities are powerfully dominated by this style may have difficulty sustaining relationships over the longer, duller run. Some, like the operatic temptress Carmen, may lose interest after the successful seduction. Others may seek affairs outside the primary relationship in order to keep the level of exciting attention sufficiently high. Others may flirt, tease, and collect admirers, while remaining sexually faithful to their partners.

Their low tolerance for boredom in relationships may inspire some Dramatic types to an inventiveness that would benefit any relationship. Rather than let the sex get boring, they may be eager to experiment and to help their partners overcome possible inhibitions. They may plan vacations, parties, and other entertainments to keep life at a high pitch. They keep making friends and populating their lives with stimulating people. If all works well, life with a Dramatic partner can be passionate and interesting. It will never be dull or quiet.

Stress!

Life with Dramatic people can also be stormy, considering their strong and immediate emotional reactions. Trouble in a relationship will be a major blow to the self-esteem of the Dramatic individual. Trouble can ensue when the partner cannot deal with the very Dramatic spouse's passionate outbursts and/or seductive behavior. It can arise when the Dramatic individual does not receive sufficient admiration, attention, or expression of feeling from his or her mate. It can result also when the couple cannot establish a routine that compensates for the extremely Dramatic partner's inability or reluctance to handle life's mundane chores—like balancing the checkbook, keeping track of important papers, saving tax receipts, or staying within the credit card limits.

To cope with stress and anxiety, Dramatic types like to look on the bright side. They prefer to repress the unpleasant in order to sustain an optimistic outlook; they keep telling themselves that everything will work out. Action helps them forget. Herbert G., a civil engineer, flew into a rage when his Dramatic wife, Gloria, neglected to record a two-thousand-dollar check. "I've bounced the mortgage payment and the car payment! How could you screw up the credit rating I've taken years to build?" he yelled, on the verge of tears. Money had always been a big problem in their marriage. Gloria believed that Herbert, who she felt was a little uptight, worried far too much about it. "You can straighten it out with them—I know they trust you and will realize it was an honest mistake," Gloria tried to reassure her husband. "I tell you what," she said, brightening. "Let's take our minds off this little misunderstanding and go dancing!" At that, fire started coming out of Herb's nostrils, or so Gloria insisted when relating this scene to her mother.

Being alone is another major source of stress for Dramatic individuals. Without a partner or lover in whose eyes to shine, many Dramatic people feel unhappy with themselves. For the Dramatic person who has never had to take care of him- or herself, having to deal with money and other responsibilities after the loss of a longtime partner may provoke extreme anxiety. The state of being alone may not last long, though. Usually a person with this personality style will attend parties and social gatherings as soon as possible, putting on a happy face and casting a delightful spell over new admirers.

The Dramatic Parent

Dramatic men and women can be emotionally understanding and accessible parents, and they encourage creativity and aesthetic appreciation in their children. But they may become disorganized and let important details slip—such as forgetting teacher conferences, field trip permissions, Little League games, even tuition payments. This can be embarrassing and confusing for a child, who may conclude that the parent doesn't care. The non-Dramatic parent should be aware of responsibilities that the Dramatic parent has toward the child and make sure that they are met.

Overall, Dramatic parents are fun, active, and energetic, offering their kids a wide range of experiences out in the world. They may need help in teaching their children restraint and frustration tolerance. And, as the style becomes extreme, some Dramatic parents may be overly needy of loving feedback from their kids and will have a hard time letting them go their own independent way. Ideally, the non-Dramatic parent will be able to reassure the Dramatic one that he or she is being a good, loving parent by knowing when to back off.

Good/Bad Matches

Because their relationships are born of seduction and passion rather than of reason, Dramatic individuals have a lot of hot beginnings with people with many different personality styles. Relationships that last tend to be with personality styles that balance and ground the Dramatic—in particular, as mentioned in chapter 4, the Conscientious.

The Dramatic-Conscientious match can work very well, for they both can gain from the other what their own personality styles lack. The Conscientious partner will take care of the Dramatic spouse and will provide him or her with steadiness, a sense of responsibility, reliability, and attentiveness to success, security, and stability. The Dramatic partner provides imagination, a spontaneous emotional life, plus an entrée into a lively social world. The Conscientious partner will be able to control the money and down-to-earth decision making, while the Dramatic partner will take the lead in the couple's social and emotional life. But if the Conscientious partner is controllingly possessive and cannot tolerate the Dramatic's pleasure in exciting admiration from others, sparks will fly. Similarly, if the Conscientious person has his or her feet stuck too firmly in the ground, and the Dramatic person is floating too high in the clouds, they won't find a plane on which they can coexist.

Serious people share similar traits with Conscientious types—particularly a steadiness and work orientation. Serious men and women may at first be swept away by the whirlwind the Dramatic person creates around them, but while this match might work for a while, it is risky in the long run. Highly Serious people cannot long share the Dramatic person's gaiety and optimism. Dramatic people cannot tolerate consistent pessimism, and will berate the Serious person as a "killjoy."

Dramatic and Self-Confident attractions are based on similarities; they are both high-energy attention-getters who can share intensely lived lives surrounded by admirers. The Self-Confident partner can deal with the real-life, down-to-earth side of life for the Dramatic spouse. A major pitfall in these relationships is the Self-Confident person's relative inattentiveness to others. Another is the tendency of both styles to compete for attention.

Two Dramatic individuals can powerfully attract each other, but their similarities will lead to confrontation and conflict. This is a strong style that does best with a partner who will back off and let the other have the emotional way. For this reason, a match with someone with the Mercurial style (another style ruled by the Emotions domain) is destined to explode.

Individuals with a modicum of the Devoted, the Self-Sacrificing, or the Sensitive style are happy to let their mates lead from the heart. And, significantly, they provide the attention and appreciation on which the Dramatic style thrives. The Devoted person will have to be able to deal with his or her worries about the Dramatic partner's fidelity, however, and must fight against becoming too compliant when facing stresses within the relationship. Dramatic types require emotionally stable partners, no matter what the style. Sensitive individuals may appreciate their Dramatic mate's ability to socialize and to give them an entrée into the social world, but if they prove to be very anxious in public, they'll get little sympathy from the highly social Dramatic butterfly.

Although Dramatic people are often extremely attracted to the Vigilant person's apparent strength and cool control, unless the Vigilant style is moderate to slight, these matches are headed for rocky times. Vigilant individuals demand the full attention of their mates and cannot tolerate suspicion and jealousy. Similarly, Dramatic people may find the Aggressive image—the strong, tough type—appealing; but Aggressive types require a much more passive, accepting, undemanding partner.

Adventurous types appeal powerfully to the Dramatic's love of excitement. They too are spontaneous, seductive, thrilling, and fun loving. But they also share a lot of the Dramatic's bad habits, including impulsiveness and a lack of patience for certain essential responsibilities of life, which makes them a bad influence on each other. Moreover, the Adventurers tend not to commit, which can prove devastating for Dramatic individuals. (While the more extreme Dramatic types may not be given to lasting commitments themselves, they nonetheless require loyalty and faithfulness from their partners in a double-standard sort of way.)

Their responsiveness to appreciative attention, their tendency to romanticize a person's image, and their preference for looking at the bright side can make trouble for some Dramatic individuals: they are easily taken in by dashing figures whose intentions are less than honorable. This risk is greatest for individuals who suffer from Histrionic personality disorder, the extreme of the Dramatic personality style; see the case of Katy T. later in this chapter, who was continually taken in by Adventurous and Antisocial types. But it also influences the matches of less extreme individuals.

SELF: THE IMPORTANCE OF IMAGE

Outward and other-directed as they are, these intensely social beings tend to define themselves from the outside in. They see themselves as others see them. Ask a strongly Dramatic person to describe him- or herself and you might hear: "People say I'm very friendly," or, "My family is always telling me how funny I am," or, "My teachers say I'm very talented." (A Self-Confident person would say: "I'm friendly," "I'm funny," or "I'm talented.")

Similarly, because their self-definition comes from outside themselves, how they look to others—the image they present—is extremely important to them. They are what they wear. Dramatic people often are great dressers. Theirs is a talent for costume and style, for creating a visual image. Their eyes always trained outward to the reactions of others, they tend to outfit themselves in the fads and fashions of the social groups with which they identify themselves. They dress to go out with great care, never just throwing on any old thing. Some will dress, redress, and dress yet again before they are satisfied that they look right. People who are clearly dominated by this personality style may have difficulty appreciating the maxim that beauty comes from the inside.

One of the consequences of being intensely other-directed and emotionally reactive is that the Dramatic individual will, to varying degrees, lack a calm, consistent, centered sense of self. For this reason, people with this personality style usually require reassurance and feedback—call it applause—from others in order to maintain their self-confidence. They need to hear that the meal they just cooked tastes good, that they are attractive, that their artistic performances are moving, their athletic feats astonishing, and especially that they are loved.

SELF-CONTROL: RESISTING THE URGE

This passionate, pleasure-loving personality style comes with a low frustration tolerance. Unless they have personality styles balanced with some reflective, thoughtful, "head" styles, emotionally ruled Dramatic individuals will be spontaneous, impulsive, impetuous, impatient—they want what they want *now*. "*Please* let me open my present now. I can't *bear* waiting until my birthday," a Dramatic person pleads. Toby, a Dramatic playwright, couldn't find his gold-plated fountain pen when he went to write in his journal one morning. He didn't use the pen that much since he'd started writing his scripts on a word processor. But that pen was an important symbol to him, and he searched high and low for it, to no avail. He couldn't wait even until the next day to see if it turned up around his apartment, although common sense told him that it would. That afternoon he spent almost two hundred dollars on a new pen, which he could ill afford. Ten days later, when Toby cleaned his apartment, he found the old pen, which had fallen behind his bed. The department store would not take back the new pen because Toby had already used it. Toby says that if it happened again, he'd do exactly the same thing, rather than be without his lucky gold pen for ten days.

Temptations to act on impulse grow harder to resist as the degree of Dramatic style becomes greater. Self-control—in everything from eating to spending to keeping secrets to controlling a hot temper—will prove relatively difficult for a Dramatic person. This is because Dramatic individuals live best in the heartfelt moment, which makes it difficult to resist immediate gratification. Also, Dramatic types like to take their minds off their worries as soon as possible; a bit of self-indulgence can lift their spirits immensely. Another reason why this style confers a vulnerability to self-control problems is that Dramatic individuals are not natural planners. For many people, restraint in spending, for example, comes from planning and keeping to a budget or a certain level of expenditure; success in losing weight comes from determining in advance what and how much you are going to eat over how long a period. Success in keeping the lid on your anger results from anticipating the damage it may cause.

Fortunately for many Dramatic types, a healthy streak of a counterbalancing, restraining personality style (such as Conscientious, Self-Confident, Vigilant, Serious, Solitary, or Aggressive) in one's overall pattern can make it easier to resist the urge. Otherwise they may find they are continually dieting or watching their spending. Extremely Dramatic people will probably find they have a difficult time with emotional control. As the Dramatic style becomes Histrionic personality disorder, temper tantrums become increasingly common.

REAL WORLD: WISHFUL THINKING

For Dramatic men and women, the Real World is a storybook land where romance lives. They have rich fantasy lives. Like Valerie, who made a Hell's Angel out of a man on a motorcycle, they spot heroes and villains wherever they turn. Other people become larger-than-life characters in a cosmic melodrama. Talented, balanced Dramatic individuals may transform their storybook world into art and entertainment that gains and holds public attention in the Real World. Some of them have a great talent for creating inspiring and/or romantic stories with broadly drawn good guys and bad guys in which the bad guys get what's coming to them and the good guys share a happy ending.

In the world of romance, dreams come true. Dramatic men and women, although they have their despairing moods, want to believe in happy endings. Their optimism about the present and future can be inspiring. "Everything will work out" is their motto. Given their tendency to cope with stress by ignoring unpleasant reality, however, Dramatic individuals must take care not to substitute a wish for an uncomfortable truth that they'd rather not deal with.

WORK: CREATIVE FLAIR

Dramatic people love an exciting work situation in which they can make an impact. They're idea people, often brilliant in their hunches. And they can persuade others to back their projects. What they may fail to do, however, is follow through with the details. But if they can find people to do it for them, they can make their dreams a reality. Years ago, Max W., a successful trial attorney with an ability to move juries to decide cases in his favor, came up with an idea whose time had come. One night Max, who was twice divorced, was fantasizing about how to find the woman of his dreams. Wouldn't it be great, he mused, if all the available women in the world could appear to you one after another on a movie screen? You could watch them, listen to them, and pick the ones you wanted.

Although the concept of videotape dating services is old news now, no one had thought of such a thing when Max had his brilliant idea. He took a leave of absence from the law firm and traveled to major cities around the country gathering backers. Max had a deep, sonorous voice and an ability to spin a moving story. He intrigued many people from coast to coast with his project, and they dug deep into their pockets to help finance it. Within the year Max had opened thirty on-screen dating offices. He put ads in the papers and ran TV commercials featuring himself. People responded by the thousands. The only problem was that Max hadn't begun to organize the production side. He hadn't even hired a production staff. As happens so frequently to individuals with the Dramatic personality style, Max had come up with and promoted a great idea, but he had failed to execute it.

He was beginning to see his great idea collapse into a bunch of bad debts when finally he put an ad in the paper for an executive manager. Louise T. was the eighth person he interviewed. He knew as soon as she walked in that she was the person for the job. Louise was astonished to be offered the job after a five-minute interview. Max's hunch was right, and Louise put together a plan and was in production in key locations within six weeks. Max has long since sold his dating services for a huge profit. Louise, in all her Conscientious competence, has gone on to become head of production for a cable TV station.

Their tendency to operate on hunches and insights instead of reasoning things through may make life difficult for Dramatic types if the institutions they work for insist that they proceed with outlines, plans, budgets, and detailed follow-through. However, Dramatic individuals can contribute greatly in the entertainment, broadcast, advertising, and associated industries, which welcome Dramatic individuals on their creative staffs and demand less regimentation from them than from other employees. Usually the creative personnel are encouraged to dress as they please, for example, whereas suits are de rigueur for the business staff. One creative hotshot at a New York advertising agency was given a piano for his office—not because he was responsible for the music, but because playing the piano helped him relax and generate ideas. A suggestion for management: Pamper your Dramatic employees, tell them how much you appreciate them, let them work the way they please, and they'll reward you with excellent work.

Many successful entrepreneurs, like Max in his dating-service enterprise, have a strong streak of Dramatic style. These people can charm, sell, wheel and deal, promote, and, if they can manage to put together a strong organization to back them up and take care of the administrative details, they can often create quite a successful enterprise.

Management Style

Dramatic men and women can be strong managers, skilled at inspiring their subordinates to work hard. They need to have a capable and strong Conscientious secretary or assistant whom they trust to keep the work moving and to make sure the routine responsibilities are met. They openly appreciate a job well done and are generous to those who work hard on their behalf. Similarly, they do not hide their anger. They may lambast a subordinate who displeases them, even threatening to fire the unfortunate offender. Often they do not follow through on their threats. They may be emotionally changeable individuals, gruff and un-communicative on one day, cheerful and enthusiastic on another. If you work for such a person, do not take your boss's emotional reactions personally. Avoid a confrontation, lie low, maintain your own emotional balance, and wait for the boss to show a more expansive mood before you ask for your raise.

Careers for the Dramatic

The creative and performing arts or the creative sides of business and industry are natural choices for talented Dramatic people. Overall, seek careers that make use of your style's extraordinary ability to influence other people—anything from public relations, to teaching, to sales and sales promotion. This style's sensitivity to emotions can be an asset in the helping professions.

Avoid routine, repetitive, and technical work of any kind, and seek a nonregimented work environment. Working for yourself may appeal to you, but it could be your downfall unless you have an agent and/or can afford to hire someone to assist with the paperwork, help you handle the finances, and prod you to be disciplined and productive when you feel strongly tempted to goof off.

DRAMATIC ON THE INSIDE

For many people who have a heavy streak of the Dramatic style, it marks the character of their inner lives rather than their outward behavior. Other strong styles in the personality pattern will influence how "out front" a Dramatic person is. For example, if the Conscientious style shares top billing with the Dramatic, as it often does, it will add social and emotional reserve and self-control. The Sensitive and the Solitary styles will temper the Dramatic's gregariousness and emotional expression, the Vigilant style will contribute independence and caution, and the Devoted style will moderate the individual's drive to get out there and move the world. But inwardly, regardless of the outward appearance, the Dramatic individual's emotions and love of attention remain rich and strong.

TIPS ON DEALING WITH THE
DRAMATIC PERSON IN YOUR LIFE

1. You are attracted to the Dramatic person's spontaneity, passion, sensuality, and ability to have a good time. Now don't clip this bird's wings. Let the Dramatic person in your life dress you up and drag you out to social gatherings. Don't fight it when he or she insists you take romantic vacations, go out dancing, or give parties. Allow the Dramatic person in your life his or her emotional freedom, and enjoy the range of experience that will result for you.

2. Appreciate, praise, flatter, and give feedback. The Dramatic person in your life needs you to react openly and verbally, especially about your positive feelings, at all times. React to his or her appearance, cooking, business and personal successes, lovemaking, gift giving, and so on. Most important, say how much you love this person. Don't hold back; there's no such thing as too much of a good thing with this personality style. But be sure to be honest. If you don't mean the good things you are saying, the intuitive Dramatic person will know it.

3. Be romantic. Bring flowers, candy, gifts, and send valentines and mushy cards for every occasion. Even if the Dramatic person in your life is a friend, relative, or parent, these sentimental attentions will delight and thrill him or her. Similarly, neglecting these expressions of affection may make Dramatic types feel that you don't care.

4. Be realistic about this person's relative inability or reluctance to handle certain responsibilities, including money. Handle the finances or the financial planning yourself, if need be. Better, supervise or double-check essential details. For example, if your Dramatic partner writes checks, periodically ask whether he or she has recorded them all; individuals with this style frequently forget. Encourage this person to do better, but never expect him or her to do as well as you do in this aspect of life.

   Similarly, remind this person to keep track of responsibilities such as meetings and phone calls, especially those that relate to children.

5. Don't hold grudges. Dramatic people don't hold things in, and the Dramatic person in your life may be emotionally tempestuous. You and this person may have a loud fight and he or she may express ferocious anger. A few hours later the Dramatic individual will have forgotten all about it. He or she will not understand why you are still stewing. Try to let go of your own anger or annoyance. Don't take this Dramatic person's emotional reactions personally and don't be frightened by the drama.

6. Avoid jealousy. Dramatic individuals like to charm other people. If you're the jealous type, stop and think whether there's anything to be jealous about. If everything is going well between the two of you at home, it is quite possible this person is merely enjoying the reactions of others and will not carry things further. Try feeling flattered and turned on by the warm attentions of others to your mate and have a good time at the party.

MAKING THE MOST OF YOUR DRAMATIC STYLE

Your sources of self-esteem come from outside yourself, which may make your inner life unsteady. Finding sources inside yourself will help ensure some inner calm.

Exercise 1

Think about or make a list of what you like about yourself. Be sure to look at yourself through your own eyes. For example, do not say: "I'm glad that other people like me." Instead, try to rephrase from your own point of view, such as: "I like that I am friendly."

Exercise 2

Pat yourself on the back. Every time you find yourself needing somebody's reaction, reassure yourself. After cooking a meal, tell yourself how good it tastes. When you dress to go out, look in the mirror and appreciate how nice you look. When you are worried that someone doesn't love you, tell yourself that you are worthy of love whether or not that person cares.

Exercise 3

To balance your natural spontaneity, work on restraint and planning. Stop and count to ten. The next time you are about to act on impulse of any kind—to spend, to leave work, to eat, to drink, and especially to vent your feelings—stop for a moment. Count slowly to ten. Think whether you want to proceed with what you were about to do. If you don't want to but can't resist the urge, see how long you can hold out. Practice this exercise at every opportunity. Get used to stopping between urge and action.

Exercise 4

Plan. Every time you have a task to accomplish, at home or at work, write down all the steps necessary to complete it. Resist the urge to throw down your pen or pencil halfway through.

Exercise 5

You are very intuitive about other people, but you lead with your feelings, and when you are powerfully attracted to someone, your judgment may fly out the window. So, stand back and observe. Collect details and information about this person. Leave your feelings aside. What color are this person's hair and eyes? How big are his or her feet? What style shoes is this person wearing? What color are his or her clothes? Ask questions. Where does this person work? Is he or she married? Where does he or she live? Make this exercise a game: the more details you fill in, the higher your "score."

Exercise 6

Face it. You like to take your mind off unpleasant truths. However, some truths grow more unpleasant if you ignore them. Try keeping all aspects of real life in the front of your mind and see how that feels. It's okay to feel anxious. If you take action to deal directly with the difficulty, the anxiety will often go away. If you need help with anxiety, see Exercises 2 to 10 in chapter 9, "Sensitive Style" (pp. 193–96).

Also try Exercises 5 (Develop the life skills you lack) and 6 (Resist throwing yourself blindly into a new relationship) recommended for the Devoted personality style in chapter 6 (pp. 121–22).

HISTRIONIC PERSONALITY DISORDER

Men and women who have Histrionic personality disorder live in an exaggerated emotional world in which they do anything they can to get attention—because without it they are nothing, or so they feel.

DIAGNOSTIC CRITERIA

The DSM-IV describes Histrionic personality disorder as:

A pervasive pattern of excessive emotionality and attention seeking, beginning by early adulthood and present in a variety of contexts, as indicated by five (or more) of the following:

(1) is uncomfortable in situations in which he or she is not the center of attention

(2) interaction with others is often characterized by inappropriate sexually seductive or provocative behavior

(3) displays rapidly shifting and shallow expression of emotions

(4) consistently uses physical appearance to draw attention to self

(5) has a style of speech that is excessively impressionistic and lacking in detail

(6) shows self-dramatization, theatricality, and exaggerated expression of emotion

(7) is suggestible, i.e., easily influenced by others or circumstances

(8) considers relationships to be more intimate than they actually are

---

EMOTIONS OUT OF CONTROL

The men and women who suffer from this personality disorder are often unaware of or uninformed about the world around them. This is because they are so involved in their own emotional dramas. Everything is a production: a minor setback becomes a major disaster; a small pleasure becomes the greatest joy of their lives.

Yet, for all their *Sturm und Drang,* Histrionic individuals seem unconvincing. As he negotiated deals throughout the day, a middle-aged entrepreneur named Neil would go from "this is the happiest day of my life" to "I can't stand it anymore—I'm getting out of this business," depending on the way the deal went. Every day it was the same litany. "Yes, Neil," his colleagues would respond unsympathetically, no longer taking him seriously.

Their emotions often seem infantile. Like children, people with this disorder react instantly, their feelings change frequently, they can't stand frustration or disappointment, and they cannot delay gratification of their needs. They act self-centered, and when they can't get what they want, they become greatly upset. Like some youngsters, they are prone to throwing tantrums.

The sexuality of some Histrionic individuals may be equally childlike. Men and women with this disorder often dress and act very seductively. Yet for many it's just a tease; take them up on it and they run or get offended. Although some are sexually promiscuous, many persons with this disorder are sexually naive and often inhibited.

I DEMAND YOUR LOVE AND ATTENTION!

All their emotional flamboyance—tantrums and sexual seductiveness included—serves to get the attention of others. The lives of Histrionic individuals are focused on other people, on whom they depend utterly to fulfill their needs. These individuals obtain their identity from others, for inwardly they are very uncertain about who they are. Without all eyes on them, they feel powerless and unworthy. Thus, they are overly concerned with how they look to others, and will often appear in outrageous clothing in order to excite public attention. They take up any fad of the moment and believe in it completely, until the next fad sweeps them off their feet.

Histrionic individuals idealize the people in their lives and turn them into fantasy figures, like Prince Charming and the Wicked Witch. They can be very trusting of others and overly submissive, so much so that they become easy prey for unsavory people. (See the case of Katy T. at the end of this chapter.)

Their relationships may start off ecstatically, but they usually become stormy and ungratifying. For all their attempts to attract people to them, Histrionic individuals can't sustain a mature emotional relationship. They are too in need of constant approval and often maintain their self-esteem by seeking new "conquests" outside their primary relationship. Although they do not realize it, many individuals with this personality disorder are afraid of closeness and commitment; thus, they will focus on people who are emotionally or physically unavailable to them.

Also, as the DSM-IV points out, "Without being aware of it, they often act out a role (e.g., 'victim' or 'princess') in their relationships to others."

The emotionality of the person with Histrionic personality disorder can be very destructive to their relationships, and to make matters worse they are not usually contrite about their blowups. They can be vicious and cruel to their loved ones during tantrums, but when the episode passes they do not comprehend why other people remain hurt and angry.

Like Joey in chapter 5, who suffered from a mixed Narcissistic, Histrionic, Antisocial personality disorder, to get what they want they can be exploitive and manipulative. Histrionic Carla, mother of three, had great difficulty with her oldest daughter's adolescent anger toward her. During their fights, to control her daughter's behavior Carla would shriek, "Your behaving like that will send me to my grave. I swear I'll kill myself!" The troubled daughter began to feel deeply guilty. She stopped attacking her mother, lapsed into a deep depression, and at age eighteen attempted suicide herself.

Lively and spontaneous though they are, people with Histrionic personality disorder can sabotage their friendships by their constant need to be the center of attention. Moreover, as the DSM-IV mentions, their seductiveness can be very alienating, "because their sexually provocative interpersonal style may seem a threat to their friends' relationships."

HELP!

It's not easy to stay close to Histrionic people, even though they can often be charming and likable. Despite their intense need for and dependency on other people, their behavior invites rejection and disapproval from their loved ones. People with this disorder are so tuned in to other people's feelings for them that they can sense rejection coming. They grow intensely anxious and upset, and it is then that they might seek help. Just as likely, a spouse or family member who can't put up with their behavior anymore will insist that they see a therapist—or else!

Histrionic individuals are not very introspective; when they do enter therapy they have not thought about how they are contributing to their own problems or how they really feel about themselves. It may come as a great surprise to them, for example, that despite their many seductive and sexual conquests, they feel deeply unlovable, dependent, and confused about sex. They are able to shield themselves from the reality of their inner conflicts by an unconscious "what I don't know won't hurt me" attitude about themselves, and by paying more attention to what other people think about them than to what they think about themselves. They may turn to the therapist as a kind of fantasized savior who will say the magic word that will instantly enable them to have fulfilling love lives.

Many Histrionic patients come from families in which their parents were in conflict when they were very young. Women in particular often report that from the earliest days they were unable to form a satisfactory relationship with their mothers. Their fathers may have been the champions they turned to.

If they are willing to cooperate with the therapist in discovering how their choices of partners and/or their emotional conflicts keep them from feeling satisfied, these patients can begin to form mature relationships for the first time in their lives. Psychodynamic types of psychotherapy have traditionally been the treatments of choice for Histrionic personality disorder. Cognitive therapy challenges characteristic assumptions and distortions in thinking, such as, as Drs. Beck and Freeman describe it, "the distortion of emotional reasoning—taking their emotions as evidence for the truth. Thus, histrionic individuals tend to assume that if they feel inadequate, they must be inadequate; if they feel stupid, they must be stupid."

COPING WITH HISTRIONIC PEOPLE

An essential rule is not to overreact to their overreactions. This isn't easy, since they are manipulative and know how to "press your buttons." Don't engage them, and don't sulk or pout. Later, when things are quieter, be friendly but firm about what you require from the relationship. Be sure at the same time to reassure this Histrionic individual of your loving feelings for him or her—unless you no longer have these feelings, in which case you must ask yourself whether you are prepared to end the relationship. (See also the tips on dealing with Dramatic individuals, pp. 145–46.)

RISKS, PREDISPOSITIONS, AND INCIDENCE

Individuals with this disorder are vulnerable to Axis I conversion, somatization, and dissociative disorders (see chapter 2, page 19). In the first two of these disorders, psychological conflicts express themselves through bodily symptoms that have no physical cause. In dissociative disorders (which include multiple personality and some types of amnesia, among others), the conflicts express themselves through changes in identity, memory, or consciousness. Under extreme stress, such as the collapse of a love affair, some individuals who suffer from Histrionic personality disorder may experience some transient psychotic symptoms; we call this a brief reactive psychosis, and the symptoms disappear completely in hours to weeks.

Histrionic people are liable also to suffer from depressive disorders. Psychiatrists Michael Liebowitz, M.D., and Donald Klein, M.D., have described a subtype of depression called hysteroid dysphoria that seems to occur among individuals (mostly women) with many Histrionic characteristics. These individuals react to rejection with severe emotional crashes. When depressed, they oversleep and overeat (they are especially drawn to chocolate and other sweets). Monoamine oxidase (MAO) inhibitors, a class of antidepressant drugs, in combination with psychotherapy may be very helpful in stabilizing these unhappy people.

People with this personality disorder are believed to be at risk for suicidal gestures and threats. It occurs frequently along with Borderline, Narcissistic, Antisocial, and Dependent personality disorders.

Histrionic personality disorder is common. It is diagnosed much more frequently in women than in men, except possibly for homosexual men. Nevertheless, in at least one study, the prevalence rate of this disorder among men and women was found to be substantially the same.

Many authorities believe that the tendency to diagnose this personality disorder in women is "more a product of our societal expectations than a true difference in occurrence," as Beck and Freeman put it. The emotionality of Histrionic individuals, their dependency and submissiveness, and their coquettishness are all exaggerations of what are considered "feminine" traits within our culture. We know that cultural factors and pressures strongly influence the expression of personality traits. Under the influence of gender roles, male domination, and ideas of appropriate sexual behavior for women, certain women may channel their inner conflicts into stereotypically "feminine" behaviors. Similarly, stereotypically "male" cultural expectations may influence the expression of certain personality disorders—such as the Antisocial, the Aggressive, and the Conscientious—among men.

Current thinking is that people with Histrionic personality express exaggerated sex role stereotypes generally. Thus, the DSM-IV suggests that "a man with this disorder may dress and behave in a manner often identified as 'macho,' and may seek to be the center of attention by bragging about athletic skill. . . ."

Histrionic personality disorder does occur more commonly among first-degree biological relatives (parents, children, and siblings) of persons with the disorder than among the general population, which may reflect a genetic predisposition. The mood shifts and impulsivity characteristic of this style may reflect an inherited instability in various neurotransmitter systems in the brain, particularly the serotonin system.

FALLING IN LOVE WITH LOVE: THE CASE OF THE HISTRIONIC COPYWRITER

Katy T. (whom we introduced in chapter 1) was a copywriter at a major ad agency in New York. She sat at her desk composing an ad on her own behalf, for the personals in *New York* magazine. "Best of the Big Apple—tall buxom blonde, romantic, sexy, talented, giving, outgoing, athletic, dynamite, oh-so-female, 26," she scribbled, and stopped. She had all the attributes of today's woman, yet here she was, reduced to seeking love through a magazine. She stood up abruptly and sent her chair careening across the cubicle. She felt like screaming.

What Katy wanted more than anything else was a wonderful guy to whom she could give herself completely for the rest of her life. She knew she would make a perfect wife. But it seemed that all the interesting men were either gay or treated her like garbage. The rest were boring. She didn't think she could take it anymore.

Katy retrieved her chair and sat down heavily. She put her head down on her desk. Everybody in the agency knew what she was going through because of Keith. He was an account executive with the same agency, and they'd recently broken up. She still had to see him day after day, which was humiliating. Usually she didn't date men from work, but he was so gorgeous and had come on so strong that she gave in. In the beginning it was heaven. He sent her flowers every day. For work reasons they decided to keep their relationship quiet, so she couldn't reveal the identity of the man her boss, Alice, had started referring to as Katy's "secret admirer."

Keith virtually moved in with her after they had been seeing each other for only two weeks—she was giddy with how fast it went. However, he had to travel frequently, and he had many business dinners that kept him out so late he'd go back to his own place afterward. In addition, he spent at least every other weekend at his family's place in the Berkshires. But when Katy and Keith were together, it was as if they thought with one mind, breathed one breath. The sex was incredible.

The slime—he was married! Alice told her. Alice had been passing by Katy's building late one evening when Katy and Keith were returning from dining out. A week after bumping into them, Alice asked Katy if Keith was the one responsible for the daily flowers. Katy blushed and nodded. Alice said, "Katy, don't you know he's married?"

Katy's world fell apart. She became so upset she had to take a week off from work. It wasn't just Keith—it was that every time she opened her heart to a man he took advantage of her. Like that guy whose personal ad she had answered a couple of years ago. He'd promised her a ski trip to Switzerland and then didn't show up at the airport. The clothes she'd bought! Katy had been so devastated that time that she'd called in sick for two weeks.

Katy grabbed the piece of paper on which she'd been scribbling her ad, crumpled it, and tossed it out into the hallway.

"Everything all right in there?" Alice called from her office across the hall.

"Yeah," Katy answered unconvincingly.

"Are you ready with the new ad copy you promised me this morning?"

"No," Katy answered after a pause. Tears began to roll down her cheeks.

Katy hadn't been able to get much work done since the Keith business. Usually she could count on Alice's support. But this time, when Alice came in and found her sitting there crying, her work undone, Alice said that if Katy didn't get it together she'd be fired. She handed her the name of a psychiatrist.

Katy was diagnosed as having Histrionic personality disorder. She was preoccupied with a desperate quest to find the right man. The reason she couldn't find him was that she didn't know what love is. Her idea of love was straight out of a romance novel: total, magical connection to a beautiful, powerful man who would sweep her off her feet. Unfortunately for Katy, men who come on that strong are often extreme Adventurers like Keith and the Swiss-trip man, all too willing to exploit her tendency to "see no evil."

Katy made it easy for them. Liberated though she thought she was, in relation to a man Katy gave up all her power and much of her reason.

She could have found out quickly that Keith was married, but she never asked. She never questioned all his evenings and weekends away from her. She rationalized that men were different from women and needed a lot of space, when in truth she was afraid to displease him. He would call at dinnertime to cancel their evening plans and she would forgive him, as long as he told her how much he loved her and how fabulous she'd looked in the office that day. Katy was starved for reassurance, and any bit of flattery would do.

In therapy, slowly and painfully she began to see how, because of a deep feeling of inferiority and inadequacy, she created for herself a fantasy world in which excessive flattery and too-quick declarations of undying devotion masqueraded as love. Similarly, she began to understand that she couldn't be attracted to the "boring" men out there because no normal person could fulfill her distorted needs. But the fact remained that even after three years of psychotherapy, the bad guys continued to be a turn-on for Katy, and she complained to her therapist that there was nothing she could do about that. How could she force herself to love a frog, when her heart belonged to Prince Charming?

"I know," said the psychiatrist.

Then one night Katy was having dinner at her sister's apartment when her sister's friend Casey stopped by. A lawyer, Casey had been one of the men whom Katy had ruled out as uptight and boring. Casey was quiet and kind. After he left, Katy asked her sister, "Casey's really cute—what happened to him?"

"Nothing," said her sister. "He's the same as always."

Later that week, discussing this experience with her therapist, Katy recognized that *she* had changed. A nice guy like Casey really was attractive. "Will wonders never cease!" Katy declared.

She got up the nerve to invite Casey to her place, and they hit it off. They have been seeing each other for eight months. It's been rocky. Sometimes Casey's been fed up with her theatrics, her crazy clothes, her impulsive spending habits, and especially the way she flirts with other men when they're out at the parties she's always dragging him to. But Katy is learning to hear him out and not fall into tantrums or torrents of tears.

She is working hard on developing a sense of herself in her therapy. It is not going to be easy for her—how much she still wants to be swept off her feet by an all-powerful supermacho dream-come-true! Until recently Katy was still concocting personal ads that would lure in this perfect prince, and she was answering strangers' ads with long, romantic, perfumed letters on which she did not sign her name. And now in her office on slow days, Katy sometimes takes to scribbling wedding announcements on behalf of her and Casey. She imagines a splendid wedding, a honeymoon in the south of France, two children, and fabulous success for both of them in their careers. "Then again," Katy muses, "I could stay home with the children while Casey argues cases in front of the Supreme Court. I can just see him, asking for a recess so that he can call home and tell me how much he owes it all to me. . . ."

Not that Katy and Casey have come that far in their relationship. "Listen," Katy protests to her therapist, "a person's gotta have her dreams."

"True," says the therapist, thinking that when Katy can face her inner realities as enthusiastically as she clings to her still-childish fantasies— and she is starting to—she'll be free to create more mature hopes and dreams and to make them come true.

CHAPTER 8

Vigilant Style

"THE SURVIVOR"

Nothing escapes the notice of the men and women who have Vigilant personality style. These individuals possess an exceptional awareness of their environment. Call them Survivors. Their sensory antennae, continuously scanning the people and situations around them, alert them immediately to what is awry, out of place, dissonant, or dangerous, especially in their dealings with other people. Vigilant types have a special kind of hearing. They are immediately aware of the mixed messages, the hidden motivations, the evasions, and the subtlest distortions of the truth that elude or delude less gifted observers. With such a focus, Vigilant individuals naturally assume the roles of social critic, watchdog, ombudsman, and crusader in their private or our public domain, ready to spring upon the improprieties—especially the abuses of power —that poison human affairs.

THE SIX CHARACTERISTICS

The following six traits and behaviors are clues to the presence of the Vigilant style. A person who reveals a strong Vigilant tendency will demonstrate more of these behaviors more intensely than someone with less of this style in his or her personality profile.

1. *Autonomy.* Vigilant-style individuals possess a resilient independence. They keep their own counsel, they require no outside reassurance or advice, they make decisions easily, and they can take care of themselves.

2. *Caution.* They are careful in their dealings with others, preferring to size up a person before entering into a relationship.

3. *Perceptiveness.* They are good listeners, with an ear for subtlety, tone, and multiple levels of communication.

4. *Self-defense.* Individuals with Vigilant style are feisty and do not hesitate to stand up for themselves, especially when they are under attack.

5. *Alertness to criticism.* They take criticism very seriously, without becoming intimidated.

6. *Fidelity.* They place a high premium on fidelity and loyalty. They work hard to earn it, and they never take it for granted.

THE SIX DOMAINS OF VIGILANT FUNCTIONING

RELATIONSHIPS: WHO'S IN CHARGE HERE?

Individuals with Vigilant personality style are acutely aware of power and authority in their relationships. Throughout all aspects of their lives they seek to maintain their freedom and independence from domination. Vigilant individuals cannot be subordinated—this is their organizing principle. Thus, for this style, the domain of Relationships—characterized by their insistent autonomy—is key. In relation to other people, in no uncertain terms Vigilant types are always in charge of their own destiny.

Caution and reserve mark all their dealings with people. But they are not necessarily cold or unfriendly, nor do they prefer to do without relationships. Although they may be uneasy among strangers and slow to warm up, Vigilant individuals can be gregarious and comfortable among people once they get to know them. But they are slow to commit. Unlike the Devoted type, who is comfortable with dependence and will jump in with both feet, the Vigilant individual will enter one slow step at a time. Even within their established relationships, loyal though they may be, most Vigilant types hold back part of themselves.

Ted and Dorothy

Until they are certain that a person who shows interest in them can be trusted not to hurt or disappoint them, Vigilant types prefer to watch and evaluate. Vigilant men and women are gifted people-watchers. Dorothy C., who is fifty-one years old, has been dating Ted G., age fifty-five, for four years. Ted, whose personality is characterized by strong Vigilant, Conscientious, and Sensitive styles, is a bioengineering consultant; they met when he undertook a project at the company where Dorothy was working at the time. They worked together daily on the project for more than three months.

"I was attracted to him from the first day," confides Dorothy, a widow. "I didn't know much about him for a long time, since he isn't very open about himself and I was reluctant to ask. I didn't know if he was married or single, where he lived, how he liked to spend his time. But I had a lot of respect for the way he worked, I appreciated his sharp intellect and his fabulous concentration, and he was so polite to me, and so handsome—I liked his sexy Clint Eastwood reserve. I started having romantic fantasies about him."

Dorothy, whose chief personality styles are Conscientious, Dramatic, and Devoted, is not shy. She does not hesitate to initiate relationships with men ("At my age, I don't have the time to sit around and wait," she says). But she has learned not to mix business with pleasure, so she did not act on her attraction to Ted until the project ended. By that time she had learned from a colleague that Ted had never been married, although he had had a series of long involvements over the years. Since Ted had not shown any personal interest in her while he'd been consulting at her agency, she decided on an indirect approach, to test the waters. She called him and told him she was thinking of going out on her own as a consultant. Would he have lunch with her and offer some advice?

Ted said he'd be glad to. "At our lunch," Dorothy said, "he was friendly and full of good advice, but he didn't let down his professional guard. I was beginning to think this was a lost cause, when he made a comment about my relationship with my boss, Martin. He said he'd noticed that Martin and I were locked in a battle for control. I wasn't sure what he was referring to, and he reminded me of a day two months earlier when I had had a run-in with Martin over a minor matter. When I couldn't remember the incident, Ted reminded me that I had worn a red suit to work that day and that I'd had to leave early to go to my son's engagement party.

"I was dumbfounded. Ted had noticed what I'd worn, where I was going, what my boss and I had said to each other, and what was the underlying tenor of our relationship. Ted asked me whether I wanted to leave the agency because I felt politically squashed by my boss. That was it exactly—but I'd only just figured it out myself! I'd certainly never discussed this or anything else about office politics with him when he was working with us. I was flabbergasted by how perceptive he was, and flattered by how much he'd noticed about me. It turns out he knew so much about me, and how my mind worked, that it was almost as if he'd been tape-recording my thoughts and staring at me the whole time he was working there."

However, although Dorothy and Ted met for several more lunches, emotionally he moved no closer to her. He asked a number of questions about her life, her two grown children, her late husband. They discussed her work and he shared his insights about her. He didn't ask her out for an evening, and he was closemouthed about himself. He'd talk about his work, if Dorothy asked, or about his interest in sports, but he never seemed comfortable sharing his feelings. Dorothy assumed that he was involved with someone else, or that he simply wasn't interested in her. If she hadn't been invited to a business-related dance at which she felt obliged to show up with an escort, she would have given up on Ted for lack of any sign that he was interested in her as a woman.

The fourth time they met for lunch, Dorothy asked if Ted would join her at the fancy-dress ball. She said, "I was prepared for him to look embarrassed and say no. So when he said he would be glad to go, I was so surprised I blushed like a schoolgirl."

That was the first of four years' worth of dates. They had a great time, they discovered that they both loved dancing, and they kissed good night. But Ted didn't call afterward, which disappointed Dorothy tremendously. After a few days of no word, she called him. He sounded glad to hear from her. She said she had concert tickets—did he want to go? Sure, he said. They continued to see each other, usually at Dorothy's suggestion.

Vigilant-style individuals like Ted often will not actively pursue a relationship, and they are usually misunderstood as noncommittal because their reserve continues even when they've been involved with someone for a long time. But Dorothy was determined, and she worked hard to forge a relationship with Ted. She had confidence that in time he would relax with her—although a few of her close friends advised her that he was just stringing her along for the sex. He wasn't ever going to marry her, they pointed out—after all, he'd never really committed himself to anyone, and look how old he was.

Ted never wanted to talk about the relationship. He didn't want to share his feelings about her. And he never offered to take Dorothy home to meet his parents. The first time she suggested that she accompany him to Nebraska for Christmas, his eyes opened wide with alarm. The next time, two years later, he said, "Maybe next year." The third time, this year, instead of going home to the folks, Ted will be joining Dorothy and her children for the holidays.

Ted and Dorothy are not exactly engaged, but they are together virtually every night. Dorothy believes that he is only now becoming able to trust her and let down emotionally a little more. She would like to get married, but she knows him well enough not to bring that up. And she has the good sense that an ultimatum—marry me or else—would never work with Ted. Vigilant types will never succumb to a power play. She's hoping that they'll just slide into marriage, the way they've slid into everything else.

For all his reserve, and his lifetime attachment to his bachelorhood, Ted is dedicated to Dorothy. He is quietly possessive of her and acknowledges, to himself, that he is deeply involved with her. He believes in loyalty and has no interest in seeking out other women. True to his Vigilant style, though, he operates best at an emotional distance, where he is fully in possession of himself. But Dorothy has a lot going for her in his mind. She lets him be who he is, and all the other women in his life, of which there had been many, had always given him the shape-up-or-ship-out speech. So of course he shipped out. Marriage makes him very nervous; he doesn't like the idea of being tied to anybody by a legal contract. Why can't he have his cake and eat it too? ·

Underlying Motives

Vigilant individuals are almost always aware of other people's motives. A lot of Ted's reticence to become involved with Dorothy, and the women who preceded her in his affections, was due to his concerns that the woman of the moment was trying to corner him into a relationship. Or that she was just using him—she really had no intention of remaining true to him. More than other styles, the Vigilant carries with it an alertness to what people want from you.

Varying with the degree of Vigilance in their personality pattern, people with this style will watch for signs of disrespect and abuses of power in almost every relationship. Because they are on guard against it, they are not easily hoodwinked by others. They are capable of understanding the many levels of communication, spoken and otherwise. They can hear a false note, spot a forked tongue, sense ambivalence. This ability serves them well in their dealings with people. When Vigilant-style Mary's boss thanked her profusely for staying late at work one night, she recognized the boss's double message: "Thanks for staying late," plus, "I'm angry at you for always leaving at five o'clock." So she started staying late every once in a while to demonstrate her loyalty; her year-end bonus increased by 25 percent. Vigilant types are anything but naive, and if they can respond appropriately to the information they glean, like Mary they can prosper.

With increasing amounts of this style, however, they run the risk of misinterpreting the signs that they perceive. Not everyone harbors a hidden intention, and just because a woman wants to spend more time with a man doesn't mean, as Ted so often felt, that she is out to entrap him. And so what if she is? Vigilant individuals often invest others with a power that they do not have. No one can force Ted into a relationship he doesn't want. As the Vigilant personality style grows extreme, suspicion plagues these individuals and begins to undermine their relationships. They begin to overreact to others' human flaws and to assume that others are looking at them as closely as they are observing other people, which is far from true.

The Age Factor

Dorothy is not trying to force Ted into marriage. She knows not to play games with him. True, Ted chokes on the I-love-you's, but she knows he's a good, upstanding man. And Ted knows, since he's continually on the lookout, that Dorothy harbors no ulterior motives. She loves him, that's all. Ted would like to get married before he dies, and he's no spring chicken.

Both Dorothy and Ted have age on their side. Personality style, even disorder, tends to mellow with age. In her younger years Dorothy might have tried a Dramatic-style manipulation to move Ted toward the altar. Now she can accept herself, Ted, and life more on their own terms. As for Ted, he's inching closer to saying "I do." Maybe next year.

Inalienable Rights

Society needs individuals who are on guard against abuses of authority and power and who can detect ulterior motives. Even though their watchfulness and their sensitivity to flaws may hamper their personal relationships, Vigilant types often serve an important role in the world. They can be champions of the underdogs, protectors of the downtrodden, fighters for freedom from oppression. Vigilant are many of those who champion causes such as the environment and civil rights. They may serve as watchdogs over government and blow the whistle on corruption. They are good debaters, and their strong opinions, their certainty about the righteousness of their mission, and their intense concentration on their goals makes some of them attractive, even charismatic crusaders and leaders. Under attack they become all the stronger. They rise powerfully to their own defense and the defense of their cause. Their courage inspires those who follow them.

Vigilant men and women want to believe in a better world. Yet, wherever they turn they are confronted with the evidence of our flaws and wrongdoings. They take them hard. They are idealists. They expect more from the human race than it seems to deliver.

Extreme Vigilance, however, may make some individuals vulnerable to imagined fears and suspicions about other individuals, races, religions, or political organizations. These people may end up as rabble-rousers, stirring up hate and fear, championing the very organizations and causes, such as racism, that seek to oppress people and deny them their right to survive. (See "Paranoid Personality Disorder," p. 174.)

The Family Protector

As parents, Vigilant men and women are loyal and protective, perhaps overprotective if the style is very strong. They may encourage a mistrust of others in their offspring. When the kids begin to rebel or assert their independence, a Vigilant parent may feel threatened and attempt to overcontrol the kids. Nonetheless, even though Vigilant parents may be emotionally undemonstrative, they are deeply caring underneath it all, responsible, and thoroughly dedicated to the welfare of their families—determined to protect them from all harm from outside.

Stress!

Vigilant-style men and women need to feel that they are firmly in control. This is why it takes so much time for them to become comfortable in relationships and commit themselves trustingly to other people. The loss of that control causes the most extreme stress for Vigilant people.

People with this personality style will find it hard to come to terms with disappointment in a relationship. When a relationship at work or at home begins to come apart, or they feel they are losing control over their own destiny, Vigilant types will take the loss or change as a personal betrayal. It is not their style automatically to conclude, "Well, some things just don't work out," "I guess we just weren't made for each other," or, "We did the best we could—no one's to blame."

Self-defense is their principal coping style. Vigilant individuals tend to focus on the other person's errors. They don't like to hear about what they did wrong and can be very touchy about criticism. They can take it—they don't lapse into tears or collapse into self-doubt—but they feel attacked and will react by defending themselves. Vigilant individuals are not natural compromisers.

Although they may react bitterly to the end of a relationship, their resilient autonomy serves them well. They prove that they're survivors. They can and do take care of themselves. Like Conscientious people, they will often jump into hard work. They will, of course, be wary of new relationships and will not enter new ones for the long time it takes their wounds to heal.

Good/Bad Matches

Vigilant-style men and women thrive in relationships with nonthreatening people. They usually avoid those who must dominate the relationship or compete for the number-one spot. Thus, matches with ambitious Self-Confident and powerful Aggressive types can be very rocky. Overall, the Vigilant man or woman needs a mate who is predictable and even and who will reach out. Devoted, Self-Sacrificing, and Sensitive mates are most likely to bring these characteristics to a relationship.

Conscientious people can be quite similar to Vigilant types; if there are no control problems, they may often appreciate each other's intellectual capabilities and ability to work, and they will be able to count on each other's loyalty. Dorothy's combination of Conscientious, Dramatic, and Devoted works well for her in relation to Ted, even though unmitigated Dramatic style is usually the kiss of death for the Vigilant style.

Individuals who are very Dramatic or Mercurial are usually too emotionally unpredictable and too indiscriminately needy for attention to provide the safe haven necessary for Vigilant individuals, who are prone to jealousy. Vigilant men and women cannot tolerate jealousy. On the other hand, the Dramatic style provides an ease with people that proves useful to the more socially reticent Vigilant soul.

What about two Vigilant types teaming up? It helps to hold a similar worldview, and sharing the Vigilant trait may cement two people in an us-against-them union. Similarly, Serious and Vigilant people share a rather dark, suspicious mind-set. They'll appreciate each other's steady, independent, hardworking qualities.

Likewise, Leisurely and Vigilant share a mistrust of anyone in power over them and will absolutely not be pushed into a corner. But the

Leisurely approach to life may be too *mañana* for the more watchful Vigilant, and the Leisurely's tendency to do his or her own thing can provoke suspicion in the Vigilant partner.

Strongly Adventurous-style partners are out of the question.

WORK:
WHO'S IN CHARGE HERE? PART II

As you will see under "Careers for the Vigilant" (p. 167) many types of work are open to Vigilant-style individuals. They're observant, careful, perceptive, sensitive to subtlety, tactical, alert, not easily fooled—qualities that serve them and their employers well in the Work domain. They tend to be as serious and industrious about their work as they are about the rest of their lives (the Vigilant is *not* an easygoing style), especially when they have strong Conscientious or moderate Serious traits as well. They work hard, they can be very ambitious, and they can be very successful—depending on how well they handle their relationships with those who are in authority in their Work domain.

Vigilant individuals will be sensitive and alert to the power structure of any organization in which they operate. Coupled with their dislike of dependence and subordination, this sensitivity can make their place in the hierarchy unstable—unless they have a Self-Confident streak to balance it, in which case they'll use their antennae to gather information to maneuver them quickly through the organizational maze. Generally, the higher the degree of Vigilance in one's personality pattern, the greater the mistrust of authority and the greater the discomfort within the organization.

Vigilant-style individuals are inclined to feel that power will always be used against those who have less of it. This is sometimes true in the world, but not always. A strongly Vigilant person will not be able to make this essential discrimination. Being perpetually on guard against possible abuses of authority at work (or in any other domain) makes it harder for a Vigilant person to make positive use of his or her power.

Phil Versus the Corporation

A few years ago, Vigilant-Conscientious-Dramatic-style Phil, a corporate trial lawyer, joined the legal staff of a major multinational corporation. He'd been reluctant to leave his private legal practice, but the corporate officers wooed him for almost two years. They wanted him on their side, because Phil was often their all-too-worthy opponent.

They kept upping the ante and finally made him an offer he couldn't refuse. He accepted, after making sure that he would have substantial independence in his job.

Although he had no immediate supervisor, Phil was beholden to the chief counsel and the other corporate officers. Reasoning that the less he had to do with the "honchos" the better, Phil steered clear of them. He attended only those meetings that were absolutely required. He avoided socializing with the higher-ups, and he invited none of them to the elaborate party he planned when his personal staff celebrated a major courtroom victory. While it suited Phil's style to remain independent of the authorities, he couldn't have made a worse political decision. The chief counsel, Phil's mentor within the corporation, was deeply offended. Characteristic of many Vigilant individuals in the Work domain, Phil had poor political instincts in the broad sense. While he could defend his own bailiwick against the greater power, he couldn't let down his guard. Instead of establishing himself within the power structure, because of his discomfort he maintained a closed, defensive, mistrustful position. He made the organization the enemy, and himself an outsider.

Then, a couple of months later, when the chief counsel questioned how he had decided to organize the defense in a major case against the corporation, Phil became defensive. Instead of appreciating the input of this seasoned legal veteran, he took his questions as criticism. "You hired me to bring this substandard department up to par. If you don't like the way I do things, you should have hired some other guy," Phil challenged—rather than simply explaining his approach and convincing the chief counsel of its soundness. Phil could win over a judge and jury, but when it came to people who he thought were trying to interfere with his independence, he rushed to his own defense rather than to that of his cause.

The corporation officers began to leave Phil alone to do his work and to exclude him from political power. Phil sensed this change in their attitude, which only confirmed his feelings about them. After two and a half years he abruptly left to return to private practice, where he feels free. Recently the corporation for which he had worked engaged him to represent them in a trial. Now Phil and his erstwhile employers recognize that they have discovered the best relationship with one another.

Kid Gloves

Not all individuals with the Vigilant style behave so truculently. On the surface, many are eager to please, while inwardly they feel apprehensive. Others are happy to create their own little niche where they do their job and escape the notice of the powerful people. They are willing to forgo the benefits of political ties.

It takes enlightened management to deal well with Vigilant-style people. Like Conscientious types, they often do their best work when they are given independent roles and are managed with a light hand. Vigilant types rarely take advantage. Many people with this style will, however, be quick to spot and perhaps crusade against inequities in company policies and practices—serving the watchdog role that comes so naturally to many of them.

The Vigilant Manager

As managers, Vigilant-style men and women need to be assured of the loyalty of their subordinates. To earn it, they will often be generous with favors, praise, and rewards. If they suspect disloyalty, they will be angry and unforgiving. An extremely Vigilant manager may mistake ambition for disloyalty and make it difficult for a subordinate to move on in the organization. Generally, however, moderately Vigilant-style managers take good care of their staffs, while perhaps promoting a view of upper management as something ominously powerful, against which they will act as protector. Indeed, if their subordinates run afoul of the organization, or if policies seem to treat them unfairly, the Vigilant manager will not hesitate to fight for their rights.

Since individuals with this personality style need to be or to feel in complete command, as managers they will not be comfortable delegating important (i.e., politically powerful) responsibilities. Vigilant managers make it their business to be fully informed about the workings of their departments. When there is extra work to be done, they will often put in more than a manager's share of the time, not only to earn their staff's loyalty but to keep an eye on what's going on.

Like their Conscientious brethren, many individuals with the Vigilant personality style will choose a more independent track within an organization, where they can perform their duties without having to worry about managing other people.

Careers for the Vigilant

Vigilant-style individuals often work best in fields in which they can operate outside of direct, full-time authority. With their exceptional astuteness, their ability to focus their attention, and their gift of argument, they can be excellent critics, diagnosticians, academicians, lawyers, investigative reporters, and researchers. Their perceptive savvy, including their ability to understand the multiple levels of communication, helps them in detective work, as interviewers, in sales, and (as long as the style is at a moderate level) as psychotherapists. And, because many people with this style naturally identify or sympathize with the underdog or the oppressed, Vigilant people can contribute to the effectiveness of social and political causes.

Strongly Vigilant individuals may prefer working with machines rather than people. Like Conscientious people, Vigilant types are often very competent and comfortable with mechanical things. Their ability to concentrate serves them well in this area.

REAL WORLD: STANDING TALL AMID THE DANGERS

Vigilant men and women have a definite sense of themselves. Most have an inner sense of rightness; they believe that they're the sane ones in an insane world. They have strong opinions, they don't often doubt themselves, but, as mentioned earlier, they have a hard time admitting their mistakes and accepting criticism.

Their antennae are focused outward: it's easier for Vigilant types to detect the faults of other people. For the Vigilant person, the Real World is something of a minefield. It is populated with people who might take advantage. This alertness can be very useful in urban environments and unsafe neighborhoods.

Vigilant individuals don't like surprises. In anticipating danger, they are prepared for any emergency. They react quickly—like Penny K., who suddenly turned and stepped away from a stranger before she fully realized that he was trying to grab her pocketbook. Or like David T., Vigilant to an extreme, who flashes his headlights the moment he sees a car coming toward him with its brights on. David does not realize that he has a faster reaction time than most people and that he doesn't give other drivers time to lower their beams. Instead, David repeatedly gets annoyed that so many people have the effrontery to shine their lights in his eyes.

Whatever actual or exaggerated dangers Vigilant-style people perceive in the Real World, they quickly show the world that they can stand up for themselves.

The Vigilant Idealist

Vigilant men and women want to believe in a better world. Yet they are confronted wherever they turn with the evidence of our flaws and wrongdoings. They take them hard. They are idealists. They expect more from the human race than it seems to deliver—and their expectations, sometimes, as in the following example, help some of us humans to reach a little higher.

Richard Harris was a writer for *The New Yorker*. Upon his death, the following eulogy appeared in that magazine, and demonstrated the heights to which the Vigilant, as well as the Serious (chapter 17), personality style can reach:

Richard Harris was what one editor here used to call a hard case. His judgments often seemed harsh. He did not give the benefit of the doubt. He tended to find almost any situation worse than it had first appeared. When he came across a sunny scene, his eye invariably fell on what was in shadow—the unworthy motive, the cowardly evasion, the failure to measure up. He viewed the world with an unfiltered gaze. Applying that gaze as a reporter for this magazine, he was able to turn out penetrating and prodigious articles on the American legislative and judicial process. The work exhausted him, but it never mellowed him. When he died last month, at the age of sixty-one, he was still a hard case. . . .

He cared a lot. Like many deeply skeptical reporters, he was a closet idealist, accustomed to almost constant disappointment. He was, someone close to him once said, "a gloomy optimist." Unlike Diogenes the Cynic, who walked around in broad daylight with a lantern "in search of an honest man," Harris actually hoped to find one. Occasionally, he did. In a couple of cases, the honest man turned out to be, of all things, a United States senator.

. . . He set great store by old-fashioned, idealistic values. His idealism was reflected in some of the titles he used, even though he would have pointed out, somewhat testily, that they were used ironically: "A Sacred Trust" and "Honor Bound" and, most of all, "Justice."

. . . An acquaintance could disappoint as easily as a congressman could. . . . He often found himself having to cross people off his list. He was a man of great charm—his comments were often witty, his manners bordered on the courtly—but he did not consider the spreading of good cheer to be among his responsibilities. He was often angry. . . .

The people who knew him well—people who hadn't been crossed off the list, people who had somehow found their way back on, even some people who believed they were probably off for good—thought of him as a splendid companion and a fiercely loyal friend. His friends were sometimes exhilarated by contemplating the possibility that they were actually living up to his expectations. . . . "He made it difficult," the person closest to him at his death said last week, "but he was worth the trouble."

EMOTIONS AND SELF-CONTROL

Emotional reserve marks this style—except when Vigilant types feel threatened or challenged. Then they will show you, through argument or outburst of temper—that they are not to be messed with. (As the Vigilant style approaches Paranoid personality disorder, the perceived threats become more obscure and the Vigilant person is less able to recognize that his or her reactions are unreasonable.)

Otherwise, Vigilant individuals rein in their expressions of feeling and resist giving in to impulse. This is a "head," not a "heart," style. Vigilant people do not take emotional risks. Without some Dramatic, Mercurial, or Devoted style in their pattern, Vigilant individuals have a hard time abandoning themselves fully to their feelings; even sexually they may hold back to a degree. Tenderness may be difficult, at least until the person is finally ready to trust and to commit. Vigilant individuals have a hard time with I-love-you's and prefer that their mates understand them and not require verbal reassurance. They are possessive and can be extremely jealous, although they probably won't talk about it.

Humor may be their only outlet. Some Vigilant-style men and women, with their acute awareness of subtlety, ambiguity, and irony, have a well-developed, though sometimes biting, sense of humor.

TIPS ON DEALING WITH THE
VIGILANT PERSON IN YOUR LIFE

1. The Vigilant person in your life may appear very confident, independent, tough, and assertive. You may not realize how much this person needs your respect. Express, show, and otherwise prove it often.

2. If the Vigilant person in your life is new on the scene and you would like to get to know him or her better, do not hesitate to pursue this person. Even though he or she may be painfully slow to reciprocate and to begin to trust you, persistence usually pays off. Go the whole distance. This advice is especially intended for women, who may be hesitant to initiate a relationship and to be the one to keep it going.

3. Do not misinterpret the Vigilant reserve as indifference. Unless he or she has a streak of a more emotionally outgoing style, do not expect that you can break through this wall and force the Vigilant person to show you his or her deeper feelings. Don't even try. Accept the emotional reserve, and if the relationship is solid and stable, trust that this person cares deeply for you.

4. Avoid competition and power struggles. The Vigilant person needs to feel in complete control of his or her destiny. Respect that. Otherwise the Vigilant person in your life will begin to distance him- or herself from you.

5. Expect defensiveness when you criticize or confront this person. It's a natural reaction for someone with this personality style to resist accepting blame. Let the reaction run its course and don't start defending yourself if he or she tries to shift the blame to you. The best way to confront a Vigilant person is simply to express your feelings without criticizing or finding fault. Try saying that you care and are looking for a way to better your relationship, not to blame anybody. It's easy to get into a boxing match with a Vigilant-style person, trading attack for attack, argument for argument, until one of you crumbles. Since this is presumably not your style, you be the one to steer your attempts to resolve conflict toward a more constructive end.

6. Take the lead socially. The Vigilant person in your life will appreciate your greater ease in getting to know people and making plans with them.

7. Don't tease. Vigilant people often have a good sense of humor, but not about themselves.

8. If the Vigilant person in your life is unjustifiably jealous or worried about your loyalty, don't be flippant or dismiss these concerns as silly. Don't underestimate the seriousness of such worries to a Vigilant person. Reassure your mate or lover of your devotion.

9. Accept that if you slight this person, unintentionally or otherwise, he or she will have a long memory. If the Vigilant person in your life is unforgiving, at least forgive yourself.

MAKING THE MOST OF YOUR VIGILANT STYLE

Your mind and your senses are always on, monitoring the environment and other people. Being in such a state of ready alert can make you physically and emotionally tense. Therefore, the first order of business is the following:

Exercise 1

Relax. Include more activities in your life that you know will loosen you up. Concentrate especially on relatively mindless pursuits that temporarily shut down your "scanner," i.e., go for a run, take a swim, listen to music (don't just put it on for background), do yoga, take up meditation, practice muscle relaxation exercises, get a massage. Sit in a hot bath and let the tension slip out of your body while you keep thoughts from tumbling through your head by concentrating on the heat of the water and how good you are beginning to feel. If anxiety starts to do battle with your oncoming relaxation, tell yourself it's just part of the process.

Exercise 2

Every time you find yourself wondering about someone's ulterior motive, think about or make a list of two other motives that could explain the same action. For example, at a recent wedding reception you handed the newlyweds their gift. Almost two months have passed and still no thank-you note. You think, "They hate it and are so appalled at my bad taste that they can't figure out what to say to me." Now think of two other explanations: (1) they are overwhelmed with other things; (2) they tend to procrastinate and have put off writing their thank-you notes.

Exercise 3

If someone really is harboring a hidden motive, so what? Let's say a colleague from your office tells you he has a couple of free tickets to the theater and asks if you'd like to join him. You've never been friendly with this person, and you think, "He's asking me because he knows I'm in the boss's good graces and he wants me to put in a good word for him when he comes up for promotion." So what? He can't make you do anything you don't want to. Consider taking him up on it, motive or no motive. Enjoy the play.

Exercise 4

The next time someone criticizes you, catch yourself in the act of justifying your behavior. Stop and think whether the criticizer has a point. Realize that it's okay to be in the wrong or to make an error—everybody does, all the time. If you say, "I see your point," you get a thousand points. If you think the criticizer is a fool, you earn a thousand points by saying, "I'll think about what you say," or something similar, which is no admission of guilt but will usually put an end to an unpleasant situation.

Exercise 5

After each fight with your lover or mate or parent, in private make a list of what you did to contribute to it. Pat yourself on the back for being so honest. Keep the list in mind if you find yourself getting into the same situation again with this person.

Exercise 6

Every time you find yourself thinking that what just happened is somebody else's fault, laugh at yourself for being so Vigilant. Shrug your shoulders and say, "Sometimes things just go wrong. Nobody's to blame."

If you're a Vigilant type without additional strength in one of the more socially or emotionally comfortable personality styles, try the next two exercises.

Exercise 7

Once or twice each week, telephone a friend just to chat. If you feel uncomfortable on the phone, remember that most people like getting calls from their friends, even if they don't have anything special to talk about.

Exercise 8

You married or otherwise paired Vigilant types probably let your spouses make all the social arrangements. Every once in a while, make some of these plans yourself. Telephone your tennis partner and see if he and his wife want to go to a movie. Won't your mate be surprised!

Finally, to make the most of your relationships, refer to Exercise 7 in chapter 4 for the Conscientious style: Practice sharing your feelings with your loved ones. It couldn't be more important. You might try, too, a variation of Self-Confident Exercise 4 (p. 97), in which you collect data about people you interact with a lot. For you, who is all too skilled in collecting negative information, look only for positive points —things you like and admire.

PARANOID PERSONALITY DISORDER

Paranoid people expect the worst of others. They're apprehensive, suspicious, uncompromising, and argumentative, and they're convinced of their rightness beyond the shadow of a doubt. Individuals with Paranoid personality disorder are on guard against a hostile universe, where bad things happen or are always about to happen to them at the hands of other people. (Note that Paranoid personality disorder is different from paranoid or delusional disorder and paranoid schizophrenia; these are discussed in more detail on p. 178 and in chapter 12.

DIAGNOSTIC CRITERIA

The DSM-IV describes Paranoid personality disorder as:

A. A pervasive distrust and suspiciousness of others such that their motives are interpreted as malevolent, beginning by early adulthood and present in a variety of contexts, as indicated by four (or more) of the following:

(1) suspects, without sufficient basis, that others are exploiting, harming, or deceiving him or her

(2) is preoccupied with unjustified doubts about the loyalty or trustworthiness of friends or associates

(3) is reluctant to confide in others because of unwarranted fear that the information will be used maliciously against him or her

(4) reads hidden demeaning or threatening meanings into benign remarks or events

(5) persistently bears grudges, i.e., is unforgiving of insults, injuries, or slights

(6) perceives attacks on his or her character or reputation that are not apparent to others and is quick to react angrily or to counterattack

(7) has recurrent suspicions, without justification, regarding fidelity of spouse or sexual partner

B. Does not occur exclusively during the course of Schizophrenia, a Mood Disorder With Psychotic Features, or another Psychotic Disorder and is not due to the direct physiological effects of a general medical condition.

ENEMIES

The men and women who suffer from this personality disorder are consumed with mistrust. They are sure that other people mean them harm or humiliation, or at least will let them down. They may be hostile, stubborn, uncooperative, hypersensitive to the tiniest slights, defensive, sarcastic, belligerent, cold, envious, rigid, secretive, argumentative —all these behaviors serving to keep them from getting too close to other people. Individuals with Paranoid personality disorder must not let down their guard and give way to trust and intimacy, lest the other person take advantage of their weakness.

It is obvious that their relationships are troubled, both at work and in their private lives. Although their often superior intelligence, alertness, forcefulness, and ambition can make them quite successful at their work, Paranoid personalities will have difficulty with bosses and co-workers. Their envy of people in authority betrays itself in their belligerence or sometimes in their attempts to ingratiate themselves. In either case, they are quite uncomfortable with people of higher rank or position. Individuals with Paranoid personality disorder will be able to sustain relationships only with those whom they perceive as nonthreatening. George C., a high school assistant principal, claimed his only real friend was the school janitor, with whom he could let down his hair and have a good time. While those who have severe personality disorders may never marry, others may find comfort with spouses who are compliant and dependent.

It's Your Fault

Most people with this disorder do not betray their innermost thoughts to other people. And they are careful about how they appear. As a result, the people in their lives may not suspect the extent of their suspicions and mistrust.

They are perpetually searching the environment to find confirmation of their doubts about other people. And they always find what they are looking for—often because they provoke it themselves. If a Paranoid person is sure that you will not remain loyal, he or she may voice so many suspicions that you throw up your hands and say, "I've got to go out with other people! I can't stand this anymore!"

"You see," declares the Paranoid individual, "I knew I couldn't trust you!"

A Paranoid person is never wrong. It's always the other person's fault or the fault of fate. When Robert W. lost a big sale, he came home and blamed his wife. If she hadn't been arguing with him so much, he wouldn't have been so tense during the negotiations, he told her. After she divorced him, he blamed fate for dealing him a bad hand.

"To live with a paranoid person is to live perpetually in the defendant's box," comments Dr. Michael Stone. Although Stone means his comment to be taken figuratively, interactions with people with this disorder all too often lead literally to the courtroom. These men and women may magnify every slight—and then sue you for it. Many Paranoid individuals threaten lawsuits and often follow through.

PROJECTING THE UNACCEPTABLE

The fact that they are never wrong—or weak or harbor ill intent—is the giveaway to the quality of their inner lives. Unconsciously (they cannot admit this to themselves) Paranoid individuals feel so wrong, blameworthy, helpless, weak, shameful, and beset by unacceptable impulses and temptations that they have to project all their negative feelings about themselves onto other people in order to protect their fragile self-esteem. They detect the tiniest weaknesses in others and disdain them for it, because they feel so weak themselves. Although they blame others for making it impossible to trust and get close, they must fight everybody off—because inside they may yearn for dependency, and that, they fear, would be their undoing. They must maintain their autonomy in order to survive.

They do not dare doubt themselves. Instead, they doubt others, or they may see others as doubting them. For example, after Robert lost the sale, he became certain that his boss thought the worst of him. "I can see it in his face," he said. In reality, his boss had tried to reassure him that a salesman can never expect to close all his deals. What Robert saw in his boss's face was more likely a projection of what Robert felt about his own failure, combined with his boss's uneasiness in dealing with a difficult person like Robert.

Like Narcissistic types, people with Paranoid personality disorder can be extremely self-concerned. The self-righteousness, harsh morality, and punitiveness of some Paranoid individuals, combined with their certainty that people who disagree with them are wrong, and their rigid strength of purpose, can be all too attractive to some needy people. Some Paranoid types end up as cult leaders, rabble-rousers, and hate mongers; they project their self-hatred onto outside groups and spearhead the attack. According to the DSM-IV, people with this personality disorder "tend to develop negative stereotypes of others, particularly those from population groups distinct from their own."

HELP!

Individuals who are suffering from Paranoid personality disorder usually feel confident that they see the world the way it is; they do not see themselves as suffering from a personality disorder. And if they have trouble with their relationships, they do not believe that they are to blame. Therefore, a Paranoid person is not likely to seek help from, much less to trust, a therapist. Individuals with this disorder generally can and do take care of themselves, but they may live in isolation from real intimacy.

These troubled men and women may seek help, however, when under extreme stress they begin to suffer transient psychotic delusions that people are out to get them. When they begin to behave bizarrely, other people in their lives may insist, often by threatening them, that they seek help. Some people who suffer from a mild Paranoid personality disorder may at some point in their lives begin to suspect that things could be better for them. Feeling lonely, different from everybody else, and unfulfilled, they may find the courage to reach out. Others may come into treatment to deal with specific life problems and stresses and may conceal the extent of their suspiciousness from the therapist. Drs. Beck and Freeman point out that "paranoid individuals are likely to recognize that it is prudent to keep their thoughts to themselves."

The therapist must be extremely well trained and honest and have great reserves of empathy and patience. It is not easy to build an alliance with a Paranoid person, who will have a hard time maintaining trust. "Such patients often try, like a cross-examining attorney, to polarize subtle comments of a therapist into the language of 'black-and-white,'" comments Dr. Stone. "A therapist may, for example, speak of having been annoyed, momentarily and to a modest degree, with the patient. To the paranoid patient this may sound like proof that 'you hate me.' It becomes necessary to teach the patient about the shades of grey ordinary folk recognize and adapt to. This is not a matter of ten easy lessons; rather, of a thousand painful lessons."

The skilled psychodynamic psychotherapist will be sensitive to the individual's feelings about others, and, as cooperation mounts, will be able to begin to make the person aware of his or her real pain buried deep inside.

Behavioral therapy may sometimes help people with this personality disorder to become less sensitive to criticism and to improve their social skills. In Cognitive therapy, clinicians help these individuals recognize and change maladaptive thinking patterns, such as, "If I am not careful, people will abuse or take advantage of me." Helping them to increase their self-confidence in their abilities to solve specific problems may help them to relax their defensiveness before going on to tackle the thought patterns that do them in.

Medication is sometimes helpful for the patient who is under extreme stress and suffering transient psychotic symptoms.

RISKS, PREDISPOSITIONS, AND INCIDENCE

Although they may suffer from brief psychotic symptoms (becoming convinced, for example, that people are whispering about them), individuals with Paranoid personality disorder do not suffer from the persistent delusions and hallucinations that characterize the Axis I delusional disorder and paranoid schizophrenia. Many researchers believe that there is some as-yet undefined relationship between Paranoid personality disorder and these severe Axis I conditions. Some theorize that there is a genetic predisposition to a wide spectrum of related disorders, ranging from chronic schizophrenia at the most malignant extreme to Schizotypal personality disorder (chapter 12) and Paranoid personality disorder at the most benign. There is limited evidence for a genetic relationship between Paranoid personality disorder and schizophrenia; studies have established an increase in this disorder among close relatives of people suffering from schizophrenia. The familial relationship with delusional disorder (in which the individual appears to be relatively clear-thinking, except for a circumscribed delusion, such as being repeatedly followed by somebody) appears to be stronger.

This does not mean that people with the personality style will develop the psychosis, although some may. They are also at risk for depression, agoraphobia, the Axis I obsessive-compulsive disorder, and alcohol and substance abuse problems. Other personality disorders that commonly occur along with the Paranoid include Schizotypal, Schizoid, Narcissistic, Avoidant, and Borderline.

Paranoid personality disorder or paranoid traits may carry some serious health consequences. A study of five hundred older adults published in *Psychosomatic Medicine* showed that extremely suspicious people had a greater risk of mortality or of overall poor health as rated by their physicians than did those who were not so mistrustful of others.

Some studies have suggested that Paranoid personality disorder runs in families. Often the families of Paranoid individuals are extremely rigid, unspontaneous, and uncommunicative. As children, some people who later develop Paranoid personality disorder are aloof from others and have problematic relationships with friends, suffer from social anxiety, and are underachievers; they're overly sensitive, seem odd, and are frequent targets of teasing.

The actual gender distribution of the disorder within the population is not known, but it is more frequently diagnosed among men. It occurs in up to 2.5 percent of the population, in as much as 10 percent of people seeking help in outpatient mental health settings.

COPING WITH PARANOID PEOPLE

You have to love a Paranoid person completely. Any criticism or annoyance you express will hurt this person intolerably, and you will find yourself on the long list of people who have wronged him or her. To cope with such a person, back off. Don't try to talk him or her out of any suspicions, or you will soon be seen as a co-conspirator yourself. Avoid confrontations and try to stay clear of arguments. If this person is important to you, try to get him or her to seek help. Consider going for help as a couple. See also the earlier tips for dealing with Vigilant individuals (p. 170), some of which may help.

CHAPTER 9

Sensitive Style

"THE HOMEBODY"

Sensitive people come into possession of their powers when their world is small and they know the people in it. For this commonly occurring personality style, familiarity breeds comfort, contentment, and inspiration. These men and women—although they avoid a wide social network and shun celebrity—can achieve great recognition for their creativity. Nestled in an emotionally secure environment, with a few dear family members or friends, the Sensitive style's imagination and spirit of exploration know no bounds. With their minds, feelings, and fantasies, Sensitive people find freedom.

THE SIX CHARACTERISTICS

The following six traits and behaviors are clues to the presence of the Sensitive style. A person who reveals a strong Sensitive tendency will demonstrate more of these behaviors more intensely than someone with less of this style in his or her personality profile.

1. *Familiarity.* Individuals with the Sensitive personality style prefer the known to the unknown. They are comfortable with, even inspired by, habit, repetition, and routine.

2. *Concern.* Sensitive individuals care deeply about what other people think of them.

3. *Circumspection.* They behave with deliberate discretion in their dealings with others. They do not make hasty judgments or jump in before they know what is appropriate.

4. *Polite reserve.* Socially they take care to maintain a courteous, self-restrained demeanor.

5. *Role.* They function best in scripted settings, vocationally and socially: when they know precisely what is expected of them, how they are supposed to relate to others, and what they are expected to say.

6. *Privacy.* Sensitive men and women are not quick to share their innermost thoughts and feelings with others, even those they know well.

THE SIX DOMAINS OF SENSITIVE FUNCTIONING

Two domains—Emotions and Relationships—in tandem shape the experience of the Sensitive individual.

EMOTIONS: SAFE AT HOME

Each of the fourteen styles offers a way of ensuring emotional security. The Devoted, for example, finds it through attachment to another person, the Vigilant through independence and self-reliance. Individuals with the Sensitive personality style gain emotional security by building a small world they can call their own. They're territorial and family centered. They form deep, lifelong personal attachments with their families and/or a few close friends. Their home is their castle, which they make comfortable, personal, and attractive. They are always glad to be home.

Inside the bounds of their own territory, they are emotionally free. They can be warm, giving, open, spontaneous, creative. But outside their secure spheres, like fish out of water, Sensitive types feel vulnerable. They move into new situations uneasily, becoming cautious and holding themselves in emotional reserve. Among strangers they are rarely in top form. They may even feel vaguely threatened, out of their element, guarded, anxious, worried; but they mask their discomfort beneath a polite, if cool, facade. Few of the strangers they encounter at a large gathering would guess how uneasy they feel.

The Sensitive "Snow Queen"

Joel T., an internist and medical school faculty member, tells about his initial impressions of his wife, Emily, a surgeon:

"We met at a hospital function. Emily was a new resident. My chairman was talking to her, and when I came up he introduced us. We shook hands, but in a moment Emily politely excused herself and stepped away. I kept talking to my chairman, but I followed Emily out of the corner of my eye. She went to the bar and got a drink, then stood off to the side, looking rather cool and arrogant. Surgeons, you know, have a reputation for being holier-than-thou, and I assumed she had stepped on her pedestal to escape us common folk. My chairman caught me watching Emily, and he said, 'She's a nice person. You should get to know her.' I said, 'Somehow I don't think "nice" is the word for her,' and my chairman laughed.

"I kept running into Emily around the hospital, and she was always pleasant, but distant. But really attractive—I like that dark, deep, mysterious look. And she had a very good reputation as a surgeon, although nobody seemed to know her very well.

"When Christmas came around, I went to visit my old college roommate, Eddie, and his new wife, Tish, at their country place. We were invited for Christmas Eve to a gathering at the weekend home of some family friends of Tish's. I had never met these people. We get to their house, and who do you think is standing there ladling eggnog? Emily! It turns out it was her family's country house, and she and Tish had known each other since they were children. I expected the usual cool hello, but when she looked over and saw me, her eyes lit up. She immediately came over and extended her hand. 'Joel, how wonderful to see you here. So you're Eddie's old buddy. Small world!'

"I couldn't believe it! The Snow Queen greeting me like some long-lost friend! We were together all evening. I swear, she was the warmest, sweetest, and yes, nicest, woman I'd ever met. We made plans to see each other back in the city. Later, when I told Tish about Emily's behavior toward me all those months, she told me that Emily was actually quite shy. She said she was a homebody, not interested in a whole lot of people, but very close to her family and a few old friends."

By entering into Emily's familiar world, Joel could see the relaxed, easy, warm side of Emily. And once he became part of that world, Emily could relax and be comfortable with him no matter where they were. They began to date in the city. Emily invited him to her apartment. Joel was impressed by how comfortable and homey she had made it. His place was nondescript—just a place to spend the night. But hers was a nest, a home. The centerpiece was an ebony grand piano, where, Emily told him, she spent some of her happiest hours. Joel asked if she'd play for him. She said no. The piano was a private experience for her, she said, not for entertaining other people. Joel, a highly Dramatic person, was smitten—he was ready to run out and get married by their fourth date. Emily didn't exactly jump into his arms, though. Sensitive types take their time getting to know people, and they're very slow to open up. Several times she had to tell Joel that she wasn't ready to be as serious as he wished. Joel tried not to pressure her, and slowly she grew attached to him. They spent a lot of time with Eddie and Tish and with Emily's family. Eventually she grew comfortable enough to play the piano in his presence. More than two years went by before she agreed to become his wife. They had a small wedding, just the immediate families and a few close friends. Eddie and Tish were the best man and the matron of honor.

Joel and Emily live a quiet life, keeping much to themselves. Emily's career keeps her very busy outside their home, but she returns with pleasure and obvious relief. She tries to avoid socializing with colleagues, but she'll go if Joel will come with her. She prefers not to go to Joel's obligatory functions, but she will if it's important to him. He likes for her to accompany him but occasionally they agree that she'll stay home, if he feels she'll cramp his political style.

Joel likes to travel and Emily always puts up a fuss about going, claiming she's too busy or that she has to plant the garden in the country or some such excuse. But she always has a good time once she overcomes her reluctance. She'd never been to Europe, and Joel finally dragged her to Paris a couple of years ago. She loved it there, although she didn't like going off to sightsee or to shop by herself. They went to Paris again this year, where Joel had a conference. Having been there before, Emily was clearly more relaxed and willing to go out on her own. Joel suggested they go to Italy next year, but Emily says she'd like to return to Paris a third time and really get to know the place.

The Sensitive Explorer

Emily is not a reticent person. In the operating room she quite confidently wields her scalpel. The human body, inside and out, is familiar territory to her, and, like other Sensitive people, she likes to know every detail about everything in her environment. Sensitive types are not dilettantes. The more they know about something, the more they are inspired to know. Emily studies, experiments, learns in her work, in her music, in her gardening, and in her cooking.

Sensitive types prefer to explore the known rather than the unknown. That's why Emily would be happy to return to Paris a third time. Some Sensitive people travel easily within their own regions or within the country but are reluctant to go abroad. Many moderately Sensitive individuals may love to travel, as long as they can go with someone they're used to being with. Others will travel anywhere, as long as they know someone who lives there.

The Counterphobic Sensitive Explorer

In other words, it is usual for the Sensitive style to be content with the known or to search for the familiar within the unfamiliar in order to move farther out into the world. But some Sensitive types reveal an opposite tendency: they leap right into the unknown, despite, or rather because of, their inner anxiety. These Sensitive individuals demonstrate what we call a *counterphobic* coping style.

For example, Mack, a Sensitive travel photographer, had never liked to go off to strange places by himself. He got into that type of photography when an editor friend, thinking he was doing him a favor, offered him an opportunity to cover an African safari. Only Mack's psychiatrist knew the anxiety the offer caused him: Mack was scared to death of going off to a country he'd never been to—a *continent* he'd never set foot on—and having to perform at his best. He was sure he would fail or fall apart or reveal himself a jerk.

Even so, Mack didn't want to turn down the opportunity. He said he'd be terribly disappointed in himself if he let his fears control him. Several times before the departure he was tempted to cancel the whole thing, but he managed to go on the safari and do the piece. The resulting work was so good that Mack received more travel assignments. This result is not untypical for counterphobic Sensitive people; in their efforts to demystify the strange and unfamiliar, and tame the terror, Sensitive types become sharply aware of their environment and what they have to do within it. Mack's anxious attention to the details all around him translated into remarkable photographs.

Mack has been traveling around the world for years now, and he's not as nervous about it as he used to be. Yet still he worries and grows fearful, especially before he sets out. He can't completely explain what he's alarmed about. "I think it's that my feeling of inner safety and security is upset each time I go. Even though nothing bad has ever happened, and even though I'm always glad to have gone, I always feel this dread, this sense of foreboding. I have a very interesting life," Mack acknowledges, "and I guess this is the price I pay. It's ironic—me, a travel photographer—but I never really feel comfortable unless I'm home." And invariably when he travels Mack suffers from constipation; he just can't untie the knots inside himself until he returns home.

Be Prepared

Sensitive men and women are worriers. What if there's a hurricane while we're in the Caribbean? What if I lose my camera? What if the heat goes off while we're away and the pipes burst? What if the babysitter loses our number and can't call to tell us that the baby is sick?

How do Sensitive people deal with the what-if's? If their Sensitivity is extreme, they stay home. If they're like most reasonably Sensitive people, however, they invoke the Boy Scout motto: Be Prepared.

In one way or another, because they can't bear the possibility of surprise, Sensitive people are prepared for any contingency. They generally gather information on everything they're about to undertake. They pack everything they could possibly need on a trip, they call home frequently, they carry an umbrella when there's a chance of rain. They carry numerous guidebooks, phone numbers, extra pairs of glasses. Sensitive Nicole, besides the usual wallet, checkbook, lipstick, and so on, no matter where she goes always carries these items in her pocketbook: a first-aid kit, a Swiss army knife, a whistle (to call for help!), a sewing kit, two checkbooks, allergy pills, and an extra pair of prescription glasses. When she and her family go away, she never fails to overpack. But she's always prepared for everything, she says, and her kids joke that in case they step on a rattlesnake on their upcoming trip to Washington, D.C., Mom will have the antivenom on her!

Nicole's husband, Lawrence, who has a much more complacent personality style, never asked himself, "What if I marry a woman who has to take everything in the world with her when she goes away for the weekend?" After eight years, he finally started to deal with certain realities of married life. Instead of repeating the same old refrain—"For God's sake, Nicole, what do you need all this stuff for?"—he got smart and bought a mini-van.

Inner Journeys

Just because they become uneasy when they're tackling the unfamiliar doesn't mean Sensitive types are not curious or adventurous in their own way. They're avid readers, for example. Surgeon Emily, for one, delights in every word and photograph in *National Geographic,* to which she has subscribed for years. She's a great lover of literature and somehow manages to read at least a novel a month, on top of everything else she has to do.

While they may impose some limits on their physical world, or cross boundaries with discomfort, Sensitive types can often invest an explorer's energy in fantasy, imagination, and creation, their minds and feelings free and easy in the unknowns of "inner space." Emily's piano jazz improvisations transport her (and anyone who happens to be nearby) untold distances. Then there's Sensitive Hugh, an unmarried theoretical physicist. He may have turned down a visiting professorship in China out of reluctance to be so far from home during his sabbatical, yet in his work he explores the existence of undiscovered dimensions, impossible for most mortal minds to begin to comprehend.

RELATIONSHIPS: A FEW FAMILIAR FACES

The Sensitive personality style is other-directed. These people need the approval of others in order to feel best about themselves and comfortable in the world. Individuals with this style genuinely like other people and want them in their lives, but only to a degree. In a warm, solid relationship with one person, or with a small group of friends or family members, their self-confidence peaks. But put Sensitive individuals in a large gathering and they'll begin thinking of ways to excuse themselves and head for home.

Sensitive self-confidence exists in an inverse ratio to the number of people, especially strangers, whom they must endure at one time. Unlike Vigilant types, who tend to doubt strangers until their intentions are known, Sensitive individuals doubt themselves in the presence of people they don't know. They want to feel that they have made a good impression, but as the crowd increases, the number of people to impress becomes overwhelming. They begin to feel self-conscious, to worry that their discomfort will cause them to say something stupid or silly. As the Sensitive style approaches Avoidant personality disorder, the anguish these individuals experience over other people's reactions to them becomes so great that they must refuse all social functions, no matter how much they'd like to go. With more moderate amounts of the style, these people will be most comfortable socializing on the arm of someone else, or if they came alone to hunt out someone that they know, or, failing that, to count the minutes until they can go home.

When they know the people around them and are sure of their affection and respect, Sensitive types are relieved of their social anxieties and their personalities shine forth. Thus, they usually build their lives around a few people around whom they are happy. "You're always welcome here—you're family," they will say to their close friends. But they will be slow to establish new ties. Until they begin to trust a new person's feelings for them, they'll seal off their emotions and confidences behind a polite, well-mannered, emotionally distant facade.

When at last they let down their guard with someone, as Emily did with Joel, the coolness is not likely to return. Sensitive souls are loyal, devoted, and caring. They often marry for life. Those who remain single (like Vigilant-Sensitive Ted in chapter 8, whose Vigilance has kept him from the altar all his life) nonetheless prefer long-term relationships. They settle happily into the comforts of home and the routine of domestic life.

The Facade Problem

Because they are so reticent with new people, extremely Sensitive people can have great difficulty establishing a truly intimate relationship with anyone. They may begin relationships only to see them dissipate and fade away. The problem comes from the Sensitive tendency to hold themselves in reserve and their reticence to be themselves. All Sensitive people are private with their innermost thoughts and feelings. To some extent, they all believe that to impress somebody new they have to put on a facade. Very Sensitive types are sure that if they reveal their so-called true selves, they won't measure up to what the other person wants. So they end up masking what in fact makes them interesting and attractive—their likes and dislikes, their quirks and idiosyncrasies, their very individuality. Sensitive Raul was known among his friends and family for his outrageous sense of humor and his strong opinions. Yet every time he'd take a woman out, he'd stop himself from uttering a single funny comment, lest he "turn her off." And he'd end up agreeing with everything she said rather than state a possibly offensive opinion. Probably because he made himself so bland and uninteresting, and so difficult to know for who he really was, no one he liked continued to go out with him for long.

Sensitive Parents

They're good parents, attentive to their offspring and watchful of their safety. The moderately Sensitive parent will anticipate and protect the kids from the dangers "out there": wear your boots, because it's supposed to snow; don't talk to strangers, because you never know, and if someone bothers you, here's what to do; carry your name and address in your pocket in case you get lost; and so on. These parents will worry that something might happen when the kids go off to camp or to college or out on a date. Similarly, they usually give their children a strong sense of home and family; the kids know they always have a place to turn. The children feel secure and later will look back and appreciate that they were so well cared for and that they learned so well how to take care of themselves. The extremely Sensitive or Avoidant parent, however, must take care not to impose his or her anxieties on the children and make them fearful of taking chances.

Stress!

Stress for this personality style comes from having to brave the unfamiliar. It also comes from criticism. Sensitive men and women care so greatly about how people react to them that disapproval and criticism hurt a lot—although sometimes you'd never know it from their reserved demeanor. They react either by staying clear of the criticizer if he or she is outside their central sphere; or by trying to improve their behavior or performance in order to win back the favor of a person who is important to them.

To deal with the stress of the unknown, Sensitive types cope in one of three ways: they find someone else to brave it with, they back off from the challenge, or, in some cases, they jump right in. This last is a counterphobic coping style mentioned earlier: like Mack the travel photographer, you do what you fear the most in order to master the terror, or at least to avoid being mastered by it. Many Sensitive types, however, are quite happy to structure their lives around comfort and predictability and feel little need to wrestle with their inner demons.

Since Sensitive individuals count on having one close person in their lives to rely on, breakups are highly anxiety provoking. To cope, they'll seek familiar faces. They will be reluctant to get out and meet new people, and they often attempt to return to former relationships. If they have no old loves to take up with, their social reserve may make it hard for them to meet new people and get a relationship going, which they will find very depressing.

Good/Bad Matches

Sensitive types are best off with people who are also family centered but who can take the lead socially and help their mates enjoy an easier social life. Solitary types, who are content to do without others, generally do not match up well with Sensitive individuals.

People who have a balanced combination of Conscientious and a socially comfortable style, such as Self-Confident or Dramatic, have a lot to offer their Sensitive partner. (Emily's husband, Joel, had a predominantly Dramatic-Conscientious-Self-Confident pattern.) Too much Conscientious style, however, may cause the mate to feel rather uncomfortable or awkward socially him- or herself. A mate with an overabundance of Self-Confident style will not be tolerant of the limits the Sensitive person often imposes on his or her universe. Too much Dramatic and the mate will want to be socializing all the time—too stressful for the Sensitive partner.

A Devoted partner will be extremely accepting, but with an abundance of this style he or she may lack the decisiveness to step out and take the lead when the Sensitive mate needs someone to rely on.

Leisurely and Self-Sacrificing individuals may be workable matches for the Sensitive, because they each form strong family ties. A mate with at least some Sensitive, Vigilant, and/or Serious style will be content to live in his or her partner's small world, but each will reinforce the other's social or global discomforts rather than make life easier in that regard.

The Adventurous is among the worst matches for this type, since Adventurers need to take risks and to explore. Idiosyncratic people, interesting though they may be, may intensify the Sensitive's social anxieties. Idiosyncratic eccentricities in dress or behavior may be embarrassing to Sensitive types, who are always careful to conform in company and prefer not to call attention to themselves.

SELF, SELF-CONTROL, AND REAL WORLD: FACING THE UNKNOWN

In the safety of their known worlds, Sensitive individuals have a good sense of who they are and what they can do. Outside these boundaries, however, in the wide world of strangers and in relation to people with whom they are not yet comfortable, they may temporarily lose perspective. Other people become huge, powerful, and potentially threatening, whereas they themselves shrink and weaken or go into hiding. In this "Alice in Wonderland" transformation, Sensitive men and women lose their certainty about themselves.

They have good self-discipline and self-control, though. They use it to shape their behavior and to keep their feelings and discomforts to themselves. The last thing they want to do is make waves and call attention to themselves. Their only risk of self-control problems is if they begin to medicate their social unease with alcohol, recreational drugs, or tranquilizers and come to depend on these substances for "chemical courage." (If appropriately prescribed and their use supervised, however, tranquilizers can be a very useful part of treatment for people with debilitating anxiety.)

To the Sensitive person, the Real World is full of threats. Beyond the limits of their territory, there are beasts in the forest. So they stick close to the hearth, or return relieved after venturing away, and all is safe and well.

WORK: HOME AWAY FROM HOME

Individuals with the Sensitive style bring many good qualities to the workplace—*if* they can build a comfortable work "nest" and find a structured role from which to operate. Then they are reliable, steady, and effective.

Highly Sensitive people work best with few coworkers, with whom in time they become familiar. The workplace, office, or department becomes their little family, their safe haven to which they return day after day. They like to stay put in their jobs, having little need to seek variety for its own sake.

Sensitive types tend to be thorough and they concentrate well on their work. Because they care what other people think of them, they try hard to do good work. They are uneasy dealing with management, unless their workplace is small and has a family-type environment. In general, they don't like to deal with unfamiliar people (they can deal with clients, though; see additional discussion under "Careers"). Some very Sensitive people are reluctant to telephone strangers even in the course of their personal work, such as calling a repairman.

Structure and Role

Contributing to their effectiveness at work is their comfort with routine. Every type of work, in or out of the home, has its daily repetitions. For some personality styles, the Dramatic included, routine is tantamount to drudgery; it saps their strength and motivation. For the Sensitive individual, however, routine provides a welcome structure to the day.

For similar reasons, Sensitive types like defined roles, in which they know what is expected of them and don't have to readjust each day.

Indeed, their vocational roles often provide a welcome identity that they can use in their interactions with others in unfamiliar settings. Radio reporter Rita T. knew how to conduct probing interviews with people for her work. Yet in a social situation, she'd become tongue-tied when trying to talk to a new person. She figured out that if she thought of herself as a reporter even in her private life, she could approach people and ask questions. Celebrities with a strong streak of Sensitive style inching up behind a more "out-there" style—and there are a surprising number of famous people who are certain that as themselves no one would find them appealing—frequently cope with people in just such a way, by carrying their professional personas wherever they go. In fact, Sensitive people role-play automatically. Emily could go to medical conventions and speak comfortably from her role as a surgeon, or to a PTA meeting and chat in her role as parent. But at gatherings that were purely social, she couldn't open her mouth.

The Sensitive Manager

Men and women with this style often are more ambitious on behalf of their work than on their own behalf politically. They'll do the best work they can and are happy to please higher-ups. They may wish to be promoted to management in order to do more challenging work, but they are not eager to increase their exposure to upper management. Sensitive managers do not like to deal with people outside their immediate unit and may appoint a subordinate to act as their liaison. If they also have a counterbalancing socially capable style, though, such as the Dramatic, they'll be able to work the hierarchy—and attend necessary work-related social situations—despite their inner queasiness about exposing their "real" selves.

A Sensitive person can benefit from a long-term relationship with a mentor on whose sensible opinion and guidance he or she can comfortably rely.

Sensitive managers promote a family environment among their own staffs. They will appear aloof and cold to newcomers until they are sure of them and their performance. They work best with staffs in which there is little turnover.

Careers for the Sensitive

If this is your predominant style, seek a career in which you have a defined role—an accountant, a computer programmer, or a doctor, for example—and in which your exposure to the public is limited or your interactions are structured. Sensitive individuals may do well with clients because they can take refuge in professionalism, which allows them to be involved with their clients' interests yet not emotionally involved. But Sensitive types are uneasy with strangers whom they must consult or influence. So steer clear of such fields as contracting, public relations, or sales, for example. Also avoid jobs or careers that will require public speaking.

Due to the Sensitive style's ease with routine, repetition, and habit, as well as their ability to concentrate, they do very well in the technological fields.

TIPS ON DEALING WITH THE
SENSITIVE PERSON IN YOUR LIFE

1. Count your blessings. Treasure the closeness and loyalty that your Sensitive person offers you. Recognize that you are among a favored few in this person's life. Appreciate the home life this person makes possible and his or her dedication to friendship and family values.

2. Accept the Sensitive person complete with shortcomings. If your Sensitive mate becomes stiff or withdrawn among strangers or is otherwise not him- or herself in company, so what? It's no reflection on you.

3. Avoid emotional torture. Don't insist that a Sensitive person do things he or she shuns just to please you. Sensitive individuals want you to be happy with them, but there are some things they just can't stand doing. The reluctance has nothing to do with you, so don't hold it against your Sensitive friend or partner. If you like to socialize or to ski, for example, and the Sensitive person in your life prefers to stay home, consider going by yourself occasionally. Sensitive people often are happy to spend time alone, as long as there's someone in their lives whom they will soon be with again.

4. Compromise. If you want to fly to Thailand for vacation and your not-so-adventurous Sensitive companion wants to stay closer to home, consider a third alternative—perhaps going to a country where he or she can understand the language. Sensitive people want to please the important people in their lives, so your willingness to compromise may encourage them to take a few steps farther out than they would ordinarily go.

5. Help. Act as a guide to the unfamiliar. Go to social events with this person and accompany him or her on jaunts into unfamiliar territory. But don't overdo it. You want to help this person overcome certain limitations, not to make him or her dependent on you. Reassure, encourage, and praise every step forward. Remember that if you can help this person over a few barriers, you'll both have a good time, and your Sensitive partner, family member, or friend will remember the experience with pleasure.

6. Recognize the signs. You're both due to leave for a dinner with your new boss and his wife. Your Sensitive companion suddenly feels ill, gets cranky, or is late getting ready. Avoid a fight. Say, "I'll bet you're nervous about tonight." Reassure the Sensitive person that everyone is going to like him or her—what's not to like?

7. Talk about it. If the Sensitive person's anxieties are cramping your style, don't keep it to yourself. Don't attack your loved one for having these difficulties. Rather, express the problems openly and directly. Say you are interested in finding a solution that accommodates both of you.

MAKING THE MOST OF YOUR SENSITIVE STYLE

Your love of the familiar allows you to build a comfortable personal environment. It could get you into a rut, too, so practice a little preventive medicine.

Exercise 1

Do something different. Every once in a while, change one or more of your routines just for the sake of change. Try a new restaurant, take a different route to work, rearrange the furniture in your living room, take a different kind of vacation—anything.

You Sensitives are worriers and get yourselves tied up in knots. Refer to Exercise 1 for the Vigilant personality style (p. 172): Relax. Concentrate especially on meditation techniques, which are very helpful in managing anxiety.

You're likable, friendly, warm, loyal, imaginative, kind—but your "danger-alert system" is extremely sensitive. The following exercises introduce numerous methods of taming, bypassing, or even mastering your particular anxieties.

Exercise 2

Do it anyway. The less you expose yourself to uncomfortable situations, the harder it will be to overcome the anxiety in the future. Conversely, the more you expose yourself, the easier it is to dissolve the discomfort. So do what it is you would prefer to avoid. Every time you find yourself tempted to avoid a challenge or to refuse an opportunity because of your anxiety, do the opposite. If somebody invites you to a party and you are inclined to say no, say yes: go. If you want to leave the party, stay. Take small steps—don't expect to conquer everything in one leap. Give yourself credit for even the tiniest progress.

Exercise 3

Be who you are. Your imperfections give you character and make you interesting and appealing. It's your efforts to hide your human imperfections that make you stiff, uncomfortable, and possibly unapproachable. If you accept your flaws, others may find it easier to accept you with them.

Exercise 4

Stay inside yourself. Many Sensitive people look at themselves as if through other people's eyes. When playing the piano, you think that the neighbors think you're playing terribly. When you give a speech, you think the audience thinks you're stupid and uninteresting. When you're at a social gathering, you think that the stranger you're talking to thinks you're boring. You try to change your behavior or performance in order to please someone *you think* is criticizing you. You're guaranteed to lose your concentration on your task at hand each time you start focusing on other people's thoughts about you. You end up hitting the wrong note, losing your place in your speech, finding yourself at a loss for words. Every time you find yourself thinking about what another person is thinking, immediately stop those thoughts and continue with what you are doing. Like most of these exercises, this one gets easier with practice.

Exercise 5

When you have the feeling that people are looking at you in an uncomplimentary way, ask yourself whether that feeling might be coming from you. Are you feeling insecure? Are you feeling negative about yourself and therefore thinking that other people are thinking negative things about you? Realize that your self-consciousness comes from inside yourself. Other people have better things to do than stop and evaluate you.

Exercise 6

When talking to somebody, periodically look him or her in the eye. Reluctance or inability to establish eye contact can indicate that you feel in some way threatened by that person. But if you can establish moments of eye contact despite your discomfort, you'll find it easier to gain acceptance and confidence. If you can't do it, at least hold your head higher, so that it's not comfortable to look down at the floor; this posture also signals confidence to others and perhaps you'll even begin to feel a little more certain after a while.

Exercise 7

Every time someone criticizes you, stand back from yourself and observe how you (over)react. Check to see whether you are equating criticism with hate or rejection. Imagine that you are turning a knob that will modulate the volume of your inner reaction.

Exercise 8

Do what you *can* do. Perhaps you'd like to go off to Bora Bora but you just can't get yourself to do it on your own. Rather than spend another vacation at home, consider going to Florida to stay with your cousin. You can't face going to a singles' place to meet someone new, but maybe you can ask a friend to fix you up with somebody. Ask yourself what you *can* do in every situation in which you feel limited or stuck.

Exercise 9

Sensitive anxiety is only a feeling (albeit an unpleasant one); it signals a dangerous inner state, not an outer reality—so have faith that things will work out. For example, if you're afraid of flying because you think the plane will crash or you'll make a fool of yourself by screaming hysterically, rise above it into a "faith mode." Have faith that planes almost always stay in the air, that you will behave appropriately, that you are and will be accepted and liked by many people—in other words, have faith that you are as protected as the next person from most disastrous happenings. Have faith in yourself.

Exercise 10

If you rely on your spouse to help you through unpleasant experiences or to do things for you that you hate or are reluctant to do, try giving your partner a break. Stop and see it from his or her point of view. You may not realize that you may strain the limits of your partner's tolerance by having him or her take over for you. For example, some Sensitive people don't like to drive, so their mates end up being the family chauffeur. While the Sensitive person may be grateful to be relieved of this discomfort, he or she may not comprehend the burden this places on the other person. Avoid a crisis in your relationship by understanding the hardship you may be forcing on your loved one. Consider attempting to deal with your anxiety instead of having him or her protect you from it.

AVOIDANT PERSONALITY DISORDER

The unhappy individuals with Avoidant personality disorder are always on the outside looking in. They yearn to be involved with other people, but they can't endure the feeling that they get around others—that they're unacceptable, incapable of being loved, and, unaccountably, incapable of being any different. So they withdraw, in order to survive.

DIAGNOSTIC CRITERIA

The DSM-IV describes Avoidant personality disorder as:

A pervasive pattern of social inhibition, feelings of inadequacy, and hypersensitivity to negative evaluation beginning by early adulthood and present in a variety of contexts, as indicated by four (or more) of the following:

(1) avoids occupational activities that involve significant inter-personal contact, because of fears of criticism, disapproval, or rejection

(2) is unwilling to get involved with people unless certain of being liked

(3) shows restraint within intimate relationships because of the fear of being shamed or ridiculed

(4) is preoccupied with being criticized or rejected in social situations

(5) is inhibited in new interpersonal situations because of feelings of inadequacy

(6) views self as socially inept, personally unappealing, or inferior to others

(7) is unusually reluctant to take personal risks or to engage in
any new activities because they may prove embarrassing

DAMNED IF YOU DO,
DAMNED IF YOU DON'T

Avoidant men and women are trapped in a most distressing universe.
They're so afraid of being rejected by other people, and so convinced
that they will be, that they retreat from others to spare themselves the
agony they anticipate. When they can't avoid others, they stand aloof,
looking down or away rather than making contact. As a result, they live
socially impoverished lives. The painful irony for people with this personality disorder is that although the avoidance of close relationships
relieves them of the anxiety of waiting for the rejecting ax to fall, it
removes them from what they deeply (and sometimes unconsciously)
desire: the acceptance, approval, and love of other people. Unlike people with Schizoid personality disorder (chapter 13), who don't want
anything to do with others, Avoidant individuals are lonely loners; they
are aching to be a part of things, if only they knew how.

No wonder they withdraw: their experiences with other people are
like recurring nightmares. On one hand, they are sure that others are
going to treat them badly. On the other hand, their awkward self-
consciousness is indeed off-putting. What Avoidant people fear seems
always to happen: people don't accept them. In truth, others don't
know what to make of Avoidant people. Because of their detachment,
others often conclude that Avoidant people are cold and don't want to
be included.

So, Avoidant individuals feel isolated, unwanted, painfully different,
and incompetent no matter what they do. Emotionally, they rarely feel
comfortable. If they're not anxious, they're depressed—often they are
both. But at least when they are away from others they don't have to
experience that terrible anticipation of humiliation and rejection.

LOVE ME UNCONDITIONALLY

Like Paranoid men and women, Avoidant individuals have highly sensitive "danger-alert systems." They are always on the lookout for criticism or disapproval. The problem is that even the smallest signs—one cross word or a strange look—will sound the alarm. Avoidant individuals are so oversensitive to negative and even neutral evaluation that anything less than total, open acceptance feels like rejection. The expectations of relationships are immature and unrealistic. They believe that acceptance means unconditional love. They believe that people who care for each other never become angry with each other, never point out flaws, never hurt each other, and always accept each other without reservation.

At the same time, they believe that to be accepted and loved, one can have no imperfections. When Avoidant people walk into a room full of people, they are hyperaware of their inabilities and flaws—not least of which is their inability to compete and succeed socially—and they are terrified that they might reveal themselves for the "defective" individuals they are. They don't realize that the vast majority of people experience at least some social anxiety and that great numbers find it very upsetting. In one study, for example, 40 percent of late adolescents and young adults believed that social anxiety was a big part of their personalities; one of the authors of that study concludes that 15 to 20 percent of all adults experience distressing social anxiety. Avoidant individuals are convinced that they are horribly different from others. They enter a social situation just waiting to be found out. What if people think there's something wrong with them? What if they blush and reveal their discomfort? What if they say something stupid or seem uninformed? What if they forget somebody's name? Their self-consciousness is unremitting; they anxiously scan other people, as it sinks in once again that they have not achieved total unconditional acceptance and love from anyone. With such a painfully distorted inner world, it follows that individuals suffering from Avoidant personality disorder have a great deal of difficulty experiencing real love, for others or for themselves. They feel contempt for themselves, anger toward others.

CREATURES OF HABIT

Escape from anxiety is the motivating force in their daily lives. Individuals with Avoidant personality disorder develop fixed routines. Day after day they do the same things the same way. By sticking to their routines they prevent having to deal with surprises. If they are asked or are tempted to alter their patterns, they will focus on the risks and dangers and blow them far out of proportion. For example, Joe A.'s mother asked him to travel to another city to straighten out a matter concerning his father's estate. He said he would take care of it. A few days before he was supposed to go, he read about an outbreak of flu in that city and began to worry that he would catch it. What if he got so sick he couldn't come back? What if he died? What if he caught it and gave it to his mother and she died? He canceled the trip. Joe's brother went in his place.

Their comfort with routine can serve some Avoidant people well in the workplace, but only if they don't feel that they have to be involved with their coworkers or to deal with the public, and only if they do not become so preoccupied with their anxiety that they can't concentrate. Unfortunately, their lack of assertiveness usually counteracts any significant progress they might accomplish in their careers. They usually can work alongside others, but they generally remain aloof and to their coworkers seem anything from standoffish to cold to strange to painfully shy.

However, their work habits are sometimes a boon to creative production. Avoidant individuals, like their Sensitive-style counterparts, can often find freedom by turning inward and allowing creative imagination to take them far away from their anxieties.

AVOIDANT PERSONALITY DISORDER OR SOCIAL PHOBIA?

There is currently much debate within the psychiatric community about whether Avoidant personality disorder isn't really a severe form of social phobia, an Axis I anxiety disorder. People with Avoidant personality disorder suffer many of the same symptoms as do those with the generalized form of social phobia: extreme anxiety in all settings in which they might be evaluated by others, with physical symptoms such as sweating and shortness of breath as well as self-deprecation and fear of humiliating themselves. The condition, once thought rare, is now recognized as the third most common mental disorder among Americans. People who suffer from it can be extremely hampered in their occupational and social lives. Many social phobia experts are adamant that what we call a personality disorder ceases upon successful intervention for social phobia. Treatment consists of short-term cognitive-behavioral psychotherapy and/or medications, including antidepressants (particularly the type known as monoamine oxidase, or

MAO, inhibitors, such as Nardil; or the selective serotonin reuptake inhibitors, or SSRIs, of which Prozac is one example), and benzodiazepine tranquilizers (such as Xanax).

Others suggest that people with Avoidant personality disorder are extraordinarily vulnerable to social phobia, as they are to other anxiety disorders (about which more below). One study has found that 22 percent of people with social phobia also received a diagnosis of Avoidant personality disorder. (The social phobia contingent argues that the two conditions occur together as much as 90 percent of the time.) Some contend that those who fail to recover from social phobia after adequate treatment are in fact suffering from Avoidant personality disorder and require additional treatment.

RISKS, PREDISPOSITIONS, AND INCIDENCE

Human beings are social animals. Our physical and emotional welfare and well-being depend in large measure on the social supports and bonds we form with one another. Their lack of satisfactory ties to other people may make Avoidant men and women especially vulnerable to numerous Axis I mental health problems. Most prominent among these are mood and anxiety disorders, including panic disorder, agoraphobia, and especially, as mentioned above, social phobia. Alcohol and substance abuse problems are a substantial risk. Other personality disorders that commonly occur along with Avoidant include Dependent, Borderline, and Paranoid, Schizoid, or Schizotypal.

Avoidant personality disorder, to which men and women are equally vulnerable, occurs in about 1 percent of the population, and in 10 percent of patients of outpatient mental health clinics.

Inborn temperament may predispose an individual to the development of this personality disorder. Psychiatrists Alexander Thomas and Stella Chess have identified the "slow-to-warm-up" temperament in 15 percent of children in their important studies (see chapter 18). These children do not respond comfortably or adapt quickly to new stimuli. In combination with their experiences with their parents, siblings, and peers, their temperaments may make them vulnerable to this disorder as they grow up. At the Harvard Infant Study Laboratory, psychologist Jerome Kagan has found as well that 15 percent of children are born dispositionally inhibited and shy; current research indicates that this inhibition predicts anxiety disorders later, perhaps eventually Avoidant personality disorder as well. Anxiety disorders do run in families.

"Allergic" to Anxiety

Everyone experiences anxiety—those butterflies in the stomach, the wide-open eyes, the pounding heart, the sweaty palms—but people who suffer from Avoidant personality disorder are unusually sensitive to that state of physical arousal. Anxiety is the body's physiological response to threat, actual or imagined. Everyone responds by becoming tense and alert, among other natural reactions. But Avoidant people become extremely tense, overalert; they are flooded with anxiety, and to stem their overreaction, they withdraw from the source.

There is some evidence to suggest that genetically or constitutionally the nervous systems of some individuals with this disorder may be more aroused than the norm. When some stimulus from the environment arouses them even further, they go into "overload." (The brains of individuals with Antisocial personality disorder may be underaroused, so the theory goes; thus they may seek thrills to "wake up" their nervous systems; see chapter 11.)

HELP!

People with Avoidant personality disorder are luckier than they may think. Their problems can be approached in many ways, including the very practical methods for desensitizing their anxiety, for learning social skills, and for consciously changing some of their self-destructive thinking patterns. These are some of the methods that are used to treat social phobia, and the medications that are prescribed for that condition (p. 199) can be useful for Avoidant personality disorders as well. Keep in mind that not any tranquilizer or antidepressant will do; medication is best prescribed by a psychiatrist expert in the pharmacotherapy of anxiety.

Psychotherapy can be highly beneficial for the Avoidant person who has the courage to face—instead of running away from—his or her problems. The empathic psychotherapist will appreciate how difficult it is for this person to trust and open up and will not push the patient into going faster than he or she can. In time, the Avoidant patient may grow more self-confident, may be able to make some changes in the constricting routines of his or her life, and may be willing to explore the past, with the help of the therapist. Often the history of Avoidant individuals reveals that they were humiliated or shamed or made to feel guilty or inadequate by their parents, or that they could not always count on their parents for comfort and protection. They grew up feeling insecure and bad about themselves and therefore could move neither confidently out into the world nor closer to other people.

Group therapy can enable some Avoidant individuals to deal with their feelings about themselves and other people and to learn how to relate to others.

COPING WITH AVOIDANT PEOPLE

Because Avoidant people withdraw from others, unless you are part of their families few of you will find yourself deeply involved with an Avoidant person. The way to cope is to recognize the reality of Avoidant anxiety and sensitivity to criticism and how it impairs these people. To deal with the mildly Avoidant person, consult the tips on p. 192–93. Otherwise, be very kind and reassuring and completely accepting. But don't start doing for them what they are afraid to do for themselves. Instead, encourage them to seek professional help.

And look around. See how many people you encounter in your life (at work, for example) who fit the Avoidant description: aloof, ill at ease, awkward, tense. Instead of dismissing these people as cold or unfriendly, take a second look. Maybe they really would like you to befriend them. Reach out.

CHAPTER 10

Leisurely Style

"CALIFORNIA DREAMING"

Free to be me—no one can take away this right from a person who has a Leisurely personality style. These men and women play by the rules and fulfill their responsibilities and obligations. But once they've put in their time, they will let no person, institution, or even culture deprive them of their personal pursuit of happiness, for to the Leisurely person this is what life is all about. Some Leisurely individuals find their happiness through creative pursuits, some by relaxing with a good book. What's important to them is not how they choose to enjoy themselves but that they are guaranteed this opportunity. If threatened, these normally easygoing individuals will vigorously defend their fundamental right to do their "own thing."

THE SEVEN CHARACTERISTICS

The following seven traits and behaviors are clues to the presence of the Leisurely style. A person who reveals a strong Leisurely tendency will demonstrate more of these behaviors more intensely than someone with less of this style in his or her personality profile.

1. *Inalienable rights.* Leisurely men and women believe in their right to enjoy themselves on their own terms in their own time. They value and protect their comfort, their free time, and their individual pursuit of happiness.

2. *Enough is enough.* They agree to play by the rules. They deliver

what is expected of them and no more. They expect others to recognize and respect that limit.

3. *The right to resist.* Leisurely individuals cannot be exploited. They can comfortably resist acceding to demands that they deem unreasonable or above and beyond the call of duty.

4. *Mañana.* Leisurely men and women are relaxed about time. Unlike Type-A individuals, they are not obsessed by time urgency or the demands of the clock. To these individuals, haste makes waste and unnecessary anxiety. They are easygoing and optimistic that whatever needs to get done will get done, eventually.

5. *I'm okay.* They are not overawed by authority. They accept themselves and their approach to life.

6. *Wheel of fortune.* Leisurely people believe that they are just as good as everyone else and as entitled to the best things in life. They maintain that blind luck often accounts for who fares well and who fares poorly.

7. *Mixed feelings.* Although they feel impelled to proceed in their own direction, when their choices put them in conflict with the people they care for, Leisurely people are often of two minds about how to proceed. They do not like to risk important relationships, yet they need to feel free.

THE SIX DOMAINS OF LEISURELY FUNCTIONING

Leisurely is another "double domain" style. For individuals with this not-uncommon style, their domains of Self and of Relationships together are key to their personal destinies.

SELF: THE RIGHT TO BE ME

The inviolable independence of the self is the first priority for Leisurely individuals. They have the God-given right to be who they are, to feel good, to pursue their own pleasures and comforts in their own way, and no person or institution can take these rights away from them. If the Conscientious style is associated with the high-powered East Coast and the inevitable question, "What do you do?"—then the Leisurely style is more a relaxed West Coast personality stereotype, associated with the question, "What are you into?" But no matter where they are found, Leisurely men and women believe in themselves and in their inalienable right to use their personal time however they choose.

They can operate well within systems—the family, the workplace, the community; indeed, they need these complexes of other people in order to fulfill their basic human needs. But they do not identify with any outer authority. Unlike the Conscientious person, who has a strong superego and works extra-hard to be an upstanding member of the work force, the family, and the community, the Leisurely person carries no such weighty, self-critical burdens. After meeting his or her obligations, including those to the family, the Leisurely person turns to what is most important: the pursuit of his or her private pleasure in life, be it sports, art, contemplating nature, or drinking a beer and watching TV.

Unlike Self-Confident types, who feel that they are inherently special, better than others, closer to the center of the universe than most people, Leisurely people perceive that along with everybody else they are small cogs in the cosmic wheel. That's okay with them; Leisurely folks are comfortable with themselves. But even small cogs are entitled to lucky breaks—which is how Leisurely people perceive the differences between the haves and have-nots. They dream of winning the lottery, and they send in their ten-million-dollar sweepstakes entries—why not? It could happen.

Most of all, they feel entitled to be happy, and Leisurely individuals claim this right vigorously. Leisurely individuals will not enslave themselves to anyone or anything or substitute anyone else's values for their own. They have a role to play, a job to do, certain services to perform. But they are independent and separate, subject to their own dictates. Leisurely individuals do their part, but beyond that they are free to feel good privately.

RELATIONSHIPS:
YOU DON'T OWN ME

People who have a predominance of this personality style are deeply entwined with other people. They are family oriented and comfortable in groups. They like or even need to be taken care of, and they enter into relationships easily. At the same time, like Vigilant types they are vaguely suspicious of others, especially of people in authority. Leisurely types expect others to ask too much of them. But while Vigilant people stand emotionally clear of people until they are certain their autonomy is assured, Leisurely men and women have a greater immediate need of companionship as well as a foolproof defense against being ill-used: If anyone asks them to sacrifice their self-determination, they simply re-fuse. Leisurely individuals are very skilled at saying no. They'll use the word as often as they must to ensure that they hold on to their own identities and the right to lead their lives their own way.

Some men with this style might come off as "macho" or "male chau-vinist," like Archie Bunker on the old *All in the Family* TV series. Archie went to work, provided for his family, and saw himself as a responsible, upstanding citizen. But he led his life the way he wanted when his workday was finished. After dinner, he did his own thing—sat in *his* chair to watch TV, went out to a bar with his buddies, whatever he pleased. Edith (a Self-Sacrificing type if there ever was one; see chap-ter 15) rarely interfered with anything that gave her husband pleasure—and life functioned smoothly for them as long as she played by these rules. Archie was created as a caricature of a disagreeable, if comic, old-fashioned Leisurely guy. Leisurely types, both male and female, in real life need not be intimidating, rigid, or unpleasant—but within their relationships they will always be protective of their individual free-doms. And unlike Archie Bunker, they're likely to experience emotional pain when their desires and those of their loved ones conflict. Usually they'll go their own way in the end, but not without a lot of soul searching and even guilt.

Phyllis Wants to Change the Rules; Suzannah Wants Anton

Anton Z. is a fairly well-known artist. He is glad to be selling his paintings, finally, but he understands that recognition for an artist is often short-lived. He's never catered to the whims of any authority, the art market included, and he never will. He's forty-seven, and his art is his joy and meaning in life. He'll get by whether he sells or he doesn't sell; all he needs is the time to paint. Suzannah, his wife, has her own catering business, which has seen them through the rough times. Her business pays for their son's private school. Anton wouldn't mind if the child went to public school, but Suzannah wants smaller classes and a more persona! environment for their son, so she pays for it.

Suzannah is Anton's second wife. They've been married for twelve years. They met shortly after Anton's first wife, Phyllis, had left him. Phyllis had gotten fed up with Anton. As she saw it, she was the one who had to go out and work, who had to cook and clean up, when "all Anton ever did was hang out in his studio and paint that *stuff*." Phyllis believed that if Anton would only paint the kinds of pictures people were buying at the time, he could earn a good living and treat her better. Anton agreed that if he prostituted himself to the market, they'd be much better off financially. If others were making it now, it was just a matter of luck, not talent, he told her contemptuously. But he was an artist, dedicated not to money but to creation. In that he would never change, he told his young, disillusioned wife. And he pointed out that he had never promised her any other life. Since the day they'd met, back when she was nineteen and he was twenty-eight, had he ever said he'd do anything besides paint his own way?

"Well, no," Phyllis had conceded, "but I thought you'd be discovered and get famous and it would all be okay."

How romantic it had been for Phyllis, just out of high school, to meet this tall, big-boned, long-haired, intellectual artist and to live *la vie bohème*. She loved taking care of her man, cooking inexpensive stews, ironing his shirts, sleeping next to him on a mattress on the floor of his loft. Five days a week she went to work as a secretary at a plumbing supply company. Seven nights a week she dined by candlelight with her young genius. They lived together before they were married, which her parents had tolerated. But when Phyllis told them she and Anton had decided to get married, they objected. "What will you live on?" they wanted to know. "What kind of future can this man offer you?"

Phyllis was twenty. These questions meant little to her. Her needs at that age were few—to be with and take care of the most exciting man she had ever known. "I know Anton will be a great artist," she told her parents proudly. "And anyway, he can always go out and get a job."

Four years later, Phyllis was tired of all the hard, dreary work. So Anton had his art. Big deal. Nobody was buying. "A job?" He looked at her as if she were crazy. "Why should I get a job?"

"Because I'm sick of doing everything," Phyllis cried. "What kind of a life do you think this is for me? I don't even have any decent clothes. We can't afford to go to a movie or eat out."

That's when Anton pointed out that nothing at all had changed. It's not as if things had taken a turn for the worse, that he'd started withholding anything from her, that he'd stopped caring for her. He loved her and their life together as much as he ever had—he regretted that what they'd had was collapsing.

Over the next few weeks, Anton wavered between guilt and contrition (maybe he did owe it to her to make a better living; maybe her unhappiness was his fault) and anger and determination. (No! I won't get a job—I can't give up my art!) Finally, after one last confrontation, Anton told Phyllis that if she wanted to be with him, this was the deal. He wanted her to stay, he said, but he'd never be anybody except who he was.

Phyllis decided she wanted something different out of life. Anton was very unhappy without her but despite renewed agonizing he didn't try to get her back. What was the point? She would never be happy sharing his life, and he wouldn't be happy living any other way.

Suzannah, on the other hand, wanted nothing more than to share Anton's life. She was much older than Phyllis—the same age as Anton, in fact. She had built a satisfying career for herself but had not found a man she loved enough to marry, until she met Anton. She was mature enough to recognize that Anton was always going to be himself—he was not going to change. She admired his dedication to his art and his belief in himself no matter how well or how badly things were going for him success-wise. Unlike Phyllis, Suzannah loved Anton's work. She understood it, was moved by it, and felt that what he painted and his ideas about art strengthened the bond between them. After making love, Suzannah and Anton often ended up in passionate discussions about art that took them through the wee hours of the morning.

It mattered little to Suzannah that Anton had not achieved success and perhaps never would. She could take care of the two of them if need be.

And she knew that he loved her. One look at the tender, loving portraits of Suzannah he began painting was enough to tell the world how he felt about her. Once his art was understood and accepted, Anton could be a generous, appreciative, grateful, kind, fun-loving, passionate man. He was very physical and loved to hold Suzannah tightly in his arms.

Suzannah determined that no matter what, she would never try to change Anton or to mold him to a different standard. But it wasn't always easy to avoid frustration. Anton, typical of the Leisurely style, could dig in his heels. Because he was finishing an important painting, he wouldn't come home from his studio to let the exterminator in when they had a terrible invasion of cockroaches and Suzannah had to cater a large luncheon. He left most child-care responsibilities to her, especially when their son was an infant, and he wouldn't ever cook or clean up. He procrastinated so much over the income taxes that Suzannah finally took charge of them. He'd always feel contrite, but not enough to change his ways.

"All right, so I make more compromises than he does," Suzannah says. "Perhaps I do more work to keep the relationship going and the family functioning. So what? I can handle these things. My husband gives me so much love and feeling, and such great art—and he's so grateful that I allow him the time to devote to his work—well, I feel so lucky in my life. I don't believe you can measure a marriage in terms of who does how much of what. I do what I can do. Anton does what he can do. We are both happy and productive. What more could I want?"

Mara Says: "You're Lazy!"
Jonathan Says: "You're Driven!"

Suzannah has never viewed her husband as lazy or irresponsible. Phyllis, however, to this day tells tales of her "lazy, good-for-nothing, daydreaming ex-husband." People with the Leisurely personality style often appear lazy to those who do not share their values. It's not laziness, however. It's the Leisurely insistence that a large portion of their time is absolutely their own to use as they please, free of any outside encumbrance. They are not rebels, mavericks, or angrily defiant individuals. If someone tries to force them into something that they consider above and beyond the call of duty, they won't argue or yell; they'll simply refuse.

Jonathan, as we learned in chapter 1, is married to Mara. They are both high-school teachers. Mara always takes private tutoring jobs during the long summer holiday. Jonathan refuses to take summer work. He chose teaching, he says, because he likes to have the summer off. To him, that's worth the whole rest of the year. "But you don't *do* anything with the time," complains Conscientious Mara. "What you mean"—Jonathan corrects her—"is that I don't do anything that *you* want me to do, like all the laundry and cooking and housecleaning. I do garden, as you know, and I read a lot, and I walk in the woods, and I paint watercolors. I contribute as much to the household chores as I do the rest of the year. I'm busy all day, but not productive in the ways that you would be if you were here.

"Listen," he adds, "you don't have to take on the extra work in summer. We'd get by. You *want* to work all year."

Mara acknowledges that Jonathan is right. She's too Conscientious just to putter around. She thinks it's important to work and work hard. Jonathan's a good teacher, but he doesn't spend much time at school after the day is over. Mara, on the other hand, makes herself available to advise students in various extracurricular activities. She has a terrible time accepting the differences in their approach to their work, and, try as she might, she persists in judging him as lazy.

Theirs is a clash in personality styles and value systems. Jonathan says, "Work is a means to an end, not the end itself." Mara says, "Work, what you *do,* is what's important in life." Jonathan does what he must. Mara gives as much as she can. But she's growing tired, as Phyllis did, of giving so much. They've been married less than three years, and unless Jonathan changes—which appears doubtful, because Mara wants him to change what he sees as the core of himself—or unless Mara learns to accept his personality style, their future looks cloudy.

Good/Bad Matches

People who have a very strong Leisurely style need accepting, under-standing, giving mates who are content to be in orbit around them. Leisurely types will not put the needs of the relationship first, and they will not go too far out of their way to please people, except as a brief act of contrition. But they do value their relationships, they like being cared for, and all will be well if their partners accept the responsibility not only for keeping the relationship together, but for doing what may seem like more than a fair share of chores. Then they will prove respon-sive, appreciative, loyal, and loving mates. But their partners will need to have a strong degree of either the Devoted or the Self-Sacrificing style to tolerate the Leisurely person's fundamental self-interest. Suzannah's personality had strength in both these styles as well as in the Conscien-tious style.

People whose personalities are unquestionably dominated by Consci-entious style, however, should look elsewhere. The problems that Mara is having with Jonathan are typical of Conscientious-Leisurely mis-matches; strongly Conscientious types simply can't accept a Leisurely person's approach to life. They get involved with each other in the first place in part because Conscientious people are doers and their ability to take care of the nasty details of life is very attractive to a Leisurely person. The Leisurely person's gratitude flatters the Conscientious per-son. But eventually the honeymoon is over, and their differences start to draw blood. Neither style is much good at compromising, and each wants the other to do things *my* way.

Similar problems may develop between Self-Confident and Leisurely people. Anton's young first wife, Phyllis, grew into her Self-Confident personality style during their brief marriage. When the drudgery of her life supplanted the dreams of her adolescence, she Self-Confidently ex-pected Anton to abandon his lifestyle to suit her needs.

Leisurely and Vigilant people often feel comfortable with each other's worldview, since they both mistrust authority. The Vigilant person will be very responsible and take care of things that need to be done in case the Leisurely person lets them slide. A Leisurely person may be attracted to another Leisurely person, and each will respect the other's rights, but they both like to be taken care of, so at least one of them will need strength as well in the Devoted or the Self-Sacrificing style; also, one of them must be able to take charge when less desirable things need to be done.

Somewhat Serious mates provide the sense of resigned responsibility that can help keep the relationship together. Even if the Serious partner feels put upon, he or she does not necessarily expect life to be rewarding. The Serious mate will likely support the highly Leisurely person's belief that people who have it better just have more luck, as well as their passive wishfulness (if only I could win the lottery). Serious mates may not be able to share in the Leisurely partner's all-important pleasures, though, but they won't prevent him or her from pursuing them. Very Leisurely people who pair off with Serious mates will find themselves sharing a very sour attitude toward those who "have all the luck."

Leisurely individuals will not be comfortable in matches with emotionally demanding styles, including the Dramatic and the Mercurial. Relationships with Sensitive types may work, unless the Leisurely person can't be there for the Sensitive one when he or she needs support to face personal challenges.

The Adventurous style, like the Leisurely, is a pleasure-seeking style. But Leisurely folks need to play by the rules, and Adventurous types prefer to break them, so forget this match.

Leisurely Parents

They're responsible breadwinners who are concerned about their children's basic needs. Their family life is a significant source of pleasure and is important to them. Leisurely parents have a gift for enjoying themselves and can share in their children's lives more memorably when they are all having a plain old wonderful time.

Leisurely parents tend to believe that what is best for them is best for the children, so they do not generally go out of their way to adapt to their children's needs or wants if these are different from their own—a traditional parenting style. But they are not inflexible and will bend if someone can get through to them that they must. As the Leisurely style becomes Passive-Aggressive personality disorder, though, Dad or Mom will be less likely to comprehend that the child could possibly have different needs. The parent will be remembered as a stubborn and selfish person, more interested in his or her own comfort than in the child's welfare. With luck, this child will have one non-Leisurely parent who will be more attentive.

WORK: IT'S JUST A JOB

Predominantly Leisurely types often run into the same clash of values at work as in their personal relationships. They tend not to be get-ahead types, since they work not for the sake of fame or success but for security, for a pension, to finance their pursuit of pleasure, or just to have fun. Leisurely individuals are cooperative, good workers, but they don't take work home, they don't worry about it after hours, they won't do work that they do not believe is their responsibility, and they won't do more than what is asked of them to please the boss or to feel better about themselves. They feel just fine about themselves. However, they don't necessarily see that their lack of apparent ambition and unwillingness to prove their dedication to their work might account for why they receive less approval, encouragement, or rewards than their colleagues or coworkers who do go that extra distance. And they may resent another person's success as unjustified. Still, they fulfill the requirements and can take pride in what they do. But they generally don't find their meaning in life in the workplace and they will not allow themselves to be exploited by someone who does.

With a mixed personality pattern consisting of Conscientious and/or Self-Confident trends along with the Leisurely, however, many people do manage to find pleasure somewhere in the workplace. Some, like Anton, will be able to merge business and pleasure. This is easiest to accomplish in creative work, which can be highly and immediately pleasurable. Others will find pleasure in some aspects of their work (while putting off the rest of it). For example, Alexander, the accountant suffering a midlife crisis whom we discussed in chapters 1 and 6, loved the client-relations part of his work. He spent hours talking to his clients when he should have been preparing their tax forms. He'd have to sprint toward the tax-filing deadline in a last-minute frenzy. Still other Leisurely types with mixed patterns will be fortunate enough to discover rewarding activities that are incidental to what they were hired to do. Jay E., who is also an accountant, found happiness on the company baseball team. His colleagues and supervisors think he's a so-so accountant but a truly inspired pitcher. Jay lives for baseball season.

"It's Not My Job"

This is the oft-heard refrain of a Leisurely employee when a boss demands work that is above and beyond the call of the Leisurely person's job responsibilities. This attitude often annoys employers or supervisors, because people in authority usually expect their employees to share their dedication and values, even though they receive a smaller share of the rewards. But the Leisurely person may well point out that he or she is not paid to empty wastebaskets, photocopy bills, work past five, and so on.

Belle, a Leisurely child-care worker, was hired primarily to watch the Smiths' three children after school until Mrs. Smith returned home from her job. The children and the friends who often came to play with them generally made a mess of the house. Belle didn't clean up after them. Every evening Mrs. Smith came home to dirty dishes in the sink and a house in disarray. Finally she spoke to Belle about it. Belle said she was paid to watch the kids. "You don't pay me to clean up after them."

From Mrs. Smith's point of view, anyone who had Belle's job would want to pick up after them. But Belle wasn't about to be exploited, as she saw it. She was dedicated to the kids, though, and they liked her. So Mrs. Smith offered to pay Belle more to clean up as well, but to her surprise Belle refused. She didn't want to be a housekeeper, she said. She just wanted to look after kids. Mrs. Smith acknowledged, intellectually, that Belle had the right to draw the line; but when she walked into the messy house every afternoon, she couldn't help feeling that Belle had a "bad attitude." Finally the kids grew old enough to clean up after themselves. But then they didn't need Belle to take care of them anymore.

Leisurely people are not Type A's. They work slowly and comfortably. They don't rush to beat the clock or meet what they believe is an unreasonable deadline. They are not driven to please the boss or to create perfection. They can do very good work, and they can often stand a lot of tedium, but the job is rarely going to be the central focus of their lives. For Leisurely individuals, including some civil servants, union members, and career military people, work means putting in your twenty or thirty years so you can get your pension; then you can do what you really want to do.

Workers' Rights

Leisurely types are at least mildly suspicious of authority in the workplace. They expect that the boss will want more than they are willing to give, which is often true, especially when the job has no precise description or when the boss is Conscientious, Self-Confident, Aggressive, or Serious. Leisurely individuals attempt to fulfill their obligations; they feel ill-used if their supervisors or colleagues do not accept this as sufficient. If the boss asks them to do more, or to work faster, they are likely to feel that they are being treated unfairly. Should the boss insist that they do more than their fair share, a Leisurely person will threaten to file a grievance.

Leisurely individuals are always aware of their rights. Fair is fair; anything else is exploitation. They take advantage of all their rights, such as taking all the days off they are allowed, and because of this they may be unreasonably judged by their bosses as lazy or unmotivated. They are not necessarily tempted to work overtime by the promise of extra pay, but they may be interested if they are promised compensatory time off. Quitting time brings smiles to their faces.

Self-employed Leisurely men and women have much the same attitude toward authority. They don't let their clients make excessive demands on them. Ardis O. is a free-lance graphics designer with a good streak of Leisurely style in her personality pattern. She never takes rush jobs (fortunately she doesn't have to, because her husband brings in a good income), and regardless of what she has to get done that day, she will not work from 2:00 to 3:00 P.M., so that she can eat her lunch and watch the soap opera she has been following for years.

Leisurely Housework

Leisurely homemakers need to have time to themselves too. Their house will be neat enough, the meals good if not elaborate (unless they get their kicks out of gourmet cooking), but nothing will be perfectly well kept or prepared. Taking care of a house and a family is one of the more demanding jobs, and Leisurely individuals know where to set their limits. But they'll run into trouble with spouses who don't think of housework as "real" work and who will see their need to entertain themselves as self-indulgent.

In addition, Leisurely types who work outside the home may not recognize that their at-home mates have had much to do all day. When they come home from a long hard day at their "real" jobs, they may not be inclined to pitch in. They treasure their nonwork hours too much to sacrifice them easily to chores, especially if they feel that someone else in the family can and should take care of those responsibilities.

Success Isn't Everything

Leisurely-style individuals can be found in virtually all jobs and careers but rarely at the top of any, which is fine with them. Since their overall comfort in life comes from how they enjoy themselves away from work, they'll rarely devote the time or push that hard. A pitfall of the Leisurely style may be that some very Leisurely people drift off course or lose direction in their lives. But this needn't happen. Leisurely individuals can do well and make good lives for themselves—even if other people think that they haven't done as well as they "should."

Selma T. is a good example. She is a very bright biochemist who left a job at a prestigious university in a major city to take a position at a relatively unknown college in a small town with less adequate research facilities. Her choice struck her ambitious colleagues as peculiar. But with the move Selma became a full professor, received immediate tenure and a lot more money, and could afford to buy a house with several acres. She would no longer have to struggle, compete, and prove herself. Most important, she would have the space and the time to breed and raise Alaskan malamutes. Her work is interesting and provides good security. So what if she hasn't "made the most of her career," as her father, the president of a major corporation, sees it. She has no desire to win a Nobel Prize, to be recognized, or even to publish anything. She likes to teach and to raise dogs. She's happy.

Managing the Status Quo

You won't find many predominantly Leisurely types above middle-management levels, because they're not ambitious in their careers. They don't want to devote themselves to getting ahead, don't care too much about working hard enough to make a lot of money, and are extremely reluctant to make the necessary sacrifices of personal time that the fast track demands. Since Leisurely individuals often work for the same company, government agency, or military branch their entire careers, through the years they may rise to middle-management levels. As managers they expect of their subordinates what they expect of themselves: a day's work for a day's pay. They don't push anybody too hard, but they do expect their staffs to follow the rules and not make life difficult for them. They are not particularly creative managers and they're not great motivators, but in the bureaucracies in which they may find themselves, they don't rock the boat, they enable the wheels to keep turning, and they fit right in.

Careers for the Leisurely

If this is your leading style, consider being born rich. Too late? Then seek a nine-to-five job in which you know exactly what is expected of you. You may wish to seek a job with plenty of routine, since people with your personality style often prefer their challenges outside the workplace. Whatever you choose to do, just be sure that you will not be expected to demonstrate devotion that is above and beyond the call of duty, as can happen, for example, in legal careers. Seek secure jobs, such as in the civil service, in union shops, and in the military, or a tenured teaching position, where the rewards for just doing your job can be great, especially in terms of pensions and benefits. But be aware that people who are more dedicated to their work will still receive the greater share of the approval, encouragement, and advancement.

Self-employment may be a way to ensure that you have hours to yourself when you want them, but think first about whether you have sufficient self-discipline. Can you shift from play to work without someone else setting the rules? If your Personality Self-Portrait reveals a Conscientious trend in addition, working free-lance or becoming a consultant may be a way of resolving conflicting trends within your personality—and Leisurely style can be as much a problem within individuals who have this along with ambitious styles as it is between people who represent the differing personality patterns. Perhaps you can focus on your Conscientiousness now by working hard for a fixed number of years and socking the money away; then you can retire young and let your Leisurely side take over. You might also try to combine business and pleasure by seeking work in an area that interests you on your own time. For example, if you spend a lot of time listening to music, perhaps you would enjoy working in a record store, for a music publisher, or for a radio station. You may also satisfy your strong need for pleasure by doing creative work. Or perhaps you can learn to schedule time for your Leisurely yearnings in an otherwise hard-driving day.

EMOTIONS AND SELF-CONTROL:
RELAX. ENJOY. AVOID STRESS.

People with a predominance of the Leisurely style are like lizards warming in the sun—placid, patient, slow-moving, steady, not likely to get upset. Mellow fellows, in other words. They're not all tied up in knots, they don't worry, they're not running to get their blood pressure checked every other day or sending their secretaries to the drugstore for antacids. They make their daily lives as comfortable as they can and may well postpone the more onerous tasks—work deadlines, income taxes, bill paying, Christmas shopping, cleaning the house, mowing the lawn—to the last possible minute.

Generally they're emotionally even, except when they're pushed to do more than they think is fair or when someone pressures them to change their priorities. These are primary sources of stress to Leisurely individuals. In response they feel drawn to do things the other person's way, but then they react by resisting in a more demonstrative way. Even so, when they're angry Leisurely types tend to be indirect about it. They'll become grouchy and sullen, they'll dawdle and procrastinate, they'll assign blame elsewhere, but they will avoid a head-on confrontation. Maybe a Leisurely man will come home late the night that his wife has insisted *he* cook dinner. Or maybe he'll cook an awful dinner, so that she'll never insist again. If a man asks his Leisurely wife to sew his torn shirt, maybe she'll "forget" to do it. But if the problems don't go away—if she still wants him to share in the responsibilities of the house or he insists that she do more for him, or if the boss insists that the Leisurely employee take on more work or come in on Saturday—the Leisurely person will indignantly justify his or her behavior and even try to rally others to his or her side. ("Kids, you tell Daddy that Mommy doesn't have to sew his shirts just because she's a woman. Mommies have their rights too—you tell Daddy what you think.") But if their relationships are consistently stressed by mates or supervisors who keep trying to make them do "their fair share," the sullenness may well become a way of life.

If left alone to do their thing, Leisurely people are blessed with the ability to find emotional comfort. They don't need much except a little leisure time in order to enjoy themselves. The Leisurely style is, after all, a slow, easy, pleasure-seeking one. Happiness can come from just sitting in front of the TV with a bag of chips and a beer. Generally these individuals have good self-control; they're not driven to excesses. But any pleasure-seeking style can backfire. Beware of growing fat, flabby, and alcoholic or drug dependent out of sheer habit.

REAL WORLD: KEEPING A LOW PROFILE

To people with a predominance of this personality style, the Real World is a fairly straightforward place, if populated with a lot of folks who claim authority over others and would have you working all the time at unimportant tasks. Leisurely individuals have a built-in immunity to these claims, for they perceive that work is only part of the Real World. They protect their identities by keeping a low profile, fulfilling only those obligations to the system that they must, wishing for a stroke of good fortune, to which they feel as entitled as the next guy, and then concentrating on what they want to do with their own time—now *that's* living.

▆▆ TIPS ON DEALING WITH THE LEISURELY PERSON IN YOUR LIFE ▆▆

1. Accept the Leisurely person in your life as he or she is. Don't approach a relationship with such a person with the expectation of changing him or her to suit your needs. Rather, ask yourself what it is in this person that you like and are attracted to. Appreciate all your Leisurely friends, parents, lovers, children, or spouses for the qualities they possess rather than those they lack.

2. If you are having difficulty with a Leisurely person, ask yourself whether the problems arise because you two have different value systems. Perhaps you come from a push-hard, get-ahead, make-a-success-of-yourself tradition, while the Leisurely person in your life sees more value in doing his or her own thing. Instead of judging one system as better than the other, ask yourself whether your two value systems can coexist or merge. Perhaps you can take responsibility for the ambition and the Leisurely individual can take the lead in the comfort and self-fulfillment side of things, and together you can share the benefits. In any case, try to understand this person's philosophy of life and point of view.

3. Be realistic. Life with a Leisurely person may demand more sacrifices from you than from him or her. Can you make these without bitterness or resentment?

4. Make life easier for yourself. People with the Leisurely personality style don't automatically tune in to what's important to you. Instead of waiting for this person to figure it out, let him or her know your basic, essential expectations. If need be, let him or her know how to fulfill these expectations. For example, if you want your Leisurely spouse to come to a meeting at your child's school, say that it's important to you that you both attend. Mention the time, the place, and, if necessary, what to wear. If your Leisurely partner objects, ask him or her to do it *for you*—but save that special request for occasions that are deeply important to you.

5. Leisurely types can be stubborn about protecting their rights to do or to be as they please. Offer to assist in projects that need doing and/or make a deal. ("Tell me what part I have to buy in order to fix the stereo. I'll go out and get it. Then all you have to do is put it in and we'll be able to listen to music again. Okay?") But if he or she simply doesn't get around to it, don't nag or complain, and don't take it personally. Be practical. Try to find another way to accom-

plish what you want the Leisurely person to do—take the stereo in for repairs.

6. When the Leisurely person in your life starts stalling, refusing, or forgetting, ask, "Are you angry about something?" People with this personality style have a hard time expressing their anger directly.

7. Try to share in the Leisurely person's pleasures. Observe his or her habits and routines and join in. If he or she likes to go for a walk before or after dinner, go along. Pull up a chair and watch TV with your Leisurely partner, or play a hand of gin together. Learn to bowl or play tennis, if necessary. Leisurely people don't need to be alone when they're doing their own thing. You'll enrich your relationship and endear yourself to this person if you can rearrange your schedule or preferences to be with the Leisurely person at the moments that are most comfortable and enjoyable in his or her day. And you never know, he or she may become more willing to accommodate you.

8. Take good care of him or her. Leisurely people are suckers for pampering and loving attention.

MAKING THE MOST OF YOUR LEISURELY STYLE

Your Self-driven style leads you to look inward more than outward. Broaden your perspective with Exercise 4 for the Self-Confident style (p. 97): Who *is* this person? Look back and see how this exercise teaches you to gather information about people. In your case, focus additionally on the ways the people in your life achieve pleasure. What's important to them? What makes them happy?

Exercise 1

Ask yourself whether there's anything you can do to help other people better enjoy their sources of happiness. For example, if your spouse achieves real pleasure from having an orderly yard, can you contribute? Maybe your spouse would appreciate some private time; what a gift it would be if you could take over the child care or some other task, even for an hour. Don't think of it as *work* but as a source of real pleasure to your spouse and to you. For the more pleasure you can help another person achieve, the greater your shared pleasure. Think about this. We'll have more other-people exercises to conclude this section.

Exercise 2

Procrastination is the Leisurely way to maximize the pleasurable moments in life as well as to resist the demands of authority as long as possible. But procrastinating can get you in trouble with other people and make you and those around you crazy at deadline time. So, think about this: It is a major pleasure in life to get things done on or before deadline. Former procrastinators will testify to this. Think about this also: If you do it today, you'll have more free time tomorrow, without anybody being angry at you.

The following four exercises offer suggestions for dealing with procrastination. Be sure to applaud yourself for your accomplishments.

Exercise 3

Make it fun. For every chore or assignment you are supposed to complete, find a way to enjoy yourself now or later. For example, wear a Walkman while raking leaves or washing the floor; or watch a movie on TV or a VCR while getting your tax receipts together. If you have to do something at the office, reward yourself later. As soon as you complete the task, go out to a special restaurant. Or go to the theater that night. Or see a travel agent to start planning your next vacation. Or make love with your mate.

Exercise 4

Do *some* of it. It's easier to tackle major tasks if you realize that you don't have to do the whole job at once. If you do it little by little, you don't have to give up all the fun in your life. For example, if you have a paper or report to prepare, instead of doing it all in one long effort over many hours, days, weeks, or months, just sit down and sketch out a rough outline right now. Or tell yourself you can get up as soon as you've written the first two pages. Then put it aside and go play. Later, or tomorrow, take on the next small piece. Small pieces add up quickly if you do them consistently.

Exercise 5

Do it *now*. As soon as you find yourself thinking about something you have to do that you are inclined to put off, do some of it right now. Then feel virtuous for having done it.

Exercise 6

See the bright side. Leisurely types groan when they think about all the things they are obliged to do. Look instead at the pleasurable consequences. "If I do this now, I'll be so relieved to have it done and I won't have to worry about it later." "If I finish this, my wife/husband/parent/child/boss/friend will be pleased and happy with me and/or will stop picking on me, which would be a wonderful change of pace." "If I complete this paper, I won't have to take this course over again." In case you can't see the bright side, at least let go of the downside. When you find yourself thinking how this task is going to cut into your pleasure time, immediately move away from this thought; think about anything else.

Indecisiveness is often a byproduct of procrastination—I don't want to do *that*, but what should I do? For exercises to combat difficulty making decisions, see the suggestions included in Exercise 3 for Conscientious (chapter 4, p. 75).

Leisurely types are into habits. You habitually put off work you don't want to do, but also you tend to pursue your particular pleasures out of habit. You watch TV every night after dinner, you sleep late every Saturday, and so on. To avoid ruts, try Exercise 1 for the Sensitive style (p. 193): Do something different. Alter any of your patterns from time to time to experience flexibility and change, to prevent boredom, and to steer clear of possible substance use/abuse problems. Try the following:

Exercise 7

Double the fun. Leisurely people are so good at finding ways to entertain themselves that they may unwittingly become oblivious to others. If you are used to sitting down with a good book or the newspaper or taking long solitary bike rides, ask the people in your household to join you. You can discuss the news, read aloud to one another, or pedal together.

Exercise 8

When you find yourself waffling between doing what you want and acceding to someone's demands so that they won't be angry at you, to resolve your struggle try to accomplish both aims. For example, agree to cooperate in a requested task for a specific time period, then schedule an activity for yourself. Also, ask yourself whether you really don't want to do it or whether it's your habit to refuse to do things you're asked. If you find you're an automatic refuser, evaluate the task to see whether it's really objectionable; it may not be so bad. In any case, resist being resentful of the person whom you are trying to please. Look at the bright side: now you're both happy.

Finally, to enhance your pleasure and happiness in your relationships with other people, practice Exercise 2 for the Devoted style (p. 120): Get it off your chest. Express your anger directly.

PASSIVE-AGGRESSIVE
PERSONALITY DISORDER

Individuals with this disorder raise contrariness to an art form. They stall, they complain, they oppose, they dawdle, they "forget," they scorn those who try to help—and then they feel cheated that life hasn't offered them a better deal. Their inner and outer experience of life is bitter and unpleasurable, yet they cannot see that they themselves routinely close off all avenues of reward.

DIAGNOSTIC CRITERIA

The DSM-IV describes Passive-Aggressive personality disorder as:

A pervasive pattern of negativistic attitudes and passive resistance to demands for adequate performance, beginning by early adulthood and present in a variety of contexts, as indicated by four (or more) of the following:

(1) passively resists fulfilling routine social and occupational tasks

(2) complains of being misunderstood and unappreciated by others

(3) is sullen and argumentative

(4) unreasonably criticizes and scorns authority

(5) expresses envy and resentment toward those apparently more fortunate

(6) voices exaggerated and persistent complaints of personal misfortune

(7) alternates between hostile defiance and contrition

GARY, GARY, QUITE CONTRARY

In chapter 2 we presented the case of Gary, the forty-four-year-old industrial engineer who was put on probation at work for having erased from the computer all the documentation files and backup copies for an important company project. As a result, the company did not meet a high-priority deadline for a major contractor. Gary, who has lost three jobs in ten years, was sullen and sour about the experience. It wasn't *his* fault, he insisted, launching into a tirade about inept management. The only reason Gary sought professional help was that his wife said she would leave him if he didn't. Ordinarily Gary does not accede to anyone's demands, even the smallest ones, at least not for long. And in a way he didn't comply with this one either, since after his first session he didn't show up for the next appointment. His escapes from demands put on him are Gary's only "victories" in life. Like others who suffer from Passive-Aggressive personality disorder, Gary achieves freedom in the Self domain by thwarting all those who expect him to live up to their expectations. But by doing so, he and other Passive-Aggressive people sabotage their own lives.

They get you coming and going. Gary complained that he fouled up the computer because his incompetent boss had not given him sufficient time to learn the system. When his supervisors later gave him a week just to familiarize himself with the software, he complained that his eyes couldn't take staring at that screen for so many hours.

Drs. Michael Liebowitz, Michael Stone, and Ira Turkat have described a similar no-win situation with a Passive-Aggressive patient who repeatedly failed to finish writing a book. When the therapist advised this man "to ask for an advance—making him morally obligated to complete the work, he countered with, '. . . but then I would feel too hemmed in; it would cramp my style.' When told that he would just have to do the best he could without the advance, he complained, 'Yes, but then I have no incentive.' "

Because of their contrariness, people with this personality disorder are among the most difficult to deal with. In one way or another they dig in their heels in response to every demand you make of them. But they don't face you and say no. Instead, they just don't do what you ask, or they drag it out, or they do it incorrectly, or they forget. Ask a Passive-Aggressive person to do something for you—"Honey, could you pick up a pizza for dinner on your way home from work?"—and you can be sure your beloved will forget to stop, or there will be anchovies all over it, which "Honey" knows full well you detest. "Oh, yeah, anchovies. I forgot."

THE PASSIVE-AGGRESSIVE TRAP

Passive-Aggressive people do not recognize that they have done anything to make you angry or to cause them to fail. If things go wrong, it's your fault or the employer's. They are never openly defiant; their actions are so indirect, so passive, that they evade responsibility. "You know how busy I am. I can't remember everything. So I forgot you don't like anchovies. You should have reminded me."

To the individuals who suffer from this disorder, compliance feels like submission. And submission, to their tender, fragile selves, is tantamount to humiliation. These are individuals who are both very angry and very needy. They are angry over deep, forgotten hurts inflicted on them early in their childhoods by their parents or care givers on whom they depended completely for love, attention, and protection. As adults, they remain very dependent on the important people in their lives, including parents, spouses, and employers. But their neediness scares them and revives the same old wounds. They can't get close without feeling angry and resentful, but they can't live without these people either.

What do they do with all their inner rage and hostility? They are afraid of acting aggressively toward those on whom they are so dependent. Instead, they resort to oppositional behavior, which expresses their aggressive feelings in a covert, passive way, hence the name Passive-Aggressive personality disorder.

Trapped between love and hate, passivity and assertion, these troubled human beings find small comfort, happiness, or pleasure. Like Paranoid people, they externalize their suffering rather than look inward toward their pain. What happens to them is everybody else's fault, not their own. Then, when they passively drive spouses or employers to fury and punishment, they experience the feelings of injustice that they have carried with them all their lives.

They subvert their love lives and their work lives. In one long-term study of a group of men, of all the personality disorders the Passive-Aggressive proved to be the one most associated with downward job mobility.

HELP!

The work of the psychodynamic psychotherapist is to enable Passive-Aggressive people to locate the inner sources of their anger and hurt. Very often their parents gave them extremely contradictory, inconsistent, or confused messages about what was expected of them, or tried to control their lives. Others reveal a childhood in which their parents were indifferent to them or clearly preferred another sibling, or in which a parent was openly hostile. Alcoholism is a common thread in Passive-Aggressive family backgrounds.

In cognitive therapy, the therapist will help the person to confront maladaptive attitudes and assumptions, such as: "Being direct with people could be dangerous." Behavioral forms of treatment, such as assertiveness training, may also help some people with this personality disorder to change entrenched patterns.

Whatever the approach, the therapist will require great patience and fortitude, for these individuals resist the efforts of their therapists just as they resist the demands of everyone else in their lives. Passive-Aggressive individuals have little perspective on the sources of their problems. The skilled clinician will need constantly, carefully, and kindly to confront the patient on the real reasons why he or she is late, is withholding payment, is critical, or is argumentative. Group or family therapy may help the Passive-Aggressive person and therapist face some inescapable truths. The therapist must be able to deal constructively with his or her own anger that these patients inspire. If the Passive-Aggressive person has the strength, courage, and faith to begin to see his or her behavior for what it's worth, there is great hope of change.

QUESTIONS, RISKS, PREDISPOSITIONS, AND INCIDENCE

Passive-Aggressive personality disorder has appeared in previous editions of the DSM, and the concept has had a long history in clinical literature. The term *passive-aggressive* first appeared in a 1945 military publication, describing soldiers who opposed their superiors in an indirect way. Nonetheless, when the DSM-IV was being prepared, strong questions were raised whether this was a true personality disorder, or just a trait that could be shared by many people with various personality disorders. Indeed, the diagnostic criteria for this personality disorder in DSM-III-R focused almost entirely on passive resistance to authority. Now, for the DSM-IV, the disorder has been reformulated (its name was even changed—briefly—to Negativistic). The current criteria, which we presented on pp. 222–23, present a broader diagnostic picture. However, because these criteria now need to be validated scientifically, Passive-Aggressive personality disorder currently appears in the section of the DSM-IV reserved for conditions that require further study.

Needless to say, numerous individuals behave passive-aggressively (the stalling, procrastinating, "forgetting" maneuvers) from time to time. These include people with the Leisurely style as well as with other styles and disorders (including Conscientious personality style and Obsessive-Compulsive personality disorder). Far fewer people suffer from Passive-Aggressive personality disorder, whatever its formulation, although the precise number and sexual distribution are unknown.

In the past, alcoholism, drug dependence, depression, anxiety, suicide, and psychosomatic illnesses have all been associated with Passive-Aggressive personality disorder.

The so-called Difficult Child temperament identified by Drs. Thomas and Chess (about which more in chapter 18) may predispose a boy or girl to develop this personality disorder by adulthood, especially if the parents are inflexible and insensitive or too wrapped up in their own problems to meet the child's needs. The Difficult Child has frequent bad moods, dislikes change in his or her routine, and doesn't adapt well to feeding or sleeping schedules, among other qualities. Oppositional defiant disorder, a developmental disorder whose name portrays what the parents and teachers of these children or adolescents experience, may set the stage for Passive-Aggressive personality disorder in adulthood.

COPING WITH PASSIVE-AGGRESSIVE PEOPLE

It's very hard to get through to these people about what they are doing to you and to themselves. Concentrate on tips 3 through 6 (pp. 218-19). Keep in mind that deep down, most Passive-Aggressive people are very needy and may not risk losing you should it come to that. A Passive-Aggressive person who begins to suffer extreme anxiety or depression (perhaps as a result of the relationship coming apart) may agree to seek help. In any case, get help for your relationship.

CHAPTER 11

Adventurous Style

"THE CHALLENGER"

Throw caution to the winds—here comes the Adventurer. Who but Adventurers would have taken those long leaps for mankind—crossed the oceans, broken the sound barrier, walked on the moon? The men and women with this personality style venture where most mortals fear to tread. They are not bound by the same terrors and worries that limit most of us. They live on the edge, challenging boundaries and restrictions, pitting themselves for better or for worse in a thrilling game against their own mortality. No risk, no reward, they say. Indeed, for people with the Adventurous personality style, the risk is the reward.

THE EIGHT CHARACTERISTICS

The following eight traits and behaviors are clues to the presence of the Adventurous style. A person who reveals a strong Adventurous tendency will demonstrate more of these behaviors more intensely than someone with less of this style in his or her personality profile.

1. *Nonconformity.* Men and women who have the Adventurous personality style live by their own internal code of values. They are not strongly influenced by other people or by the norms of society.

2. *Challenge.* To live is to dare. Adventurers love the thrill of risk and routinely engage in high-risk activities.

3. *Mutual independence.* They do not worry too much about others, for they expect each human being to be responsible for him- or herself.

4. *Persuasiveness.* They are silver-tongued, gifted in the gentle art of winning friends and influencing people.

5. *Wanderlust.* They love to keep moving. They settle down only to have the urge to pick up and go, explore, move out, move on. They do not worry about finding work, and live well by their talents, skills, ingenuity, and wits.

6. *Wild oats.* In their childhood and adolescence, people with the Adventurous personality style were usually high-spirited hell-raisers and mischief makers.

7. *True grit.* They are courageous, physically bold, and tough. They will stand up to anyone who dares to take advantage of them.

8. *No regrets.* Adventurers live in the present. They do not feel guilty about the past or anxious about the future. Life is meant to be experienced *now*.

THE SIX DOMAINS OF ADVENTUROUS FUNCTIONING

The Self-Control and the Self domains dominate the Adventurous life.

SELF AND SELF-CONTROL: IT'S A THRILL TO BE ALIVE

Adventurous men and women are action-oriented extroverts, hungry for the peak experience that lets them know just how powerfully alive they are. They need thrilling challenge the way most of us need food and shelter. Whether in sports, in their careers, in their sex lives, in the stock market, or on the gambling tables, fulfilling their thrill quotient is the raison d'être for all levels of Adventurers. How they do it is key. Will they risk other people's lives along with their own? Will they flaunt social order to get what they want? Will they calculate their own or others' risks? A little of the Adventurous personality style goes a long way. With some of it a person can often build a meaningful, certainly interesting life for him- or herself. Too much is a real problem, especially for other people, which we'll discuss in "Antisocial Personality Disorder," pp. 245–51.

In It for Me

As with all the styles for which the Self domain is key, Adventurous types are fundamentally out for themselves. They seek intense, visceral experience for their own sakes. If they have strength in the Self-Confident personality style as well, they'll be ambitious to break records and make a name for themselves in the process. Otherwise, the rush of adrenaline that results from triumphing over danger may suffice.

Adventurous types do not need others to fuel their self-esteem or to provide purpose to their lives, and they don't make sacrifices for other people, at least not easily. This does not mean that they cannot or do not relate to others, as we will see when we discuss their Relationships domain, or that (like some warriors, for example) they cannot also advance a cause while in the service of their own experience. Other people often figure into Adventurers' exciting plans, as in a sexual experience or on a team of Antarctic explorers. But the meaning of the experience is not the fusing of souls or the love of a person, a country, or a cause; rather, what counts most is the aliveness that they experience at the moment.

Neither do Adventurous types require anyone's approval for what they seek out of life. As with Self-Confident types, belief in themselves is among their strong points. They have a definite inner sense of what's right and wrong for them, and if something is important to them, they'll do it no matter what anyone thinks. When Ginny cries, "Hank, how can you even consider racing your motorcycle? We have a baby now. What if you hurt yourself? What would we do?" Hank can only reply, "Hold on—this is what I do." Hank supports his family, he does his chores. But motorcycle racing is his soul. If Ginny wants to be with him she's going to have to accept that.

The Here and Now

The Adventurous personality style confers a freedom unknown to other personality styles. Depending on the degree of this style in their overall patterns, these men and women are relatively free of concern about consequences. They experience life as it unfolds in the present. They don't think ahead and they don't look back. They are alive to the impulse of the moment and can act on it more easily than someone who worries about the future or feels guilty about the past.

Living in the moment as they do, Adventurous individuals experience fear more as thrilling than chilling. Danger is a challenge, not a fear of what might happen. Thus, they may seem reckless—sailing into a storm, driving fast around mountain curves, or speculating in an uncertain economy. They count on their wits, ingenuity, physical prowess, and sheer guts to carry them through. Fear heightens their excitement, focuses their concentration, and sharpens their senses. The hunter, stumbling upon a crocodile, shoots true.

Living for present experience without much thought for tomorrow, those who are dominated by this personality style are not planners; they do not plot courses toward future goals. They don't tolerate frustration and they resist discipline, especially that imposed by others and by society. (But they may be exceedingly disciplined in their risk-taking pursuits; see the Work domain, p. 235.) They don't anticipate; they are happy to deal with what happens when it happens.

Andy G. had bought thousands of dollars' worth of stocks on margin. He had few liquid assets, but that didn't worry him. The last time the stock market crashed, he couldn't come up with the cash. He still didn't worry about it. He turned to his father, who said sorry, he couldn't help him. Then he turned to his father-in-law, telling him calmly that if he couldn't help him cover his losses, he and his wife and kids would be wiped out. Terrified of the consequences for his daughter and grandchildren, Andy's father-in-law came through for him. But Andy knew that even if his father-in-law refused him, he'd get by one way or another; such is the typical Adventurous view of the future. Adventurous types like Andy can make a million, lose two, and make another five. Within a year after the crash, Andy had repaid his father-in-law with interest.

Because they don't worry about going under, Adventurous people are remarkably easy with money. Investing, gambling, spending, even giving it away is stimulating, it makes them feel powerful, it's *living,* and with a good gut sense, they can sometimes make a bundle. Or they can lose everything, which, as with Andy, is no big deal. They'll get back in the game again. They'll pay off that credit card someday—no sense in getting upset about it. Of course, other people are hardly so complacent when the money lost is their own. When the gamble pays off they are glad to rake profits in; when the bottom falls out of risky investments that the Adventurer has made on their behalf, they express outrage that this person would have put them in such peril. Read about Brooke E. (p. 232).

As the Spirit Moves

Nobody is more fun, more appreciative of the possibilities inherent in any moment, than these eternal optimists. Back in the sixties when they were newlyweds, Betsy and Dick F. met Adventurous Sean T. and his wife, Gemma. The two couples quickly became friends. Betsy and Dick, who were more conventional, were delighted with Sean and Gemma's spontaneity. Sean would call Dick at the ad agency where he worked and say, "Hey, you don't really want to work late tonight. Gemma and I are going to pick up Betsy, then you, and we're all going dancing." They'd get home at 3:00 or 4:00 A.M., and Dick would then have to stay up to complete his work. At Sean and Gemma's urging, they all experimented with drugs. They took LSD and expanded their minds as well as their rock music repertoire. They even considered group sex, but Betsy and Dick decided against it.

Dick and Betsy had never lived this way and were glad to cast off their conventionality for a while at a time when everyone else seemed to be doing it. But after a year or so of their fun-loving, spur-of-the-moment lifestyle, consequences started to pile up. Too tired and "spaced out," Dick blew an important presentation, and the agency didn't get the client they were pitching. He was very close to being fired. He and Betsy talked. They realized that the future was too important to them to take chances with it. They guiltily told Sean and Gemma that they couldn't keep up the pace with them. Sean and Gemma thought Dick should abandon his soul-restricting career and move to the country and live off the land, as they had decided to do.

Now, many years later, Dick and Betsy run a small literary publishing company. Their lives are centered around their work and their two kids, who are now in graduate school. They remember the sixties and Sean and Gemma and are glad to have known them and done the things that they did. But they're not strongly Adventurous, so to be fulfilled they needed to follow a path that was truer to their own personalities.

Sean and Gemma moved to the country and lived in a commune for a while. Gemma gave birth to a boy. She discovered that Sean was involved in a ménage à trois with two women in the commune. They declared theirs an open marriage, an arrangement that was quite popular at the time, but Gemma became overwhelmed with jealousy and moved back to the city with the baby. She went back to school, remarried, and now is a special education teacher and has three grown children.

Sean, true to his Adventurous personality style, was happy to keep doing his thing. He farmed for a while, then turned to woodworking and sold his little boxes from time to time at craft fairs and flea markets. He's had a couple of brushes with the law over possession of small amounts of drugs, but he's never had to serve time. Now he and June, the woman he's lived with for a few years, sell used clothing at flea markets. They're happy as can be, moving around the West as the spirit moves. Sean's over fifty, but he says he feels nineteen. He's not admitting the truth: for the first time in his life he's begun to recognize that he *doesn't*, and never again will, feel like a teenager. While the women he's been with often end up worrying about security in their old age, the thought never crossed Sean's mind until recently. But he shrugs it off, insisting he's always been able to figure out how to survive. This is the life he knows how to live, and it's always worked for him.

You Can't Win 'Em All

Living in the now, reacting immediately to impulse, enjoying an unrestrained, nonconformist existence, and taking numerous risks can lead to a very exciting, full life. It can also exact a huge toll. Living according to whim, without self-control or thought of consequence, leads the extremely Adventurous, more than any other personality style except the Mercurial, quickly down the path toward drug problems, economic trouble, sexually transmitted diseases, difficulties with the law, and accidental injury.

The individual with a mixed personality pattern that includes the Adventurous style may be protected by strengths from other styles. Conscientious, Self-Confident, and Vigilant styles, for example, offer the foresight necessary to calculate the risks. The Devoted style will bring a sensitivity to what loved ones feel and think. Even when the bets are hedged, though, and training and preparation are thorough, death, injury, and/or substantial loss can be the unfortunate result of severely dangerous sports, career brinkmanship, or high rolling.

Brooke and Her Clients Lose Big

But strength in a more responsible and restrained personality style may only conceal the person's Adventurous streak from the outside world, possibly even from him- or herself. Brooke E. made a name for herself in investments on behalf of nonprofit organizations. She seemed the essence of Conscientiousness: A person of extraordinarily regular habits (as just one example, she ate lunch at the same restaurant at exactly the same time every day) and conservative demeanor (she wore only gray or navy suits), she devoted all her energies to her work. Also typical of a Conscientious person, she was very thrifty with her own money and indeed kept her own funds in low-risk investments like certificates of deposit at a time when interest rates were quite low and riskier investment schemes were paying off. She knew well about these rewards because her client organizations were seeing returns on the much-less-than-A-rated investments she'd been making for them.

Although Conscientiously averse to taking chances with her own money (she recognized her fearfulness and laughed at herself for it), Brooke was comfortable indulging her Adventurous love of risk in her professional work—which was why she'd been in the investment business and done so well her whole career. Up till now, she'd always mixed just enough professional caution with an ability to move fast and take chances when conditions were ripe. When in rather difficult economic times she spotted an opportunity for her clients to profit handsomely, she acted all too Adventurously and converted conservative holdings into speculations that paid off spectacularly—until market conditions abruptly changed and her paper empire crumbled. Most of the risks she had taken in her professional life had worked out over the years. This one didn't—and when Adventurous bets fail, they fail big. Because of Brooke, some very worthy organizations ceased to exist.

The community was shocked to discover the "two sides" of this prominent person. Predominantly Adventurous people don't necessarily suffer from their falls as much as some others, but Brooke was more Conscientious than Adventurous and experienced emotional as well as professional collapse. Perhaps Brooke (and her clients) would have been better off if she'd been able to be a bit more Adventurous in her personal life, and more Conscientious on behalf of her clients. Many people have such contradictions in their personalities, as discussed in chapter 3. The challenge is to recognize all the trends, understand their effects on all the domains of functioning, and to direct their influences into life expansion rather than self-defeating conflict.

EMOTIONS: WHAT, ME WORRY?

Predominantly Adventurous types don't hide their feelings. You know immediately when they're feeling sexual, enthusiastic, or angry. Restraint does not mark this style, so if a very Adventurous person has a bone to pick with you, stand back.

Most of the time Adventurous people are cheerful and eager to enjoy life. Whatever negative feelings or disappointments they experience are immediately routed into action and derring-do. They don't feel much stress, except when they are frustrated and confined and can't act. Then they become restless, angry, and disgruntled—like a caged animal. They're good at righting themselves quickly, though, and returning to their optimistic state.

But age has a way of creeping up on very Adventurous people. They're adolescents at heart. Unfortunately, as they age, the gap with the genuinely youthful grows larger. They become less attractive to others. Infirmities and other age-related limitations can be exceedingly difficult for them to accept. Whereas in their thirties or forties most people have been dealing with the reality of their mortality and the narrowing of their omnipotence, for Adventurers the facts of limited life hit late and hard. Suddenly, depressing thoughts about the future intrude. Maybe life isn't the never-ending, exciting game they always thought it was. Despite a lifetime of challenging the odds, it's never occurred to them before now that death always wins.

However, most Adventurous people cope well. They almost always land on their feet. They'll figure out some way to survive. Maybe now at last they'll begin to lead a calmer life, maybe get married late in life, or become serious about commitment for the first time.

Or perhaps they'll maneuver their old bones into a wheelchair and go out and enter a marathon—hell, you only live once.

An Adventurous Phase

Personality style, as we have mentioned before, tends to mellow with age. This is especially true of the Adventurous style, which is much more common, appropriate, and culturally acceptable in younger people.

Many adults with the Adventurous personality style were rowdy, rebellious kids. They may have been a handful for their parents, but they weren't criminals—just high-energy, high-spirited youngsters. Maybe you were Dennis (or Denise) the Menace when you were ten. Maybe you stole a Hershey bar from the candy store. Perhaps you experimented with drugs or alcohol, or you drag-raced with your buddies when you first got your driver's license, or trashed your neighbor's mailbox. Or perhaps you rebelled in college or graduate school and started cutting classes and not studying, until the dean told you to shape up or ship out. Maybe you bummed around South America for two years with no money, just picking up odd jobs and staying with new-found friends who would feed you for a while. Maybe you were into sexual conquest, picking up people at bars and parties—never the same body twice.

We expect young people to sow their wild oats—"Don't worry, dear, Junior is just going through his Adventurous phase." But we count on that part of their personality to smooth out and lose intensity, or expect other styles to grow stronger, so that these individuals can go on to productive, safer, socially acceptable, secure lives. Usually this is the case. The wisdom that comes with age tempers even Adventurers, although it leaves them with residues of mischievousness and a strong appreciation of challenge.

REAL WORLD: PLAYING THE GAME

Adventurers know what's what in the Real World—and they don't care. Life is a game of getting around the rules and the conventional obligations and going beyond the established limits. Adventurers are determined to prove that they are the world's greatest players.

WORK: A ROLLING STONE GATHERS NO MOSS

To highly Adventurous people, life is one big opportunity to do what they please; they are slaves of no system. Their primary rule of life, and of work, is that they must be faced with a challenge. They can work well, with discipline, concentration, and responsibility, if their work (and here we include their risk-taking sports and hobbies) provides this necessary challenge. Thus, people with this style can be skilled fighter pilots, stuntpersons, tightrope walkers, skydiving instructors, combat soldiers, and so on—careers in which one false move could be their last one.

If their personality combines a "head style" such as the Conscientious with the "gut-style" Adventurous, they might rise to considerable accomplishment in their careers—as heart surgeons, perhaps, or criminal lawyers—just the kind of challenges an Adventurer can appreciate. Furthermore, Adventurous types can be good talkers; they can talk anybody into anything—judges and juries included. (But, as described in the discussion of Brooke E. earlier, personality-style combinations such as this can also backfire when the individual fails to calculate the risks.)

With or without moderating influences, Adventurous types are good workers when they want to be, as long as the work provides constant challenge, new projects, and renewed excitement. Although they may be entrepreneurs, they're not what one would call management material. Adventurers operate on instinct and ingenuity rather than on intellect. They tend to resist authority, they are poor planners, they deplore tedious follow-through, they do not accept responsibility for other people, and they don't handle money or budgets well.

Adventurers are easily bored. When they are not stimulated by their work, no matter how successful they are, they'll peter out or move on. Financial reward usually is not sufficient motivation for Adventurers to keep going when they lose interest.

Tom E. commands a high fee as a systems consultant for manufacturers of high-tech weaponry. But, to his wife's chagrin, he accepts only one or two jobs a year. They have just enough money to live on, whereas they could be quite comfortable if Tom took even half the jobs that are offered to him. But Tom is bored by most of the proposed projects. He'll work only if the assignment really stimulates him. He'd rather travel. He just came back from four months trekking in the Himalayas. Sandra, his wife, who stayed home with their two-year-old, thinks that they should build a nest egg, buy a house instead of renting. She wants the conventional, secure rewards of life. But Tom doesn't think there's anything they "should" do, except enjoy their lives to the fullest.

Innovative and resourceful as they usually are, Adventurous types can often find some way to outwit the conventional obligations that most people feel they can't escape. They create their own opportunities. They frequently manage to live happily without a permanent job, moving around from place to place, working as lifeguards, ski instructors, salespeople, entrepreneurs, stockbrokers, journalists, waiters and waitresses, bouncers, truckdrivers, or by marketing whatever skill they may have when they need money.

They may outwit the system entirely. Adventurers live by an inner sense of right and wrong; they don't necessarily buy the official version. Like Aggressive types (chapter 16) they may bend or break rules for expediency or if they think the rules don't make sense. They can become extremely successful, especially if they have some Aggressive style in their personalities as well. Some build their own commercial empires by wheeling and dealing and bending the rules wherever they find a flexible spot. Some tread in deeper waters—for example, to use historical examples, trading arms for hostages, or striking it rich with insiders' stock tips.

Careers for the Adventurous

If the Adventurous is your leading style, you don't need us to tell you what to do. But if it's *one* of your styles, you might be more satisfied with your life if you recognized and accepted your Adventurous need for action, excitement, and change. Avoid routine and drudgery. Look for work that involves frequent, time-limited new projects, such as in magazine or newspaper publishing. Stay clear of middle management or any other position in which you must be subordinate to others. In other words, be on a solo track. Look for work in a high-glamour, high-excitement field, such as investment banking, arbitrage, advertising, and entertainment. Sales may appeal to you; you are a good persuader and may enjoy the challenge of working on commission. Consider marketing your skills on a free-lance or consulting basis. Explore the possibility of turning a hobby into an income-producer. Or hang in there when you're going through a boring phase in your work; remember, as soon as you're finished for the day, you can go take your flying lesson. But remember to hedge your bets; predominantly Adventurous people can pick themselves up and go on after a big fall, but can you?

Management Style

It is rare to find a predominantly Adventurous style in a regular nine-to-five job, let alone in management, and certainly not in a corporate setting. But sometimes, in nontraditional, creative enterprise, a highly Adventurous person will have a brilliant idea and enough magnetism to attract others to join in the excitement and carry the idea through. Adventurous people certainly have style, but they're not managers in any effective sense. They have charisma, though, and if the rewards keep coming in, "real" managers may stick around and make sure bets are adequately hedged and the enterprise keeps functioning. But the Adventurous manager may well lose interest once everything's up and running, become inattentive to what others are doing, and put at risk everything he or she has inspired.

RELATIONSHIPS: NO STRINGS

What fun would life be without someone to share the good adventures? Adventurers are drawn to people like themselves, who like action and risk and will go for broke. Many people are attracted to them, and not just those who identify with them. Relatively "straight" people like Betsy and Dick F., mentioned earlier, find it easier to break loose a little with an Adventurous person leading the way.

Adventurous men and women make extraordinary lovers and playmates. The pleasures of the flesh couldn't be more important to them. For a hot and heavy affair, look no farther than an Adventurer. But don't count on this person to settle down. Adventurers are not in it for the long term. When the fire dies, or simply when the newness fades, they become restless. While they enjoy companionship, they place little emotional stock in togetherness or love. They do not understand the spiritual and/or moral significance it has for many people, and they don't comprehend dependency. For the Adventurer, a relationship is important mostly for the pleasurable excitement it can provide.

Individuals with this style do not easily make sacrifices for other people; certainly they make few sacrifices for the sake of fidelity. Even when the mixed-pattern Adventurer continues in a relationship past the exciting, passionate time, he or she will rarely remain sexually faithful. More than the other styles, Adventurousness brings with it a powerful need for a variety of sexual experiences. The moderately Adventurous person may tolerate a marriage as long as he or she can have extramarital affairs and one-night stands. The infidelity is not meant to punish or to hurt the spouse. Nonetheless, the effect is almost always deeply hurtful, often intolerable. Sean and Gemma T.'s breakup was triggered by Sean's sexual activity in the commune. Gemma, trying to be very "advanced," went along with the open-marriage concept, but she couldn't live with it for long.

Not My Brother's Keeper

Sexually or otherwise, Adventurous individuals simply do not see themselves as obligated to anyone. They will remain in a relationship as long as it feels right to them. They believe that every individual on the planet —including themselves—is responsible for him- or herself. They don't have their antennae focused on the feelings of others, they don't worry about anyone, and they allow others plenty of room to do as they please. They feel no moral pressure to save a relationship just for the sake of saving it or because they feel they owe the partner something for having been involved in the first place. As in other aspects of their lives, they don't build, together or alone, for the future.

Thus, if it isn't infidelity that breaks up a couple, it may simply be that the Adventurous partner has no incentive to endure the tempering of passions that almost always occurs as a relationship grows and changes. Few relationships can offer the perpetual peak experiences that the Adventurer may require, but a new partner will provide that stimulation.

The strongly Adventurous are not, in a word, monogamous. They may never marry, preferring a series of relationships instead. If they do marry, they'll likely be unfaithful; or they may have a series of marriages, taking each for what it's worth and then moving on.

However, this trait does not mean that an Adventurer can never have a long-lasting, meaningful relationship. It can happen, eventually.

Marshall Meets His Match

Marshall is a longtime movie cowboy-stuntman, and Ramona is a dancer-aerobics instructor. They met at a circus, where they had each taken their kids, and ended up sitting in the same row. Marshall had been married twice, briefly, once when he was nineteen, then again when he was twenty-eight. The child he brought to the circus was his with a woman he'd lived with for a few years during his forties. Marshall was fifty-one and Ramona was thirty-five when they met. Within days they were tumbling in each other's arms—nothing new for Marshall. Nor for Ramona either; she'd been married once before and she "hadn't exactly been a nun" since her divorce, as she put it.

Ramona knew Marshall's type—rugged, tough, hungry, not the kind to settle down with one woman. From day one she never kidded herself about him. She never said, "Where were you last night when I called?" or, "When am I going to see you next?" or even, "Please understand how I feel about your coming and going." She didn't get upset when he left to do a western in Italy for a couple of months, or when he went deep-sea fishing off Florida or any of his other jaunts. Sometimes she even went with him, if her mother would take her little girl. Her attitude toward Marshall, and any other man, was: "I don't need a man to *give* me a life, or to *ruin* my life either. If he's going to do his thing, who am I to stop him? I'll stick around as long as there's something in it for me. If I don't like it, or if I want something he can't give, I'm not going to get myself hurt—I'll leave and take care of myself."

Ramona's attitude was learned "in the school of hard knocks. I graduated with honors," she says. Expecting more of men than they were willing to give always turned into heartbreak. One day when she was in her early thirties she suddenly "woke up to reality," as she puts it. "I looked around and saw that I was always having fantasies about how life with a man was supposed to turn out. Well, it wasn't turning out," says the Dramatic-Devoted-Conscientious-style Ramona. "So I decided: no more expectations!" She adds, "But if I want a guy, I'll fight for him. With my eyes wide open."

Marshall was intrigued with the redheaded Ramona. He'd never before met a woman quite like her. She was gorgeous, passionate, and she didn't feel compelled to talk about their relationship or to make him tell her his feelings, to make plans, or to expect him to feel guilty. She was willing to try new things—she even went skydiving with him, though she was scared out of her wits and never did it again. But if he went off on his own, she didn't complain about it. And she didn't ask whom he'd slept with when he wasn't with her.

Marshall moved in with Ramona after a few months. There were problems, of course. The biggest ones were about money. Marshall didn't work regularly; he could have, but he didn't want to. He didn't save money either, and Ramona sometimes resented contributing more to the household upkeep than he did. But when he worked he was well paid and would buy things for her and her daughter and for the house. It was the irregularity of the income, his lack of concern about it, and the way that it went through his fingers that bothered her. But then

Ramona thought it through. She decided he wasn't leeching off her. She was a big girl and could support herself—and Marshall too, if she chose to.

The other big issue was the way he treated her daughter and his son; the boy stayed with them one weekend a month and for much of the summer. She thought that Marshall was insensitive to the kids' feelings about things. If they wanted to go to a movie, for instance, he'd take them to see something *he* wanted to see. And she thought he took unnecessary risks with them. Once, when he was supposed to be looking after them, he went out and left them alone in the house for three hours, although they were only six and eight years old. Ramona lost her temper over that. Marshall looked blank. What was the big deal? Nothing had happened. "What if there'd been a fire?" she screamed. "But there wasn't," he said. So Ramona finally figured out that she would have to be responsible for the kids at all times.

Neither Marshall nor Ramona believed the relationship would last. They thought it would be a temporary, physical thing that would burn itself out. But it's lasted eight years now and there's still plenty of fire between them. Ramona believes it could go at any moment. "I'm a realist," she declares frequently, meaning that she harbors no fantasies about Marshall. She is willing to live in a long, extended present with him, not to think ahead, not to worry about what will become of them.

Financially Ramona is set. She inherited some money from her father, and she put half of it in trust for her daughter, the other in long-term investments for her old age. She owns and operates a fitness center now. Marshall still does some movie work, but more and more he's been working with her in her business, teaching karate and offering his services as a personal trainer. She doesn't push him. Sometimes he likes to take off for a month at a time. She always feels a little surprised when he comes back, and relieved down deep in her heart, although she doesn't like to admit it. She refuses to allow herself to think about Marshall's staying or Marshall's leaving.

Marshall has never told Ramona that increasingly he looks forward to coming home to her. He thinks about her a lot when he's away. Sexually he's slowing down; he's not so interested in other women. Ramona, however, isn't cooling—and it amazes Marshall that she still turns him on. She turns on other men, too—he's seen the way they eye her at the fitness center. Marshall's nearly sixty years old now. He's never counted the years before, but looking at sixty shocks him. How'd that happen? He doesn't look a day over forty. Hardly a gray hair on his head, and no fat on his body.

In truth, Marshall's feeling kind of creaky. And the younger guys are getting all the work in the movie business. "Ramona's only in her mid-forties. What's she doing with an old guy like me?" he found himself thinking recently. Marshall turned off the TV and shaved off his two-day growth of beard. He went out and bought a dozen roses and a bottle of brandy. He put on some country music and waited for Ramona.

Good/Bad Matches

Adventurers like Marshall need a partner who will ask little of them but give a lot. While Ramona may appear tough and self-interested like Marshall, in fact she made a lot of room in her life for him. She bent to his needs and asked little of the same from him. At the same time, she was sufficiently mature to make sure that she didn't sacrifice her own best interests in the process.

The personality types that have the best chance for a relationship with an Adventurer over the long run would be a combination of the other-directed Dramatic, the Self-Sacrificing, and the Conscientious. The Dramatic offers the necessary extroverted liveliness and sexuality, the Self-Sacrificing provides the flexibility, and the Conscientious provides the sense of responsibility that at least one partner in the relationship must have. But when any of these styles becomes needy of attention or dependent on the Adventurer to fulfill major life responsibilities, it's the end.

It's safer to think of matches for this fundamentally nonmonogamous style for the short term. Then the Dramatic, the selfsame Adventurous, and the Mercurial—all out for an intense experience of life—will hit it off best. The Leisurely is another possibility, since these individuals too are pleasure seekers; they tend to be more passive in their entertainments, however, and they like to live by the rules rather than bend them.

Adventurous Parents

They're not the best in any long-term relationship, including those with children. They're not reliably there, since their wanderlust draws them away from home so often. They may care a lot for their children and may feel some sadness that they can't come through for them more. But they have to go their own way.

When they are there with the kids, Adventurers tend to assume that what's good for them is good for the kids, or that what they want for their kids is in the kids' best interests. They may expose their children to unnecessary risks and may not teach them caution. Nor do they think of the consequences to the family of the risks they take on their own behalf. They are not naturally tuned in to other people's feelings.

Yet, for all the not-goods, Adventurous-style parents are exciting, interesting, and noncritical, and can open up a big world for their children. They may prove irresponsible, impatient, and hot-tempered, but they are full of energy, curiosity, and good spirit. They're romantic, swashbuckling figures. What is essential for their kids is one full-time, on-the-scene, non-Adventurous parent who will be sensitive, supportive, reliable, and protective.

TIPS ON DEALING WITH
THE ADVENTUROUS PERSON IN YOUR LIFE

1. Have fun. But make sure you know exactly what's going on. The Adventurous person in your life can make an exciting companion, but don't confuse what you may want out of a relationship with what he or she is actually offering you. Adventurous types are charming and disarming. This person may flatter, persuade, cajole, or even manipulate you into an affair or an adventure, but just because you share this intimacy doesn't mean the Adventurer loves you or feels any responsibility toward you. If you are the traditional love-and-marriage type, look at the Adventurous behavior closely. Ask questions. Understand that this person may be seeing or sleeping with others besides you. Realize that, romantic, sexy, and exciting as he or she may be, this person will not satisfy your more traditional needs.

2. No illusions. Once you are in a relationship with an Adventurous person, don't think, "Aha! Now I can change him or her." Accept what this person gives you, and recognize that he or she is not likely to start adapting to your needs. You be the flexible one. If that's not your style, and if the Adventurer does not provide what you need, it's up to you to get out.

3. Don't crowd. The Adventurous person in your life needs freedom to do as he or she pleases. Be satisfied with a nontraditional relationship that includes, perhaps, separate vacations. Don't try to prevent the Adventurer from taking off. This person is more likely to come back to you if you let him or her go in the first place.

4. Be responsible. The Adventurous person in your life may not make decisions about money, children's safety, safe sex, or other things the

way you would. Don't wait for him or her to do the right thing. You take appropriate measures for birth control and disease prevention, for financial security, and for the protection of your kids. Don't be a passive partner.

5. Know your limits. Adventurous types have a great tolerance and capacity for drugs and alcohol, for fear, and for risk. The Adventurous person in your life will probably assume that you like what he or she likes, unless you make your preferences clear. If you are terrified of white-water rafting, don't go. Stop after one or two drinks if that's enough for you.

6. Expect a lot of yourself, not of the Adventurous person in your life. To maintain a relationship with an Adventurous person requires that you have strong self-esteem and don't need him or her to support you emotionally and help you love yourself. Adventurous people are not spontaneously sensitive to other people's feelings or needs. So you have to be able to find sources of self-esteem from within yourself and to be able to say without anger or resentment, "This is who I am, what I feel, and what I need."

7. Stay as sexy as you are. Keep your sexual relationship interesting and lively. Toss your inhibitions and be ready and willing to experiment.

MAKING THE MOST OF YOUR ADVENTUROUS STYLE

Your strong points include your spontaneity, your ability to act, your strength, your fearlessness, your ability to experience pleasure, and your tendency to live life to the fullest. The trouble you run into results from impulsiveness and lack of forethought. In this way you resemble people with Dramatic and Mercurial personality styles. Practice Exercises 3 (Stop and count to ten) and 4 (Plan) from chapter 7 (p. 147); from chapter 14 (p. 311) try Exercise 7 (Time it).

Exercise 1

Think from your head, not from your appetites. Urges, desires, and whims are compelling and have their own satisfying, feeling logic. Acting in direct response to impulse bypasses the cerebral cortex, the thinking part of your brain. While you are counting to ten, concentrate on the thinking part of your brain and try to experience the difference between that and the feeling, sensation-satisfying part of your brain.

Exercise 2

Your style is remarkably free of anxiety, thus the consequences of your actions or lifestyle may not occur to you. So, worry a little. Each time you are about to take a risk—to invest money or to gamble, to go in an airplane or on a motorcycle, to drink or take drugs, to climb a mountain, anything at all—use your cerebral cortex to consider what could possibly go wrong. Think of two or more unfortunate possibilities. For example, if you are about to climb up on a bucking bronco at a rodeo, you might think: (1) I could get killed, (2) I could get maimed.

Exercise 3

Safeguard yourself. For each of the possibilities on your risk list, figure out at least one way to protect yourself in advance. For example, if you could get killed competing in the rodeo, you could protect yourself by staying sober and competing with your wits about you. To safeguard yourself against at least some of the consequences of life as a disabled person, you could take out health and disability insurance, or you could make sure you had a job that offered these benefits. If you are unable to figure out a safeguard for any of the risks on your list, consider not indulging in those activities.

The next two exercises are the same as the first two, but with a twist.

Exercise 4

Worry about other people. Observe your interactions with others and note all the possible ways in which your behavior or decisions put them at risk. For example, your baby is napping and you want to go across the street for a while. What could go wrong if you leave him alone for fifteen minutes? (1) The house could catch fire and the baby wouldn't be able to get out of his crib; (2) the baby could vomit and choke and you wouldn't be there to save him.

Exercise 5

Safeguard other people from the risks of your behavior. Wait to go across the street until your spouse comes back, or get someone in to look after the sleeping baby just in case something happens. Or don't go at all.

If you find it difficult to understand how you may put others at risk, you may need to see things from their point of view. Try Exercise 4 for the Self-Confident style (p. 97): "Who *is* this person?" Concentrate on what the people who are important to you like, dislike, think, and feel. Try to see things through their eyes instead of your own. Look especially for ways in which they differ from you.

Exercise 6

Think about this: What do you want out of your life five, ten, twenty years from now?

ANTISOCIAL PERSONALITY DISORDER

Individuals with Antisocial personality disorder, also known as psychopaths or sociopaths, couldn't care less about the feelings of others or the rules of society. Where others seek to build, they destroy.

DIAGNOSTIC CRITERIA

The DSM-IV describes Antisocial personality disorder as follows:

A. There is a pervasive pattern of disregard for and violation of the rights of others occurring since age 15 years, as indicated by three (or more) of the following:

(1) failure to conform to social norms with respect to lawful behaviors as indicated by repeatedly performing acts that are grounds for arrest

(2) deceitfulness, as indicated by repeated lying, use of aliases, or conning others for personal profit or pleasure

(3) impulsivity or failure to plan ahead

(4) irritability and aggressiveness, as indicated by repeated physical fights or assaults

(5) reckless disregard for safety of self or others

(6) consistent irresponsibility, as indicated by repeated failure to sustain consistent work behavior or honor financial obligations

(7) lack of remorse, as indicated by being indifferent to or rationalizing having hurt, mistreated, or stolen from another

B. The individual is at least age 18 years.

C. There is evidence of Conduct Disorder with onset before age 15 years.

D. The occurrence of antisocial behavior is not exclusively during the course of Schizophrenia or a Manic Episode.

MISSING: CONSCIENCE AND COMPASSION

Most of us internalize into our personal conscience the basic rules of society and culture. We believe that it is wrong to hurt or exploit others. We believe we should obey the intent or the letter of the law. We feel it is right to support and protect our children, and so on. When we fail to live up to our moral codes, we feel guilty. Some people (such as Conscientious types) have a stronger conscience and resulting sense of guilt than do others, but those with Antisocial personality disorder have little or none of either. They disdain the rules of society. They want what they want and they'll take it, be it property, sex, or even life. They know the difference between right and wrong in the legal sense; they just don't care about it. They have little compassion or empathy for others and can often justify every cruel, destructive, malicious, or manipulative act.

You'll find many of the people with this disorder in jail, now or eventually. Antisocial personality disorder is among the two most common diagnoses among convicted felons, occurring in as much as 75 percent of the prison population. (Alcohol abuse is the other diagnosis that vies for top place in forensic settings.)

But unscrupulous, exploitive, thoroughly self-interested behavior is not restricted to convicted criminals. The majority of Antisocial persons are not criminals. In public and private life, they use and abuse, outdo and outsmart other people, and suffer little or no remorse. They can be extremely shrewd and size up your weaknesses in no time. To get what they want they will manipulate your conscience and compassion. Somewhere along the Adventurous-Antisocial continuum are people who commit professional ethics violations and think they're perfectly entitled, yet who lie convincingly when caught or confronted; those who take pride in saying anything to a woman just to get her into bed, then blame her for seducing them. They'll charm and disarm you, telling you what you want to hear or what will touch your tender heartstrings. An Antisocial individual can con an elderly person out of his or her meager savings and feel thrilled with the victory.

Obviously, individuals with Antisocial personality disorder can rarely form deep, warm, close, responsible relationships. Their ability to love and to empathize with others is so impaired that few of them can sustain a relationship with one person for as long as a year. They do have children, since their sexual needs are powerful and they rarely concern themselves with the consequences. Unfortunately, Antisocial parents do not take care of their children or consider their future well-being. Child abuse, sexual and otherwise, runs rampant in their families.

ACT BEFORE YOU THINK

Antisocial individuals can bear no frustration. If thwarted or simply annoyed, they will often lash out violently, against their own families or whoever else is around. They do not consider consequences, they do not plan ahead, and they do not learn from experience. In other words, Antisocial individuals do not think before they act. Impulse rules. Moreover, they are unafraid; they seem to suffer none of the anticipatory anxiety that would stop most of us in our ill-intended tracks. Again and again, their aggressiveness, impulsiveness, and recklessness land Antisocial individuals in court, in jail, or in hospital emergency rooms. As the DSM-IV notes, people with this disorder "are more likely than people in the general population to die prematurely by violent means (e.g., suicide, accidents, and homicides)."

REMISSION OF SINS

Antisocial behavior appears early in life and tends to diminish early as well. Without exception (and by definition), the men and women with Antisocial personality disorder suffered from Conduct Disorders as kids. They were vandals, bullies, thieves, truants, early substance abusers, and sexually active far younger than their peers. Note that only a minority of children with Conduct Disorder go on to develop the adult pattern; most grow or are helped out of it. Note too, as we will discuss shortly, that these disordered kids who go on to develop the adult disorder are not apples that turn bad for no reason. They were almost always "nurtured" in extremely unstable, chaotic, violent families.

Should they survive into their thirties, however, there's a good chance that these individuals will stop behaving so destructively toward others. This does not mean that they are "cured." Even if many Antisocial individuals calm down in later life, they remain isolated and unable to establish close, responsible relationships. As they were in their youth, they continue to be irritable, angry, isolated, and tense. They may suffer as well from anxiety, depression, and numerous physical complaints.

INCIDENCE, PREDISPOSITIONS, AND RISKS

Approximately 3 percent of American males and fewer than 1 percent of American females suffer from Antisocial personality disorder, although there's been concern that it is underdiagnosed in women. It seems to be more common among lower socioeconomic classes, especially in poverty-stricken urban environments where families are fragmented. The DSM-IV raises a cautionary flag, however, in applying this diagnosis: "Concerns have been raised that the diagnosis may at times be misapplied to individuals in settings in which seemingly antisocial behavior may be part of a protective survival strategy. In assessing antisocial traits, it is helpful for the clinician to consider the social and economic context in which the behaviors occur."

Antisocial personality disorder shows a strongly family-related pattern. It is much more common among immediate relatives of people with the disorder than among the general population. "The risk to biological relatives of females with the disorder tends to be higher than the risk to biological relatives of males with the disorder," reports the DSM-IV, although reasons for this correlation remain unclear. Family history of alcohol and substance abuse problems as well as somatization disorder (marked by significant physical symptoms that cannot be explained by any medical condition) is also common.

Anxiety, depression, substance abuse, and pathological gambling are common among this group. Borderline, Histrionic and Narcissistic personality disorders often co-occur.

Biological Factors

Studies of children born to Antisocial parents reveal that they are more likely than the general population to develop this personality disorder even if they are adopted soon after birth. This evidence strongly supports the existence of a genetic factor involved in the development of Antisocial personality disorder among some individuals.

Among the biological factors that may prove to be inherited is the brain-arousal pattern characteristic of many people with Antisocial symptoms. Brain-activity studies have shown that the nervous systems of some Antisocial individuals are relatively underaroused. Unlike over-anxious Avoidant individuals, who withdraw from stimuli because they are overly excitable (see chapter 9, p. 201), underanxious Antisocial people may need excessive stimulation in order to keep themselves turned on. This would explain their characteristic sensation-seeking behavior (we'll talk more about this in chapter 18).

Some studies have found that although Antisocial individuals react normally to an unpleasant stimulus (such as an electrical shock), their physiological response to anticipation of this stimulus is abnormally weak. After a few of these jolts, most other people will know the next is coming and will show evidence of anticipatory anxiety. This finding may provide some biologic evidence for what is often observed in Antisocial people: they do not become afraid, even in situations (such as violent confrontations with police) that they've been in before that have produced disastrous consequences. In other words, they do not become conditioned to fear—one reason, perhaps, why they do not learn from experience.

Evidence has been accumulating that some Antisocial individuals have low brain levels of serotonin, a neurotransmitter that helps to suppress aggressive behavior, among its many roles in regulating the nervous system. Low levels of serotonin have been linked to violent, impulsive behavior. Now neuroscientists are finding that the Antisocial person's aggression against others may actually result from a combination of a serotonin deficit plus an excess of the activating neurotransmitter noradrenaline—which is linked to a tendency to overreact to the environment. (See "The Biochemistry of Dominance and Violence ," in chapter 16, p. 364.)

Environmental Realities

Biological factors are not entirely responsible. Being born to an Antisocial parent increases the risk to the offspring—and so does being adopted by an Antisocial parent. Antisocial parents form chaotic, unstable, violent families, in which discipline and supervision are absent, inappropriate, or inconsistent. Very often individuals with Antisocial personality disorder reveal a history in which they were severely abused, removed from their homes, and/or grew up without any parental figures. (Abusive, neglectful parenting is not a guarantee that the child will become Antisocial. Far from it. One recent study found that 86 percent of the people they studied who had been abused/neglected as children *did not* show evidence of this personality disorder.) Extreme poverty has also been identified as a risk factor. Others may have been born with difficult temperaments that incited the hostility and rejection of insensitive, uncaring, immature, or cruel parents. Some researchers believe that the behavior in children results from a lack of adequate bonding to a parent within the first year of life.

Children who must suffer these indignities learn immediately that the world is hostile, frustrating, and mean. They have no responsible adult models to teach them how to control or to channel their own impulses. They learn to trust and care for no one except themselves. They may learn too that vicious behavior is one way to vent their feelings.

And the results are apparent early. Canadian psychologist Richard Tremblay and his colleagues have been conducting a long-term study of boys in Montreal since their kindergarten year. They found that boys who exhibited delinquent behavior at age thirteen had already been identified in kindergarten as impulsive, excitable, and otherwise troublesome. (These are traits that are also typical of children with attention deficit/hyperactivity disorder, or ADHD. ADHD is a risk factor for the development of Antisocial personality disorder in adulthood if it occurs along with conduct problems in early childhood.)

HELP!

Antisocial individuals rarely wish to change. However, they may end up in treatment because of impulsive suicide attempts, substance abuse problems, discipline difficulties, or sometimes a shattering life experience, or because of threats by family members or as a condition of probation. Some come faking symptoms in order to get psychoactive medication. "They do not seek help for their bad character," Dr. Stone points out. "I have never heard a patient announce as his 'chief complaint': 'Doc, you have to help me get control of myself. I treat people shabbily, I cheat on my fiancée, I pad my expense account . . . you gotta help me stop!' What I have heard instead are complaints like: 'I'm turning forty now and I worry that my hairline is receding. I go to the beach to see if I can still attract girls of eighteen or nineteen. My wife pissed me off the other day when she came home unexpectedly and caught me talking to one of them on the phone. What do you think, Doc? Do I look forty?' "

In one-on-one psychodynamic therapy, they tend to try to con, outfox, and humiliate the therapist, with whom, as with everyone else, they fail to form an emotional bond. Treatment success is more likely with those Antisocial individuals who are least destructive and possess some measure of empathy.

Cognitive therapy for Antisocial personality disorder is designed to help these people learn to anticipate the future and to stop thinking in concrete, here-and-now terms. Typical dysfunctional Antisocial beliefs that need to be challenged include: "My thoughts and feelings are completely accurate, simply because they occur to me," and "I know I am right because I feel right about what I do."

People with Antisocial personality disorder can often be helped on a problem-by-problem basis. For example, successful treatment of the substance abuse problems that commonly accompany Antisocial personality disorder will often lead to improvement of mood and health problems as well as their behavior toward their families. Sometimes Alcoholics Anonymous and other Twelve-Step programs can achieve results that therapeutic treatment programs don't. Men and women with this disorder are perhaps most effectively treated in strict, disciplined, live-in therapeutic environments in which they are treated with care and respect, as in a good family, but in which they can't get away with breaking the rules and manipulating other people. Also, there is some evidence that the drug lithium can help some of them stop and think before they misbehave.

COPING WITH ANTISOCIAL PEOPLE

While it may go against your own beliefs, do not assume that you can trust, help, or reform an Antisocial person. Remember that these people can be very cunning and manipulative. Don't be conned. Protect your own interests and back out. If you can't pull yourself away from such a person, get help for yourself.

CHAPTER 12

Idiosyncratic Style

"THE DIFFERENT DRUMMER"

Idiosyncratic men and women are not like anyone else. They are dreamers, seekers of the spirit, visionaries, mystics. They march to a distinctive beat, different from the conventional rhythms that most people follow. They are true originals and often they stand out, sometimes as eccentrics, sometimes as geniuses.

THE SIX CHARACTERISTICS

The following six traits and behaviors are clues to the presence of the Idiosyncratic style. A person who reveals a strong Idiosyncratic tendency will demonstrate more of these behaviors more intensely than someone with less of this style in his or her personality profile.

1. *Inner life.* Idiosyncratic individuals are tuned in to and sustained by their own feelings and belief systems, whether or not others accept or understand their particular worldview or approach to life.

2. *Own world.* They are self-directed and independent, requiring few close relationships.

3. *Own thing.* Oblivious to convention, Idiosyncratic individuals create interesting, unusual, often eccentric lifestyles.

4. *Expanded reality.* Open to anything, they are interested in the occult, the extrasensory, and the supernatural.

5. *Metaphysics.* They are drawn to abstract and speculative thinking.

6. *Outward view.* Though they are inner-directed and follow their own hearts and minds, Idiosyncratic men and women are keen observers of others, particularly sensitive to how other people react to them.

THE SIX DOMAINS
OF IDIOSYNCRATIC FUNCTIONING

The Idiosyncratic is the only style for which the Real World, coupled with the Self domain, is the central determining domain of functioning.

REAL WORLD:
THINGS AREN'T ALWAYS WHAT THEY SEEM

Antonia R., a best-selling writer of detective novels, lives in a twenty-room Victorian mansion. She volunteered her house for the movie version of one of her murder mysteries. Three rooms in a closed-off wing of the house were refurbished for the film. After several days of preparation and setting up, the actors took their places and the cameramen were poised to begin shooting the bedroom murder scene. No sooner had the director given the word than they heard a loud crashing noise from somewhere above their heads. Then another.

"Cut!" yelled the director. He looked around for Antonia. "What's going on up there?"

"I'll go see," she said.

"Fred, go with her," the director ordered a young crew member.

The two of them looked around the attic and found nothing out of place or unusual. After a fifteen-minute delay, the shooting resumed and nothing untoward happened for the rest of the day. The same noise recurred, in different parts of the house, on the second and again on the last day of shooting. No explanation was ever discovered, although each time it happened Antonia went off to look, with Fred trailing close behind. "I can't explain it," Antonia said, shaking her head.

After the crew finished filming at the house and returned to California to complete the movie, Antonia's husband, Russell, came back from a business trip abroad. They talked about the strange incidents. "The ghost," they both agreed.

Antonia had refrained from telling the director what she believed was the cause of the peculiar noises. She had heard them before, always in that unused wing of the old New England house. She had no doubt that a ghost dwelled there. Russell didn't really believe it, but he went along with that explanation for lack of any other. Besides, the idea of having one's own resident ghost amused him.

The couple mentioned their ghost to very few others and certainly not to the film crew. They knew that people would think that Antonia, who believed thoroughly in such unearthly manifestations, was crazy.

Open Minds

Idiosyncratic individuals like Antonia are not crazy, but they often strike people that way because they perceive the Real World so differently from everyone else. It's not that they all believe in ghosts, have a sixth sense, experience past lives, or hear the music of the spheres. It's that Idiosyncratic individuals do not feel compelled to accept the customary explanations of what's going on in this world. Thus, in some settings they may be viewed as weird or eccentric (meaning off-center)—or even heretical, as were those Puritans in early Massachusetts who did *not* believe in witches.

The minds and imaginations of Idiosyncratic types range far and wide. They are willing to consider anything as real. The open-mindedness of this style is a boon to creative and intellectual exploration and discovery, and Idiosyncratic personality style frequently accompanies creative and intellectual genius. People such as Albert Einstein, Isaac Newton, Glenn Gould, Salvador Dali, and Lewis Carroll, to name a few, perceived something different out there because they were not locked into the accepted explanations and interpretations that seem unequivocally true to most people.

Genius or otherwise, Idiosyncratic men and women are creatively curious. They're always asking: What if . . . ? What if I represented reality with one black line down the center of this canvas? What if I played the Bach Partitas at twice the tempo? What if there really were a Santa Claus? "There's no Santa Claus, Henry. *I* put the keys to the new Pontiac under the Christmas tree and *I* paid for it. Here's the bill if you don't believe me." But if Henry's personality is sufficiently Idiosyncratic, he may perceive a spirit of Christmas that you cannot begin to imagine.

Idiosyncratic individuals are by no means oblivious to what other people think and believe. Henry knows that most people over the age of seven no longer believe in Santa Claus. Antonia is aware that few people believe in ghosts. It doesn't matter to them what other people think. Always their own understandings come from inside themselves, not from other people, books, or newspapers. Idiosyncratic types are driven to live their lives according to the sensations, feelings, and ideas that spring from inside them. They are true nonconformists.

A New Age Personality Style?

By definition, Idiosyncratic is an uncommon personality style. But you may find many people with this style involved in some way with the New Age movement, for it provides them a forum and setting for their unconventional beliefs and their personal spiritual seeking. An Idiosyncratic individual can attend a New Age workshop on past lives or shamanistic healing or spend months meditating at an ashram without fear of being thought peculiar. Individuals with this personality style are very aware that other people may think them rather strange, so they often seek the company of like-minded others in order to be more comfortable in life. This doesn't mean that everyone who identifies with the New Age movement necessarily has an Idiosyncratic personality style, or that all Idiosyncratic people participate in New Age activities. People come to new movements for many reasons: because the ideas or beliefs appeal to them; because their old belief systems no longer work for them; because they have a strong need to affiliate and to be accepted; because they need a person or a cause to lend new structure to their lives; and so on. However, Idiosyncratic people are not "joiners"—they do not affiliate or conform, no matter who's in charge. They are not inclined to accept or espouse anyone else's principles and beliefs. Their quest is entirely personal, their beliefs original.

SELF: MY WORLD IS REAL

The greatest reality for Idiosyncratic types derives from their internal worlds—from the domain of Self. If they believe in something or their personal experiences suggest, for example, that they have ESP, then it exists and they don't need scientific proof. They heed their inner voices, not those of other people. Unlike Conscientious or Sensitive-style people, their self-esteem is not based on following protocol or being correct from someone else's point of view. Thus, an Idiosyncratic artist can break with tradition without worrying what the public or the dealers or the critics might think. With sufficient talent and genius, this artistic vision may be a huge groundbreaker. Or it may offend throughout history. No matter, the artist with this personality style will follow his or her inclinations.

. . . And I'll Live in It However I Please

Idiosyncratic individuals tend to have odd habits and to build strange, eccentric lifestyles—and to be judged by more conventional types as slightly or substantially strange.

There is no end of stories about Idiosyncratic peculiarities. Antonia, to discourage mosquitoes indoors, invited a number of bats to live inside her house. When Russell was away on a business trip she had the handyman hang several bat houses. Then she removed the screens from the windows in two of the guest rooms, and soon she had a number of flying mammalian mosquito-eaters swooping around at night. But Russell, normally very accommodating to his wife, put his foot down at that one. A ghost was enough.

The late Canadian pianist Glenn Gould slept by day and worked by night. He liked to wear several layers of clothing—turtleneck, sweater, jacket, and coat—indoors. He hummed along with his music in performance and as he recorded, unconcerned that listeners could hear his unmistakable drone.

Charlotte G., a landscape designer, wears only green clothing since she discovered that in that color she feels deeply peaceful. Ronald H., a self-made multimillionaire, prefers to sleep outdoors, often in the gardens of some of the finest hotels of the world.

All these individuals are (or were) indifferent to what other people think about their habits. They don't try to fit in—they wouldn't even know how.

. . . Whether You Like It or Not

Somehow, many Idiosyncratic people live and work and succeed, sometimes phenomenally well, in the same world we live in, only they do it their way. (Individuals with Schizotypal personality disorder, the extreme of the Idiosyncratic style, do not manage to adapt to "our" world.) Still, predominantly Idiosyncratic people may find acceptance by others difficult, and in this country they are frequent subjects of ridicule (see the Timothy Leary story on pp. 259–60, for example). The degree to which their Idiosyncrasy will be a problem for them depends on the setting, on the prevailing culture, on their successes or talents, and on the degree to which they need the warmth, support, and acceptance of other people. In the sixties, weird behavior and alternate lifestyles were "in." But neither then nor now could an Idiosyncratic wife of a military officer or corporate executive get along well on the base or in the traditional corporate culture, where proper form and procedure are everything.

The fact is, the numbers of settings where highly Idiosyncratic individuals can fit in are few. An Idiosyncratic actor, writer, musician, intellectual, or psychic healer may be able to find his or her niche. With great talent, achievement, or wealth, an Idiosyncratic individual (the late Howard Hughes comes to mind) will be courted by others no matter how bizarrely he or she behaves. But the quirky Idiosyncratic individual who has nothing extraordinary to offer to mainstream society may find the going rough if he or she cannot locate a welcoming or at least tolerant environment.

Moderately Idiosyncratic people, especially if they have a more dominant conforming style (such as the Conscientious), usually find it easier to accommodate to traditional external expectations, while keeping their beliefs and ideas to themselves. Even so, in extremely "straight" environments they may seem a bit unusual—refreshingly original to some, a little "off" to others.

Just Another Typical (English) Eccentric

The English seem to favor Idiosyncrasy. *Time* magazine writer Pico Iyer described one Charles Waterton, for example, as

> just another typical eccentric. In his 80s the eminent country squire was to be seen clambering around the upper branches of an oak tree with what was aptly described as the agility of an "adolescent gorilla." The beloved 27th lord of Walton Hall also devoted his distinguished old age to scratching the back part of his head with his right big toe. Such displays of animal high spirits were not, however, confined to the gentleman's later years. When young, Waterton made four separate trips to South America, where he sought the wourali poison (a cure, he was convinced, for hydrophobia), and once spent months on end with one foot dangling from his hammock in the quixotic hope of having his toe sucked by a vampire bat.

Stress and the Uncertainty Factor

Freethinking has its limitations. Idiosyncratics' rejection of standard explanations and conventions, plus their reliance on inner experience alone to assess the nature of the Real World, can lead to doubt and uncertainty. It is characteristic of this personality style to question and to wonder. Among the "what-ifs" that Idiosyncratic individuals may ask is: "What if there's yet another way to explain things?" Idiosyncratic types may experience anything from mild confusion to serious crises of confidence when their personal systems begin to rearrange themselves into new worldviews.

"I wish," sighed Idiosyncratic Benjamin W., "that I'd been able to accept the Orthodox Judaism I was brought up in. My dad never had a doubt in his life. He never had to make up his mind. His father, the Talmud, and the rabbis told him what to believe, what to do, what not to do, what to think, what to eat, who to marry." Benjamin is now in his late thirties. His spiritual quest is his reason for being. He has studied with mystics in South America, he has experienced his own personal god while on an acid trip, and he considered entering a Buddhist monastery.

Benjamin, like many Idiosyncratic people, is constantly reinventing the universe in his search for reality and truth. He could no more accept an orthodox explanation of the Real World than his father could have lived in an ashram. But in part he envies his father his lifetime consistency of faith and his ability to accept conventional interpretations of things without wondering whether they're true for him personally. Benjamin wants a Real World that can satisfy him intellectually, spiritually, and emotionally, but his self-styled system is in constant flux. As a seeker, he will always be looking for something more, something else, something better. Usually that's fine with him; the quest itself is a source of joy and fulfillment for him. But in times of difficulty, as when his marriage ended last year, it would have been easier for Benjamin to have an established set of beliefs to make sense of things. As it was, he found nothing in his understandings of the universe to explain what had happened to his life. He lost faith and became deeply dispirited.

Doubt and disillusionment often accompany Idiosyncratic seeking. These, along with having to conform to someone else's reality, are this personality style's most significant sources of stress. But inner strength is also characteristic of this style, and Idiosyncratic individuals will often find a suitable metaphysical explanation for their crises of confidence and then move on to embrace a new belief system or at least solace themselves with music or art. (Yale-educated Benjamin was heard to say recently, "Maybe I'll take up East Coast intellectualism again.") If, however, the stresses come from the pressures of a conformist society, Idiosyncratic types may find it easier to cope by withdrawing from the mainstream.

The Cosmic Answer(s)

Dr. Timothy Leary, the brilliant ex-Harvard social psychology professor (who in the 1950s made important contributions to the understanding of personality assessment), earned a notorious place in the annals of social history in the 1960s for experimenting with and popularizing the use of LSD. He was thrown out of Harvard, but that hardly ended his Idiosyncratic saga. "It becomes apparent that computers are the new Cosmic Answer to It All for Dr. Tim. He's always prescribing *something* as the Cosmic Answer, although the Answer has tended to change—*evolve,* he'd say—fairly frequently," reported Ron Rosenbaum in *Vanity Fair* magazine in 1988, when Leary was in his late sixties and living in Los Angeles.

Psychedelic "peace and love" was the Answer for a long time. But then, in 1971, after his escape from prison, when he found refuge with the Black Panthers in Algeria, revolutionary violence became the Answer. . . . But this Cosmic Answer didn't last long: after the Black Panthers put Leary under house arrest in Algiers for being "too frivolous" for revolutionary discipline, after he escaped from their custody to Switzerland, where he stayed in the ski chalets of various wealthy heirs to European fortunes (including the Opels), for a brief while it seemed as if *skiing* might be the Cosmic Answer: Dr. Tim rhapsodized over "the ski satori, the velocity revelation . . . like the first acid experience . . . high speed philosophy . . . kinaesthetic yoga."

Then after he'd been recaptured by the U.S. drug agents in Afghanistan and thrown into the maximum-security hole in Folsom prison, he took up the idea that space migration and extraterrestrial intelligence might really be where it's at: he prophesied that the comet Kahoutek might be heading here specifically to take him out of jail and onto a mission to the stars.

When the comet failed to live up to expectations and Leary faced the prospect of years in the clink, the Cosmic Answer became "truth telling"—although others called it "informing" in return for reduced time. . . . "I know some people might get hurt," Leary said then. . . . "But if I can tell my story and get it all out, karmically, I think I'm free within. And if I'm free within, it will reflect without. . . . When I look at Socrates, I see that all they wanted him to do was say he was sorry. He didn't have to drink the hemlock."

. . . But, in his enthusiasm for his most recent Cosmic Answer—interactive software and "cyberpunk" computer-freak consciousness—he seems to have embraced his psychedelic past as well, proclaiming that "the psychedelic revolution was the forerunner of the Cybernetic Revolution."

EMOTIONS AND SELF-CONTROL: TESTING THE LIMITS

The Idiosyncratic is a powerful thinking and feeling style. How these individuals *feel* within themselves is as important as what they *think* is going on in there. Like Dramatic individuals, they seek emotional experience in life, the difference being that the Dramatic emotional expression has so much to do with other people. Not so for the Idiosyncratic, for whom emotions are felt in all their intensity for their own sake.

These individuals seek mind/emotional/spiritual expansion. They crave new experiences to send them to new peaks of feeling and awareness of their inner being. To achieve this, many Idiosyncratics will experiment with varieties of intense experience, from primal-scream therapy, to fasting and long hours of meditation, to psychedelic drugs, to hours and hours of deep thinking or listening to music. Since they tend not to be constrained by convention and will experiment with the forbidden, others may view them as out of control. Those who experiment heavily with drugs often suffer from extreme emotional and behavioral difficulties; these may have more to do with their drug use than with their personality styles, however.

Idiosyncratic types test the limits of emotional and spiritual experience. They seek rapture. They are also eager to explore their inner darkness. During a summer break in college, Idiosyncratic Harriet volunteered for a sleep study. For more than a month she lived in a room with no natural light, no clocks, no TV or radio, no cues to the external environment. She slept and woke when she felt like it. As the time went on, she became increasingly depressed. The more depressed she became, the more she felt she was approaching an important understanding. She began to write down her inner experiences and soon spent all her waking moments with pad and pencil, sleeping less and less. When the study concluded, Harriet, for all her depression, felt she had had a profoundly creative, insightful experience.

An objective observer might have concluded that Harriet had experienced an emotional disorientation that often occurs when a person's internal biological clock loses the external light/dark, day/night cues on which it depends for proper functioning. An Idiosyncratic person, however, would consider that explanation as missing the point. To Harriet the experience *was* the point, not the manipulation of the environment that caused it.

Idiosyncratic people always give priority to their inner emotional experience over what others consider to be objective, external reality. No one's going to tell these types that what they feel isn't really happening. "I feel the presence of his spirit hovering over us," exclaimed Bertha at her husband's deathbed. "Oh, Mother, don't start this now," snapped her daughter Rachel. To which Bertha responded, "Rachel, who are *you* to say what's real?"—at which Bertha's son, Daniel, intervened to cut short the familiar mother-daughter go-around. Similarly, Antonia will declare to Russell, "Something terrible is going to happen. I know, I can feel it." She'll walk around the house in a dark, worried mood, and nothing he can do or say will talk her out of it. And Barry will exclaim to the new woman in his life, "I know I've been close to you in another life." She may feel closer to him in this life as a result of his declaration, or she may think he's off the wall.

The emotional reactions of Idiosyncratic types may be based more on their subjective experiences at a given moment than on what's happening around them—which may make their behavior at times seem strange and inappropriate. Extremely Idiosyncratic individuals will often start to laugh in public because something inside them strikes them as funny. Sometimes they seem kind of "spaced out," because they're tuned inward, not outward toward others. They express their feelings and thoughts in their own way, because conforming is no motivation for them. Still, they may become anxious and self-conscious when they have to be around others who dwell securely in the "regular" world. They know they're different and that people don't always respect or appreciate them for it. They can display quite a temper around rigid, narrow-minded people who insist that their Idiosyncratic way of life is "wrong" and who try to make them mold themselves to "normal" behavior standards.

WORK: FINDING A NICHE

Two key factors in the quality of Idiosyncratic lives are, first, whether they can find an accepting environment and, second, how far they can go to adapt to others' expectations. Not many work settings tolerate eccentricities of behavior—unless the Idiosyncratic person has a great deal to offer by way of intelligence, talent, or skills. Still, the rent has to be paid; like most people, Idiosyncratic types have to work. Those who can keep their eccentricities to themselves do best. Some Idiosyncratics can do well with one ear tuned in to their own little worlds and one outward to what the boss expects of them. Others, however, have a hard time understanding or accepting authority.

Idiosyncratic Pamela, a word processor, could not figure out why her boss insisted that she work from nine to five, when she could often concentrate best in the wee hours. She continued to ask that she be allowed to come into the office at midnight instead. Monica, her boss, at first mildly amused by "kooky" Pamela's requests, would repeat that the office opened at nine and closed at five. But she became increasingly annoyed by Pamela's "weirdness." Although Pamela's work was better than average, when the firm needed to cut back on employees, Pamela was the first to go.

Idiosyncratic types frequently are not ambitious or competitive in the conventional sense and can do well (if they can play by the rules) in routine work that doesn't much interest or challenge them. They are often capable of intense concentration or can "tune out" and still accomplish a day's work well. Kevin H. is a postal worker by day, despite his considerable achievement at college. He's into meditating and can sort mail in a trancelike state.

The Idiosyncratic Manager

Idiosyncratic people aren't often interested in managing others, certainly not in any traditional way. They're not very efficient at the day-to-day requirements of a supervisory role, and they are not necessarily tuned into others' feelings. With competent people to whom they can delegate the routine matters of running an office or department and instituting disciplined practices, however, they can often inspire creativity in others and bring a fresh view to the work. Don't expect the usual sorts of meetings and process reports and overall concern for form, though.

Careers for the Idiosyncratic

Issues of security, benefits, and daily structure do not mean much to people with a predominance of this style. More important are freedom from rules and conformist expectations. If your Personality Self-Portrait includes get-ahead, ambitious styles such as the Self-Confident, the Conscientious, and the Vigilant in addition to the Idiosyncratic, your prime requirement will be to seek out a challenging work environment in which your Idiosyncrasy will be accepted or in which it is not too stressful to keep it to yourself. Even if you are very bright and talented, you will not be able to contribute in settings in which everyone is expected to behave similarly, such as in the corporate world. Even if you do manage to produce, be aware that in traditional settings—including, perhaps, the family business—you may be an irritant to others and may not be politically successful no matter how much you can contribute. Seek out creative work environments, which are generally more tolerant of individual eccentricities provided the work gets done. In professions such as medicine or law, you may be able to find a niche for yourself in your own practice or in partnership with others who are similarly freethinking. Consider, perhaps, a career associated with one of your personal concerns or hobbies. For example, you could sell New Age publications or goods, or work in some capacity for an organization or cause that interests you.

For those of you who are not especially ambitious in the Work domain, or who need to earn money only to support your personal interests or endeavors, find a nondemanding job that provides stability and freedom from economic worry. With good concentration, Idiosyncratic individuals often make skilled word processors, typists, secretaries, baggage handlers, postal employees—work in which you can keep your mind to yourself while still performing. Idiosyncratic individuals often thrive as part-timers or temps, free of the pressures of performance evaluations and nine-to-five expectations. Consider freelance consulting work as well, if you have a skill or talent you can market; clients are often more tolerant of unusual personality styles as long as you can do the work and deliver it on time.

RELATIONSHIPS: GOING MY WAY?

Russell R. adores his accomplished Idiosyncratic Antonia. He takes care of her, he caters to her eccentricities, and he adopts her ghost (if not her bats) as his own. Her emotional intensity excites him. He feels that she gives him an experience of life that he never would have created on his own. He can't imagine life without Antonia, but he knows that she probably could do without him if she had to. "Darling," she gasps, "I would never leave you!" But Russell poses this question to his wife: "If a little green man from Mars came down and said, 'We want to take *you* but not *him*,' wouldn't you go?" After a pause she answers, "I would have to think about it."

The fact is, Idiosyncratic individuals do not necessarily need other people, certainly not to give their lives definition, direction, or meaning. They go their own way, with or without relationships. They have no need to be like other people; thus they do not team up with others just because it's expected of them. It is not uncommon for very Idiosyncratic individuals to remain unpaired throughout life, with few or no attachments. Some become downright reclusive. Their removal from society may have much to do with the pressures that may be put on them to drop their Idiosyncrasy—to become someone they're not. Under such pressure, Idiosyncratic people simply can't live in the mainstream. They may gravitate toward similar types of people, in the New Age movement perhaps (see p. 255), or in creative circles. Or they may be sufficiently self-contained to go it alone. But Idiosyncratic people frequently report that they feel lonely. Their differences from others make it difficult to connect with people. They are aware that others are often uncomfortable with their Idiosyncratic ideas and intensity, which may sadden them and make them anxious or uncomfortable in groups. They may wish to share life with others more closely, but they cannot reshape themselves to fit in. They may be tolerant of your world; they wish only that you be tolerant of theirs. But a person who is not Idiosyncratic may have a difficult time relating to the highly Idiosyncratic person's unusual behavior and emotions.

In the artistic world, talented, successful Idiosyncratic individuals are courted and admired. Unless their personalities have some Self-Confident streaks as well, the adulation won't turn their heads. On the contrary, they may be indifferent to applause or even, in the interests of artistic authenticity, remove themselves from it (as did Vladimir Horowitz, arguably the finest pianist of the twentieth century, who absented himself from the concert stage at the peak of his career for more than a decade).

Sometimes two Idiosyncratic individuals will find each other and create their own intense little world together—as did the late, great English actors Elsa Lanchester and Charles Laughton, who were fiercely dedicated to their craft and to each other, Laughton's homosexuality notwithstanding.

Other Idiosyncratic individuals may experience several relationships throughout their lives, none of them lasting (Timothy Leary, for example, has had five wives) or achieving the emotional intensity and unconditional love that an Idiosyncratic person may crave within a relationship. Their mates may be unable to tolerate their peculiarities or to find fulfilling lives outside their conventional framework. They may be unable to endure the Idiosyncratic partner's constant need for an intensely emotional experience and his or her inability to manage the lower-level, day-to-day love and emotionality that sustains close relationships over the long term. Sometimes, too, partners of Idiosyncratic people complain that while their mates experience intense emotions in their inner lives, they can't share these feelings or endure a shared emotional experience. But many other Idiosyncratics, with moderate amounts of the style and/or strength in some of the more other-directed or earthbound styles, will often come to appreciate a giving, loving, accepting life companion.

Good/Bad Matches

Idiosyncratic men and women do not, as a rule, adjust to others' needs. Therefore, they will not match well with anyone who is primarily Self-Confident, Vigilant, Adventurous, or Aggressive. Idiosyncratics need to find mates who will accept them for who they are, let them be, take care of them, and perhaps act as a liaison to the regular world. Individuals with Devoted and Self-Sacrificing styles have these characteristics. A little Dramatic style helps too, for sharing or at least appreciating the Idiosyncratic partner's emotional experience of life.

As always, a bit of the Conscientious contributes a sense of responsibility, which helps keep the bills paid and the Idiosyncratic life on track. But if there is too much of the conformist Conscientious style, the mate will be horrified by the oddities. Russell R.'s personality, which works so well with Antonia's Idiosyncratic-Dramatic-Self-Confident combo, is dominated by the Conscientious, with Dramatic and Devoted following close behind. Leisurely is another possibility. Two Idiosyncratic individuals, should they find each other, can sometimes build a tight little world together, with the conventional Real World rarely intervening.

Although Serious personality style resembles the Conscientious in terms of responsibility and hard work, this style's preference for routine and avoidance of novelty does not match up well with the Idiosyncratic creativity, curiosity, and openness.

Zany Parents

Having Idiosyncratic parents can be difficult. Children usually model themselves after their parents. At the same time, once they enter school they tend to be conformists, needing the acceptance of their peers and a chance to do the "normal" thing. If a parent is highly unconventional and leading a lifestyle markedly different from those of the parents of the other kids, the child will feel in conflict. He or she may begin to feel ashamed of the parent and guilty about harboring such "bad" feelings. And a highly Idiosyncratic parent might pressure the child toward an unconventionality with which he or she is uncomfortable. Similarly, Idiosyncratic parents often push their children to be more creative and expressive than they may be by nature.

The Idiosyncratic parent needs to be sensitive to the child's own personality and tolerant of the Real World that the child must negotiate.

He or she must also be willing to bend a little for the sake of the child's world. Benjamin's eleven-year-old daughter, Ella, for example, told him recently that she wanted him to stop jogging. After his divorce from Ella's mother, on the two days a week that his daughter stayed with him, Benjamin liked to jog about five miles before he picked her up from her after-school activities. He'd arrive sweaty and smelly, and Ella, it turned out, was embarrassed in front of her more "proper" friends. Benjamin launched into a little lecture about how she shouldn't let her friends' uptightness get to her, but he stopped himself in the middle of it. He looked at the child's sweet, unhappy face and said sure, he'd go home and change first. Childhood is hard enough without Daddy trying to change all the rules, he realized.

Now for the bright side: A mildly or moderately Idiosyncratic parent may encourage creativity in a gifted child and provide a wide range of experiences for him or her. Most important, such parents very often teach their children to accept themselves in all their individual uniqueness, which is a strength that they carry with them all their lives.

TIPS ON DEALING WITH
THE IDIOSYNCRATIC PERSON IN YOUR LIFE

1. The Idiosyncratic person is one-of-a-kind. Accept, tolerate, and treasure this person *for* his or her uniqueness, not *despite* it. That is, do not assume that the Idiosyncratic quirkiness is incidental to his or her personality. If you are looking for the "normal," conventional human being you think is lurking inside the Idiosyncratic person, you miss the point of who he or she really is.

2. Do not pressure the Idiosyncratic person to conform to the Real World—and do not be pressured into conforming to his or her world either. Instead, recognize the ways in which your realities differ, discuss these differences, and prepare to compromise or to go your separate ways occasionally.

3. To widen your life together and to bring you closer, share the interests of the Idiosyncratic person in your life. At least be willing to learn about his or her interests.

4. Help the Idiosyncratic person to have more time for his or her spiritual or otherwise special interests. Many individuals with a moderate amount of this style are so bound up in conventional Real World responsibilities that they cannot indulge their special pursuits; as a result, they feel and act unhappy and unfulfilled.

5. To deal with a very Idiosyncratic person, accept that you are the one who is more attached to conventional reality; take charge of meeting the fundamental responsibilities of life. Many Idiosyncratic individuals are "absentminded professors"; they're so involved in their own inner world that they need to be reminded it's time to pay the rent, buy groceries, get the car serviced, buy new clothes for the kids, or turn off the light and go to sleep.

MAKING THE MOST OF YOUR IDIOSYNCRATIC STYLE

You are interesting, original, spiritual, maybe even highly creative and gifted. Because of your uniqueness, however, you may find that you pay a price in both your personal and professional relationships with others. You may not realize just how different you really are, so try the following exercises.

Exercise 1

Make a list of all the ways in which you differ in habits, beliefs, and feelings from the important people in your life. Your list might include, for example, "I believe I have special spiritual gifts. My family believes that there's no such thing as special spiritual gifts." Or, "I think success in life can be sought only through the spirit; I do not believe it is measurable in terms of money or possessions. My spouse, however, works hard for material possessions." Or, "I am an emotionally intense person. My spouse prefers to be more even."

Exercise 2

Look at your list and visualize a world in which everyone, including you, is capable of accepting, tolerating, and living comfortably with all these differences in one another. Continue to go through your list and imagine yourself accepting each person's right to believe in whatever he or she pleases. Then imagine each person accepting you for all your differences—and all of you living harmoniously in the world.

The next set of exercises will provide some practical help in negotiating life with other people.

Exercise 3

Make it easier on yourself: compromise. You can't always make your own rules and succeed in all important areas of life. For example, if your boss is a stickler for punctuality, make sure you get to work on time. If your spouse wants you to dress conventionally to attend a social event, do it to keep the peace.

Exercise 4

Very few people are like you, so to stay in touch with them, do something conventional. Pitch in with the dishes, help out with the laundry, child care, household or garden chores, and so on. Give a conventional gift.

Exercise 5

Do something that someone else wants you to do. Your personality style is Self-intense; you become consumed with your own desires, interests, and ideas. You may not realize that others do not share your enthusiasms. For example, while you may be excited about giving your mate or child an exotic knickknack you brought back from your travels, has it occurred to you that he or she might be happier with a bicycle, a comic book, a microwave, a pearl necklace, or something else from this person's own frame of reference? If you are in doubt about what others want for themselves, ask. Exercise 4 for the Self-Confident style (Who *is* this person?) will help too (p. 97).

If you suffer from social anxiety and terror around mainstream people, refer to Exercises 1 through 8 for the Sensitive style (pp. 193-95).

SCHIZOTYPAL PERSONALITY DISORDER

Individuals who suffer from this very incapacitating personality disorder do not live in the same world as the rest of us. They experience little pleasure, they can't find a way to relate appropriately to other people, and they lose the boundaries of their selves.

DIAGNOSTIC CRITERIA

The DSM-IV describes Schizotypal personality disorder as:

A. A pervasive pattern of social and interpersonal deficits marked by acute discomfort with, and reduced capacity for, close relationships as well as by cognitive or perceptual distortions and eccentricities of behavior, beginning by early adulthood and present in a variety of contexts, as indicated by five (or more) of the following:

(1) ideas of reference (excluding delusions of reference) [for example, a belief that one is being talked about by others in the room]

(2) odd beliefs or magical thinking that influences behavior and is inconsistent with subcultural norms (e.g., superstitiousness, belief in clairvoyance, telepathy, or "sixth sense"; in children and adolescents, bizarre fantasies or preoccupations)

(3) unusual perceptual experiences, including bodily illusions [for example, interpreting the feeling of a breeze on one's skin as being touched by someone]

(4) odd thinking and speech (e.g., vague, circumstantial, metaphorical, overelaborate, or stereotyped)

(5) suspiciousness or paranoid ideation

(6) inappropriate or constricted affect

(7) behavior or appearance that is odd, eccentric, or peculiar

(8) lack of close friends or confidants other than first-degree relatives

(9) excessive social anxiety that does not diminish with familiarity and tends to be associated with paranoid fears rather than negative judgments about self

B. Does not occur exclusively during the course of Schizophrenia, a Mood Disorder With Psychotic Features, another Psychotic Disorder, or a Pervasive Developmental Disorder.

ANOTHER WORLD

The men and women who suffer from Schizotypal personality disorder are estranged from the world of other people. Yet, they are just as removed from a coherent, satisfying inner world.

Outwardly they are shy, aloof, withdrawn. They dress in a weird manner, and they often appear disheveled. When they speak to you they can't communicate effectively. They get lost in a tumble of irrelevancies and vague thoughts, they don't use or respond to the usual social gestures or cues, such as smiling or nodding, and their emotions are inappropriate to the situation. They just can't connect with other people, and when they are faced with strangers their anxiety may be extreme.

While they generally prefer to be alone, forming no close friendships, their inner life offers them little pleasure. A Schizotypal person often feels disembodied, unreal, lost.

These men and women need to believe that they have extraordinary, supernatural powers in order to give their impoverished, powerless, empty selves some meaning in this world. Thus, they often believe that they can predict the future, that if they eat some special substance they will be immune to misfortune, that they can see, feel, and perhaps communicate with dead people, and that if they think of something it will happen. Their special powers bring them a significance that is not always pleasant. Schizotypal individuals often are certain that other people are aware of their dark inner feelings, that if they are angry they will cause someone harm, and, like Paranoid individuals, that other people are out to get them.

"THE CASE OF HARRY THE TURTLE"

Mildly Schizotypal individuals may get along in the world by keeping to themselves at work and socially. Extremely Schizotypal people, because of their ideas and behavior, may be severely disabled. They may be unable to hold a job or to exist at all in the world of others, as you will see in the following case description, reported by Drs. Samuel Perry, Allen Frances, and John Clarkin.

Mr. L is brought to a psychiatry clinic for the first time at the age of 36 by his mother, who would like him "fixed." He is a pudgy, short fellow in a striped T-shirt and carpenter's overalls. This outfit, along with his unbrushed bushy hair and whimsical distant stare, gives [him] the appearance of an overgrown boy. When Mr. L enters the consultant's office, he looks bewildered and slumps down in a corner chair as though he would be content to sit there for hours if left undisturbed.

The history, obtained mostly from the mother, reveals that this kind of inertia has been a lifelong problem for Mr. L. Born out of wedlock in a remote rural area when his mother was only 15, Mr. L was raised first by his grandparents while his mother worked as a waitress in a nearby town. When Mr. L was seven, his mother left the area to waitress in a larger metropolitan area, leaving Mr. L to stay with his cousins and to drift through a small country school, where he was accepted with benign neglect simply as a creature who could not pull his weight or earn his feed.

Sixteen years ago when the cousins sold their farm, Mr. L (now age 20) was "shipped" to the city to stay with his mother. She had been married a couple of times during the interim but was once again living alone. With little choice, she agreed to make room in her small apartment for her son, a relative stranger. The original plan was that when Mr. L got used to the city and found a job, he would live at a place of his own—but he never made even a tentative first step.

The mother soon resigned herself to the situation, viewing Mr. L not as a son but more as a strange pet (she teasingly called him "Harry the Turtle"). Mr. L was content with this view. He never liked people and believed they did not like him. To avoid their ridicule, real or imagined, he kept to himself, closing himself up in his small room, eating his meals alone while listening to talk shows or country music on the radio, and avoiding even his mother whenever she tentatively challenged some of his unusual ideas. These beliefs . . . centered on nutrition and the prevention of disease, such as the benefits of drinking ocean water in large volumes and the value of darkness during the day for improving dreams at night. These ideas were apparently elaborations and distortions of opinions he had heard expressed on late night radio programs.

. . . The incident that had occurred recently [that prompted Mr. L's mother to seek treatment for him] was a rather casual comment made by Mr. L to his mother regarding reincarnation and the virtues of suicide, death being merely a transitional phase towards a higher order. Mr. L mentioned these ideas first in relationship to his pet turtle (which he had named Harry). He told her that Harry might have to be sacrificed and "become less to be more." The mother had become accustomed to Mr. L discussing his own feelings in relationship to this turtle because, as Mr. L admitted during the interview, "We're a lot alike except Harry doesn't have to talk."

HELP!

Schizotypal individuals like Mr. L suffer frequent bouts of severe depression and anxiety (especially social anxiety), and they are at risk for psychotic episodes. Many have obsessive-compulsive and hypochondriacal symptoms. Mr. L's psychiatrist, fearing impending suicide or a psychotic break, recommended hospitalization. But Mr. L refused all offers of help, including antidepressant medication to alleviate his despair. He thought the best thing to do was drink an extra quart of ocean water a day.

In addition to treatment for acute conditions, Schizotypal individuals can benefit substantially from vocational, social-skills, and anxiety-management training. Group therapy can be very beneficial in helping these individuals overcome their social anxiety. Cognitive therapists report some success in helping people deal with their bizarre thoughts, such as by teaching them to seek objective evidence for a thought before acting on it. Drs. Beck and Freeman describe a Schizotypal patient who "was able to address paranoid thoughts in this way: When she would drink out of a glass at home, the thought would come to mind that there might be small pieces of glass in the drink. Since there was no objective evidence of this, she was able to discount these thoughts after some practice."

Low doses of antipsychotic medication can be helpful for their more bizarre symptoms or for psychotic episodes.

In supportive psychotherapy, the therapist generally does not delve deeply into the patient's psyche, but rather offers understanding, advice, and support. The Schizotypal person who is willing to be helped may make his or her first real emotional contact in a relationship with a sensitive, accepting, empathic therapist.

INCIDENCE, PREDISPOSITIONS, AND RISKS: THE SCHIZOPHRENIA CONNECTION

Schizotypal personality disorder occurs in about 3 percent of the population. It appears to be somewhat more common in men. There is some suggestion that it is less severe and disabling among women. Schizotypal personality disorder commonly co-occurs with Schizoid, Paranoid, Avoidant, and Borderline personality disorders.

Evidence continues to mount that this personality disorder has a strong genetic component and a relationship to schizophrenia. According to one study of twins with Schizotypal personality disorder, in one-third of all cases, when one identical twin had the disorder, the other identical twin (who has identical genes) also had it. Where one fraternal (nonidentical) twin had this personality disorder, however, the other twin suffered from it only 4 percent of the time. These results suggest the role of genetic inheritance in the development of Schizotypal personality disorder.

Its relationship to schizophrenia has been revealed by a number of studies that seem to show that Schizotypal personality disorder occurs more frequently in first-degree relatives (parents, children, siblings) of schizophrenics than among the general population. Many researchers now theorize that Schizotypal personality disorder, together with Paranoid personality disorder (see p. 178) and Schizoid personality disorder (p. 291), is one of a number of related disorders on the so-called schizophrenic spectrum for which one may inherit a predisposition. These disorders range from schizophrenia on the severest extreme to the three personality disorders as the mildest manifestations. Although Schizotypal personality disorder is the most severe of the three, it is important to note that a person with Schizotypal personality disorder is *not* likely to develop full-blown schizophrenia. Although men and women with this personality disorder may experience brief psychotic episodes, they are at very small risk of developing the chronic disorder. And their offspring are no more likely to become schizophrenic than is anyone else.

Researchers have found that some people with Schizotypal personality disorder show some of the same neurological dysfunctions and brain structure abnormalities as do those with schizophrenia, although the consequences are less severe. We'll talk more about this in chapter 18.

Genetic and environmental factors no doubt act together in the development of any personality style or disorder. Possibly, in Mr. L's and other cases, an inherited predisposition was exacerbated by detached, cold, uncommunicative care givers, who deprived him of social involvement and experiences, and who allowed him to drift into a world of his own thoughts and fantasies.

COPING WITH SCHIZOTYPAL PEOPLE

Schizotypal individuals maintain few or no relationships, except possibly with family members. If you feel that someone in your family suffers from this disorder, encourage him or her to seek help. Try to avoid keeping these individuals dependent on you for everything; they can learn to take care of themselves. Family therapy could turn out to be of benefit to you all.

CHAPTER 13

Solitary Style

"THE LONER"

Solitary men and women need no one but themselves. They are unmoved by the madding crowd, liberated from the drive to impress and to please. Solitary people are remarkably free of the emotions and involvements that distract so many others. What they may give up in terms of sentiment and intimacy, however, they may gain in clarity of vision. Left to their own devices, Solitary anthropologists, naturalists, mathematicians, physical scientists, filmmakers, writers, and poets can uncover and record the facts of our existence to which our passions so often blind us.

THE SIX CHARACTERISTICS

The following six traits and behaviors are clues to the presence of the Solitary style. A person who reveals a strong Solitary tendency will demonstrate more of these behaviors more intensely than someone with less of this style in his or her personality profile.

1. *Solitude.* Individuals with the Solitary personality style have small need of companionship and are most comfortable alone.

2. *Independence.* They are self-contained and do not require interaction with others in order to enjoy their experiences or to get on in life.

3. *Sangfroid.* Solitary men and women are even-tempered, calm, dispassionate, unsentimental, and unflappable.

4. *Stoicism.* They display an apparent indifference to pain and pleasure.

5. *Sexual composure.* They are not driven by sexual needs. They enjoy sex but will not suffer in its absence.

6. *Feet on the ground.* They are unswayed by either praise or criticism and can confidently come to terms with their own behavior.

THE SIX DOMAINS OF SOLITARY FUNCTIONING

The Self and the Emotions domains are key to the Solitary personality style. For moderately Solitary people with mixed personality patterns, either of these two domains may exert a more powerful influence. For clearly Solitary patterns, Self and Emotions will merge to shape the Solitary character.

SELF: THE INNER SANCTUM

Solitary individuals are self-contained. They are their own truest, most trusted companions, providing the most important resources they need. They require no one else to guide them, to admire them, to provide emotional sustenance, to entertain them, or to share their experiences. Although they may marry or otherwise become involved with others, at heart they remain separate and they find greatest comfort, reassurance, and freedom alone with themselves.

Their desire for solitude is not an apparent reaction or an avoidance. Sensitive people, for example, often avoid others because they just can't be themselves around them. Some Idiosyncratic types remove themselves from society because they can't conform to conventional rules of behavior. Solitary types, however, simply prefer their own company. They like to be alone. Certainly they need no one to buttress their self-esteem or to rescue them from boredom. They can be remarkably free of loneliness.

Solitary Virginia J. cannot figure out why so many people seem incapable of doing things alone. Her young acquaintance Sally N. invited her to go to a play, but Virginia had already seen it. Sally was upset because she'd phoned almost everyone she knew and she still couldn't find anyone to go with.

Virginia asked, "Why don't you go by yourself?" Sally replied, "I just couldn't enjoy myself if I went alone."

Virginia thought Sally was being ridiculous. What did anyone else have to do with her enjoyment of a play? If she needed to share the experience, why couldn't Sally just call someone up and tell him or her about it afterward? Sally gave up trying to explain. "Virginia, you just don't *get* it," she said.

EMOTIONS:
THE LANGUAGE OF DISPASSION

Virginia's personality is strongly dominated by the Solitary style. She's never understood people who always have to have someone else around. She met twenty-two-year-old Dramatic/Sensitive Sally in Vietnam. They were on the same university-sponsored travel tour. Sally, a graduate student in drama, joined the tour because she wanted to see that part of the world but didn't want to travel alone. Virginia, fifty-three, an adjunct professor of botany, joined it only because she had limited time and was unable to make arrangements to get to all the destinations on the tour's Southeast Asian itinerary by herself, as she would have preferred. On the tour she kept to herself. At their destinations she would walk off to explore on her own, while the others clustered around the tour guide. At meals she was friendly and responsive if seated with a group, but she was just as happy to dine alone.

Sally frequently sought out the older woman and began to trail after her when they were sightseeing. She was fascinated with Virginia, who knew so much and could look out over a seemingly barren site and point out details that chatty, emotive Sally would never have noticed. "Don't you just love this place!" Sally once exclaimed when they arrived at a picturesque village.

Virginia responded by pointing out to Sally how poor this village was. She drew the younger woman's attention to the tumbledown houses and the tattered clothes of some of the children. This time Sally seemed annoyed by the older woman's dry observations. "Sometimes you're a real downer," she said, laughing uneasily. "Don't you have any romance in you at all?"

Virginia looked at Sally quizzically—rather like the way *Star Trek*'s half-human/half-Vulcan Mr. Spock regarded Dr. McCoy when the other criticized his lack of emotionality and sentimentality. The alien first officer on the star ship *Enterprise,* like others from the planet Vulcan, was all reason, no heart—or hardly any, since he did have one Earthling parent. (Androids such as Mr. Data, of a later *Star Trek* generation, of course, need not contend with even a hint of human emotion.) Spock was an extraordinarily pure scientist and consummate observer. You could count on him never to be distracted by his feelings. Virginia and her Solitary style mates are not unlike such half-Vulcans. They do not experience emotions as intensely as do most others on this planet. They are not feelers, not emoters. Emotionally, like Spock they are imperturbable. Strongly Solitary individuals, Virginia among them, have little emotional need of intimacy. Moderately Solitary people, though, may feel frustrated by their inability to connect with anyone on a deep feeling level (see additional discussion under "Relationships," pp. 281–84).

But Solitary people are not necessarily unhappy—as long as others do not demand more of them than they can give. People are always pushing Solitary types to reveal themselves and express their feelings, trying to get a rise out of them, as if (like some Conscientious people) they are keeping them hidden and not sharing what is actually there. But for many Solitary people who have no compensating emotional styles, the repertoire of emotions may truly be small. They do not speak the language of emotions—which is hard for many of us to comprehend.

The Dispassionate Observer—and Lover

Solitary individuals are, in a word, dispassionate. In some ways they are richer for it. They may not be feelers, but they are doers and watchers. Free of the passionate need for others that often clouds our minds, they can stand back and watch the curious things people do. Similarly free of sentimental reverie, they can observe the world around them in strikingly clear focus. Gifted Solitary individuals can be highly creative, if reclusive, poets, scientists, and intellectuals.

Virginia is a superb observer of nature and even of relationships among people because she does not identify with their feelings. She does not become lonely, so she can do as she pleases. She'll go off into the mountains and camp by herself for weeks at a time. She takes books, notebooks, cameras, and food to sustain her. She is comfortable with silence. She watches everything around her, makes notes, learns, feels satisfied.

On one of her solo treks some years ago, she met Oliver, who was enjoying some time away from his busy law practice in the city and had come up to the mountains to fish. They camped together for nearly a week, each going off separately by day, returning to camp at nightfall. Oliver was quite taken with Virginia's competence, her no-nonsense independence, her sensitivity to her environment, and her looks. A very tall, striking blonde, she had a shapely, muscular body; Oliver could tell by the confident way she moved that she felt comfortable with herself.

The two would often sit quietly together by the campfire, Oliver thinking how delightful it was to be with someone who appreciated silence.

The night before Oliver had to return to the city, he quietly, tenderly
suggested that they make love. They had never even touched, yet somehow he felt that Virginia would accept. She did. The next morning, as
he was packing up, Oliver declared that he had to see her again. After
such a remarkable week together, and their lovemaking of the night
before, he could not imagine returning to real life without her. He felt
so close to her, he told her, so comfortable with himself in her presence.
He needed someone like her in his life.

"This is my real life," Virginia said, looking up unmoved from the
brook where she was rinsing the coffeepot and frying pan.

"You know what I mean," said Oliver. "Don't you feel close to me
after the time we've spent together? Don't you want to make love together again and again?"

Virginia shrugged. She said she had enjoyed meeting him and camping together and reminded him that she lived alone. "Yes, but you don't
have to stay alone," he urged. "I've been alone since my divorce, but
that's not something I mean to do forever"—as if she were just the same
as he.

Virginia suggested that he call her sometime. They might have dinner
or take in a movie. Now she felt quite uncomfortable with him.

Oliver went home thinking that she must be gay. It was the only
explanation he could think of for her rejection of him.

Virginia is not gay—but, as is true of many Solitary individuals of any
sexual preference, sex is not an overwhelming force in her life. She
experiences sexual pleasure, but she can take it or leave it. She does not
require or want a sustained sexual relationship.

Most of all, she doesn't have the same need as Oliver for lasting
closeness and intimacy. She'd had encounters with others, but she had
not wanted to make them permanent. She'd been married in her early
twenties, to her English professor. It lasted three months. Virginia
couldn't stand his demands on her once they were married. Before, he'd
accepted and admired her as Oliver had during their week in the mountains—no insistence that she relate to him in a more apparently involved, responsive way. She was sorry that he wouldn't let her be
herself, sad that the marriage broke up, but relieved to discover something essential about herself. She never again attempted to live with, let
alone marry, anyone.

Virginia is content to have chosen a path in life that diverges from
that of most other people. Sometimes after experiences such as that
with Oliver, with whom she was able to share a week of her life *her*

way, she feels sad that no man can seem to accept her as herself for long. But, true to her Solitary style, these emotions do not last long. Virginia packed her bedroll and headed higher up into the mountains.

SELF-CONTROL:
TOO MUCH OF A GOOD THING?

It's hard to tempt a Solitary person to overindulge his or her visceral appetites. Impulses, hungers, and delight in the pleasures of the flesh are all driven by spontaneous emotion—which is not this style's strong suit. Unless these individuals have a competing streak of an impulsive or pleasure-seeking style in their personalities (e.g., the Dramatic or the Leisurely), or unless they experiment with dependency-producing recreational drugs to help them relate or to intensify their emotional experience, they will be protected by their very natures from excesses of human passion.

They may also discover within themselves a stoic disregard of pain as well as passion. Virginia seems to have an exceptional gift in this regard. More than thirty years ago, when she was a graduate student, she took a bad fall on a rocky peak. For months afterward the back pain was so debilitating that she could hardly turn or move. The doctors told her to abandon her hopes for an active career. Never, she told them. On own, Virginia determined to get up and get on with it, despite her agony. Against doctors' orders, she began to get up and walk. Each time the pain attacked, by force of will she began to ignore it. Eventually it receded and finally disappeared. She was back to her studies within two months of her decision to take control of her experience.

There may be a downside to overdoing the emotional self-control for some people with certain Solitary traits, though. A 1987 study reviewing psychological and medical records of male doctors who had been students at Johns Hopkins University School of Medicine between 1948 and 1964 showed that those who were both unemotional and lonely were the most likely to develop cancer in the following years. Those men who were the most anxious, emotional, and easily upset proved in this study to be the least cancer-prone. While this study does *not* show that the Solitary personality style is associated with risk of cancer, it may possibly suggest that becoming aware of your feelings and getting them out, especially the bad ones, is better for you in the long run. See Exercises 2 and 3 on p. 287 for some help.

RELATIONSHIPS:
TAKE THEM OR LEAVE THEM

Without other-directed personality styles to offset the Solitary tendency, the individual will be more or less indifferent to the emotional ties that bind others together. Extremely Solitary types will not be likely to pair up or involve themselves intensely with others, even friends. While they may have a rather detached interest in people, they will not naturally be responsive to many of them or wish to draw them intimately close.

It's not that Solitary people don't like people. They are not hostile or angry at anyone. They may enjoy the company of others in many of their activities. Some—those with a mixed personality pattern—may even marry. But in their relationships they need much time to themselves and there will always be a wall of greater or lesser thickness between them.

Stress!

Even moderately Solitary people may not intuitively comprehend others' feelings or respond to their emotional cues. "You don't love me!" is a common lament of partners of Solitary people. This may be true as defined in the emotional language that most people speak. The more the partner pushes for emotional reactions and a depth of intimate feeling, the greater will be the stress on the Solitary partner. To cope, the Solitary person will retreat.

Richard and His Girlfriends

The Solitary person who has other-directed styles in a mixed personality pattern may feel frustrated and in conflict in his or her relationships. On one hand, he or she will be motivated toward people; on the other hand, the Solitary need to protect solitude may be so strong as to prevent any deeply intimate relationship.

Richard F., a brilliant chemist, is a case in point. He has a mixed Solitary-Conscientious-Dramatic personality pattern. Forty-two years old, he has not been married, nor has he lived with anyone for long. But he has dated a great many women; he's rarely gone without. Typically he sees the woman of the moment one, two, three times a week, meeting her late at night and staying over at her place; his apartment is off-limits. The relationship can go on for many months, with no increase in intensity. Richard becomes quite comfortable, but the woman usually starts expecting the relationship to grow. She begins to pressure him to spend more time with her, to tell her he loves her, to live together, to commit. At this point Richard invariably realizes he'd rather be home by himself. The woman in question becomes hurt and outraged that Richard is withholding something from her, deliberately stringing her along, using her for his own purposes. But in fact Richard is doing the best he can.

"I mean, it would be different if I *loved* her," he said recently to a friend as he was telling him how Joanne, the latest woman, had thrown him out of her apartment. He has always clung to the notion that someday he would meet a woman whom he would love—a feeling he's never in reality experienced. He's always believed that when he met the woman he loved, then he'd know what love was. They'd marry and have children—Richard's always hoped for a family. But now that he's crossed the forty barrier, it occasionally occurs to him that life may not afford him this opportunity. He feels stymied and sometimes depressed that he may never meet a woman whom he will love.

On the other hand, he's just met another woman, Sandra, and has begun his usual pattern with her. He will be comfortable as always, until she begins to demand more from him than he can give. Maybe he'll luck out this time, though, and find that Sandra wants no more of him than he wants of her. Then, possibly, the relationship could go on indeterminately, a few hours a day, two, three, four, even seven days a week.

If he really wanted to change, Richard could consider psychotherapy. But Richard likes his life and himself and he figures it's okay if things don't work out the way he's always dreamed they would. To the extent that society says a deeply committed emotional relationship with one person is important, Richard is underequipped or maladapted. But our culture gives mixed messages: it's good to build a marriage and it's okay to be single. Richard lives in New York City, where single people of all ages abound. He has companionship when he wants it, and he has numerous hobbies and interests and can entertain himself alone better than most people can. He'll buy single tickets to the opera and the theater, he'll eat out alone, all quite contentedly. He can, and does, find many rewards in his life.

Some predominantly Solitary people may commit to marriage because of family pressure, because they think they should, or, especially if they are women, because of practical necessity. Although it may not prove easy for these individuals to feel emotionally connected to their mates, they may grow attached to their marital responsibilities and roles. As long as no one expects fireworks from them, or a social network outside the family, these nonemotional, nonsentimental, nonromantic, not passionately sexual unions can survive.

The Solitary Parent

The birth of a child is one of those extraordinary life experiences referred to in chapter 2, that can trigger the Solitary person's unrealized genetic potential. Especially for the mother, once the bonding occurs, love comes and she is forever changed. Without pairing up, of course, the Solitary individual is not likely to have this experience. Moreover, many Solitary individuals are not interested in having children.

However, Solitary individuals who do become parents discover a path to emotional experience and "togetherness" that they never perceived before. Not that they will cast off their lifetime personality patterns and be "reborn." They will continue to experience at least some difficulty in meeting and responding to some or many of the child's emotional needs. The other parent may be able to fill in what's missing. In any case, Solitary individuals, in their usual autonomous competence, will be reliable and be able to meet at least the nonemotional needs of their families.

Good/Bad Matches

Relationships are difficult for predominantly Solitary people. They do not naturally gravitate toward or stick with others. If Solitary is one of your personality styles, for a relationship to work you'll need a mate who is high on acceptance and forbearance and low on emotional need. A Conscientious person will probably be your best bet, considering that style's lack of emotionality and high regard for marriage as an institution. Self-Sacrificing people too are extremely accepting and giving, without demanding much in return. Some moderately Self-Confident people may be attracted to your self-containment and competence and may be able to tolerate your aloofness. But stay clear of the emotion-driven, emotionally needy, and highly social styles, including the Dramatic, the Mercurial, the Adventurous, the Devoted, the Idiosyncratic, and the Leisurely. Sensitive individuals may seem as unsocial as you are, but they need mates who will make it easier, not harder, to be with people. You might be attracted to a Vigilant person, but you're probably not the type for him or her; Vigilant types need their mates to stay within their watchful eye, but you need to go your own way. Two moderately Solitary people would be able to respect each other's privacy. A match with a Serious person would last, in a dull, uninspired, don't-rock-the-boat way.

WORK: GOING IT ALONE

Solitary types can function very well in the Work domain. They get down to work, concentrate, don't waste time with personal calls or concerns, and are not easily bored. Characteristically self-contained, they do not require a lot of feedback and can take criticism. The setting is the crucial factor for their performance, however. Extremely Solitary individuals are not team players and do not relate well to the public. It's not that they are uncooperative. Rather, they can be clumsy and impatient with the give-and-take necessary to maintain most types of relationships. They tend not to be sensitive, diplomatic, or responsive to indirect and subtle forms of communication. They have little patience with office politics. As managers, they tend not to understand their subordinates' personalities and they usually can't handle personnel problems.

But when left alone to their work—and this goes for leisure-time activities as well—they can put their mind to it without distraction. They can fix a car, write poetry, deliver mail, design a bridge, or study for an exam with equanimity. Their previously mentioned ability to observe and collect information serves them well in many undertakings. And they can be sent far away to do their work—to repair an offshore oil rig, to man a remote lighthouse, to watch for fires deep in a forest, to dig in the desert for ancient artifacts—without feeling lonely, bored, or isolated. Or they can retreat from society and work productively, without much thought to recognition. The poet Emily Dickinson was a great literary recluse, who may have had some of this style (plus the Idiosyncratic and Sensitive, among others) in her personality. She withdrew into her Amherst, Massachusetts, home before she was thirty (she lived from 1830 to 1886), began to dress only in white, and eventually she never ventured out. She wrote well over a thousand poems, only a handful of which were published during her lifetime. It is said that "she . . . became exhausted by emotional contact with others. Her mode of existence, although circumscribed, was evidently satisfying, even essential, to her."

Solitary Careers

Unless you also have other-directed styles such as the Dramatic within your pattern, steer clear of careers that involve you deeply with people to whom you must be responsive. You may be brilliant at your work, but success may elude you because you do not deal comfortably or naturally within the political framework. Do not hesitate to remove yourself from that fray. Reroute yourself toward autonomy, working from your own office, laboratory, or home. You may be able to work with clients who seek no more from you than the service you provide—as an accountant, for instance. Freelance careers may also work for your style.

Your ability to concentrate in solitude and to be completely comfortable in your inner sanctum will be a boon to you throughout your working life—in creative and scientific exploration, in research, in technological and mechanical work, and in security work in which you are paid to watch and to wait.

Be aware that the more you wish to take on in your career, the greater the number of people with whom you may have to be involved. Solitary independent filmmaker Christopher J., while still in his twenties, has made a name for himself among connoisseurs of short subjects. Colleagues have begun to urge him to make feature-length films, and backers are willing to come forth with the financing. He is in a position that many other young filmmakers could only pray for. So why is Christopher so uncomfortable? In his award-winning short films he has done all the work himself—he writes the scripts, shoots the films, edits them, sometimes he even writes the scores. He loves it that way. To expand, he would have to bring others in and work closely with them. He does *not* wish to do this. But he also knows that financial success in his field means feature-length films. Christopher now has to decide whether he wants to be a happy albeit starving creative solo filmmaker with a tiny following, or if he wants to make it big in the world of feature films. Can he find a way to work with others and still be content? No small decision—and one that some of you Solitary folks may have to face. Remember, you have to be true to yourself to achieve fulfillment and contentment. But you don't have to feel limited by your style, either. See "Making the Most of Your Solitary Style" (p. 287) for some pointers.

REAL WORLD: PRIVACY, PLEASE

The Solitary individual, like *Star Trek*'s Mr. Spock, in a way has been transported away from his or her home planet. In the ideal Solitary world, there are very few people and they go about their business without bothering one another. But the Real World is regrettably overpopulated with intrusive aliens who spend the majority of their time impeding each other's progress. So, Solitary folks do the best they can to create little pockets of solitude around themselves and try to spend as much time in them as they can.

TIPS ON DEALING WITH THE SOLITARY PERSON IN YOUR LIFE

1. Let this person be. The most common mistake people make in dealing with Solitary types is trying to push them to be like everybody else. But Solitary individuals are who they are. They may not mix much in the Real World or react deeply to you, but they are competent and responsible, and their inner worlds can be very interesting.

2. Do not assume that the Solitary person is uncomfortable or unhappy because he or she is alone. For many Solitary individuals, a life filled with people is hell. Indeed, they may pity you for your social and emotional needs.

3. Do not assume that the Solitary person in your life is uncomfortable with you because he or she prefers to spend much time outside your presence or just sitting quietly instead of interacting with you. This person will be quite comfortable with you if you don't try to engage him or her, insist on filling up the silence with chatter, or try to smother the Solitary person with togetherness.

4. Look for signs of caring that are different from the standard I-want-you, I-need-you, I-love-you's. The fact that this person is in your life at all says a lot about his or her attachment to you, considering that Solitary individuals can do so well without others.

5. Ensure this person plenty of time to be alone. Anyone with even a small amount of Solitary style requires time to him- or herself to feel sane, well adjusted, and productive. Try not to consider a Solitary person's private time your enemy. But if it is at variance with your own strong social and emotional needs, be honest with yourself in admitting that this relationship isn't going to work out.

6. Take up hobbies or find activities to occupy yourself while the Solitary person is off on his or her own.

7. When you need to work out a problem with a nonemotional Solitary person, appeal to logic instead of emotion. A Solitary person may have a good head on his or her shoulders. Speak to it.

▬▬▬ MAKING THE MOST OF YOUR SOLITARY STYLE ▬▬▬

In your ability to entertain yourself and be comfortable alone, you have no peers. You may want to improve your relationships with people, however, if only to be able to go about your self-determined business more easily. You will need, first, to collect information about other people and then to learn to speak their language.

To begin, turn to Exercise 4 for the Self-Confident style: "Who *is* this person?" (see p. 97).

Exercise 1

Observe emotion. Watch how people express their feelings in their interactions with you and with one another. Look first for obvious emotions, such as joy and misery. After you get good at spotting those, look for the more subtle, delicate expressions of feeling. Accept that feelings are very important to most people and that they are injured very easily.

Exercise 2

Search for your own feelings. In your comfortable privacy, stand in front of a mirror or sit with paper and pencil and search for what you feel at that moment. If you are at a loss for an emotion, think about what you felt the last time you had difficulty with someone. For example, if a companion pressured you to spend more time with him or her, or a colleague gave you a hard time at work, did you feel frustrated? angry? sad? hurt? misunderstood? annoyed?

Exercise 3

Now express a feeling. Pretend or act, if need be. If you think you are or were angry, let out a yell. Sad? Pretend to cry.

Exercise 4

Practice endurance. Instead of retreating when you feel pressured by people, tolerate your discomfort a little longer. If you are in the city and want to escape to the country, just hang in there one day longer. If you are with a companion and you want to be by yourself, wait another hour. If you are in a meeting and you just want to go off and do your own work, stay until the meeting breaks. Be your stoic self about it. Say to yourself, "I can handle this discomfort." The point of this exercise is not to make you do things you don't want to do, but to extend your flexibility and give you more freedom of choice. Should you begin to feel anxious by extending your involvements with others in this way, try the anxiety-management exercises for the Sensitive style (see pp. 193-96).

Exercise 5

Negotiate with others to find a way for you to do things your way without affecting the cooperative effort. For example, make a deal with your spouse that Saturday is your day for yourself, but Sunday is for family. Try telling your boss that you don't function well in meetings, and if he or she will excuse you, you'll contribute extra in some other way. It might not work, but it can't hurt to try.

Exercise 6

Talk about it. Don't expect other people automatically to understand you—and don't expect yourself automatically to understand other people. Others may assume, from your Solitary behavior, that you do not care for them or do not wish to cooperate. Tell them that your need to be alone has nothing to do with them. If you run into difficulty with others in your work, say frankly that you are used to working on your own. If others are not straightforward with you and seem to be sending emotional messages instead, ask them to explain what's on their minds.

Exercise 7

Learn to say things that please other people. Even though you may be immune to compliments or praise, many people need to hear them. Tell whoever cooked the dinner that it tastes good, even if you are not used to expressing yourself in this manner. Tell your lover that you care. If you did your homework in the first two exercises (Self-Confident 4 and Solitary 1), you'll know what to say.

Exercise 8

Remove the blinders. If time after time you refuse commitment because you think the right person hasn't come along, realize that your Solitary personality style may have something to do with why you can't find happiness with one person. Think about how much you hold yourself back from other people.

Exercise 9

Take a leap—share with someone something deeply personal about yourself.

SCHIZOID
PERSONALITY DISORDER

Emotionally and often physically, Schizoid individuals are cut off from people. Neither happy nor sad, they are careful to build lives that protect them from all human intimacy.

DIAGNOSTIC CRITERIA

The DSM-IV describes Schizoid personality disorder as:

A. A pervasive pattern of detachment from social relationships and a restricted range of emotions in interpersonal settings, beginning by early adulthood and present in a variety of contexts, as indicated by four (or more) of the following:

(1) neither desires nor enjoys close relationships, including being part of a family

(2) almost always chooses solitary activities

(3) has little, if any, interest in having sexual experiences with another person

(4) takes pleasure in few, if any, activities

(5) lacks close friends or confidants other than first-degree relatives

(6) appears indifferent to the praise and criticism of others

(7) shows emotional coldness, detachment, or flattened affectivity

B. Does not occur exclusively during the course of Schizophrenia, a Mood Disorder With Psychotic Features, another Psychotic Disorder, or a Pervasive Developmental Disorder and is not due to the direct physiological effects of a general medical condition.

THE WALLED CITY

To others, individuals with Schizoid personality disorder are impenetrable. They reside in a "walled city" deep inside themselves, far away from other people. They're not *anti*social; they're *a*social—they want nothing to do with you. Even those mildly Schizoid men and women who on the surface seem somewhat sociable prove flat, empty, passive, unresponsive, or just indifferent when you try to get to know them. Some mildly Schizoid individuals may gravitate toward religious cults, in which relationships among members are highly structured; there they can carry on the semblance of interpersonal relationships while managing to avoid close contact. More detached Schizoid men and women may choose to live their entire adult lives alone in one room, with no contact with friends or even family. Every day they go to and from work—where they can be very productive if left to work in isolation—without sharing a warm moment with anyone, except perhaps a pet. Or they may live on the streets. A study of personality disorders among the homeless population in Baltimore, for example, showed a substantial prevalence of Schizoid and Paranoid personality disorders.

Schizoid people are not without an inner life, however. Inside the "walled city," where no other person is admitted, they can have rich interests and fantasies—but almost no feelings. Inwardly and outwardly, Schizoid people are emotionally unmovable—no thrills, no chills, no happiness or unhappiness, no anger, no joy.

HELP!

Individuals suffering from Schizoid personality don't often seek help. They claim they are more or less satisfied with what we would regard as a highly impoverished existence. Often family members bring them for help. Sometimes, when demands from others at home or at work are inescapable, they will begin to suffer more disturbing experiences, including anxiety and panic, perhaps even brief psychotic episodes. Or their isolation itself will bring feelings of depersonalization; they may begin to feel that they are unreal, nothing, empty.

Psychotherapy can, of course, be extremely threatening to someone who wishes to remain detached from everyone. Some Schizoid men and women will have a sense that their lives could be better, though, and will accept guidance from an empathic psychotherapist. Many, too, are burdened with the knowledge that they are social misfits. As with Schizotypal individuals, the therapist can provide the first meaningful, trustworthy relationship in the experience of the Schizoid person. In psychotherapy, the aim is to make patients comfortable and trusting, not to intrude upon their privacy and never to push them to relate more closely than they are able. Therapy often is supportive and practical. The therapist will encourage the Schizoid individual to begin to take part in social activities, if only as a spectator at a sports event. As the person's tolerance for such activities increases, he or she may begin to increase the amount of personal involvement, perhaps by joining a computer or stamp-collecting club. The therapist will need to help the Schizoid person learn social skills, since, like Schizotypal individuals, they are not attuned to social cues or rules of propriety.

For some people with this disorder, group therapy, in which they realize there are many people with the same or similar problems and in which they can learn the social skills they lack, can be very beneficial.

INCIDENCE, PREDISPOSITIONS, AND RISKS

No one knows how prevalent Schizoid personality disorder is in the general population. In mental health settings it is very rare, seen less commonly than all the other personality disorders. It is diagnosed somewhat more often in men, among whom it seems to cause more disability than among women. Whether this personality disorder, along with the Schizotypal and Paranoid, is on the so-called schizophrenic spectrum of inherited predispositions (see p. 273) remains unclear. There is some evidence that it is more common among relatives of people with schizophrenia or Schizotypal personality disorder than among the general population. Possibly some Schizoid individuals are born without the "emotional machinery" needed to relate to others. Sometimes people with Schizoid personality disorder later develop a delusional disorder or schizophrenia. Some Schizoid individuals respond to severe stress with a brief psychotic episode.

A child born with an introverted, shy temperament may be constitutionally predisposed to developing this disorder, especially if the earliest parenting is cold, neglectful, insensitive, or hostile to the infant's disposition. Some psychodynamic theorists believe that individuals with this disorder remain completely unattached to people because they gave up early on any hope of gratification from others. Following their inborn temperamental style, perhaps they adapted to their unsatisfying environment by turning inward, away from any attachment to anyone. Certainly the men and women who suffer from this personality disorder do not trust people. Moreover, they detach from their own feelings and anxieties, so that they do not feel hurt. Unfortunately, they do not feel pleasure either.

Schizoid personality disorder often occurs in mixed patterns along with Schizotypal, Paranoid, and Avoidant personality disorders.

COPING WITH SCHIZOID PEOPLE

Anyone (including a member of the clergy, a colleague, or a helping family member) who can reach out in an accepting, friendly, respectful, and utterly nonintrusive manner to a Schizoid individual can help improve his or her quality of life. Don't be put off by these people's apparent indifference to you and your feelings, and don't force them to interact with you. Show your friendship and interest, and maintain a respectful distance. Some of the earlier tips on dealing with Solitary people may prove helpful.

CHAPTER 14

Mercurial Style

"FIRE AND ICE"

Life is a roller coaster for those with the Mercurial personality style—and they'll insist that you come along for the ride. From the peaks to the valleys, intensity imbues their every breath. Mercurial women and men yearn for experience, and they jump into a new love or a new lifestyle with both feet, without even a glance backward. No other style, the Dramatic included, is so ardent in its desire to connect with life and with other people. And no other style is quite so capable of enduring the changes in emotional weather that such a fervidly lived life will bring.

THE SEVEN CHARACTERISTICS

The following seven traits and behaviors are clues to the presence of the Mercurial style. A person who reveals a strong Mercurial tendency will demonstrate more of these behaviors more intensely than someone with less of this style in his or her personality profile.

1. *Romantic attachment.* Mercurial individuals must always be deeply involved in a romantic relationship with one person.

2. *Intensity.* They experience a passionate, focused attachment in all their relationships. Nothing that goes on between them and other people is trivial, nothing taken lightly.

3. *Heart.* They show what they feel. They are emotionally active and reactive. Mercurial types put their hearts into everything.

4. *Unconstraint.* They are uninhibited, spontaneous, fun-loving, and undaunted by risk.

5. *Activity.* Energy marks the Mercurial style. These individuals are lively, creative, busy, and engaging. They show initiative and can stir others to activity.

6. *Open mind.* They are imaginative and curious, willing to experience and experiment with other cultures, roles, and value systems and to follow new paths.

7. *Alternate states.* People with Mercurial style are skilled at distancing or distracting themselves from reality when it is painful or harsh.

THE SIX DOMAINS OF MERCURIAL FUNCTIONING

Take the Relationship domain, add Emotions and Self-Control, and you have the recipe for this tempestuous personality style.

RELATIONSHIPS:
TO POSSESS AND BE POSSESSED

Adam M., a music critic, met Ursula T. at a reception following her famous brother's cello recital. After speaking to her for less than ten minutes, this predominantly Mercurial and Dramatic man told her he knew that they were meant to be involved in each other's lives. "I will fall in love with you," declared the tall, tuxedoed, well-spoken middle-aged gentleman. Ursula, a thirty-one-year-old music teacher and some-time performer, could only blush. This elegant man was coming on to her so strongly; ordinarily she would have made her polite excuses and moved off. But he seemed so genuine, and his eyes seemed truly to pierce her soul. Uncharacteristically, this normally reticent woman took him at his word and gave him her telephone number at his request.

Notwithstanding his cutting review of her brother's performance, Adam phoned Ursula the next day. He had to attend an opera that evening—would she grace him with her presence? Ursula had other plans, but at Adam's urging she agreed to go with him. Never previously married or even deeply involved with anyone, the sober woman had never experienced such attention. Adam was intense, emotional, insistent—he wouldn't allow her to be slow, cautious, quiet, restrained.

"This is meant to be," he continued to tell her, and although in the back of her mind a voice said, "Slow down," she let loose with this intensely romantic, beautiful, changeable man. "You are the world to me," he would tell her. Even after their love affair was over and his passion and fury were spent, and years after Adam had died, Ursula knew that during the time they had been together, she really had been his entire world.

It's in the Stars

Mercurial individuals like Adam are never casual about the people they care for. As between Adam and Ursula, they immediately feel a magnetic involvement and a powerful sense that the relationship is destined. The relationship then becomes the center of their lives, the heart of their beings, and they pursue it with an intensity unlike any of the other personality styles. A love affair—even a friendship—with a Mercurial individual is unforgettable. These individuals put their lovers, friends, even colleagues on pedestals; they worship their perfection; they thank the heavens for blessing them with such a person. They must talk to the other person every day, sometimes several times a day. They must know everything the other thinks, does, and feels. They must fill themselves up with the other person. If the other person resists, dark clouds gather; Mercurial hurt and fury mount, as we will see later.

Adam drew Ursula closer than anyone had ever before desired her to be. "We breathed life into each other," she says now with shy embarrassment about the early days of their relationship. He had to have her with him everywhere—at every concert, at every meal, to visit friends, to shop for groceries. He introduced her to his vast circle of friends and insisted that they welcome her with open arms. He wanted to attend her music classes, he insisted on hearing her play her violin, he suggested new music to her, he urged her to perform at his weekly music salon—and he introduced her to new sensual pleasures in the bedroom.

Ursula's famous brother disapproved. He thought Adam was arrogant, grandiose, and a poor judge of musical performance. The cellist believed that Adam's feelings for a performer got the better of his judgment of the performance. It was true that on occasion Adam would be so taken with a performer that he would hear nothing short of perfection, whereas the audiences and other critics might hear an off-register note, sloppy technique, or an ineffectual interpretation. Similarly, he could get a bad feeling about a performer—and perhaps Ursula's brother was among these—and pan a performance that others considered accomplished or even exquisite. While Adam was not the most universally respected music critic, and although he was rather poor at the business details of his life, he had a wide audience who enjoyed his critiques on music and musicians. On the radio program he hosted for nearly a decade, he was considered fascinating, erudite, outspoken, controversial, and invariably interesting.

Giving All

Adam could be difficult, agreed virtually every one of the hundreds of people who attended his funeral. But once he reached out and pulled you forcibly into his life, you were forever changed by his love. Despite his shifting moods, his incessant demands, and the ease with which he became disappointed in people, he created for himself a permanent place in the hearts of many throughout the world. One conductor known widely throughout Europe eulogized that one of Adam's greatest gifts was his encouragement and backing of talented, gifted young musicians. Many musicians who now have careers in classical and even popular music credit their success to Adam's ability to urge them to greater heights, to recommend them to gifted teachers, and to put in good reviews for them.

There was nothing Adam would not do for the people he cared for. He had his Self-Confident side, too. The way he saw it, he and "his people" were special, superior, different—and not because of class, wealth, or education. In his Mercurial way, Adam was open to anyone. When someone struck him as belonging in his life, he did everything in his power to bring that person in. He could be sharply critical and unforgiving if the individual wasn't interested in being his friend, and he would fight to hang on to someone who he felt was slipping away from him.

A month after the emotional end of their yearlong affair, Ursula retreated to her tiny mountain cabin 250 miles away. The next day she heard a car drive up, and there was Adam, with his three cats, his typewriter, a suitcase full of cassettes, and a huge wicker basket filled with cheeses, sausages, breads, caviar, smoked fish, and two bottles of cognac. Indulging his Dramatic theatricality, he threw himself on her couch, sighed, and said, "It is simply that I cannot be without you." He said he'd driven up only for the day, but he stayed the week. He cooked for her, tended her garden, read to her, filled the cabin with recorded music, and sipped rare cognac. "All I ask from you is that you play for me," he'd plead. Each time she played, Adam wept. Then, on the seventh day, he heatedly took issue with her interpretation of a sonata. His irritation grew to intense anger at her. "I don't want you, Ursula!" he shouted. He cast her a look of pure hatred and walked out.

Stay Close

How deeply Ursula had loved Adam! Still, she had been the one to end their affair. It all just got too much for her. She had wanted to settle into a quieter, calmer love life with Adam once the infatuation began to subside into a more abiding love. But that wasn't Adam's style. His ceaseless activity, his pushing, his intensity, and not least his changeable feelings began to drain her.

For all his enthusiasms, Adam, like most Mercurial people, was a brooder. He'd go through more moods in a day than Ursula would in a month. Ursula was mature enough to allow him his moods, but they all seemed to involve her. If she was quiet and thoughtful, Adam would worry that she was withdrawing from him. If she played particularly well, Adam would be in ecstasy. If she played badly, he would snap at her as if she were a child who hadn't practiced her lessons. He seemed always to be watching her; she couldn't escape his eyes.

Adam needed to be involved in everything Ursula felt, and vice versa. If one day he felt that there was no meaning in his life, he insisted that she cleave so closely to him that she experienced his ennui. Many times she tried to explain to him that she was a separate human being with individual feelings, and that if he didn't always pull so very close she wouldn't need to establish a distance from him. She had never experienced such ardent moments as when she and he truly connected with each other, but she found she could not sustain that intensity as a way of life. Ursula began to feel pulled in two directions—toward the man she most assuredly loved and admired, and toward her own independent identity. Increasingly, Ursula needed time away from Adam to marshal her inner resources for her teaching and for her own performances.

Needless to say, Adam took her need for emotional distance badly. He became angry, critical, convinced that she was letting him down. Here he had given her his whole world and she could only think of herself. "Ursula, my Ursula," he would sigh sadly. "You and I are among the very few special people in this world. We understand what life really is. It is music, it is love, it is beauty, it is knowledge, it is, after all, you and me. Why am I not the world for you? Why do you break my heart? What have I done to you that is so terrible? I *love* you!"

Ursula could not make him understand that she wasn't like him, that she had needs that had nothing to do with him, but that she still loved him. She could not get through to Adam that he demanded more than a "regular" person like herself could consistently give. "Ah, don't put yourself down," he would insist. "You are a superior being, capable of more than you think."

It caused her unbearable pain to end the most passionate and beautiful experience of her life, but emotionally Ursula could not endure it any longer. Even as she broke off with him, she knew no one would ever give her the kind of love Adam had—and that she would probably never care for anyone as much as she still cared for him.

Indeed, no one but a Mercurial individual like Adam is quite so focused on you, so endowed with attention, totally filled up with you, and so generous. Adam gave Ursula his entire Heifetz recording collection after she mentioned that she admired the virtuoso.

More!

In an individual with a moderate amount of Mercurial style among a balanced pattern, this focused attentiveness and generosity can contribute to a powerful, romantic, lasting love—the kind that songs are written about. However, Adam's personality was powerfully dominated both by the Mercurial and the Dramatic styles, each of them emotionally unrestrained and intensely needy. If his pattern had been balanced by more of the stop-and-think styles, such as the Conscientious, he might have been more inclined to give Ursula some breathing space and plan for a longer, more mutually fulfilling life together. But, like other very Mercurial individuals, Adam's needs and expectations of others were enormous, his reactions to them strong and immediate. He needed from others exactly what he gave to them: constant, intense passion and attention. But very few of his friends, although they loved him dearly, were able to give him back the intensity of emotion he required. Again in Mercurial fashion, he sometimes manipulated his friends and lovers to give him more. He would berate friends for not telephoning or visiting enough when he was ill, making them think that their occasional lapses had made his condition worse. One close friend, Eric, became angry at Adam for making him feel guilty. "You know, Adam, if you needed me, you could call and ask me to come over. I never hear from you, yet you expect me always to know what you want."

Adam was hurt by Eric's remarks and felt that he did not deserve them. Mercurial individuals are not, as a rule, skilled at patching things up with people. They tend to feel that they are the ones who give most (often true), and they have trouble recognizing the ways in which they contribute to difficulties within their relationships. If a relationship ends badly, Mercurial individuals will often look back at their whole time together as dark and terrible; they may conclude that the other person was unworthy of them and that they themselves had been blind to this unfortunate reality.

Stress!

Relationship problems are the greatest sources of stress for Mercurial individuals. Trouble comes when they feel that they are not being recognized and treated as special. Like Self-Confident people, Mercurial types feel entitled to *more,* and when they don't get it, or when the other person tries to establish distance, they feel threatened. They react to such stresses very intensely, of course. Often they'll throw themselves into a powerful, passionate experience—sex, music, alcohol, or drugs—to distract themselves from the abyss that is widening before them. Or they'll step back and act as if it isn't happening, which can seem a little strange. But unless the stress itself diminishes, sooner or later they'll react full force, often feeling that rejection is tantamount to the end of the world. If their outbursts of emotion fail to influence the other person, they may cope by suddenly turning their backs on that person and becoming intensely involved with someone else (itself a distraction from the pain). They hate being without love, and they don't stay that way for long.

Adam's End

Adam was never capable of sustaining a romantic relationship for more than three years. But he thrived on romantic love, so after any breakup he would give of himself completely to someone new.

　　After Ursula came Rinaldo, an Italian tenor. Adam had never before (except briefly in his boyhood) had a homosexual affair. But in his debut at La Scala one glittering night, Rinaldo sang straight into Adam's heart. Mercurial individuals, as we will see shortly, are intrigued rather than put off by others' differences. They tend not to categorize people and can experiment with different identities and roles. They attempt new lifestyles easily, and Adam had little difficulty experiencing the love of a man and being comfortable at homosexual gatherings. He didn't see himself as changed in any way, and he resented the gossip that he had at last "come out" and declared his "true self." This was shortly before the HIV virus was identified. Rinaldo became ill within a few months of their meeting. No one knew what his illness was. By the time the world became aware of AIDS, Rinaldo was dead and Adam was dying.

　　In the last months of his illness, Adam confided to a new friend, Amy, that his friends had all deserted him. At his funeral, when she saw how many tears were shed and heard literally hundreds of people speaking of Adam's profound effect on their lives, she was shocked. How could Adam not have felt the strength of the bonds of loving friendship that he had forged in his sixty-year life? But the sad truth for some extremely Mercurial people is that sometimes, because they feel hurt and abandoned when others simply assert their own needs, and because they expect others to give to them with equivalent intensity, they are the last to recognize how much they mean to the people in their lives.

The Mercurial versus the Dramatic

While in certain respects the Mercurial resembles the Dramatic personality style in passion and feeling, and although the two styles often coexist within the same personality, they differ in important ways. Dramatic men and women are other-directed. This means that they will be alert to you, to learn what you want in order to draw your love and become the center of your attention. Dramatic men and women can be deeply sensitive and intuitive to the desires and needs of other people, and they can orchestrate their own behavior to draw you to them (as Adam often did).

Mercurial individuals are much more intense and demanding. They are not content simply to dance in the light you shine on them; they need you to step in there with them. They want to fill up their whole world with you. They dream of being together with you as one throughout eternity. Their needs for such a relationship will dominate the picture. Generous and outgoing though they may be, Mercurial individuals are less inclined to moderate their behavior for your sake or to adapt to anyone else's ways of looking at things.

The Mercurial Parent

Never stodgy, Mercurial people can be wonderfully fun, entertaining, interesting, energetic, and involving parents—when they're in the mood. As we will soon see, Mercurial men and women have highly reactive moods and can be emotionally inconsistent in all their relationships. But they greatly enjoy the emotional intensity of parent-child relationships, especially in the child's earliest years. Dealing well with the child's emerging autonomy will be more difficult for them; Mercurial parents need to work hard to allow the youngster his or her independence and distance. Also, as the child becomes contrary, they may need their spouse to help shore up their patience and forbearance. Since theirs is an impulsive style (discussed in more detail later in this chapter), they may also need some support in teaching their kids to control their own impulses and appetites. But a moderately Mercurial parent can encourage emotional depth, generosity, creativity, courage, romance, and spirit in his or her offspring.

Good/Bad Matches

The stronger the Mercurial streak, the more difficult it becomes to sustain a long-term relationship. Mercurial types require hot intensity, but the heat they need usually burns itself out rather quickly. As with the Dramatic style, theoretically the best match for the long haul would be with a sober, steady, responsible Conscientious type. Unlike a predominantly Dramatic person, however, a strongly Mercurial type would get bored with such a person in no time, if the Conscientious person didn't get overwhelmed by the fireworks first.

Mercurial people need partners who are interesting, strong, exciting, passionate, and romantic, yet fully responsive to their demands—Prince or Princess Charming, in other words. And this is their problem in seeking a long-lasting relationship: their idealized perfect union doesn't exist in the world. But, like Adam, they may find fulfilling, intense loves for memorable, if brief, relationships. Adventurers often prove highly attractive to them; they are not good at fulfilling Mercurial demands, but they'll be compatible in the passion and excitement department, for a while. Two Mercurial people may have a similarly exciting affair. Dramatic partners usually need too much attention themselves, but this match too could be good and fiery over the short term.

If you have a streak of Mercurial style and wish to find a lifetime partner, you must learn to love and appreciate a partner's lower-key, steadier, less romantic qualities. Look for someone with at least some Conscientiousness. Vigilant qualities may help, for you can share your mutual sense of being somewhat separate from the rest. An Idiosyncratic individual could prove a real find, as long as this person isn't too involved with his or her own separate reality; you two are different from the usual mold and find you can build a truly unique relationship. Also, a match with a Sensitive person may surprise you both with its longevity. Sensitive people can be strong, tolerant, feeling mates who need you to open them up and make the world of other people available to them—your greatest strengths.

But watch out for a strong Serious tendency in anybody you're attracted to. You two will bring each other down in no time.

EMOTIONS: LIFE IN A VOLCANO

Emotions drive Mercurial people, and what moves them is what counts. Individuals with even moderate amounts of the Mercurial style experience all their emotions more intensely than do other people. They are all heart, and everything and everyone affects them on an emotional level. They laugh and they weep easily and openly. They can feel hot fury and ice-cold rage. And they experience profound sexual excitement and passion, encountering few inhibitions in this or any other emotional aspect of their lives.

Emotions drive even their thoughts. Listen to the strength of feeling with which a Mercurial person expresses his or her convictions. Wishy-washy they're not; Mercurial people let you know exactly where they stand.

They are emotional reactors. They hold nothing back and they take nothing lightly, especially when it comes to other people. As we noted earlier, relationships are the focus of Mercurial lives—*all* their relationships, from lovers to friends to relatives to coworkers. They react to everyone, finding emotional significance in everything another person says or does. As a result, they are easily flattered and pleased, and they are just as easily devastated and disappointed. When you bring your lover a single red rose, you take him or her deep into your heart. But when you have nothing to offer, or otherwise behave imperfectly, your romantic Mercurial lover who has so idealized you becomes openly disappointed and deeply disillusioned with you.

A Mercurial friend of Adam's, twenty-seven-year-old Marcia, an interior designer, told him how once she had fallen out of love with someone because he had worn an ugly tie. From then on she'd felt a powerful revulsion to him. The tie had revealed something vulgar and tasteless about the man, she'd told Adam. "Yes," said Adam, "you're like me. We cannot settle for anything less than perfection."

Mercurial individuals idealize emotion; they seek perfect romantic love. They may find it, too, but they cannot grasp it for long—and perhaps no one can. For the idealized lover exists only as long as no flaws, however minor, are seen. The strongly Mercurial person prefers to remain infatuated by his or her beloved. Real human imperfections become a dreadful disappointment, and a calm quiet life with a "regular" person spells boredom.

The Changing Tides of Feeling

Because their emotions are their primary source of experience and meaning, Mercurial individuals who lack a solid anchor in the "head" styles will be subject to rapid, sometimes unpredictable shifts in moods as they react to the unavoidable changes in their environments. Mercurial Terry, for example, went on a long-awaited vacation to Puerto Rico with her husband, Jim. The first day the weather was fabulous. The second and third day it was stormy. Terry's mood crashed—she just couldn't help it, she told Jim; they'd been looking forward so long to this vacation. Jim suggested they take their minds off it and try to have a good time anyway—why not try some gambling? But unlike her part-Conscientious husband, Mercurial Terry could not reason with her emotions. She brooded and snapped until the sun came out on the fourth day and the Puerto Rico of her dreams lay splendidly before her.

The greater the degree of the Mercurial style in a person's pattern, the more frequent the mood shifts. With moderate Mercurial style within a well-balanced pattern, a person may have a gift for experiencing the fullness of emotion. But as the style approaches Borderline personality disorder (p. 311), sufferers find that they lack a consistent emotional center. They can be hot for you one minute, cold to your approaches the next. Why the change? Like infants, they are at the mercy of their emotional reactions; and like young children, they sometimes overreact to the most trivial incidents. They have no control over their emotional states, and they suffer great torment as a result.

SELF-CONTROL: ACTING ON IMPULSE

Self-Control is the last of the Mercurial's three key domains. Appetites exert a huge force on the Mercurial life. Propelled by their all-powerful emotions, Mercurial men and women are hungry for and thoroughly responsive to pleasure, sensation, and experience, which also serve as all-encompassing distractions from hurt and pain that they may be unwilling to acknowledge. They're curious and interested; they love to taste and experiment. They are alive to the moment, and they find it difficult to pass up any spontaneous gratification. When Mercurial Willy gets a taste for pizza at three in the morning, he'll call for a limousine, drag his houseguests out of bed, and have them all delivered to his favorite all-night pizzeria. Willy wouldn't think of ordering in—he adores rousting everybody from sleep, hushing their complaints, hustling them into the limo, orchestrating the impulsive adventure (and his guests know what they're in for when they accept a weekend invitation at his beach house, including Willy's hurt and anger when he feels let down by his friends).

These men and women are intensely motivated to have a good time and to experience new things. They'll try anything. They are unafraid of risks and will head down a dark alley in a strange city while out partying with new friends, without stopping to think what danger may lurk in the shadows. Often they drive like demons and feast on food without a single thought about calories or cholesterol. When Ursula and Adam traveled abroad one summer, she never tired of commenting on the unhealthy way he indulged his appetite (the fat! the pastry! the helpings!), and she made sure to do all the driving, after he passed a truck in a no-passing zone and nearly collided with a bus in the oncoming lane.

Ursula envied Adam's ability to act on his urges. She was a more plodding, planning type of person. Alone, she had a hard time just dropping everything and indulging an appetite. However, while she could learn to loosen up (especially in bed with Adam), Adam would not or could not be taught to plan, to stop and think. Mercurial individuals are similar to Dramatic and especially Adventurous people in their reluctance to think things out and to plan for the future. Their skill is in living right now. Although he was relatively successful as a critic, Adam's business life was a shambles. His office was disorganized, with papers strewn around or heaped on the floor. Adam pleaded with Ursula to help him straighten out his office, but as soon as she got started he confessed that he preferred the chaos. He had not a cent in savings. He spent his money as soon as he had it—there were so many things he wanted to give people! When he became ill, his friends and family paid for his care.

For predominantly Mercurial types, their impulsiveness may reach the level of reckless self-indulgence; and their distaste for goal-directed planning and their tendency to "go for it" instead of waiting for a more opportune time may lead them to self-destruct, despite their talents and abilities. For even moderately Mercurial people, the appetites are a strong force requiring continual conscious control. Many will have a hard time passing up the dessert tray, will have trouble moderating drug or alcohol use, or will find themselves repeatedly getting carried away with their credit cards.

Many people are lucky enough to have mixtures of the Mercurial and the nose-to-the-grindstone or commonsense styles (including the Conscientious, the Leisurely, the Vigilant, the Self-Confident, and the Sensitive), which will keep them from venturing too far afield. A mate with these styles can also help to anchor them.

SELF AND REAL WORLD: FLUID IDENTITIES

Their willingness to try anything affects even the Self domain. Mercurial types tend to be extremely open-minded and curious about other ways of being. Their sense of who they are rarely is concretely fixed to any particular identity or lifestyle, and sometimes not even to a culture. Mercurial men and women have a talent for moving into new lifestyles and fitting right in, whereas others with different personality styles seem out-of-place and uncomfortable. For example, Wendy G. and Kristin T. met in Turkey when they were both in the Peace Corps in the early 1970s. Both studied hard to learn the ways of the villagers and to speak their language, but no matter what Wendy did she always looked, sounded, and acted like the American New Englander she was. Mercurial Kristin, on the other hand, whose sense of self was not etched so indelibly in her character, could lose her American definition and assimilate more of the Turkish character. Both young women were gifted in languages, but it was Kristin who absorbed the flavor and nuance of accent and inflection. She seemed to become a Turk. Later, when she traveled extensively in France, she "passed" as French. Kristin wisely centered her life around this particularly Mercurial talent. Since the early 1980s she's been working as a journalist covering Europe and the Middle East. She's known for her "local color" pieces and interviews with "average" Europeans. Her excellent linguistic ability and the ease with which she establishes herself allow people to open up to her more easily than to many other foreigners.

Mercurial men and women may demonstrate this fluidity in a number of different ways. Some Mercurial types identify easily with changing cultural movements. Some find it relatively easy to make career or role changes. Eliot C., for example, rather smoothly changed from being a lawyer to an evangelical preacher. After five years at that, he became an investment banker. Barbara N. has taken her gift to the stage, where she is a character actress who can thoroughly abandon herself to the role she is playing. Some extremely Mercurial types will immerse themselves in the lifestyles and even the identities of people with whom they become intensely involved.

I'm Not Exactly Sure Who I Am

This Mercurial sense of self may also mean that the individual is not absolutely certain of his or her own identity. As a result, one Mercurial person may have a hard time figuring out what to do in life, whereas another may feel somewhat empty inside. Some exceedingly Mercurial people may resort to "borrowing" an identity—"I think I'll be like my sister"; "I think I'll join a cult"—as a way of achieving some self-certainty.

In any case, the Self—or selves—of the Mercurial individual is likely to be painted in strongly contrasting colors. Mercurial people may be changeable but they always stand out. To them, the Real World is intense and powerful, often chaotic, often rather dark. This is a fire-and-ice personality style, inside and out.

WORK: SPECIAL TALENTS

At work, Mercurial types can be bright, outgoing, enthusiastic, energetic, original, and creative. Characteristically they become intensely involved with their coworkers and take personally everything that happens in their work relationships. They can be passionately interested and involved in office intrigues. They often put their bosses on pedestals and expect them to behave with perfect judgment and compassion, which of course can lead to disappointment. If the boss manages to maintain this idealized image, the Mercurial individual will work extremely hard to make a good impression. But he or she will need to be recognized and rewarded for being so hardworking, for the "special" relationship with the boss is much of the motivation. Mercurial types will not become selfless drones. If all their intense efforts go unnoticed, and the boss acts as if the employee is just one among equals, the Mercurial individual quickly loses interest in working so hard. Mercurial types rise to the occasion when they are admired, needed, depended on, and idealized.

Mercurial men and women are as demanding at work as in the other areas of their lives, but their insistence on being treated well can serve them in this domain. Their sense of entitlement keeps them from being ill-used and underpaid. Extremely Mercurial people may have some trouble being realistic about entitlement, though, and may insist on seeing themselves as more important to their employers than they really are. Some will also find that their tendency to react with strong emotions at work interferes with the progress of their careers. In creative fields, however, this so-called creative temperament usually will not be a hindrance. Employers often expect creative people to be "difficult."

The Mercurial Manager

The Mercurial personality style does not carry with it a gift for leadership, largely because Mercurial types are loath to establish the necessary managerial detachment from subordinates. They like to become intensely involved and they end up, as always, idealizing relationships. They expect extraordinary personal dedication and perfect performance from those who work for them. When the subordinates do not meet these expectations, Mercurial managers tend to feel personally let down. They're moody and emotional. They often split those around them into an in-group and an out-group, although affiliation among the favored few is never guaranteed for long. Moreover, like Dramatic managers, they haven't much ability in planning, in dealing with money, or in organization.

A bit of the Mercurial style, however, may well aid a manager in inspiring subordinates to give their all. Mercurial individuals are sometimes capable of brilliant ideas, and with a solidly Conscientious, noncompetitive second in command, such semi-Mercurial managers may be able both to fire up the spirit in the office and to make sure that the work gets done.

Careers for the Mercurial

To be happy and productive in your work life, you need a career preferably in a creative field where your emotive ability can work for you. You have good critical skills and enjoy sitting in judgment; consider becoming a critic. You must always be involved with others in your work; steer clear of solitary, technical, detail- and/or numbers-related work, or work that requires rigorous cerebral perseverance. You'll need the discipline of a structured work setting; in solo or independent work, you'll have a tendency to lose focus or to get sidetracked by your personal whims. Consider acting, professionally or simply as a hobby, which is a natural for many Mercurial individuals. You may thrive in the teaching and/or helping professions, considering your style's comfort in an idealized role. With moderate amounts of the Mercurial style in a balanced personality profile, you may find success and happiness in such work—if you can avoid overinvolvement with students/clients and can deal with or offset your style's generally high impatience and low frustration tolerance.

TIPS ON DEALING WITH THE MERCURIAL PERSON IN YOUR LIFE

1. Step up on your pedestal. The Mercurial person wants and needs to idealize and overvalue you. Enjoy his or her admiration of the best,

noblest, and most romantic aspects of your character, and let your relationship with this person bring out the best in you. It is inevitable that you will fall from grace by being human and fallible, which will deeply disappoint the Mercurial person in your life. Restore your image by going out of your way to do something extraordinarily loving, romantic, noble, generous, or showy.

2. Step down from your pedestal. You may need to remind the Mercurial person—and yourself—rather regularly that although you appreciate his or her feelings and expectations, you are after all a mere mortal who is at times selfish, uninteresting, weak, and even unkind. Ask for acceptance and understanding of all aspects of you. Remind the Mercurial person that he or she views people as either all good or all bad, and that nobody's really that way. Tell this person that his or her acceptance of all sides of you is very important to you.

3. Don't be surprised or thrown by the Mercurial person's changeable moods, and try not to overreact to them. Realize that little things set off Mercurial people. If you can remain steady and consistent, it will be easier for the Mercurial person in your life to see the bright side again.

4. Mercurial individuals often expect you to understand what they are reacting to and are hurt when you don't figure it out. Save time and trouble: ask for an explanation.

5. Mercurial individuals can be impulsive and excessive and may let the necessary business of life slide. You be the responsible one if you're good at that. (See Tip 4 for dealing with Dramatic types, p. 145.)

6. Show your warmth, love, devotion, and dedication frequently. Hearing how much you love them and how special they are to you is important to Mercurial people. The Mercurial person in your life may be quite a handful, for these people are tempestuous, and what they want from you can be very hard to provide. But they can be courageous, interesting, exciting, and can show you a deep and profound love unlike any you have experienced before. Openly appreciate them for all that.

MAKING THE MOST OF YOUR MERCURIAL STYLE

You know how to live and to feel and you have a tremendous appreciation for romance—these are among the strengths that infuse your life.

To feel more fulfilled and successful in life, especially in your relationships, work on developing some detachment and restraint.

Exercise 1

Read or reread chapter 13, on the Solitary style—your style's opposite. Try to imagine what it would be like not to experience emotions or to feel involved with people. Try to experience what it would be like to read a book, see a movie, listen to music, or be with a person without having an emotional reaction. Pretend that you are an actor and have to play a Solitary role. Remember that this is just an exercise (and a difficult one at that)—we're not suggesting that you try to become Solitary, only that you begin to experience the difference between thoroughly emotional and thoroughly nonemotional.

If you cannot figure out how a Solitary person would evaluate a person or a movie without depending on feelings, you may not realize the extent to which you rely on, and overreact to, your feelings.

Exercise 2

Observe your feelings. As you go through your day, imagine that you are sitting in a movie theater watching yourself on the screen. Or imagine that there is another you, an observer, inside your head who is watching everything that you experience. As you become skilled at developing this dual sense of yourself, tell your observing self to watch especially for your feelings. Keep an eye out for changes in feelings and emotions. Keep track of how and when they change. If you like, keep a running list of each time you have a change in feeling—such as the moment you become disappointed with someone.

Exercise 3

When you have developed some skill at observing your feelings and their changes, try to disown your feelings. Every time you notice a feeling or a change in feeling, say to yourself, "It's only a feeling." For example, if your lover does something stupid and you find yourself suddenly despising him or her for it, stand back from that feeling and do not claim it, or any other feeling, as your own. Let the moment pass without a feeling attached to it. Most important, do not react to that feeling. Again, this is just an exercise, not a suggestion that you no longer have feelings. If you practice it, you will find that you can develop unexpected control over what usually controls you. Try it when you get depressed. Insist to yourself that no matter how awful it feels, your depression *is only a feeling;* it is not the way the world is.

Exercise 4

Modulate your feelings. Every time you have a strong emotional reaction, imagine that you are turning a dial that lowers its intensity. Turn the reaction down 10 percent, then another 10 percent.

Exercise 5

Having observed and distanced yourself from your feelings and having consciously controlled them, try to observe your feelings about the people in your life and note exactly when they change for the worse. Each time you find yourself becoming angry or disappointed with someone, or suddenly beginning to hate that person, ask yourself whether you are reacting unfavorably to what you perceive as flaws in him or her. As soon as you catch yourself having this kind of a negative reaction, immediately return to Exercise 3 and disown the feeling. Simply observe that you have a hard time accepting a person's humanness, but do not act on your negative feeling in any way.

Exercise 6

Observe the degree to which you polarize people into categories of all-good individuals whom you love and adore, and all-bad persons whom you hate and revile. For each person you idealize, think of some of his or her traits that are not so wonderful. Similarly, for those whom you despise, force yourself to think of some of their acceptable or admirable qualities. Resist sudden shifts of feeling about any person when you do this exercise. If you find yourself suddenly beginning to hate a person whom you've been idealizing because you've thought of an unpleasant trait, try Exercises 3 and 4.

The preceding exercises should provide some preparation for the next set, aimed at helping you to develop some control over your appetites and to strengthen your ability to think before you react. You share your tendency to live spontaneously in the present with the Dramatic and the Adventurous types. Turn back to p. 147 and practice the Dramatic Exercises 3 (Stop and count to ten) and 4 (Plan). From the Adventurous exercises on pp. 243-44, concentrate on Exercises 1 (Think from your head, not from your appetites), 2 (Worry a little), and 3 (Safeguard yourself).

Exercise 7

To help prevent overindulging, time it. If you want one cookie (or one sweater) but you usually eat the whole box (or buy up the whole store), carry a stopwatch or other watch that has a timer. Take one cookie (purchase one sweater). Now set your timer to go off in one hour. You can have another cookie (make another purchase) one hour from now. Usually the urge will have passed by that time. If not, take one more cookie (make one more purchase) and set the timer to go off in another hour.

Exercise 8

Now, take your attention off yourself and focus on the other people in your life. For each important person, concentrate on identifying his or her feelings, needs, and expectations from relationships. Look especially for ways in which each person's feelings, needs, and expectations are different from yours. If you find that you have negative or disappointed feelings when you think about these differences, go back to Exercises 3 and 5.

BORDERLINE
PERSONALITY DISORDER

Despondency, rage and fury, self-hatred, arrogance, anxiety, uncertainty and emptiness, clinging dependency, defiant stubbornness, violent self-damaging impulses—these are but some of the torments of the individuals who suffer from Borderline personality disorder. They are desperate, intense, and unstable. They can't make use of their abilities and talents, they are terrified of being alone, and they destroy the relationships that they can't live without. To have this disorder is to exist in perpetual anguish. And to be with people who suffer from it is to be trapped in a maelstrom with them.

▮▮▮▮▮▮▮ DIAGNOSTIC CRITERIA ▮▮▮▮▮▮▮

The DSM-IV describes Borderline personality disorder as:

A pervasive pattern of instability of interpersonal relationships, self-image, and affects, and marked impulsivity beginning by early adulthood and present in a variety of contexts, as indicated by five (or more) of the following:

(1) frantic efforts to avoid real or imagined abandonment

(2) a pattern of unstable and intense interpersonal relationships characterized by alternating between extremes of overidealization and devaluation

(3) identity disturbance: markedly and persistently unstable self-image or sense of self

(4) impulsivity in at least two areas that are potentially self-damaging (e.g., spending, sex, substance use, reckless driving, binge eating)

(5) recurrent suicidal behavior, gestures, or threats, or self-mutilating behavior

(6) affective instability due to a marked reactivity of mood (e.g., intense episodic dysphoria, irritability, or anxiety usually lasting a few hours and only rarely more than a few days)

(7) chronic feelings of emptiness or boredom

(8) inappropriate, intense anger or difficulty controlling anger (e.g., frequent displays of temper, constant anger, recurrent physical fights)

(9) transient, stress-related paranoid ideation or severe dissociative symptoms

---

CYCLES OF DESPAIR

Life is nightmarish for those who suffer from this anguished personality disorder: Nothing ever stays the same. They fall desperately in love; no sooner done than their beloved turns into someone hateful and supremely disappointing. When they are happy, they are certain there will never again be anything or anyone to be unhappy about; with that it's gone and the world, themselves, and everyone else, all return to ashes, never to flower again. They live for love, yet they become stubborn, arrogant, and fly into a rage at the drop of a hat. They seek an identity—say, as a student, a member of a religious group, a cheerleader, a social worker—but it doesn't feel right for long, they can't find themselves, they don't know what they believe anymore, so they think they must become someone else. Who am I? What do I think? What am I going to do with myself? Their feelings, moods, sense of themselves, and their experiences with other people are supremely, tragically inconsistent. They can go nowhere but in circles.

STUDY IN BLACK AND WHITE

People with Borderline personality disorder live an all-or-nothing, black-or-white existence. Where others can tolerate mixed feelings—I love my mate, but of course he/she has plenty of flaws—the Borderline individual sees the world as made up of two kinds of people: perfectly good, kind, loving individuals, and villains. They need the love of the former, but they usually find only the latter.

They are similarly confused about themselves. One minute they think they're the greatest; then they begin again to belittle themselves. Feeling so empty inside, Borderline women and men dare not be alone with themselves. They must have the love, protection, and companionship of a nurturing, thoroughly good person. Along comes someone, and the Borderline individual can see no evil; never has there been anyone more perfectly loving or understanding. In a flash the lover, having perhaps committed the most minor indiscretion, becomes an object of hate or contempt. The world collapses again. The lover's disappointing fall from grace is inevitable; yet, even before it happens, the individual with Borderline personality disorder may begin to fear, to assume, or to predict that he or she will be rejected—so the more desperately he or she must cling: "Don't leave me! I'll do anything to keep you!" Sometimes a Borderline person will go to great extremes of self-sacrifice and self-denial in order to hold on to a relationship, only to react against the partner with fury alternating with self-pity.

Bouncing uncontrollably between black and white, all and nothing, Borderline individuals live unfulfilled lives. Mostly they feel depressed and pessimistic, and almost anything can set them off into extremes of despair, irritability, anxiety, disillusionment, guilt; occasionally, though, they experience brief episodes of euphoria. However, nothing but the usual low-level misery lasts. Their inability to maintain or perceive consistency in anything or anyone, themselves included, prevents them from being able to persevere, to learn from experience, to master challenges. They can't tolerate the mood shifts, the frustration, and the pain and disappointment of it all, especially the rejections and impending rejections. They don't know how to take their minds off their anxiety and pain; they can't focus themselves on their work, on a movie, on a bike ride, or on a good book. Instead, they flee into impulsive sex, shopping, food, or drugs. For the most severely disordered individuals, only mutilating themselves—cutting their arms, burning themselves with cigarettes, banging their heads against a wall, and suicidal gestures—will temporarily make them feel better, calmer inside.

BORDERLINE OF WHAT?

Of all fourteen personality disorders, the Borderline is today capturing the most research and clinical interest among mental health professionals. It is a puzzle with many curious pieces. The more we know about it, the more commonly occurring we find it to be, especially among individuals hospitalized for psychiatric difficulties. Some 20 percent of this population are suffering from this complex personality disorder. Many of these people enter a hospital because they are suicidal (often precipitated by a romantic rejection), self-mutilating, or suffering extreme consequences of drug and alcohol abuse; others are hospitalized for depression or because of psychotic episodes.

What *is* Borderline personality disorder? Some theoreticians and clinicians believe it is not a personality disorder at all, but rather a level of personality "disorganization." The term began to be used nearly sixty years ago to identify a group of patients who did not fit into the then-standard categories of neurosis and psychosis. These patients' enormous problems seemed to qualify them for a category midway between functional and nonfunctional. The Borderline term was also used by some earlier clinicians to categorize patients with what they believed was a mild variant of schizophrenia; today, however, these individuals would probably be diagnosed as Schizotypal (see chapter 12).

Although the framers of the DSM retained the term *Borderline,* they did not intend it to define disorders bordering on psychosis. Patients who receive the Borderline diagnosis have a personality disorder, period. Nonetheless, researchers today are intrigued by its relationship not so much to schizophrenia as to the affective (mood) disorders. The full range of Axis I depressive and manic-depressive mood-regulation disorders frequently occurs in combination with Borderline personality disorder. Perhaps, some theorize, Borderline personality disorder is related to an inherited "affective spectrum" of disorders the way Schizotypal, Paranoid, and Schizoid personality disorders may fall along a so-called schizophrenic spectrum.

Yet another "spectrum" has claimed recent research and clinical interest: the "impulse spectrum." Here Borderline personality disorder takes its place along with Antisocial personality disorder, bulimia (the binge-and-purge eating disorder), and drug and alcohol abuse, among others, as an impulse-control deficit. There is much evidence to show that people with Borderline personality disorder as well as their relatives suffer from numerous problems with impulse control. Dysregulation of both appetites and moods, with perhaps a common biological underpinning, may lie at the bottom of this terribly self-destructive personality disorder, about which more below.

INCIDENCE, PREDISPOSITIONS, AND RISKS

Borderline personality disorder is diagnosed far more frequently among women, by a ratio estimated at three to one. The reasons for this are not yet understood, but analyses to date have discovered no sex bias in the diagnostic criteria.

It is worthwhile to note that women also suffer from the clinical forms of depression much more commonly than do men, for reasons that are also unclear. Research into depression has begun to yield considerable evidence that depression (especially the manic-depressive or bipolar forms) may be an inherited illness. Individuals with Borderline personality disorder may be similarly predisposed. Their family histories often reveal a relationship both to manic depression and to alcoholism and other impulse-control disorders. Women, too, are more common victims of childhood sexual abuse and bulimia, both of which have been associated with Borderline personality disorder.

Increasingly, researchers in the biology of personality believe that individuals with Borderline personality disorder inherit a genetic predisposition to poor mood regulation and impulse control, which could explain their constantly changing feelings, their sensitivity to rejection, their unstable relationships, the eating and substance abuse disorders to which they are prone, even their suicidal tendencies. Evidence suggests that individuals with this disorder may have diminished levels of the important brain chemical serotonin, which helps to regulate the central nervous system and many of its emotional functions. Deficits in serotonin and the neurotransmitter noradrenalin could lead to the self-directed aggression (such as suicide attempts) that is so characteristic of this personality disorder. On the other hand, the sensation-seeking behavior of Borderline people could be tied to excessive secretions of noradrenalin, as in Antisocial personality disorder (p. 245). (For more about the biochemistry of personality, see chapter 18.)

In any case, such a biologic predisposition would make it hard for a vulnerable individual to deal with some of the more difficult experiences in life—and there is much evidence that these women and men have had more than their share to cope with in early life.

Many Borderline women and men come from disturbed or broken families in which there were alcoholism, abuse, violence, and traumatic separations. As children, many experienced extreme physical or verbal brutality. Studies have found the rate of childhood sexual abuse to be as high as 70 percent of Borderline individuals. Other research has determined that 25 percent of individuals with Borderline personality disorder are also diagnosed with post-traumatic stress disorder, which suggests that there is a common role of trauma in both disorders.

The vast majority of all Borderline individuals reveal a history of adverse, inconsistent, and unpredictable parenting. Some come from families that appeared well-functioning on the surface, but in which one or both parents hampered or punished the child's earliest attempts at establishing an independent identity and simultaneously discouraged closeness and intimacy.

The family members of Borderline people often suffer from Borderline or Antisocial personality disorders, substance-abuse disorders, mood disorders, and eating disorders. Borderline women and men themselves commonly suffer from additional personality disorders, including the Schizotypal, the Histrionic, the Narcissistic, and the Antisocial. Under extreme stress they may experience some transient psychotic symptoms, often marked by paranoid features. Under the same circumstances they may also experience temporary amnesia or feel completely detached from their minds or bodies. As with Antisocial individuals, their most extreme self-destructive behaviors, which explode into view by late adolescence, seem to diminish once they reach their thirties or forties, when they begin to lead their lives in quieter desperation. Unfortunately, they may not survive to that age. Because they take impulsive risks with sex and drugs and have suicidal tendencies, individuals with severe forms of Borderline disorder risk death at an early age.

Dr. Michael Stone identifies hostility as a trait that will predict whether a Borderline person continues to do well in mid- and later life. Those whose "anger and querulousness continue to smolder on into middle life eventually wear out the patience of spouses or other intimates upon whom they depend," he claims. Yet those among whom rage and anger have subsided, he says, "reach a higher plateau in their forties and fifties, such that the 'borderline' label is no longer applicable."

Borderline personality disorder appears to be on the rise. Social factors such as the disintegration of the family may provide at least a partial explanation.

HELP!

And now for the good news. Many people who have Borderline personality disorder can be helped, in short- and long-term inpatient or outpatient programs and therapies, and with pharmacotherapy. Crisis management is the goal of the shorter programs, while extended psychotherapy, usually lasting at least four years, can effect lasting change *if* the person can persevere that long. Many people who are diagnosed with this disorder eventually achieve significant successes in their lives following treatment.

Borderline individuals often seek therapy, enjoying the intensity of the idealized relationship with the therapist. But, as in all their relationships, they may suddenly begin to hate the person they so dearly loved, and they may reject one therapist, move on to another, and then another. Their frequent rage and intense moods, their demands for more and more attention, and their continual testing of the therapist, often through self-damaging acts, can provoke feelings of helplessness and anger in the unwary, inexperienced clinician. Borderline patients are not every therapist's cup of tea. But a well-trained, empathic professional will be able to recognize the source of the feelings such patients inspire and will continually but kindly confront the patient with the effects of his or her behavior on others. The therapist must be strong enough to set and enforce limits on acceptable behavior, be sufficiently patient to work toward future results, and be compassionate, caring, reliable, and consistent. It is important that the therapist be actively involved with the patient during the treatment hour rather than simply sitting and listening.

Cognitive therapeutic approaches emphasize techniques to change the "dichotomous" thinking style (e.g., a person is all good or all bad) that makes life so difficult for Borderline individuals. Individuals also learn ways to control their emotions and their impulses. Learning to substitute behaviors can help. "For example, as a stopgap measure, it is sometimes possible to substitute a minimally self-destructive behavior (such as marking oneself with a marking pen) for a more self-destructive one (such as slashing oneself)," report Drs. Beck and Freeman.

Psychologist Marsha Linehan in recent years has developed a particular form of behavioral therapy for use specifically with people suffering from Borderline personality disorder; she calls it dialectical behavior therapy. In highly structured individual and group treatment settings, therapists and participants work together to target and cope with self-destructive behaviors and those that reduce the quality of life. Importantly, they acquire new skills to help them make their lives worth living and to respect and like themselves.

As with all personality disorders, there is no medication specifically for the treatment of Borderline disorder. Rather, medications selected to relieve particular symptoms are prescribed for limited periods of time. Antidepressants, antipsychotics, anticonvulsants, and lithium have all proved helpful in this regard. The selective serotonin reuptake inhibitor (SSRI) class of antidepressants (Prozac, for example) seems promising for mood instability and impulsiveness in some people.

COPING WITH BORDERLINE PEOPLE

See the tips for dealing with Mercurial types on pp. 307–8 for help with individuals with mild Borderline personality disorder. Otherwise, recognize the inner anguish that drives Borderline people to behave as they do, and try not to perpetuate a pattern of overreacting to their overreactions to you. In other words, try to stand back emotionally from the effects of their behavior on you. This will help you keep your own feelings under control, and it will help you see a manipulation for what it is Most important, you must understand your own limits. Tell Borderline people that you love them *but* you cannot be for them everything they need you to be, and you cannot be responsible for everything that they do to themselves. Encourage them to get help; insist, if you can. If your family life is in chaos, seek help together.

CHAPTER 15.

Self-Sacrificing Style

"THE ALTRUIST"

To live is to serve; to love is to give. These are axioms for individuals who have the Self-Sacrificing personality style. The way they see it, their needs can wait until others' are well served. Knowing that they have given of themselves, they feel comfortable and at peace, secure with their place in the scheme of things. At its best and most noble, this is the selfless, magnanimous personality style of which saints and good citizens are made.

THE SEVEN CHARACTERISTICS

The following seven traits and behaviors are clues to the presence of the Self-Sacrificing personality style. A person who reveals a strong Self-Sacrificing tendency will demonstrate more of these behaviors more intensely than someone with less of this style in his or her personality profile.

1. *Generosity.* Individuals with the Self-Sacrificing personality style will give you the shirts off their backs if you need them. They do not wait to be asked.

2. *Service.* Their "prime directive" is to be helpful to others. Out of deference to others, they are noncompetitive and unambitious, comfortable coming second, even last.

3. *Consideration.* Self-Sacrificing people are always considerate in their dealings with others. They are ethical, honest, and trustworthy.

4. *Acceptance.* They are nonjudgmental, tolerant of others' foibles, and never harshly reproving. They'll stick with you through thick and thin.

5. *Humility.* They are neither boastful nor proud, and they're uncomfortable being fussed over. Self-Sacrificing men and women do not like being the center of attention; they are uneasy in the limelight.

6. *Endurance.* They are long-suffering. They prefer to shoulder their own burdens in life. They have much patience and a high tolerance for discomfort.

7. *Artlessness.* Self-Sacrificing individuals are rather naive and innocent. They are unaware of the often deep impact they make on other people's lives, and they tend never to suspect deviousness or underhanded motives in the people to whom they give so much of themselves.

THE SIX DOMAINS OF SELF-SACRIFICING FUNCTIONING

There's no question about it: Relationships is the key domain for the Self-Sacrificing personality.

RELATIONSHIPS: FOR YOU, ANYTHING

Self-Sacrificing individuals derive their meaning in life through giving to others. "I exist to serve," Self-Sacrificing Donna laughs with just a bit of self-mockery. Her husband, Bruce, has requested her homemade sourdough bread with dinner. It's late on a Sunday afternoon and Donna, a nurse practitioner, has been trying to catch up on paperwork brought home from the office. She pokes fun at Bruce for always getting his way, but it is she who generally anticipates his desires. Today she's a little annoyed with herself for not having baked the bread that he always likes to have on cool spring evenings like this. But of course today she has all this work of her own, she reminds herself. And the reason she's behind on the paperwork is that she spends so much time—too much time, some of her colleagues tell her—with her patients. But that's Donna. Her patients come to her with individual needs—it simply isn't in her character to turn anyone away before helping as much as she can.

Donna also has a streak of the Devoted style in her personality pattern, but the Self-Sacrificing is stronger. Devoted types center their lives around their principal relationships—spouses, children, dear friends. Self-Sacrificers do for and give to everyone they come in contact with. They are gentle, kind, good-deed doers; it's their built-in value system always to help others. They do for others one way or another in all their relationships.

They don't seek rewards for their helpfulness. These men and women may sacrifice their own needs in the act of service—witness Donna putting aside her work to bake the bread that her husband loves—but they don't experience their actions as self-renunciation. To do a good turn for another person makes them feel right in the world, and that's what counts. They are altruists, in other words.

Anyone with a prominent streak of this style will find meaning in laboring to make others' lives better. Some Self-Sacrificers become great philanthropists, some missionaries. These are the people who take in ill or injured foster children, who work to help victims of AIDS, who lend their untiring support to charities and causes, who sacrifice their own needs to those of the family. They are drawn to creatures in pain and in need, whose suffering and hardship they will do all they can to alleviate. Some individuals with Self-Sacrificing style are truly gifted healers.

They labor long and hard, happy to lose sight of themselves in their helpfulness to cause or person. Sometimes Bruce will say to Donna, "Darling, it's almost midnight. Forget the ironing. I'll wear something else tomorrow. You look bushed. Think of yourself, sweetheart. Come to bed." But Donna doesn't mind the never-ending labors of her life. She can fall into bed in a calm, contented, inner equilibrium; her rest is earned.

"Heavens, Don't Thank Me"

Self-Sacrificing men and women are active, vigorous, energetic, highly motivated, ever diligent—but, unless they also have one or more of the "me" styles (such as the Self-Confident) in their personalities, their efforts will always be for someone else. They routinely deflect attention away from themselves. "It's nothing special," insisted Conscientious/Self-Sacrificing Peter after he single-handedly organized and coordinated a fund-raising dinner for a local theater company. He devoted three months of his off-work time to this task. On opening night, rather than relax with the guests even for a moment, he was continually overseeing the serving, the clearing, and the overall comfort of the five hundred guests.

"Heavens, don't thank *me,*" he insisted with typical Self-Sacrificing modesty as the guests began to depart. "Why, Elizabeth baked these wonderful pies," he'd say, or, "Raymond's firm donated the linens," or, "Violet hand-lettered every envelope." Self-Sacrificers do not like to take full credit for what they do. They do not enjoy the attention. It doesn't "feel right" to them.

Indeed, some Self-Sacrificers so routinely take the attention off themselves that the important people in their lives may stop noticing their extraordinary efforts and begin to take them for granted, or even take advantage of their good natures. After these Self-Sacrificers insist time and again that they don't want to be thanked, credited, or noticed, people begin to take them at their word and stop paying attention to their contributions. *That* hurts.

They may not want to be lionized for their selfless efforts, but like most other people, Self-Sacrificers need to be loved and appreciated. They love to give, and they hate appearing prideful or pushy. But to be treated as a nonperson can cause an underrecognized Self-Sacrificer much pain and confusion. After years of telling her husband, "Honey, don't make such a fuss over the sourdough bread. Really, it's no big deal"—if Bruce ever stops fussing and begins to expect the bread to be there when he wants it, Donna will feel deeply let down. "Why," she will ask herself, "when I work so hard to make him happy, does he seem not to notice or care?"

Guilty Pleasures

All Self-Sacrificers share to some degree this discomfort with positive attention. They don't feel right standing on a pedestal, and they feel awkward (albeit flattered) when anyone says, "Let's concentrate on making *you* happy for a change." Self-Sacrificers are in their element when they are giving pleasure or assistance to others, but they are not comfortable with themselves when the tables are turned.

This discomfort may resemble guilt, as if deep down they don't feel entitled to so much attention. For example, Lorraine J.'s personality was dominated by the Dramatic style, with the Self-Sacrificing next in line. She had powerful Dramatic needs to be on center stage, but her Self-Sacrificing streak made her feel embarrassed by her wishes. After a couple of years in therapy, she was able to throw herself a lavish thirty-fifth birthday party. She dressed exquisitely and was determined to be the star of the evening, as she was. But to keep up the show in front of her seventy-five guests, Lorraine needed to become intoxicated and thus not apparently responsible for her self-entitled show-offy behavior. The next morning she had a huge hangover—and a miserable feeling of depression. She was later able to work out with her therapist that she had felt guilty for "wallowing" in all that "selfish" attention. Secretly Lorraine had always wanted and loved getting special attention, she realized, but she had been taught to be humble, that "pride goeth before the fall."

Caution: One-Way Street Ahead

Self-Sacrificers like Lorraine, who would rather give than take, may be good, even saintly people. But when it comes to getting their own needs met, because they can't accept love easily they may get involved in unbalanced relationships. They may not realize that people who ask nothing for themselves or who feel they don't deserve such attention often discourage appropriate partners who can and wish to give.

Patrick S. was the Self-Sacrificing giver in his relationship with Gail B. At first Gail was flattered by all his attentions to her—the flowers, the gifts, the back rubs, the abiding interest in what turned her on sexually. But she liked to share, not just to take. She began to surprise him too with little gifts, but to her disappointment Patrick didn't respond very much. He seemed uncomfortable. She tried to give him a sensual massage—the kind he was so good at giving her—but it didn't relax him and it didn't turn him on. Gail tried to explain that to love him she needed to be able to give to him, too. Although she had been powerfully attracted to his apparent sensitivity to her needs, Gail began to be turned off by Patrick. "How ironic," she confided later to a friend, "that after years of searching for a man who cared about how I felt, I finally found one who cared *too* much and asked too little for himself."

Anna B., the fashion designer whose case history appears on pp. 334–40, was an extraordinarily attentive and gifted lover, but with a loving partner she herself could achieve no sexual satisfaction. When a partner would attempt to satisfy her, she would become embarrassed and uncomfortable and stop him. Eventually, like many extremely Self-Sacrificing people, she began to attract only men who were all-take-and-no-give, selfish, even cruel and rapacious lovers who thought only of their own needs.

Then there's predominantly Self-Sacrificing Tony, who, to demonstrate his generosity and love, put his Jaguar and his valuable collection of old coins in his bride's name. When she left him two years later, she drove off with both.

A Fine Line

Obviously, it can be very difficult for people with a lot of this personality style—who mean only the best for other people—to know where to draw the line. Moderately Self-Sacrificing individuals can balance their giving and doing for others and can, perhaps with some effort, ask more for themselves. As the style becomes extreme and approaches Self-Defeating personality disorder, however, the constant giving and doing puts an unwelcome burden of obligation on others. ("Good Lord, now that Nina has insisted on staying to wash all the dishes after my dinner party, I suppose I'm going to have to do that for her when she gives her party. You know, I don't really want to go to her party.") Self-Sacrificers always insist on going out of their way to help, generally oblivious to the fact that some people may not want their assistance. Unsolicited let-me-do-this-for-you's often get on people's nerves.

When Bruce wants his nurse-practitioner wife, Donna, to stop ironing and come to bed, before she begins to carry her personality style too far, perhaps she ought to start asking herself whether he'd rather have her there by his side than working herself to exhaustion for his sake. Since Self-Sacrificers work to achieve acceptance through their giving, some may find it hard to comprehend that those who love them may prefer that they give a little less, or differently, for a change.

The Self-Sacrificing Parent

Successful parenting requires the ability to sacrifice for one's children and to expect little for oneself in return—to a point. Individuals with moderate Self-Sacrificing style give of themselves naturally and happily, providing the child a strong sense of security in life. Extreme Self-Sacrificers, however, may become martyrs and lay a burden of guilt on their offspring. They work themselves to the bone for the children and suffer extreme disappointment when the children appear ungrateful, or when they grow up and go their self-determined way. The very Self-Sacrificing parent who "went without so you could go to medical school" may not take kindly to the child's decision to pursue a career in rock music. "But, Mom, I never *wanted* to be a doctor. I never *asked* you to give up new clothes or a new car for my sake."

As role models, Self-Sacrificing parents may have to remind themselves to set good examples of self-assertion for their children—that it's okay to stand up for oneself and to ask that one's needs be met. They may also have to practice setting limits, expressing their anger directly, and saying no at appropriate times.

Good/Bad Matches

Self-Sacrificers get so tuned in to what others need and want that, like the Devoted and the Mercurial types, they can become involved with almost anybody. Similarly, they may not be sufficiently discriminating in choosing an appropriate mate; they run the risk of hooking up with people who take advantage of their helpful, gentle, giving, submissive natures. And because Self-Sacrificers are forgiving and tolerant, they might continue in hurtful relationships rather than bail out.

If Self-Sacrificing is your style, obviously you'll do best with those who enjoy being taken care of and lavished with attention. But beware of people who are dominated by the Adventurous or the Aggressive style, who might use or abuse you. Avoid Self-Confident people, too, for they will not notice your needs and will disappoint you, although they will be only too glad to take what you have to give. Otherwise, you will probably be able to match up well with any of the other personality styles, depending on other influences in your personality pattern.

EMOTIONS, SELF-CONTROL, AND REAL WORLD: THE PROBLEM OF PLEASURE

As we have seen, Self-Sacrificing men and women are pleasure-givers, not pleasure-takers—but they can be far more capable of the full range of satisfying emotions and appetites than they may seem. Emotionally they can feel quite positive and full, especially when they've done something good for someone.

As for their overt pleasure, the key is privacy. In the presence of others they automatically give up their comfort in order to provide for another's. They cook or serve rather than eat. They stand while others sit. They choose the uncomfortable chair in order to leave the soft chaise for someone else. In bed, they may attend to their partner's needs rather than their own. It's the way they are, and they're good at it. But since they are other-directed people pleasers they will not find it easy to relax their strict controls over their own emotions and hungers in order to have a let-loose good time. Some extreme Self-Sacrificers may seem stiff, stern, uptight—and no fun at all.

Stolen Moments

If there's no one else around, though, these same individuals may find that relaxation and self-indulgence come easily. They can relax in the comfortable chair, dish out the ice cream, watch a racy movie, and enjoy themselves.

The stronger the Self-Sacrificing style, the more time Self-Sacrificers will spend in the company of others worrying about what they need to do or might have overlooked for them. They'll indulge their own pleasures only when no one is looking, as if they have something to feel guilty about.

The Dark Side

Still, Self-Sacrificing individuals are prone to sadness and depression for many reasons. They all see the Real World as a hard, tough place—*painfully* real—in which their mission is to make things better for other people. Even those with balanced personality patterns may be more exposed than others to the pain, misery, and misfortunes of human existence through their altruistic efforts to help the needy. They will not see life as pleasant, just, or easy. Those who are more Self-Sacrificing may be weighed down by their deep inner guilt and their sense of never-ending, unfulfillable obligations to others. They may not know how to express their anger at the people they care for or even acknowledge that they harbor such feelings. Others may simply not be able to "lighten up."

For these and other reasons, Self-Sacrificing people often come across as long-suffering—but always emotionally strong and capable of shouldering whatever burdens come their way in life.

How they express their personal suffering will depend on the other styles in their profiles. With Dramatic or Mercurial streaks, a predominantly Self-Sacrificing person may loudly fuss and complain about the number of ungrateful people in his or her life. With Conscientious or some Solitary influence, another may keep his or her resentment private, leading to a chronically stiff upper lip. With considerable Serious style, they will be cynical, pessimistic, critical, and resigned to what they see as the inevitable disappointments of life.

Stress!

There are two principal sources of stress for Self-Sacrificing people. One, they take on too much, willingly giving up their leisure time to care for others. They don't kick back and put their feet up unless they dare to "steal" a moment. And they find it difficult to accept help from anyone else. Thus, they may work themselves into poor health.

Resentment, the other key stress for this style, occurs when they begin to feel that others do not appreciate, understand, or love them, despite all they do.

But Self-Sacrificing types are strong. They can take on other people's burdens as well as their own. "Such is life, whether I like it or not. I can deal with it," say these stressed-out individuals. Unless they are in a state of complete collapse, they'll roll up their sleeves and restore their emotional equilibrium by doing someone a good turn.

THE (UN)DESERVING SELF

The extent to which they seek their identities through their acts of service may reveal some Self-Sacrificers' uncertainties about their self-worth. Would they still feel good about themselves if they were stranded alone on a desert island? Can they feel at peace with themselves if they're not trying to do something for someone else?

Some Self-Sacrificers feel unworthy and undeserving of love, attention, and pleasure. Therefore, they are always trying to earn it. Others may, deep down, have a very good sense of who they are and what they want for themselves—but they may feel that they should not indulge their "selfish" desires but instead tend to the needs of others.

WORK: SERVICE COMES FIRST

Work is a comfortable domain for this personality style, for through their work they perform their service to others. They resemble Conscientious types in their competence, their loyalty, their reluctance to relax and enjoy themselves, and their giving their all to their work. Also like Conscientious types, Self-Sacrificers are respectful of those in authority.

Give Self-Sacrificing individuals a task and they'll work all night and on weekends if need be to complete it. They can handle drudgery and routine. They can adapt to many work situations and conditions. They don't complain that "it's not my job." If it's important to the boss, the spouse, the children, or the cause, they'll get it done.

They may work exceedingly hard, but unless they have an ambitious personality style in their pattern (the Self-Confident, for example), they will not be powerfully career-minded. Neither will they be as demonstrably successful as you might imagine, considering the amount and the quality of their work. Outward personal ambition, as we have said, does not mark this personality style. The value of the work itself or of the person for whom they work is more important to Self-Sacrificers than their own personal gain. A Self-Sacrificing individual may work tirelessly toward the candidate's victory, the patient's recovery, or housing for the homeless, but will be uninclined to stop and think, "Hey, what's in this for me?" What counts most is the satisfaction of the principal others involved with the work.

This altruistic pattern operates on all levels of work—from service to mankind to work for hire. In this latter category, meet Self-Sacrificing Steven C., who is a ghostwriter. He couldn't care less that he receives no credit for his work, even though he has penned some best-sellers. He makes a lot of money, but perhaps he could make more if he wrote his own books. He's not in it for the money, either, he'll tell you. What he likes best is the gratification that comes from making the people who hire him sound like good writers. He loves his work.

Many extremely bright and talented Self-Sacrificing people are content to remain secretaries throughout their working lives—and lucky are the people they work for. Self-Sacrificing types make steady, reliable, longtime, undemanding workers no matter what careers they choose.

Not all Self-Sacrificers may be so satisfied, however. Some who are very talented and would like to advance in their careers wonder why they haven't gotten anywhere. Like Self-Sacrificing/Leisurely Derek D., who was trying to break into a singing career but tended to oversleep every time he had an audition. Or speechwriter Beatrix N., who, like ghostwriter Steven, never wrote anything under her own name, yet resented nonetheless that she never got credit for what she did.

As this style begins to rule the personality, Self-Sacrificers may have difficulty taking advantage of opportunities for their own advancement—much as they may have a hard time accepting pleasure and being the center of attention in their relationships. They hate to ask favors. They may not follow up on leads or maintain contacts. Rather than compete, they may stand back so that a colleague receives the promotion or raise. Self-Sacrificing Frank O. told his wife, "Paula wanted that promotion so badly, I just didn't have it in me to try to take it from her. So I told the boss not to consider me." While Frank felt genuinely good about what he'd done, his wife was far from happy with him. The way she saw it, every time he was in a situation to assert himself and to compete, he got up and took the backseat. For all the work he was doing, he wasn't getting anywhere.

Perhaps, in his Self-Sacrificing way, Frank did not feel entitled to anything special for himself. Inside he may have wanted the promotion but then "atoned" for his "greed" by giving it away to his colleague. Note that the extreme of this personality style is called the Self-Defeating personality disorder, and for good reason. Too much of this style may mean that the individual takes active steps to cut off every avenue toward pleasure and success.

But with a balanced personality style, a moderately Self-Sacrificing person will take much pleasure in the doing of good work and be the better (if not necessarily richer) for it.

A Note to the Boss

Thank your Self-Sacrificing employees for all their untiring efforts on your behalf. You may forget these individuals are there, because Self-Sacrificing types step off into the shadows and demand so little for themselves. Now that you've noticed these dedicated souls, give them a raise—they may be reluctant to ask for what they deserve.

The Self-Sacrificing Manager

Generally Self-Sacrificers avoid becoming managers. They like to work for or on behalf of others rather than be responsible for overseeing other people's work and behavior. They may end up in middle-management positions, however, by virtue of their good work, loyalty, and devotion to their organizations or their bosses. They may have trouble delegating work and insisting it be done on time, so they do it themselves and end up seriously overworked. They may be overly solicitous of subordinates' problems and go out of their way to help them; they may later feel that these individuals are not grateful, and angry when they continue to underperform. Other Self-Sacrificing managers may display a somewhat tyrannical side, expecting their subordinates similarly to sacrifice themselves completely to the job or to them.

Careers

Look for work in which you can take care of or satisfy the needs of others. Consider any of the helping, ministering, serving, and facilitating professions—including medicine, psychology, nursing, social service, the clergy, charitable institutions, volunteer work, secretarial and administrative-assistance work, teaching, catering, interior decorating, production work, library science, daycare, homemaking, and housework. Avoid careers that involve public speaking or otherwise require you to be comfortable as the "front person" or the center of attention. Unless you have a Dramatic or Mercurial side, avoid the performing arts. With a creative bent, consider writing, editing, songwriting, or commercial art.

TIPS ON DEALING WITH
THE SELF-SACRIFICING PERSON IN YOUR LIFE

1. Remember to recognize and acknowledge this person's efforts, no matter how frequently he or she insists "it's nothing." Your Self-Sacrificer may be embarrassed by compliments but inwardly needs to know that you notice and appreciate.

2. Try to find a comfortable give-and-take formula. Self-Sacrificing people *must* keep giving, helping, and doing, but they could use a little help from you in being able to relax and enjoy themselves. Don't hesitate to insist that the Self-Sacrificing person in your life stop building your bookcase or ironing your shirts and just come and sit quietly with you.

3. Learn how to translate "Self-Sacrificing language." "Heavens, don't thank me," may mean, "I don't feel right taking the credit, but thanks for the compliment." Similarly, "I really don't want to go out dancing," often means, "I really don't think I should go out and have a good time—so please drag me."

4. Try not to reject what this person has to give, and don't be embarrassed by the constant attention. Self-Sacrificers think of you first. They love it. So relax and enjoy being so well looked after. In any case, don't get into a fight about it. When Aunt Jenny calls and tells you she's bringing yet another box of garage-sale used clothing for your children, instead of getting into your usual huff ("No! Aunt Jenny, don't! If I see another box of that stuff I think I'll scream!") say, "Fine, thank you." She's going to bring it anyway ("I'm sorry," she'll say, "I know you said you didn't want this, but just look at these sweet things. I'm sure the children could use them"). So be gracious, accept the parcel, and after she leaves, donate it to the homeless.

5. Be careful not to take advantage. Some extreme Self-Sacrificers may give away too much or go too far out of their way to please you. This person is not your slave, no matter how he or she behaves. If the Self-Sacrificer won't draw the line, you do it. But when you refuse a favor, always explain why.

6. Insist on being more helpful. Take your own clothes to the dry cleaner, even if the Self-Sacrificing person explains that it's no problem for him or her to do it. You wash the dishes or water the lawn or otherwise find a way to relieve the person of the usual Self-

Sacrificing overwork. This will help you establish balance in your relationship and make it difficult to take advantage of this person's willingness to do everything.

7. Talk about it. Try to convey to the Self-Sacrificing person in your life that the way he or she can do something really nice for you is to share your leisure time with you. Unless you provide this feedback, this person may be truly unaware that you want something other than what he or she is giving to you.

MAKING THE MOST OF YOUR SELF-SACRIFICING STYLE

You are a naturally unselfish, generous, helpful, giving human being. You work hard to please, even when no one asks or thanks you for it. You may deny your own needs and pleasures more than you realize. Work on establishing a firm or firmer balance of give-and-take by being more circumspect in the giving, more assertive in the taking.

Exercise 1

In your imagination, focus on yourself for a change. Whenever you are with people, you automatically think about taking care of their needs. The next time you are with others, try to imagine what you would like for yourself in the same situation. For example, as you run to fix the drinks for your guests, imagine someone else making the drinks or even fixing one just for you. When you are listening to a friend's problems and trying to suggest solutions, imagine that you are the talker and your friend the listener. This is just a thinking exercise, and you may find yourself uncomfortable with these fantasies, because they go against your nature. The point is to begin to recognize what *you* might really enjoy getting from other people. Keep a list of all the desires you discover. You may find it easier to do this exercise when you are alone, in which case make a list of all the things you would like other people to do for you.

Exercise 2

Learn to ask. Make your desires and expectations known. Choose one or more items from the list you wrote for Exercise 1, and ask someone to do it or provide it for you. For example, if you're the one who gets up to make the morning coffee but you can imagine your lover or spouse doing it for a change—ask. Say, "Honey, why don't you make the coffee tomorrow?" Won't he/she be surprised! Don't worry if you feel uncomfortable making such requests—you'll get used to it. But don't take it back. If your partner says, "Gee, I would but I don't know how to measure it out right," don't give in. Say, "Here, I'll show you." There's a chance, of course, that your partner will be pleasantly surprised and say, "Sure! I never really thought you wanted that." People often report that they wish Self-Sacrificing individuals would let them know what they wanted for themselves.

Exercise 3

Whenever anyone offers to do something for you or to help you out, say yes.

Exercise 4

If you feel that you are not being treated fairly, say so. Self-Sacrificers usually expect the best from others and feel justifiably hurt and let down when people take advantage. You may be able to prevent or discourage this kind of behavior, though, by speaking up sooner.

Exercise 5

Listen for the number of times and the situations in which you say "I'm sorry" on any given day. If the string beans come out too mushy or you're five minutes late or you forgot to put oil in the car although you promised, how big a deal do you make of it? If you find you apologize frequently over relatively minor matters, ask yourself whether you worry too much about pleasing other people. Try to give yourself a break and catch yourself *before* an apology comes out. Think about whether you have anything to be sorry about.

Exercise 6

Every time you are about to offer to go out of your way for somebody, ask yourself: "Is this in my best interests?" There are times in life when you have to ask, "What's in it for me?"

For example, if you volunteer to drive two hours to the airport to pick up a friend who can easily afford to rent a car or take a bus, stop and think whether sacrificing your whole day makes sense. Or if you offer to throw a party for the out-of-town guests coming to your friend's daughter's wedding, ask whether you really have the time, energy, and money, not to mention a genuine desire for such an undertaking. In other words, do you really *want* to do this, or do you think to be a good friend you *should* make this gesture?

If you are about to suggest that your drug-abusing acquaintance stay with you after he has wiped out his family's savings account and his wife has thrown him out, ask yourself what's in it for you. Kind as your intentions are, do you really think you can change him? Do you think that he would respect your giving, selfless, tender nature, not to mention your property, and not, in his condition, take advantage of you too?

Exercise 7

Before you volunteer to do anything for anybody, ask yourself, "Does this person really want me to do this?" Your lasagna may be the world's best, but before you volunteer to bring the main course to your daughter's dinner, think first whether she's still on a diet. Be aware, too, that people often like to do things for themselves, or for you. Maybe your daughter would like to cook dinner for you—that's why she invited you.

Exercise 8

Focus on relaxation. Every day devote at least fifteen minutes to absolutely nothing except unwinding. Refer to Conscientious Exercise 1 (p. 74) and Vigilant Exercise 1 (p. 172) for some suggestions. Pamper yourself. Concentrate on the luxurious feeling of being relaxed.

Exercise 9

Combat the guilt. Every time you find yourself feeling awkward or uncomfortable about having a good time, say to yourself, "It's *good* to feel good. What am I worrying about? I'm *entitled* to this."

Exercise 10

Take the pleasure; share the fun. When you're with other people you tend to be working to make them happy—but that's not much mutual fun. Try to resist the impulse only to give pleasure and not to receive or to ask for it. Go right ahead and sit in the most comfortable chair instead of reserving it for your guest.

You can combine this exercise with the preceding one and learn to relax and enjoy a massage from your love partner, for example. You can also combine it with the first and second exercises. For example, think about what you would enjoy from your partner sexually and have the courage to speak up. You may at first think you are being "selfish" by being on the receiving end, but most partners take great pleasure in being able to provide it to another, as you should well know. If your lover does *not* enjoy giving, go back to Exercise 6 and ask, "What's in this relationship for me?"

For two additional style-strengtheners, try Devoted Exercises 2 (p. 120) and 6 (p. 122).

———————

The following case history reveals the story behind the fabulous successes and secret failures of a remarkable woman. Her Self-Sacrificing pattern verges on the Self-Defeating personality disorder. This woman has had a very difficult personal life. She has missed out entirely on the joys of love and family. But change is possible for those who wish it, even late in life.

LIBERATION IN PARIS:
THE CASE OF ANNA B.

Anna B. took her place on the stage. The audience applauded wildly. It was her finest, most successful fashion line in her long career. At fifty-seven, she was perhaps the fashion world's leading trendsetter for youthful, vibrant, energetic elegance—or so one writer had put it in a cover story on her in a leading French fashion magazine.

Anna nodded and bowed, slightly embarrassed to be on the stage. She thought to herself, "I mustn't let this go to my head." Then her thoughts turned to the upcoming fall line, about which she still had some doubts. Then she looked out at the audience again, finding her tiny, ancient mother sitting stiff and unsmiling at her table. If it wasn't for her mother . . . but the ungenerous thought fled as she accepted a dozen long-stemmed roses.

Later that evening, at her estate outside Paris, Anna bid adieu to her last guests and slipped into her boudoir, where Prince Andrei had retired earlier. She wrote in her journal, then went to the window and looked out into the moonlit garden, too thoughtful still to lay her head on the soft pillow next to Andrei. She thought about her father.

Anna was the youngest of her parents' five children, all daughters. She was ten years younger than her next-older sister, born after her mother believed she could no longer bear children. The family had come to Paris from Lithuania when Anna was very young. Her father had been a milliner. "With five daughters to marry off, I must make many fine hats," her father used to say laughingly.

Anna liked to sit in her papa's shop while he deftly placed feathers and netting. Then she would peek out into the showroom as he placed the hat gently on a well-coiffed head, bowing to his elegant customer and respectfully taking a few steps backward. Anna could not have been older than three or four at the time, but she remembered these visits to her father's shop as some of the richest in all her days. How she missed her papa, she thought.

But she remembered too the hard, set, cold expression on her mother's face when she and Papa would return home. Her mother did not like her going to her father's shop. That hurt Anna so. She wanted her mama to be just as happy as she and her papa were. Sometimes through the walls of the bedroom she could hear her mother berating her father, "Why must you take the child there to see you bowing and scraping to those women? If she is to have any future she must understand that we are better than that. I have kept the other four away from that place. They are bettering themselves. Why must you defy me now?" Anna could not hear her father's reply, since he always spoke softly.

Her papa taught her how to make little hats and clothing for her dolls. "You can be my designer," he would say to her.

Anna was eighteen when her father died. She and her parents were living in London, to which they managed to escape after the Nazis occupied France during the war. Two of her sisters had insisted on staying behind. Both had been deported to concentration camps in Poland, where they had died. Her other two sisters, the eldest of the five, had emigrated to America with their husbands. Anna was not close with her sisters, who were so much older than she.

The move to London had cost her father everything. He had opened a shop in London but it had not done well. Anna now had to support herself and her aging mother. Her mother was very bitter at all the losses she had suffered—her money, her daughters, her husband—although Anna did not think her mother had ever really cared for her father. But she had needed him to provide for her. So Anna would do that now. She didn't mind. It made her feel good to take on such a big responsibility.

She had been working for a dressmaker who called herself Madame Rose, helping to take up hems and let out seams. When she was alone at home she used to like to sketch her own designs, and she began to make some of them for herself. One day Madame Rose noticed a simple little dress she was wearing and was surprised to hear that Anna had designed it herself. She asked to see other of her designs, and soon she was having Anna make them up. Into each she sewed a label: MADAME ROSE. Anna's clothing proved very successful for Madame Rose, and Anna now spent all her time designing. She did not ask for, nor did Madame Rose offer to give her, credit for her fashions. Anna, in her twenties, was happy enough that her designs were being worn by many people.

It was only ten years later, when Anna was thirty-three, that Madame Rose revealed her designer's identity. The miniskirts Anna was designing in the sixties were selling successfully in London, New York, and Paris. Madame Rose was the toast of the town, and during a press conference following a fashion show, when reporters pressed for her designer's name, she finally told them. Suddenly Anna was being besieged with job offers, and her career could have taken off had it not been for her sense of loyalty to Madame Rose. In her turn, Madame Rose, who now ran a moderately large operation, suggested that they introduce an "Anna B." line. Anna demurred. She could not take all that credit. After all, she owed everything to Madame Rose. But the "Anna B." line was in Madame Rose's best interests, now that Anna's name was known, and the line came into existence.

Anna continued to work for Madame Rose, without even a percentage of ownership in the operation, until Madame Rose died. Her son sold the company to a large fashion manufacturer. Anna finally took another job, to design for a major Parisian fashion house, for more than twice what she had earned with Madame Rose. It was a major career move for Anna, and she was alternately frightened and exhilarated. Sometimes she wanted to crawl under the covers and just go to sleep for weeks. She became frightened that she would lose her ability and inspiration. Then she would look in the mirror and say to herself, "This person—I am Anna B." But it didn't sink in that she was a celebrated designer, wined, dined, and wooed to come to Paris.

Her mother, whom she was leaving behind in London, was distressed by the disruption in her life. She and Anna had never been close and warm, but Anna had always provided for her and made a home for her. "You should stay here and get married and have babies," her mother would say, seemingly impervious to her daughter's professional success. "How much longer do you think you have to do that? You are going to be forty sooner than you think. I had you when I was forty-five, but of course that was an accident."

"Yes, Mother," Anna would say, looking away. Anna would have liked to have married and had babies, but that part of her life had never worked out. She didn't understand why. Some people said that she was very beautiful, and everyone agreed that she was very warm and kind. She knew she could be passionate. She had always attracted men, especially now that she was somewhat celebrated, but it never led anywhere, except to heartbreak.

When she was younger and just starting out, she had had many dates. Indeed, she had slept with many men. She had learned to be a skilled lover, expert at giving a man pleasure. Anything they wanted, she would do. Anything. She did not understand why after three or four weeks, possibly a few months, these men would not call her back. She felt ashamed at abasing herself in their arms.

Then there was Ethan. Ethan she had truly loved. He was a museum curator, elegant and well spoken. He didn't have much money, which had made her mother angry—"Don't even consider marrying a poor man," she had said. "Look at the mistake I made." Anna didn't care about money. She and Ethan used to go to museums and galleries, then sit for hours over tea talking about art. He told her once after their lovemaking that no woman had made him experience himself so fully. He would lie there and moan with joy as she caressed him. When he would say, "Now, my lovely, you shall see your own world of delights," she would push him lightly, fondly away. When he would persist, she would push him away more forcefully. "Why not?" he would ask, but Anna couldn't talk about it. She could barely think about it. With Ethan, Anna could not respond sexually. Yet she loved being with him more than anyone in the world. But she never even came close to having the excitement she'd experience with her uncaring lovers. She felt ashamed of herself for being, as she believed, "frigid."

For a while Ethan gave up trying to please Anna—since it obviously was *not* pleasing her. Then he would attempt to talk about it: "Why won't you let me love you?" He began to have doubts about his own manliness—it must be his fault that Anna was not responsive. "Don't think that, Ethan. It's me, not you," she would hasten to assure him. One night Ethan said, "Anna, I can't bear that our lovemaking is only for my sake. I can't enjoy it this way. I have to give. I love you. You must try to *let* me love you. Promise me you will."

For his sake, Anna said she would try. Gently and carefully Ethan would begin to caress her, ever so slowly and sensuously. Anna began to find herself responding to his touch, yet at the same time she felt miserably self-conscious, awkward, and inexplicably ashamed. Still, she began to loosen up and let herself experience the pleasure she was capable of.

But out of bed her feelings for Ethan began to diminish. She was growing bored with him. Now the endless conversations about art, which she previously had enjoyed, seemed tiresome. She began to find excuses to avoid seeing him on certain nights. Ethan began to worry that she was growing so distant from him. "You're hot in bed and cold at the breakfast table," he said to her. She looked away from him, annoyed at his crude way of expressing things.

Finally their relationship petered out. Anna felt it was for the best. Her mother had been right: Ethan was not the man for her.

There were other men over the years. Most of them did not interest her. The ones who excited her treated her badly. She had a three-year affair with a man named Gabriel, who did not tell her until the night they parted that he was married. It made sense, of course. They had seen each other only late at night. In bed he was very rough with her. Then he would get up and leave before daybreak.

The move to Paris enabled Anna to break from her past. She determined that she would give up on men and throw herself completely into her work. As her career soared—within ten years Anna B. was a household word for many of the best-dressed women throughout the world—Anna retreated from men. She had many male friends and she enjoyed their company, but she no longer pursued romantic or sexual liaisons. For Anna did not like herself with men. She did not like the way she behaved or reacted with them. Now, after half a century, at last she was becoming proud of herself in almost all other areas of her life. But she could not bear the way she would diminish and debase herself when she cared for or was aroused by a man.

How wonderful it would have been if she had been able to hold her own with a man and to create a loving family. But that was not to be.

Just before she turned fifty, Anna went into analysis in Paris. She told the analyst, "This is my fiftieth birthday gift to myself." Then she grimaced. "Would you call this a gift?"

"What would you call it?" the analyst asked.

After a moment's hesitation she said, "A gift. Yes. No. I'm not sure."

Anna had thought about entering analysis for many years. But she had always decided against it, reasoning that she had pulled herself up by her own bootstraps in life and that no one else could do it for her. She had wanted to talk about her problems with men, but she was ashamed to confess her experiences.

The analysis had helped her to liberate her creativity and her sense of entitlement in her business life. She was able to establish her own design house. But in the area of love it had been very painful for her to face some essential truths about herself. She had begun to see that Ethan had been right years and years ago—that she could not accept love. Now she knew that she had lived her whole life running from every possibility. Remembering Ethan was especially painful, for Anna reexperienced how deeply she had cared for him. Why hadn't she married him? After all these years she had to look back and see that she had destroyed the best and most promising relationship in her life—of them all, the one man who could have made her happy. But she had had to extinguish the flame that Ethan's love had set under her. She had become "bored" with him rather than face the conflict that accepting a good man's love caused for her.

Anna wept bitterly. "It is too late for me. Look what I have done with my life. Look how old I am!" Then she asked timidly, "*Is* it too late for me?"

The analyst replied, "Many people can begin to work out in middle life the conflicts that overwhelmed them earlier. For you, you have chosen this time to begin to face these things. That is very encouraging."

For weeks Anna had been talking about her new admirer, Andrei, a titled prince from a long-overthrown royal family. Andrei is sixty-seven years old, elegant the way she likes, very Old World, very proper. He reminds Anna of her father.

With Andrei, Anna has broken her self-imposed exile from men. She would not have had the courage once again to "tempt fate," as she put it, without her analyst to help her make sense of her deepest feelings and confusions. For with Andrei, Anna immediately reverted to her old patterns—needing to please, worrying how to make herself important to him, feeling diminished, becoming an abject "love servant" in bed with him, rejecting him when he wished to excite her and give her pleasure, growing bored with him the more in love with her he became. Needless to say, Anna's mother, nearing one hundred years old, does not approve of this man. "He's too old for you," she says. "He's nearly the right age for me!"

But with her analyst behind her to help untangle her experiences and feelings, Anna continues to see Andrei, who is patient and sensitive. Perhaps one day soon a healthy, fulfilling relationship with a man will be possible for this intelligent, talented, warmhearted, successful woman—but the moment Anna has such a thought she has to take it back and say, "Never! It is too late!" For she remains frightened of love. Andrei is the best of men, but Anna still cannot take all that he is willing to give.

Nonetheless, Paris is abuzz with rumors. There will be a wedding, the gossips say. Anna B. and Prince Andrei—the wedding of the century!

A cool breeze began to blow in the window through the garden. Anna turned to look at Andrei's peaceful expression as he lay asleep, snoring lightly. "What is he dreaming?" she asked herself. She drew the billowing curtains and lay down next to Andrei, hoping he was having a good dream. As she began to drift into sleep, she thought that perhaps tonight she might share his good dream with him. Or one night soon.

SELF-DEFEATING
PERSONALITY DISORDER

The men and women who suffer from this disorder are trapped in repetitive patterns of soured pleasure and missed opportunities. Happiness and fulfillment elude them, no matter how hard they work toward those goals.

DIAGNOSTIC CRITERIA

The DSM-III-R described the Self-Defeating personality disorder, which does not appear in DSM-IV (as explained near the end of this chapter), as:

A. A pervasive pattern of self-defeating behavior, beginning by early adulthood and present in a variety of contexts. The person may often avoid or undermine pleasurable experiences, be drawn to situations or relationships in which he or she will suffer, and prevent others from helping him or her, as indicated by at least *five* of the following:

(1) chooses people and situations that lead to disappointment, failure, or mistreatment even when better options are clearly available

(2) rejects or renders ineffective the attempts of others to help him or her

(3) following positive personal events (e.g., new achievement), responds with depression, guilt, or a behavior that produces pain (e.g., an accident)

(4) incites angry or rejecting responses from others and then

feels hurt, defeated, or humiliated (e.g., makes fun of spouse in public, provoking an angry retort, then feels devastated)

(5) rejects opportunities for pleasure, or is reluctant to acknowledge enjoying himself or herself (despite having adequate social skills and the capacity for pleasure)

(6) fails to accomplish tasks crucial to his or her personal objectives despite demonstrated ability to do so, e.g., helps fellow students write papers, but is unable to write his or her own

(7) is uninterested in or rejects people who consistently treat him or her well, e.g., is unattracted to caring sexual partners

(8) engages in excessive self-sacrifice that is unsolicited by the intended recipients of the sacrifice

B. The behaviors in A do not occur exclusively in response to, or in anticipation of, being physically, sexually, or psychologically abused.

C. The behaviors in A do not occur only when the person is depressed.

"WRECKED BY SUCCESS"

Individuals with this personality disorder cannot tolerate success or pleasure. Therefore, through their own actions, they unconsciously undermine or sabotage all hopes of fulfillment. In 1916 Freud used the phrase "wrecked by success" to describe these people. Their behaviors—taking a low-paying, unchallenging job when they are capable of far more, rejecting people who truly care for them, remaining in a personal or vocational relationship in which they are consistently mistreated—are seemingly avoidable. Yet, an individual with this disorder has no awareness that he or she is deliberately self-destructive.

In the case of Anna B., in her work she was able to combat her need to subjugate herself to another person. Although she spent many years avoiding taking credit for her own work, she was at last able to step forward and achieve great success. Individuals with full-blown Self-Defeating personality disorder, however, who can be similarly hard-working and talented, will not allow themselves to experience such unabashed victories. And if they do happen to be praised or celebrated, they may suddenly feel inexplicably depressed, or slip on a stair and break an ankle, or find a reason to leave the job or the relationship.

MARTYRS TO LOVE

These men and women cannot tolerate pleasure. They won't go on vacations, for example, or if they do they will not find the pleasure they seek. "Did you have a good time in Hawaii?" "No, not really."

Pleasure in loving relationships is particularly elusive. Like Anna B., they can't feel love for those who love them. Instead, they feel bored and uninterested and must flee the relationship. Very often the only people who interest them are those who exploit them. They may unwittingly elicit this behavior by being so powerless and unassertive. In their deepest reaches, they need to suffer in their relationships, although on a conscious level they may feel at a loss to explain why they always get involved in such unhappiness. As in Anna B.'s case, their love relationships are often humiliating to them. Some Self-Defeating individuals become obsessively attached to those who reject them. The people who dominate them or use them or push them away are the ones, often the only ones, who turn them on. "I know she's not nice to me—but what can I do? I adore her!"

HELP!

Self-Defeating men and women are extremely, often overly generous to others. For example, they may loan a friend their car although they need to use it themselves. They may stay up all night helping a friend prepare for an exam, but not do their own work. But try to help them, and they'll reject you. They are loath to seek help on their own behalf; they may not even call a doctor when they are quite sick. Yet, they will often complain about how ill they feel or bemoan their difficult straits, often making others feel guilty while all the time refusing what anyone tries to do for them.

Thus, the course of psychotherapy for Self-Defeating personality disorder will not be easy. So compelling is their inner need to fail and to remain submissive to powerful people that they will resist the work of the treatment more strongly than most others. It will be difficult for the therapist to make them aware of their inner terror of pleasure and success, and even more difficult to help them to change these Self-Defeating patterns, which may have developed very early in childhood. These men and women are needy of love while simultaneously they may be very frightened of their own angry and aggressive feelings, which they usually deny that they have. They often relate to those whom they love like children who have been mistreated, who, despite the suffering they experience, desperately need to be wanted by their all-powerful parents. Through their submissiveness and self-punishing behavior, Self-Defeating individuals form a kind of intimate bond with others in their lives.

And through their constant, martyred doing for others, they prove something that they have never been sure of—that someone needs them. Inside they may feel a devastating unworthiness and a nagging sense that they may have done something to deserve their miserable fate, although they can't imagine what.

Nonetheless, over the course of a long-term psychotherapy, they often can be helped greatly. Change will occur slowly, so the therapist will need reserves of patience and high frustration tolerance to help the patient build up self-esteem and face and resolve his or her painful inner conflicts. Usually, psychodynamic psychotherapy or psychoanalysis, in which the therapist helps the patient to explore and understand his or her inner conflicts, is the treatment of choice. Short-term cognitive types of therapy, in which patients learn to tackle their Self-Defeating thoughts and consequent behaviors, may also be helpful.

PREDISPOSITIONS AND RISKS

Children who have been physically, sexually, or psychologically abused are predisposed to developing Self-Defeating personality disorder, as are those who grow up in homes where a parent or caretaker is abused. Commonly, someone in the immediate family also suffers from this personality disorder.

Self-Defeating people often have other personality disorders as well, especially the Borderline, the Dependent, the Passive-Aggressive, the Obsessive-Compulsive, or the Avoidant. Depression is an ever-present risk, sometimes leading to thoughts of suicide. In addition, these excessively submissive people are at risk of being seriously abused in their adult lives.

INCIDENCE, SEX RATIOS, AND CONTROVERSY

According to some studies in the past, by a 3 to 2 or a 2 to 1 ratio, women are more likely than men to suffer from Self-Defeating personality disorder, although it is the impression of many practitioners that men and women suffer from it equally. In any case, as the DSM-III-R stated, Self-Defeating personality disorder is "one of the more common personality disorders in clinical practice."

Nonetheless, Self-Defeating personality disorder has not been included as a DSM-IV diagnosis, and in the DSM-III-R it was relegated to an appendix when feminist organizations strongly objected to it as an "official" psychiatric diagnosis. Then as now, they and others were concerned that the disorder, formerly known as Masochistic personality disorder or simply as Masochism, would be used to stigmatize women, especially those trapped by circumstance or cultural upbringing in abusive relationships. If these women were wrongly diagnosed as having a personality disorder or seen as otherwise "mentally ill," society would end up blaming the victim for her own plight—as if she brought on all her problems herself. Psychiatric diagnoses carry great weight in the courts as well. Perhaps a diagnosis of Self-Defeating personality disorder could be used to take a child away from its mother.

"A diagnosis that has the potential for misuse should be held to an especially high standard of validation before it is given any official credibility," comment DSM-IV editors and researchers. Because studies conducted on the basis of DSM-III-R criteria did not, in fact, overwhelmingly establish the validity of Self-Defeating personality disorder, it was dropped from the new manual.

Even so, a great number of clinicians agree that this is an important personality disorder to diagnose and to treat. We include it here for reasons detailed in the Introduction to this book, but we caution mental health professionals to apply it very carefully.

COPING WITH SELF-DEFEATING PEOPLE

The tips for dealing with Self-Sacrificing individuals, on pp. 330–31, may be helpful for mildly Self-Defeating types. Assure these individuals that you care, and try to encourage them to seek professional help. Resist feeling guilty about their unhappiness or suffering, and while you're at it, do everything you can to avoid taking advantage of them. Very likely, if you are closely involved with a Self-Defeating person, you are in a troubled relationship that could use some help. Seek counseling together or as a family.

CHAPTER 16

Aggressive Style

"TOP DOG"

Who's the boss? The Aggressive type, of course. While others may aspire to leadership, Aggressive men and women move instinctively to the helm. They are born to assume command as surely as is the top dog in the pack. Theirs is a strong, forceful personality style, more inherently powerful than any of the others. They can undertake huge responsibilities without fear of failure. They wield power with ease. They never back away from a fight. They compete with the supreme confidence of champions.

How these individuals use the power that seems always at their fingertips depends on other styles in their patterns. When put to the service of the greater good, the Aggressive personality style can inspire a man or woman to great leadership, especially in times of crisis.

THE SIX CHARACTERISTICS

The following six traits and behaviors are clues to the presence of the Aggressive style. A person who reveals a strong Aggressive tendency will demonstrate more of these behaviors more intensely than someone with less of this style in his or her personality profile.

1. *Command.* Aggressive individuals take charge. They are comfortable with power, authority, and responsibility.

2. *Hierarchy.* They operate best within a traditional power structure where everyone knows his or her place and the lines of authority are clear.

3. *Tight ship*. They are highly disciplined and impose rules of order that they expect others in their charge to follow.

4. *Expedience*. Aggressive men and women are highly goal-directed. They take a practical, pragmatic approach to accomplishing their objectives. They do what is necessary to get the job done.

5. *Guts*. They are neither squeamish nor fainthearted. They can function well and bravely in difficult and dangerous situations without being distracted by fear or horror.

6. *The rough-and-tumble*. Aggressive people like action and adventure. They are physically assertive and often participate in or enjoy playing competitive sports, especially contact sports.

THE SIX DOMAINS OF AGGRESSIVE FUNCTIONING

The key domains for this personality style are Relationships and Work.

RELATIONSHIPS:
I LEAD. YOU FOLLOW.

We subtitled this style "Top Dog" because in their interactions with other people, Aggressive individuals always move to the front. They have an instinctive gift for leadership and a driving need to dominate. This "organizing principle" is evident in all their relationships, at home, in the social club, on the football team, and most certainly in the workplace. Aggressive-style men and women naturally vie for control of all the groups of which they become a part, often beginning very early in their lives. (For a possible biochemical connection to this dominance pattern, see pp. 364–65.)

This Aggressive instinct to direct and to dominate need not be seen as hostile to others, however. Individuals who are strong, comfortable with power, and who can and want to bear the weight of immense responsibility for others are necessary and welcome in many groups, organizations, and families. In other words, like the rest of the dogs in the pack, the others are often glad to have someone else stepping forward to take responsibility, to make the tough decisions, and to fight the battles. Many people find it comfortable indeed to have someone strong and competent to rely on.

However, when the Aggressive style grows extreme, the need to dominate becomes more important than any concern for the interests or feelings of others. Also, the end may become far more important than the means (discussed in more detail below), and these overwhelmingly Aggressive individuals may disregard their moral and ethical values on their way to grabbing the golden ring.

All Aggressive types tend to be autocratic and dictatorial—that goes with the territory—but with balancing features from other styles in their patterns, they may well be benevolent and protective, especially if no one from the ranks steps out of line.

Hail to the Chief

In all their relationships throughout their lives, Aggressive types reach their full potential when they're in charge. At home they rule the roost; at work they run the show. They prefer a pyramid-type hierarchical structure, with themselves at the top and everyone beneath them spread out in a well-understood, fixed pecking order. They like to give orders and to establish rules.

Dominick C., Jr.—his family called him Chief—was "one macho guy," in the words of his twelve-year-old granddaughter. His father had come from an Old World paternalistic tradition in which his power as head of the family was undisputed. Dominick continued the tradition. He married May, a Southern belle with traditional views of a woman's place in regard to her husband. Dominated by the Devoted style, she was content to let Dom make important decisions and determine family policy as long as he treated her with respect and took good care of her. For his part, Dominick liked the way May leaned on him; it made him feel right in the world, a man. He provided well for May and their four children. He even supported her widowed mother and her institutionalized retarded sister.

May had a mind of her own, especially when it came to running her home and the church organizations in which she took part. But if her views conflicted with Dominick's, in front of him she rarely voiced them. She almost never crossed her husband, at least not willfully. Since May always deferred to her husband and his will prevailed, in almost twenty years together they had not experienced a serious disruption. Their family life seemed blessed. But when their youngest child and only son, Dominick III, nicknamed Theo, in his adolescence began to rebel against his father, trouble festered at their doorstep.

May found herself torn between her son and her husband. The issues between father and son were not huge—no criminal conduct, no drugs or drinking, no unsafe sex. They had become locked in an escalating battle of wills, with Dominick insisting that Theo do everything his way and Theo defiantly setting his own course. For example, Dominick ordered Theo to work in the family business one summer during high school, and Theo said he'd already gotten a job at a pizza parlor. Dom ordered Theo to turn that job down or he would take his car away from him. Theo said he'd walk. Dom, true to his word, sold the car that he had helped his son buy the year before. Theo began to stay out later than his midnight curfew. He'd come screeching up the driveway about one in the morning on the back of his friend's motorcycle. Dom grounded him. Theo stopped talking to his father.

It was war in the house. Theo's sisters, all now living away from home, were on his side and called their mother several times a week to tell her so—but never their father. He'd been a strict disciplinarian, and the girls, although they loved their father, had never dared to cross him. Instead, they waited until they left home to make their own decisions. Theo had always been his sisters' treasured Little Chief, as they had liked to tease him. Now his sisters wanted their mother to intercede with their father on their brother's behalf. May thought they were right. But she had had no experience standing up to her husband. When she tried to say, "Dom, dear, can't you let up on Theo a little—" he interrupted her abruptly: "Stay out of this, May." The harsh look he gave her was frightening to May. She retreated to their bedroom and began to cry. When Dom found her there wiping her red eyes, he became furious with her and stormed out of the house.

May tried to tell Theo to wait until he went away to college to assert his own personality. "Your father believes he knows what is best for all of us," she said. "Usually he does. He works very hard to give us all a good life. But things have to be his way as long as he's head of this family. When you go away to college you can do what you want. I trust you, Theo," May added, "but your father thinks you're being disloyal to him now, and he can't stand that. Please, just go along with him for a short while longer, for all our sakes. Whatever you do, don't do something foolish just to show your father he can't push you around." Theo listened, but he didn't answer. Likely he was hurt that his mother wouldn't defend him more strongly in front of his father.

Theo—president of his class, captain of the wrestling team, twice voted most likely to succeed—was definitely his father's son. That was a great part of their problem. The family had room for only one Chief, and through his teens Theo was jockeying to move up. Appropriate for his healthy development, Theo was competing with his father. But Aggressive-style individuals often have difficulty tolerating challenges to their authority. They instinctively lash out to quash and to punish the perceived disloyalty and to reassert their control. True to the Aggressive style, Dominick mistook his son's essentially appropriate rebellion for a defection from the fold. Dom had never flinched at imposing discipline and punishment when he felt it was necessary. When he found out that Theo had begun cutting classes at school, he hit him so hard that Theo's nose bled.

Theo seemed stunned, like a boxer about to keel over. After a moment he wheeled around and punched his father in the stomach. Dom fell to the floor. Theo ran out of the house. May was able to prevent Dominick from calling the police. Eventually Theo turned up at his grandmother's house. He was scared to death to go home. May, to Theo's everlasting gratitude, was able to urge Dominick to let Theo stay at her mother's house until everybody calmed down. Theo ended up living there for the remaining three months of school and through the summer until he left for college. This solution allowed him sufficient independence and distance from his father that he no longer needed to rebel so destructively. Dominick, for his part, in the absence of his son could once more resume his role as the unrivaled Chief. And May no longer felt torn between the two strong-willed, hot-tempered men in her life. She visited her son frequently at her mother's house, where she could express support for his decisions without upsetting her husband.

Theo did very well in college. He distinguished himself in law school, practiced law for a few years, and ran successfully for public office. He is now a third-term United States congressman, and he is planning to run for the Senate in the next election. He has never lost a race. He is ambitious, has a strong power base, and has let it be known that he wants to be president. He and Dominick (now retired from the family furniture-manufacturing business, which a son-in-law runs) have never been close or comfortable with each other since the events of Theo's adolescence. But May knows how much Dom respects his powerful son, and she tells him so whenever Theo comes back home for a visit, or when he and his wife invite her to Washington. Theo loves and respects the Chief equally, and credits him for teaching him to be tough, courageous, and ambitious. But he may never be able to share these feelings with his father. For both, "sentimentality" goes against their Aggressive grain.

The Next Generations

Theo, as Aggressive in personality style as his father, has managed to establish a well-structured, orderly, disciplined family. His two children are still in grade school, so we have yet to know how he will deal with their adolescent assertiveness. His eighth-grader, Sara, will probably be tougher to deal with than his younger child, Dominick IV. So far, Sara seems to be a chip off her dad's Aggressive block. This style is not exclusive to men. Aggressive-style women traditionally have assumed control of their families as powerful matriarchs. Girls now grow up believing themselves entitled to use the power inherent in their personalities to assert themselves and to compete in a "man's world." If Sara does go head-to-head with her dad in the coming years, one hopes that Theo will be able to deal with it more creatively than his father did. In contemporary permissive society, which does not support the Aggressive style's autocratic parenting, punishing a child's developing autonomy may serve only to push a healthy child to take too many risks (discussed in more detail below).

Theo's wife, Katharine, practices law part-time. She is bright and self-assertive, but she, like her mother-in-law, May, does not question her husband's authority in the family. She can imagine herself as First Lady strongly supporting her husband and participating in his presidency where possible. The only substantial marital problems they've had so far began when she found out Theo was having an affair with his press secretary. Theo insisted it was nothing, just a trifling, very occasional, sexual thing. Katharine sought solace in the arms of her law partner. When Theo found out about that, he took their little daughter and moved out. Typical for Aggressive types, he could not and would not accept such disloyalty. He took strong, punitive, and one might say vengeful measures to stop it. Arguing about double standards got Katharine nowhere. In time she decided that the marriage was worth continuing. Indeed, when everyone was following the expected rules, Theo in his Aggressive way was a loving, giving, generous, often understanding, and unquestionably interesting and exciting husband. Life with Theo was better than life without him, she decided. She has never regretted this decision. For his part, although it was difficult for him to admit this, Theo was immensely relieved that he had not lost his most important supporter, his wife.

More About the Aggressive-Style Parent

Men and women with the Aggressive personality style provide strong, capable role models for their children. Their kids know that they can count on them for protection against every threat from a dangerous world. They are often proud of such parents for their success and accomplishments in the world.

As we have seen, these parents are strict disciplinarians and expect their kids to obey them without question. If the style is not extreme but is tempered with flexibility and sensitivity, such a parent can help anchor the children to tradition and responsibility amid these chaotic social times. Otherwise, they'll have extra-tempestuous times with their teenagers, for whom competition with and rebellion against the parent are normal and healthy. If the Aggressive parent nips the rebellion in the bud, the child who capitulates may have trouble with self-assertion, independence, and competition throughout life. The child who continues to rebel may overdo it and get into real trouble. Advice to Aggressive-style parents: Bend a little so that your appropriately self-assertive children will be able to find more creative ways to cope with your authority. Try to understand your children's feelings. Also, if you are extremely involved in your work outside the home, as are many individuals with your style, recognize that your children may feel left out of your life. Work on listening to reason and compromising with your children, on expressing more affection, and on spending more "quality time" with them, especially when they are very young.

Good/Bad Matches

Aggressive types have to be king or queen of the hill. They do best with trusting, accepting, deferential mates who nonetheless maintain their competence, inner strength, autonomy, and self-esteem. It is all too easy for Aggressive individuals to take advantage of exceedingly Devoted or Self-Sacrificing types. Aggressive mates are not extremely sentimental or driven by romance, and they will have little patience with partners who are emotionally very needy. The most natural matches for Aggressive individuals are with moderately Devoted, Self-Sacrificing, and Sensitive types. Conscientious or Serious qualities in the mate may also contribute to a lasting match, unless the Aggressive individual is the kind who likes to bend moral and ethical rules in the service of being top dog (see "Ends and Means," pp. 353–54); Conscientious types are strong moralists.

If Aggressive is your style, avoid matches with individuals who need to control (such as the Vigilant, the Mercurial, and the very Conscientious), who will make you jealous (the Dramatic), and who have their own agendas for their lives (the Self-Confident).

Note to Aggressive-style women: Because of your inherent power and need to dominate, you may have some difficulty finding a man to accept you as you are. Seek nontraditional types—perhaps a man with a strong streak of Devoted style, who may have no qualms about being different.

WORK: THE DRIVE FOR POWER

Work is the domain in which Aggressive types can bring their need to dominate and their gift for leadership to their greatest fruition. These men and women are intensely purposeful. They *will* get ahead. They devote themselves thoroughly to the job, deterred neither by their family lives, a need for eight hours' sleep, nor any yearning to relax and have a good time.

The Aggressive personality style is actually rather unusual, but those who have it are highly visible and influential because of their drive for power. These are the political power brokers, the corporate raiders, the department chairmen, the CEOs, the Las Vegas "bosses." Scratch anyone who has accumulated a great deal of power in his or her chosen arena, and you are likely to find no small amount of the Aggressive personality style.

One reason why they do so well in their quest to take charge is that they thrive in an intensely competitive, dog-eat-dog environment in which ultimately there can be only one, or very few, winners. While the increasingly intense competition of a run for the top position discourages many a potential competitor, Aggressive individuals actually enjoy the rough-and-tumble of a fiercely competitive fight. Instead of feeling "stressed out" by the struggle to achieve and maintain power, Aggressive individuals feel wonderfully stimulated and alive.

They are not squeamish. "Killing off" a competitor does not upset them. They are not sentimental and they do not identify with the underdog. The "strong stomach" that goes along with this style makes Aggressive individuals particularly suited to make certain kinds of difficult, unpleasant decisions. For example, in wartime a commanding officer must often sacrifice the lives of some of his troops in order to gain a particular objective. Similarly, to reorganize and stay in business, a corporate executive may have to lay off hundreds of employees, whose futures will then be in doubt. A banker may have to foreclose on a home owner. A university president may have to eliminate whole departments. Aggressive individuals can size up the situation and make these decisions if they have to. Similarly, they may make excellent emergency-room specialists, heading up trauma teams. They do what they must to lead effectively.

All's Fair

Peter V., who legend has it moved from stock boy to president and CEO without pausing anywhere in between, has been running a major corporation for more than a decade. He has consistently parried all takeovers, defended against all challenges to his base of power, and kept his corporation in the black despite changes in economic climate. He holds complete control over the corporation, its finances, and its executives. Any of the principal executives to whom he allows some power must demonstrate total loyalty to Peter to remain in the inner circle. He rewards this loyalty lavishly, with money and perks. He punishes disloyalty by withholding money and reducing power and recognition. Those who do not question Peter's right to run the show and who perform up to his high expectations are assured of good treatment. But should they fail to please him, despite years of service out they go.

Recently Peter summarily fired a senior vice president, Janet G., who he felt was widening her base of power among the board members. The woman was extremely competent in the financial end of the business. To undercut her effectiveness and her support from the board, Peter leaked to the press her long affair with a powerful, well-known, and long-married director of a Wall Street brokerage firm. The newspapers gave the story all the play that Peter had hoped for. The board abhorred the unseemly publicity and fully supported Peter's decision to let this key executive go.

Some would consider Peter's action vicious. He saw it as justified. All's fair in love and war—and to the Aggressive individual, work (indeed, all of life) is strategic combat, a struggle to get and to keep power. He had known about Janet's affair for years. It became his weapon when he found he needed one. He did what he had to do, he would tell you—and he would add that if you found his means so upsetting, you don't belong in the big time.

Ends and Means

Aggressive-style individuals are strongly goal-directed. They have a job to do and they get it done. Success, victory, power, and excellence are their objectives, but they are practical and pragmatic in their pursuit of them. They use the means that are at hand. If an Aggressive individual has strength as well in the Conscientious style, he or she will also be concerned about doing the right and honorable thing. Otherwise, there is a risk that individuals whose personalities are strongly Aggressive will act unscrupulously or vindictively, without regard for morals or ethics or consequences to another person's feelings or reputation—as did the perfect fictional model of this type of highly Aggressive person, J.R. on TV's long-gone *Dallas*.

To Aggressive-style individuals, it's the objective that counts. The means tend to be expedient. For example, somewhat Aggressive-style

Ilene is trying to sell the company car that has persistent transmission problems. A young man has seen her advertisement and calls to inquire about the car. He says he's never bought a car before. He doesn't ask about the car's problems, and Ilene doesn't tell him. If he did inquire, she would probably say something about it, downplaying the problem. It would be up to the potential buyer to have a mechanic check it out before coming to a decision. Ilene is not a criminal and she's not a cheat. But she wants to sell the car quickly at the best price, and, like many people in a similar situation, she thinks it's not her problem if the buyer negotiates a bad deal. As an Aggressive person, Ilene in most business situations makes decisions in a similar style. She is less concerned with following the "right" or "honorable" course as with finding a practical, efficient, effective solution. Another example of Aggressive problem solving would be selling arms covertly to a hostile government in order to free political hostages. Or toppling a rival by uncovering ostensible corruption, without concern for one's own similar wrongdoing.

The accumulation of power and the tendency to use expedient means can lead some extra-Aggressive types, like their Adventurous cousins, to cross the line into outright criminal behavior; this becomes more probable if they have considerable Adventurous style in their own personalities. However, most Aggressive types will have in their profiles "mitigating" styles that will protect them from crossing moral and ethical boundaries. Or they will have someone with a conscience—a Conscientious second in command—sitting at a desk nearby to keep them honest, or to turn them in.

Management Style

Aggressive individuals make excellent, interesting managers and administrators. With unflagging energy they create structure and organization, perceive short- and long-term goals, and plan effective strategies. They can see the big picture and can juggle numerous major responsibilities and projects at one time, without becoming disorganized or distracted. They run a tight, disciplined ship, and they demand loyalty and reward it generously. Some Aggressive managers divide staffs into a loyal inner circle (those who share their dedication and sense of purpose) and an out-group ("regular," less privileged others). The most extremely Aggressive managers, who attract a loyal cadre on their climb to the top, may experience a mass defection of top lieutenants who become disillusioned with their unscrupulous or unethical behavior. For example, watch, in times of government scandal, how many of an agency leader's most trusted subordinates get disgusted, come to their senses, and abandon ship.

Aggressive managers focus on results, not feelings. Subordinates may think them hard-hearted or insensitive. They set high performance standards for themselves and for their subordinates, having little patience with inefficiency, error, and waste, and none with disloyalty. Aggressive managers have little difficulty punishing or dismissing employees who do not meet their approval. Emotional appeals may hasten the execution.

Besides disloyalty, there's only one thing that Aggressive managers—indeed, any Aggressive-style person in the workplace—may not be able to deal with creatively: boredom. Work is strategic combat, accomplishment is winning. Like some military officers at the end of a war, once the battle is won, they don't know what to do with themselves. They must function at high stimulation levels at all times, and may end up creating an internal political conflict just to keep the juices flowing.

For tips on working for an Aggressive manager, see the general suggestions on pp. 358–59. See also Tips 1 and 3 for working for Self-Confident people (pp. 95 and 96).

Stress!

Lack of power, serious competitive threats, and defeat or failure are the greatest sources of stress for Aggressive types. They cope by establishing or strengthening their power base, planning a strategy, and fighting back, often with fury. For example, when Aggressive Audrey did not get promoted to manager of her bank branch, instead of biding her time until something else opened up (as her boss at headquarters suggested), she filed a sex-discrimination lawsuit. She had a strong case, and the bank ultimately suggested she take over their smallest, sleepiest branch. Audrey refused. They gave her another branch, and she withdrew her suit. Now she's managing the bank's credit card division.

No one with substantial Aggressive personality style will accept loss or failure and go quietly into the sunset. These folks are survivors, winners. They fight their way to the top, claw their way if they have to.

Power Careers

Politics, government, the military, education, the corporation—look for a career in any area that offers a power structure you can climb. You may do equally well as an entrepreneur in your own business, where you create the structure yourself. You must in all cases be working with and around people, so that you can aspire to being in charge of them.

SELF AND REAL WORLD: AGGRESSIVE VERSUS SELF-CONFIDENT

Individuals with these two styles reveal a fiercely competitive, "me first" approach to life, but their differences can best be seen in the way each of them views the Self and its relative position in the Real World domain.

The Aggressive person, driven primarily by Relationships and Work domains, needs to dominate others, to be in charge. Like Vigilant types, their issue is control. It's a jungle out there, and only those who can show their strength over the others can survive. Aggressive men and women have tremendous faith in their own abilities to win and to lead, but perhaps unconsciously they feel that unless they plunge in and take control, they will lose their power and have to give in. Submitting to a greater power is nothing short of humiliating for people with large amounts of the Aggressive personality style. They need to maintain and reinforce their sense of self by being the undisputed ruler of the kingdom.

Self-Confident individuals, governed by the Self domain, don't worry about other people. What other people? These types, as we have seen, are turned in toward their own wonderful possibilities and frequently must be reminded that other people exist. They hardly need to buttress their sense of self, since they already feel secure in the center of the Real World. They expect to be very successful, powerful, rich, famous—it's their birthright. Nobody else presents a serious threat.

Both Self-Confident and Aggressive individuals compete easily and move up the power structure. Self-Confident types are successful because they are so confident of their abilities and their inherent personal stardom. Aggressive types succeed because they know so well how to take, use, manipulate, and keep power—and to keep everybody else down. They stand victorious, assured, and skilled at the top of the dominance hierarchy.

EMOTIONS AND SELF-CONTROL: STRONG IN BOTH

Although Aggressive men and women do not necessarily respond to other people's feelings, they have very strong feelings of their own. This is a powerful personality style in every domain, Emotions included.

Their feelings tend not to be of the soft, "mushy," delicate, or otherwise sentimental variety, of course, although they can be very romantic once they are securely in control of the relationship.

Aggressive types can have a powerful sex drive, too. These personality types are very physical people; they need to express themselves with their bodies. Like Adventurers, they need action and adventure, but whereas Adventurers are turned on by physical risk in the present, Aggressive types are motivated by the excitement of the win to come. Thus, they often engage vigorously in competitive and contact sports; frequently they are stimulated by combat and violence, if only on the pages of a book or on the movie screen.

Although failure may temporarily bring them down, Aggressive individuals are not prone to depression or anxiety. Battling, competing, and winning are such a pleasure that for them "the cure" is the fray. Don't ask them to relax, though. Aggressive individuals cannot let go of their sense of purpose. They'll be glad to go on a cruise to participate in a conference, but not to relax in a deck chair. (The Conscientious person will go too, if he or she can spend the time between ports plotting a sightseeing plan for the next three hours ashore.)

The key to this style, as we have mentioned, is control. Aggressive types generally have extraordinary control over their emotions and their appetites for pleasure. These individuals will not let anything get in the way of their drive to the top. They generally do not react impulsively, no matter how strongly they feel about something—unless they're angry, in which case only the most extreme Aggressive types as well as those with Sadistic personality disorder will lose the all-important control and lash out violently. Their anger can be particularly powerful and can be used as a mighty weapon to keep others in line. Those on the receiving end will most likely be family and subordinates, with whom these overly Aggressive types may feel they have a right to do as they please.

Fortunately, most individuals with the Aggressive style will avoid riding roughshod over those whom they wish to control. They will channel their aggressive energy into being crafty, strategic, shrewd. You'll rarely find even the most Aggressive types having a temper tantrum in the boardroom after they have been outmaneuvered. Instead, they will convert the rage into a brilliant new plot to reestablish themselves and gain the day.

TIPS ON DEALING WITH
THE AGGRESSIVE PERSON IN YOUR LIFE

1. Know yourself. In a personal relationship, this individual can be very easy to deal with if you understand and accept that he or she must be the boss. Even if you are a very strong person yourself, although you might come close you will never be equal in power if you pair up with an Aggressive type. Is your personality style one that is comfortable coming second in your love relationships? Or does your self-esteem demand that you present yourself in all ways as an equal? These people can be wonderfully exciting, even charismatic to be around and to share a big life with, *if* you can be content with a hierarchical relationship. If you can't, you'll be miserable.

2. Beware of competing with an Aggressive person. Never try to undermine this person's authority or to unseat him or her—unless you don't care about maintaining your relationship. If you expect to gain this person's respect by being more powerful than he or she is, think again. Aggressive people like to have strong, worthy, *loyal* individuals around them, in positions lower in the hierarchy. If you do find yourself in competition with an Aggressive person, allow him or her a way to save face in case you win. Otherwise, you may find yourself with a very powerful enemy.

3. Know the precise parameters of your job and/or your role so that you do not overstep the boundaries that the Aggressive person may have set. In military terms, you need to know your orders and then to carry them out, no more, no less.

4. Be strong and maintain your self-esteem. Just because you are in the presence of power doesn't mean you must fawn or fall back into a weak position. It is all too easy for an Aggressive person to push people around and overwhelm them. But the Aggressive person in your personal or business life doesn't have much use for "wimps" or yes-types. To obtain an Aggressive person's respect or love, show your natural mettle. Present a worthy and self-assertive but not competitive or defiant front, and negotiate strongly on your own behalf. If you allow an Aggressive person to take advantage of you, you risk his or her contempt and a fall to the ignominious bottom of the heap.

5. To resolve conflicts that crop up in your personal life with an Aggressive person, do not go after the win. Do not, in other words, insist that he or she do it your way or admit guilt or error. The

Aggressive individual cannot tolerate losing, so don't seek all-or-nothing, I'm-right-you're-wrong solutions. Work toward compromises in which the Aggressive person can still maintain his or her top-dog self-esteem. Try trading concessions. Say, for example: "Okay, I'll change my plans and go to that convention with you next month, if you'll change your plans and come to the meeting at Jimmy's private school." Should you find that winning the battle is as important to you as it is to your Aggressive partner, ask yourself whether the victory is worth a sacrifice of this relationship, when there may be other ways to accomplish what you need.

6. Appeal to reason, not to feelings. Aggressive people often give little weight to how a person feels. If you want to make your point, paint a very reasonable case; with a show of emotion, you'll be up against a brick wall. Point out how your plan or approach directly benefits the Aggressive person. Instead of saying, "You'll do this if you love me," put it this way: "If you come to the meeting at Jimmy's school on Tuesday, the admissions committee may keep our family's interest in the school in mind when they consider little Timmy, who we both know is not very smart."

7. If the Aggressive person in your life is your parent, look for ways to cope creatively with his or her possibly harsh rules and regulations. Don't take the bull by the horns. Instead of being defiant and demanding that your parent let you do what you want to do, or openly and self-destructively rebelling, try showing respect and agreeing with his or her way of looking at things—and then quietly going about your business.

   This advice may come in handy for those who must deal with an Aggressive person in the workplace, too.

8. Accept that the Aggressive person in your life has a temper and avoid pushing the predictable buttons that will ignite it. Look for other ways to solve your problems. To deal with this person's anger, don't fight back and don't blow off your steam in his or her face. Back off and let the anger wind down.

MAKING THE MOST OF YOUR AGGRESSIVE STYLE

Your personality style gives you enormous potential for success, especially in the Work domain. The exercises that follow are designed to help smooth your sometimes overbossy side and to make all parts of your life similarly rewarding. Being the boss and in total control of everyone in the workplace may work brilliantly for you—but the same authoritarian style may cause conflict for you at home.

Exercise 1

When you come home from the office, practice leaving your authoritarian style on the doorstep. Observe yourself interacting in a bosslike way with your family or friends. Realize that many people do not appreciate being ordered around. Try to experience yourself as an equal with others rather than as the commandant.

Exercise 2

Give people a chance to make their own mistakes. You run a tight ship and get things done extremely well your way. But others—children in particular—need to gain experience and to learn for themselves. Give them some rope—you can always tug them back in if they go seriously off the mark. Let your teenagers make some of their own decisions and mistakes so that they can forge a strong, self-directed path through their lives, and so that they don't have to go to extremes to prove they can do things for themselves.

Exercise 3

Learn to compromise and even to give in. Instead of insisting on your will being done, negotiate a solution that pleases everyone. Remember, there's no war. In a conflict in your personal life, it's not a matter of win or lose—try to keep that in mind.

Exercise 4

Practice doing things someone else's way. Keep an ear open to disagreements over how things should be done. Although you are used to getting your way, try letting the other person take responsibility for a change. Get used to saying, "Fine, let's do it your way."

Exercise 5

At least once a week, ask the people who are closest to you in your personal life what you can do for them. Be open to all suggestions, including emotional ones—such as, "I really wish you would show that you *care* for me a little more." Find a way to come through for each person and not to reject the request based on its merits. For example, suppose your teenager says, "Yeah, well, now that you mention it, you can let me stay out all night on prom night." Instead of rejecting the request out of hand, perhaps you can extend the usual curfew a bit or otherwise find a way to lighten up on some of the rigid rules you impose on your child.

If you practice this exercise faithfully, you'll soon be able to anticipate your loved ones' most important needs, and you'll find that they're not always accusing you in one way or another of hurting their feelings.

Should you have difficulty with this exercise, try Self-Confident Exercise 4 (p. 97): "Who *is* this person?"

Exercise 6

Relax your control over your life (and the lives of those around you) and just have a good time for a while. Learn to meditate, perhaps. See Conscientious Exercise 1 (p. 74) and Vigilant Exercise 1 (p. 172) for other relaxation suggestions. Letting down your iron grip occasionally will prove advantageous to your health and may well prolong your vigor, and it will also allow you to retake the reins of your powerful life with renewed strength. Relaxing with your family will strengthen the bonds among you all.

That is, relax your control in all areas of life but one:

Exercise 7

Control your temper. Concentrate on holding back when you are about to explode or fight back. If necessary, turn around and walk out of the room, punch a pillow, even leave the house until you have cooled down. Do not permit yourself to believe that anyone deserves your powerful, Aggressive response. Someone can make you angry, but no one except yourself can "cause" a ferocious, punitive reaction.

Exercise 8

Keep a list of what makes you really angry. Ask yourself whether your anger boils down to issues of dominance and control. Do you become angriest when somebody close to you does something differently from the way you want it done or otherwise challenges your authority? Ask yourself whether you overreact to these issues. Run this through your mind: Other people will respect you even more if you accept that you have power and cease being quite so touchy about who's being defiant or who's trying to take it away. No one can take away the inner power of your personality.

SADISTIC PERSONALITY DISORDER

As the name implies, people with Sadistic personality disorder are cruel, coldhearted, and ruthlessly intimidating. They may be violent and will take pleasure in humiliating those around them.

DIAGNOSTIC CRITERIA

This personality disorder, as will be discussed later in this chapter, does not appear in the DSM-IV. The DSM-III-R described Sadistic personality disorder as:

A. A pervasive pattern of cruel, demeaning, and aggressive behavior, beginning by early adulthood, as indicated by the repeated occurrence of at least *four* of the following:

(1) has used physical cruelty or violence for the purpose of establishing dominance in a relationship (not merely to achieve some noninterpersonal goal, such as striking someone in order to rob him or her)

(2) humiliates or demeans people in the presence of others

(3) has treated or disciplined someone under his or her control unusually harshly, e.g., a child, student, prisoner, or patient

(4) is amused by, or takes pleasure in, the psychological or physical suffering of others (including animals)

(5) has lied for the purpose of harming or inflicting pain on others (not merely to achieve some other goal)

(6) gets other people to do what he or she wants by frightening them (through intimidation or even terror)

(7) restricts the autonomy of people with whom he or she has a close relationship, e.g., will not let spouse leave the house unaccompanied or permit teenage daughter to attend social functions

(8) is fascinated by violence, weapons, martial arts, injury, or torture

B. The behavior in A has not been directed toward only one person (e.g., spouse, one child) and has not been solely for the purpose of sexual arousal (as in Sexual Sadism).

DOMINANCE BY FORCE

Sadistic individuals will hurt, humiliate, punish, bully, threaten, and intimidate in order to control the members of their family and those who are subordinate or dependent on them in their work. Unlike Antisocial individuals, they do not hurt just anyone; they may even show a benign, respectful face to those who are in authority over them. But where they feel they are entitled to be in charge, they establish their dominance through psychological and physical torture—especially when their victims prepare to fight back or rebel against their cruel control. When their lovers or spouses threaten to leave them, Sadistic individuals don't get depressed—they get even. Sadistic individuals are wife beaters and child abusers. They are vicious bosses. They are people who inflict pain on others just to keep command or get their way.

It's easy for them to inflict pain, for they have no empathy for people whom they dominate or control. They may enjoy the suffering they inflict in the act of dominating—like the Sadistic policeman who beats up his prisoners or the Sadistic ex-wife who lies to her ex-husband over the phone that their son has been badly hurt in an accident.

They are disciplinarians, meting out harsh punishment to children, students, spouses, prisoners, or anyone else who is subordinate to them for the most minor indiscretions or errors. They are angry individuals; they turn violent when crossed or irritated by the people whom they feel are supposed to follow their orders. They often pick on people who suffer from Self-Defeating personality disorder, who may be all-too-easy victims.

BUT IS IT A REAL DISORDER?

No one can doubt that many individuals display such malevolent behavior. The question nonetheless remains whether it qualifies as a bona fide personality disorder. It was proposed for inclusion in the DSM-III-R after women's organizations objected that the Self-Defeating personality disorder, also being added at that time, was biased against women who are victims of abusive situations; it "blames" the victim for her situation, they claimed (see chapter 15). Based on clinicians' case reports, an equivalent personality disorder category was thus created to cover much of the population of abusers, thought to be largely male. But a related objection was then made to the Sadistic personality disorder: it provides wife beaters and child abusers a psychiatric diagnosis that could be used as a defense to spare them the legal consequences of their actions.

Now, along with its "sibling" Self-Defeating diagnosis, Sadistic personality disorder has been eliminated from the DSM-IV. The editors decided there was insufficient research to merit its inclusion, and that the diagnosis could indeed be misused.

We include it here, however, with the same caveat we added for Self-Defeating personality disorder: clinicians, apply with caution. As explained in the Introduction, in forensic settings, mental health professionals continue to find evidence of this disorder.

Frequently, people with Sadistic behaviors share many of the features of the Narcissistic, Antisocial, Mercurial, and sometimes Paranoid personality disorders. They may suffer from the consequences of alcohol and drug abuse, and their lives are rife with marital, work, and legal problems. Physical, sexual, or psychological abuse in childhood, or growing up in a home where a parent is abused, may predispose an individual to the development of Sadistic behaviors.

THE BIOCHEMISTRY OF DOMINANCE AND VIOLENCE

Serotonin, an important neurotransmitter, appears to have an intriguing relationship to both violent and dominant behavior. As mentioned in relation to Antisocial and Borderline disorders, low levels of serotonin have been linked to impulsive, violent behavior, perhaps because serotonin serves in part to slow down or inhibit the central nervous system. Thus, with a serotonin deficiency, perhaps combined with an excess of noradrenalin, a person may not be able to stop and cool down before reacting to the impulse to lash out in a violent rage.

But there's another side to the serotonin mystery, as far as this chapter is concerned. Although violence-prone people may have low levels of serotonin, individuals who are strong leaders may have *high* levels of this intriguing brain chemical! Researchers measured serotonin levels in monkeys and in college fraternity members. They found that the dominant monkeys as well as the fraternity officers had higher levels of the neurotransmitter than did their "brethren" lower down the totem pole. In the monkey studies, the serotonin levels went down when the dominant monkey was separated from the others, suggesting that serotonin may be influenced by social interactions, and vice versa.

Is there some serotonin-regulation connection between violence, dominance, and Aggressive or Sadistic personality patterns? Additional research in neuropsychiatric laboratories may someday reveal the answer—and help supply a pharmacological "antidote" for those who are violently out of control. See chapter 18 for more.

COPING WITH SADISTIC PEOPLE

Remember that interactions with Sadistic individuals are no-win situations. You cannot work it out with them except by giving in completely, and even then they may inflict pain gratuitously, without a detectable reason. If the Sadistic person you are trying to cope with is not so extreme or totally hard-hearted, try some of the tips for dealing with Aggressive types. Rather than try to cope with a Sadistic boss, quit or transfer. If you are the victim of Sadistic behavior at home, move out. Should you lack resources and/or be fearful for your safety, move to a shelter for battered spouses, consult women's organizations in your area, or go to the police. If leaving is possible but you find you cannot extricate yourself emotionally from a relationship with a Sadistic person, ask yourself whether you may have an unconscious need to suffer. If so, you can be helped; see chapter 15.

CHAPTER 17

Serious Style

"THE REALIST"

Serious men and women suffer no illusions. They don't hitch their wagons to a star, count their chickens before they're hatched, sing that life is just a bowl of cherries, or don rose-colored glasses to paint their existence in a more beguiling hue. Even when things are not so pleasant, they see them as they are. Of course, since the current culture favors individuals who "think positive," look on the bright side, and attempt always to improve themselves, somebody with Serious style may not exactly fit the image. But Serious people don't expect to be popular.

What they sacrifice in silver linings, they gain in ability to carry on in even the worst of circumstances. No other personality style is quite so able to endure when a harsh climate seems to descend on the planet. This is a no-frills, no-nonsense, just-do-it personality style, whose strength in hard times can help everyone to survive. Like many of the other personality styles, it is one where a little goes a long way.

THE SEVEN CHARACTERISTICS

1. *Straight face.* Individuals with the Serious personality style maintain a sober demeanor. They are solemn and not given to emotional expression.

2. *No pretentions.* They are realistically aware of their own capabilities, but they are also aware of their own limitations; they are not tempted by vanity or self-importance.

3. *Accountability.* Serious people hold themselves responsible for their

actions. They will not soft-pedal their own faults and do not let themselves off the hook.

4. *Cogitation.* They're thinkers, analyzers, evaluators, ruminators: They'll always play things over in their minds before they act.

5. *Nobody's fool.* Men and women with Serious personality style are sharp appraisers of others. In their ability to critique other people, they are as unhesitating as in their own self-evaluation.

6. *No surprises.* They anticipate problems and when the worst happens, they're prepared to deal with it.

7. *Contrition.* Serious people suffer greatly when they realize they've been thoughtless or impolite to others.

THE SIX DOMAINS OF SERIOUS FUNCTIONING

Work and Emotions are the key domains for people with Serious personality style.

WORK:
LIFE IS WORK

For predominantly Serious people, work truly is the metaphor for existence. Life is work, work is life. In the workplace or during personal time, everything is a series of chores. It's hard, it may even be a grind, but you do what you have to do to survive. Serious people see no choice in this approach to life, and they do not expect to find pleasure in it (as you'll see when we discuss Emotions) or to achieve some possible hidden creative potential. In this way they differ considerably from people with the two other personality styles in which Work is a key domain: Conscientious types, who find a sense of themselves and a meaning to their lives through their efforts; and Aggressive individuals, who experience positive fulfillment from their wielding of power.

To Toil and Travail

This is a personality style especially adapted to adversity. People with this style have the strength to keep on doing their duty, which can be a particular asset to their families and to the community. April M. gets up at four-thirty in the morning in order to get to work as a cook's assistant. She has four children and she organizes the young ones' clothing and meals before she wakes up the older two, who will feed their little siblings and take them to day-care on their own way to school. April's husband works the night shift, which means they hardly see each other, except on weekends. Although they live extremely frugally, both paychecks barely cover the bills; food stamps help. April lost her last job because she couldn't afford the carfare. Although in her seemingly thankless travails she is an inspiration to others around her, she takes no pride in her achievements. She sees it as drudgery, not heroism. Typical of the Serious personality, she feels that this is her lot. It's a sour one, and she does not question it.

Picture the stereotypically dour farmer of days gone by. He toils on his dry, barren land though little comes of it. When crops fail he sells what he can and heads west with his family, surviving harsh winds off the prairie, snow and sleet, the death of his wife and two of his five children. This is the tale Dinah tells of her great-grandfather, Peder, who emigrated from Scandinavia to Minnesota. Peder never smiled and when he spoke it was usually to complain. But he kept on, eventually to California; though he became a legend to his progeny, he saw little romance to his labors. You're born, you work, you die. Although Serious people like Peder press on where others might give up, they get no thrill from it, as would an Adventurous person who survived a frightening challenge. Neither do they get particular gratification for doing things for others, as would a Self-Sacrificing individual.

Serious types are normally cautious, avoiding risks, but when their path is strewn with hardships they'll keep on plodding.

In the Workplace

Life is hard work for Serious people whether or not their personal circumstances are extreme. They do their duty as they see it, but the doing of it may feel like toiling on a treadmill. What it feels like is irrelevant to them. They persevere whether or not they like what they are doing or they are rewarded for their efforts—a trait that's easy to take advantage of in the modern workplace. They'll do the job responsibly no matter what; they may gripe about having too much work to do, but they'll do it. Without any of the ambitious, self-promoting styles (Self-Confident, Aggressive) in their personalities, people who are dominated by the Serious style will not map out their careers in a series of stepping stones toward the big prize. It's survival, and for that they'll work singlemindedly to stay in place rather than to conquer new challenges. They're not activists and do not assert their rights as others might see them. Unlike the Self-Sacrificing person, who works just as hard with similar humility, the Serious individual doesn't long for the appreciation that he or she fails to insist on.

The ability of Serious types to endure discomfort enables them to tolerate routine and tedium and prodigious amounts of work. They are steadfast, loyal, and trustworthy. They take their jobs extremely seriously and, though they may lack the overt enthusiasm that some employers prefer, they come through.

Moderate Seriousness at Work

Serious people are likely to be disappointed with themselves and cynical about others and the future. Yet, in moderation, such traits can contribute to a very accomplished career. For an example of a person who made an important contribution, see the eulogy of Richard Harris that we quote on pp. 169–70, in the Vigilant chapter. Richard Harris was a reporter who showed characteristics typical of a combination of Vigilant and Serious styles. He "viewed the world with an unfiltered gaze." Putting that trait to use on behalf of *The New Yorker,* he turned out "penetrating and prodigious articles on the American legislative and judicial process. The work exhausted him, but it never mellowed him."

As with Peder the nineteenth-century farmer/pioneer, Richard Harris's accomplishments benefited others without necessarily lightening his own burden. And, though much admired, he proved trying, in part because, as the eulogist phrased it, "he did not consider the spreading of good cheer to be among his responsibilities."

The Serious Manager

Predominantly Serious people are not eager for authority and thus are unlikely to seek management-level positions. They may be promoted to lower or middle management because of their productivity and years of service, however. Someone with another predominant style and a moderate amount of the Serious is more likely to rise to management level.

The Serious manager will expect others to take on a great deal of work regardless of whether they like any particular assignment. The manager won't shirk his or her own responsibilities, though. The atmosphere will not necessarily be upbeat, personally encouraging, or even supportive, but a lot can be learned from such a "doer" for the subordinate who is self-motivated and does not require inspiration from on high. Serious managers can be quite critical of those who work for them. It may help to know that they usually don't get too out of shape about it, since they don't expect things to go right.

Lacking political skills, the manager may not be able to fight for subordinates' rights when necessary. But, whether they say so or not, they will appreciate the steady, reliable worker who shows up and does the job day after day.

Careers for the Serious

Because you are so responsible and hard-working, and can put up with routine, you will do well in virtually any kind of work that does not force you continually to demonstrate initiative, problem-solve, or deal with people in an ever-cheerful way. For many Serious people, civil service, government, and union-regulated employment offers the opportunity to work hard without having to compete to stay alive (although the competitive in these and all other settings will almost always go farther). A moderate amount of Seriousness often enhances other styles to help you put your personality strengths to work in investigative journalism, research, law, accounting, secretarial work, health care. Avoid sales and public relations, which require that you manage the interpersonal atmosphere more creatively than is your style. Consulting work is a possibility, but be careful that you don't underprice yourself.

EMOTIONS: THE GLASS IS HALF EMPTY

Emotions represent the second of the Serious style's ruling domains. Mostly these individuals evince a sober, unspontaneous emotional style. Their seeming joylessness is inherent, not a cover, as it may be for Self-Sacrificing people, whom they may often resemble. Self-Sacrificing Sid and Serious Doug sometimes play golf together. Both say they don't really enjoy the game all that much. But Sid tends to feel guilty about leaving his family home and having a good time on his own, whereas Doug, though he plays well, really doesn't get more than perhaps an occasional surge of pleasure from his exertions.

The glass is invariably half-empty to Serious men and women. They see the dark side of life in sharp focus and are constitutionally incapable of coloring it with a positive brush. Mind you, they are just as accurate in their depiction of this container as are those who insist it is half-full, even if contemporary culture accords extra credit to those who "think positive." Pain and loss are impossible to avoid in life, to be sure. To this reality the fourteen personality styles all react differently. A Mercurial person, for example, will try to escape into pleasure, and a Dramatic type will want to shift his or her eyes immediately to the bright side. A highly Solitary person may not feel much of anything very strongly. A Serious person will stay with the dark side, even when the intense agony has faded. This style is incapable of the self-sustaining illusions that many others require to keep their chin up. "Things will work out," a Self-Confident person might say, which may or may not be true. "I'll believe it when I see it" is a more likely response from the Serious person, whom, as you'll note, we dub "the realist."

Continually confronted with the harsh realities of life, Serious types can't flip the channel, as it were, to take their minds off it. Irritability is therefore common, and as the style becomes extreme, depression becomes a real possibility, as we'll see in the second half of this chapter. But even a somewhat Serious person will display a characteristic pessimism, regardless of his or her capacity for emotional heights from time to time.

Almost invariably, upbeat, optimistic people see the Serious emotional darkness as willful (see "Stress!" p. 373), as if they can just snap out of it. Right before the real estate boom of the seventies and eighties, Jackie W. sold her house for more than twice what she'd paid for it twenty years before. Five years later she could have gotten that amount twice over. All she could see was her *loss* in this transaction, not the actual, appreciable gain. Of her two grown children, Jackie's son was most like her and commiserated. Her daughter—whom she long before had nicknamed "Pollyanna"—never failed to tell Jackie that she was making herself miserable with the way she always looked at life. But Jackie's daughter was wrong in believing her mother was unhappy. She mistook a lack of overt happiness for its opposite. But Serious people may be quite satisfied with their dark view of things. And they may believe, perhaps accurately, that they're more tuned in to the rough terrain of the world than most people are.

Serious Plus Outgoing Emotional Styles

Even though this is a characteristically dark style, it often coexists along with normally outgoing, emotionally expressive personality styles. Its effects may be subtle. A mixed Dramatic-Serious person, for instance, would probably be able to act more emotionally engaged than she or he really felt inside. And this person would not be as startled by misfortune as would a more predominantly Dramatic individual. A person who was both Serious and Mercurial would be particularly vulnerable to depression and perhaps both drawn to and frightened by risk.

"Lightening Up"

Reality is the best medicine for Serious people. When they want to relax and take it easy, they read or watch the news, always finding their view of life affirmed by the latest unemployment statistics, reports of disasters, accusations of political corruption, and the like. Though these subjects may not be very relaxing or cheering to most people, Serious individuals expect such events, and find them interesting and curiously reassuring.

RELATIONSHIPS: LIFE IN THE SLOW LANE

Predominantly Serious people bring the same virtues to their personal lives that they demonstrate in the workplace. They are dependable, trustworthy, steady, and predictable in their relationships. They are not socially outgoing, which might cause some difficulty in meeting potential partners. Once they find a mate, though, they'll invest sincerely in the long haul. They will provide for their families and perform all the responsibilities necessary to their daily lives. They'll remain faithful, even if a partner is not.

They do not expect the relationship to be perfect. If anything, they expect a rocky course and surrender in advance. Olivia D. found out from a friend that her husband had been cheating on her. Rather than confronting him and insisting on better behavior, she told her friend sourly, "They all cheat, don't they?" and resigned herself to this bitter pill. Still, although some people may think that the Serious ability to accept the worst in others is harmful to themselves, Olivia and her husband did manage to weather the strains of their marriage and are now, after forty years together, clearly devoted to one another in their old age.

Whether or not they assert themselves in their relationships or face conflict creatively, Serious types tend to be critical of their mates. This trait is a logical extension of their "half-empty" approach to life. Like Vigilant people, they see what is off or not right in any situation or person. Unlike Vigilant types, however, they are not suspicious. What they see is real. Even so, they do not see the whole picture, since they are blind to the prettier realities. This can be quite stressful to their mates, who may justifiably insist that their qualities and actions are not being weighed on a balanced scale.

Remorse

Accused of an unkindness, however, a Serious person will suffer greatly. People with this style, though they may be unable to express positive feelings, are very dependent on their loved ones. They get no self-righteous pleasure in finding fault. When they recognize that they have caused pain, they become regretful and readily take the blame. They often chalk up others' as well as their own shortcomings to the imperfections of the world, and they trudge on—so you might as well try to let go of your hurt and trudge along yourself.

Stress!

Serious people can't stand the pressure that people often put on them to change. Loved ones commonly insist that they look at the bright side—as if their point of view was not authentic. Others also may have higher expectations for them than they may have for themselves and therefore attempt to push them to be more assertive: "Be ambitious! You could get a promotion if you really tried!" In the face of increasing stress, the natural Serious pessimism may turn to gloom and eventually to true depression. But most of the time their very cynicism helps them cope, overcoming any unsettling wistfulness. As mentioned earlier, just because they're Serious doesn't mean they're unhappy.

Good/Bad Matches

Serious people require mates who are highly accepting and will let them be. The best matches are with moderately Devoted and Self-Sacrificing people, who are very eager to please. Conscientious types have a similar work ethic and strong sense of responsibility, which will prove comfortable, but beware of the Conscientious need to be "right," since Serious people have a very definite point of view.

Serious-Serious matches can work, because both partners will have a common understanding of the world. But it might be better to pair up with someone who can socialize with greater comfort and drag you into activities in which you find yourself enjoying yourself despite yourself! But steer clear of predominantly Adventurous, Mercurial, Self-Confident, and Dramatic people.

Serious Parents

They're responsible, cautious parents who try to make their children aware of life's unavoidable hard knocks. Whereas Sensitive parents will try to control the child's world in order to make it safe (wear boots even if it's not snowing, just in case it starts, you get chilled, and God forbid get pneumonia), Serious parents teach them not to be surprised by misfortune (even if you wear boots, scarves, parkas, you can't avoid getting sick in winter). Like Sensitive parents, they will not encourage their children to take risks, but, as in the just-cited example, they will not overprotect them. They won't fight the children's battles for them. Their children will not expect easy street, and they'll have a role model in how to endure adversity. But they'll need one non-Serious parent from whom to learn that a person can change things for the better as well as how to prevent or overcome difficulty.

Like Conscientious and Aggressive parents, Serious mothers and fathers will inculcate the value of work, but they must take care to allow kids time for activities other than homework and chores. The non-Serious parent, one hopes, will impart the benefits of fun and the joy of novelty.

SELF, REAL WORLD, AND SELF-CONTROL: WATCH OUT—SOME THINGS NEVER CHANGE

Serious people have a clear sense of who they are: they're limited people in an imperfect world. They work extremely hard, since they see the world as harsh and hard work as a necessity just to stay in place. Their self-critical humility, when moderate, can be appealing. These people do not struggle to present a better face, to pull the wool over anybody's eyes, to improve themselves, or to fit an image. Their sense of Self becomes vulnerable, however, when they're under stress or when the Serious style becomes extreme; in such cases their self-esteem can hit bottom and require some shoring up.

The Real World of the Serious person is a forbidding, inauspicious place. One way these individuals come to terms with it is to dwell on their past failures or their helplessness in the face of forces beyond their control: "If only I hadn't sold that stock fourteen years ago, I'd be well off today." "My life would have taken a different course if I had been born with a different temperament." Often these thoughts run through their mind repeatedly.

The other, more adaptive way they come to terms with the harsh Real World is to continually prepare for the worst and in so doing prevent other potential calamities. In this they take great satisfaction.

Dylan L., for instance, who is both Serious and Conscientious, is always expecting his car to break down. So he trades it in for a new one every few years. He's never actually had a serious car problem, and believes he has averted the inevitable by being one step ahead of the game. He doesn't take special pleasure in his new cars, but he does appreciate beating the odds. Similarly, Marilyn A. refuses to invest in the stock market because she is certain of its instability. For years she has maintained fully insured bank savings accounts and occasionally certificates of deposit. Her savings have grown modestly but steadily over the decades. She is proud to say she has never lost a cent.

Finally, Serious people prepare for the worst of the Real World by removing any potential for surprise. Through sheer Self-Control, they keep their noses to the grindstone, adhere to routine, and remain undistracted by impulse or passion. Serious types think everything through before acting, they do not take risks or challenge fate, and they don't escape into pleasure or appetites. Extremely Serious people may take too little initiative, however, which may give them good cause for feeling limited in life.

For the moderately Serious person, however, this sober, dour approach to life may provide a literal survival advantage. Health psychologist Howard S. Friedman reviewed results of a sixty-year project following over a thousand California men and women from age eleven into their seventies. To his surprise, he found that those who had been somewhat cheerless, dutiful, and dependable since childhood tended to live longer than the happy-go-lucky optimists.

TIPS ON DEALING WITH THE SERIOUS PERSON IN YOUR LIFE

1. Acceptance is key. Refrain from trying to get the Serious person in your life to see the bright side of every situation, or to be more outgoing, to show more enthusiasm, or to set higher goals . . . whatever might be bothering you about this person. Trying to change him or her is fruitless, as it is with most personality styles.

2. Look on the bright side yourself. This person is steady, responsible, loyal, hard-working, and caring (if not expressively so). You can count on the Serious person through thick and thin. These traits are extremely positive indicators for a long-term relationship.

3. Don't assume that the Serious person's dark view means he or she is miserable. Although your own pessimism may result from your oc-

casional bad moods, the attitude is utterly normal for the Serious person. But if the Serious "bah humbug!" outlook influences your own moods, think twice about getting involved.

4. You're allowed to be happy. Don't inhibit your own natural emotions just because the Serious person doesn't respond as you would like. If he or she doesn't exactly jump for joy over your promotion, there's no reason to curb your own excitement.

5. Compliment the Serious person for what he or she adds to your life. Expressions of caring are very important to people with this personality style, although they themselves often have trouble sharing any positive feelings with you. If you praise him or her, the habit may rub off.

6. The Serious person will usually comment first on what is not right in any situation. Such criticism is par for the course. For example, when you've just had an exceptional haircut, expect the Serious person to comment first on your muddy raincoat or unshined shoes. Let the person get this stuff off his or her chest, and then you can get on to what's right about things. In any case, don't assume that the Serious person in your life hates how you look. Do you like your own haircut? Then say so.

7. Be honest without being manipulative, punitive, or indeed critical yourself. Tell the Serious person in your life that being complimented and directly appreciated is very important to you. Say that you realize these sorts of comments don't come easily to him or her. Pay attention in days that follow for at least some subtle signs that he or she heard you. You may not realize how sensitive a Serious person is to your feelings for him or her.

8. Don't be put off by the Serious person's apparent lack of enthusiasm for you in the beginning of a relationship or for the activities you do together later on. Remember that this style is very very slow to lighten up. Just because he or she fails to rave about the wonderful time being had by all doesn't mean you should not ask this person to accompany you in the future. Often a Serious person's ability to show satisfaction or levity has little relation to how important being with you really is. Serious people have needs like everybody else.

9. Don't wait for a Serious person to be spontaneous—do it for both of you. Show initiative in all aspects of your life together. You'll enlarge your mutual scope of experience.

MAKING THE MOST OF YOUR SERIOUS STYLE

You are a hard worker, you persevere in all your tasks, and you feel the weight of the world on your shoulders. In order to protect yourself from stress, to enhance your relationships, and to preserve your strength for truly difficult times, you need to develop some flexibility. Approach the following exercises as tasks like others you do throughout your day.

Exercise 1

Make one list of ten things you would like to have happen to you in your relationships, and another one concerning your work life. Avoid expressing your wishes as negatives (e.g., instead of saying "I would like *not* to always do the dirty work at the office," phrase it as: "I would like to do more responsible work," or name specific tasks you would prefer to be doing.

Exercise 2

For each item on your two lists, write down at least one practical action that you could take in order to make it happen. This is just an exercise, remember—not something you are going to *have* to do if you don't want to. The only point is to think up a way to achieve the goal, if in imagination only. For instance, to use the example from Exercise 1, one action might be to request a transfer to another site or department.

Exercise 3

Again, consult your two lists. Now, sit back, close your eyes, and, item by item, step by step, imagine first that you are taking the action and achieving your goal. If you get used to rehearsing it in your mind, you may find it easier to approach in real life.

Exercise 4

After completing the previous exercise, again relax and close your eyes. Now, one by one, imagine that you have achieved each of these goals. What does it feel like? Try to visualize as many details as you can.

Exercise 5

Keep a confidential daily journal for at least one month. Each day, after recording what occurred that day, and anything else you might wish to say, sum up with a positive comment about the day. What good of any kind came out of this day? This requirement may seem an artificial constraint—and it is!—but remember, it's only an exercise.

Exercise 6

If you have difficulty putting yourself forward in social situations, when seeking employment, or on the job, consider taking an assertiveness training course to learn the necessary skills. Also see Exercises 4 through 6 for the Sensitive personality style (pp. 194–95) for some tips for overcoming reticence with others.

Exercise 7

To relax, practice *not* thinking. See Exercise 5 for Conscientious style: Take time out—turn off your brain (p. 75). For Serious style, clear your mind immediately when you find yourself thinking and rethinking the same point or issue.

Exercise 8

Think of or better yet write down (perhaps in your daily journal) ten things you like about yourself.

Exercise 9

Think of/write down ten things you like about the significant others in your life.

Exercise 10

Every day, try to compliment the important people in your life and do something just to please them. You care about them, but they may not always realize it.

Exercise 11

Every time you are about to criticize somebody, think of something favorable to say first. This will make the substance of your criticism easier to take, since the person will not immediately be on the defensive. You can use this same exercise when you're about to criticize yourself!

Finally, consult Exercise 1 from Sensitive style (p. 193): Do something different. Like Sensitive people, you are a creature of habit. You're quite happy with your routines, but for flexibility's sake, to make sure you keep up your ability to solve vexing problems when you must, develop a repertoire of alternatives.

DEPRESSIVE PERSONALITY DISORDER

They think there's no hope, now or ever. They seem incapable of pleasure. They can't relax. They're critical and angry, heaping most abuse on themselves. All told, sadness and gloom dominate the perceptions of people with Depressive personality disorder.

DIAGNOSTIC CRITERIA

The DSM-IV describes the Depressive personality disorder as:

A. A pervasive pattern of depressive cognitions and behaviors beginning by early adulthood and present in a variety of contexts, as indicated by five (or more) of the following:

(1) usual mood is dominated by dejection, gloominess, cheerlessness, joylessness, unhappiness

(2) self-concept centers around beliefs of inadequacy, worthlessness, and low self-esteem

(3) is critical, blaming, and derogatory toward self

(4) is brooding and given to worry

(5) is negativistic, critical, and judgmental toward others

(6) is pessimistic

(7) is prone to feeling guilty or remorseful

B. Does not occur exclusively during Major Depressive Episodes and is not better accounted for by Dysthymic Disorder.

WHEN THE SUN NEVER SHINES

It is a dreary world that people with Depressive personality disorder inhabit, and there's no escape hatch for them. They look inward and find themselves inadequate and worthy of reproach. Outwardly they perceive an existence without hope. In others they find cause for complaint. They're passive, helpless, hopeless. They attend to what must be done in their unhappy lives, which feels like pushing a huge weight up a steep incline. If they let go, they'll be crushed, so they have no choice but to keep up the terrible task.

Clearly, individuals with this personality disorder are in pain. They dwell on their faults and the unhappiness they perceive everywhere. They find no relief outside themselves, no letting down and getting away from it all. They don't even have the "luxury" of blaming others for all their misery, as do those with Paranoid and Passive-Aggressive personality disorders, to name two; to people with Depressive personality disorder, they only have themselves to blame. Not that their self-censure leads to an objective appraisal of their attitudes and behaviors; most do not see that the gloom comes from inside them and colors their every perception and behavior. Even if they do, they believe there is no hope—none at all—for change.

OR ARE THEY "JUST" DEPRESSED?

The DSM-IV marks the debut of Depressive personality disorder in the American diagnostic nomenclature. Although it is an accepted diagnosis among European psychiatrists, and one that has been employed by many American practitioners, it is not yet an official U.S. diagnosis, appearing only in the appendix of the DSM-IV that is reserved for conditions that require further study. But the inclusion of Depressive personality disorder at all reintroduces an old question about the relationship between an acute symptomatic disorder, such as major depression, and a personality pattern that is a way of life. Fundamentally, the debate concerns the very nature of the relationship of mind and body, of biology and psychology, and of lasting trait vs. temporary state.

At present, the DSM-IV offers two principal diagnoses for depression in its Depressive Disorders section: major depressive disorder (major depression) and dysthymic disorder (dysthymia). Since 1980, these have been conceptualized as Axis I psychiatric disorders, which, as explained in the Introduction, consist of discrete symptomatic conditions that wax and wane. They happen to some people, as if superimposed on who they are—rather like a person with diabetes. And indeed, Axis I conditions are considered to have a highly biological underpinning.

Major depression is the acute, severe form of suffering; people who are stricken by it often cannot work, think, sleep, eat, or experience pleasure; they lose hope, they may hate themselves, and they may wish to die. Bouts of major depression usually recur throughout life. Dysthymia is the chronic, milder form, characterized by low self-esteem, low energy, gloominess, appetite disturbances, and other problems; those who suffer from it can continue with their lives, but they feel and often are diminished by it. Those who suffer from dysthymia may also suffer from major depression from time to time.

Importantly, both major depression and dysthymia principally affect mood and the so-called "vegetative" functions, such as eating, sleeping, sexual desire, and energy. Such symptoms are usually considered indications that biological treatment—that is, antidepressant medication—will work.

The diagnostic criteria for Depressive personality disorder, however, focus on cognitive and behavioral symptoms: how a person thinks and acts in life, including his or her relationships with others. Although people with this personality disorder are considered vulnerable to major depression and dysthymia, they are seen as having a negative, hopeless, self-limiting way of life and thinking style that is distinct from the somatic and mood symptoms of depression itself.

THE AFFECTIVE SPECTRUM

In the past, before the era of neuropsychiatry and the introduction of technology that has begun to reveal the workings of the mind/brain at the cellular level, it was easier to see psychiatric problems as either biological or psychological. Personality disorders (which used to be known as character disorders or neuroses) would have fallen in the realm of the psychological. As these distinctions fade with the discoveries about the biological underpinnings of all states of mind, and about how mental events influence physiological processes, the concept of a spectrum of disorders becomes more enlightening.

In previous chapters we have discussed Schizotypal, Schizoid, and Paranoid personality disorders as perhaps being mild manifestations along a spectrum, or continuum, of disorders with Schizophrenia at the most extreme and of course most limiting. Likewise, Borderline and Antisocial personality disorders may fall on a spectrum of impulse disorders along with bulimia, and drug and alcohol abuse, among others. In addition, because mood instability is one of the defining criteria of Borderline personality disorder, numerous researchers have suggested that it may overlap with the affective (mood) spectrum disorders. Certainly, Depressive personality would come at the mild end of this continuum. Those who are diagnosed with the Axis I mood disorders would be in an intense state of depression. Somebody with the personality disorder variant would have lifelong depressive traits or temperament. A vulnerability to any of these disorders, either Axis I or Axis II, could be genetically transmitted.

Indeed, the trend to conceptualize a continuum between Axis I and Axis II (personality) disorders was a principal reason why the personality disorders work group recommended that Depressive personality disorder be included in DSM-IV. As psychiatrist Katharine A. Phillips and her colleagues stated: "This recommendation reflects the Work Group's belief that certain Axis II disorders may be on a spectrum with certain Axis I disorders—that is, that certain personality disorders may be early-onset, enduring, traitlike variants of the more episodic and severely symptomatic Axis I disorders; and may share similar family history, treatment response, and perhaps etiology."

Family history studies do suggest a relationship between these various manifestations of depression.

INCIDENCE, PREDISPOSITIONS, AND RISKS

Despite the use of this diagnosis in Europe, little is yet known about how common Depressive personality disorder is. It is believed to occur equally among women and men, unlike major depression and dysthymia, which are diagnosed far more frequently among women. Theoretically, individuals with this personality disorder are highly vulnerable to major depression and dysthymia. In fact, some researchers have found that nearly half of these mood disorders occur in people who have an underlying Depressive personality. Dysthymia is so common that the editors of the DSM-IV have remarked, "It remains controversial whether the distinction between Depressive Personality Disorder and Dysthymic Disorder is useful."

HELP!

When biologically driven syndromes (such as major depression) were believed to be entirely separated from personality disorders, a similar distinction was made in treatment approaches: medication plus at least some psychotherapy for the former, psychotherapy alone for the latter. Now that many Axis I and Axis II conditions are being conceptualized along a spectrum of related mind/body disorders, however, these treatment distinctions are also beginning to fade. Certainly medication is often useful in personality disorder that produces symptoms of depression, anxiety, or confusion. But, as we have maintained throughout this book, medication cannot "cure" a personality disorder, which is a pattern of habits and reactions and beliefs that has existed for years.

Or can it? In *Listening to Prozac*, psychiatrist Peter Kramer has made a popular though highly controversial case for the ability of a particular class of antidepressants—the selective serotonin reuptake inhibitors (SSRIs)—to transform the lives of many people who are inhibited, pessimistic, hard-working underachievers with low self-esteem who are reluctant to take risks. These traits describe people with Depressive personality disorder or even Serious personality style. "In an era when personality was understood to be the summation of psychological defenses, and the defenses were understood as responses to trauma during development, it was threatening to see personality as responding to medication," writes Kramer. "It may be that Prozac [and other drugs in its class] is special in its effect on temperament, or that Prozac arrived at a propitious moment and as a result . . . Prozac has allowed us to see an effect of medications that we should have attended to long ago."

It is quite clear that this new class of medication is extremely helpful for many people. Most researchers would agree, though, that this benefit is not the result of a primary effect of the medication on one's personality, but rather that some form of depression was present that responded to the drug. Medication could seem to change personality in people whose mood disorder has been longstanding and unrecognized; now that they feel so much better, they can engage in many activities they previously shunned.

Further research will clarify whether Depressive personality disorder exists or whether it is really a form of chronic depression, and the degree to which medication is beneficial for anyone who suffers from it. Clinicians who treat men and women with this pattern of symptoms often do advocate the use of various antidepressants if the individual's complaints seem to warrant them.

Numerous types of psychotherapy can be brought to bear on Depressive personality disorder, from the psychodynamic to the supportive to the cognitive. Most clinicians would agree that with or without medication, treatment of any personality disorder is not a "quick cure"; no matter what its cause, the pattern has been in place for a lifetime, and, although medication may ease the way for some, personality doesn't change without significant effort.

COPING WITH PEOPLE WITH DEPRESSIVE PERSONALITY DISORDER

People who are constantly unhappy and who think that nothing will ever change are difficult to deal with, because nothing you say helps. Becoming angry may help you vent your feelings, but it will accomplish little that is constructive, since a person with this personality disorder may react to your anger with such guilt that *you'll* end up feeling guilty. The tips on pp. 375–76 for dealing with a Serious person may help. In any case, keep in mind that relationships with others are very important to people with Depressive personality disorder, although their sourness may make you think otherwise. If you have been a significant person in his or her life, be compassionate but firm about going for help. Consider going together if you are a couple.

CHAPTER 18

Your Style and Your Destiny

WHERE YOU'VE COME FROM AND
WHERE YOU'RE HEADED

Now you see it: Your personality style is a kind of map of both your inner geography and the outward direction of your life. You follow its pathway every day of your life. You seek and react to experiences and people according to your own style. You change, or stay the same, according to your own style.

In the final chapter, we'll tell you about ways to alter or at least broaden your personality's horizons. Here, we'll consider in more detail how style develops throughout the life cycle.

BORN WITH IT

As we said in chapter 2, temperament is what you're born with, and character is the result of what you learn and experience. Temperament is the hand you're dealt at conception, which sets the stage for all later experiences. The development of your personality style depends on what you bring to your environment and what it brings to you: nature *and* nurture, heredity *and* environment.

Not long ago, child development specialists believed that life experiences alone shaped an individual's personality. Now, thanks to the work of psychiatrists Sibylle Escalona, Alexander Thomas, Stella Chess, and Daniel Stern, and psychologist Jerome Kagan, among others, researchers have taken a renewed interest in the biologic "givens" of individual personality. In the words of some researchers in this field, "What IQ has been to our understanding of cognition, temperament is becoming to our comprehension of personality development."

Parents who have more than one child know that each child is undeniably unique and that the differences among their children are apparent almost from the first moments of life. Some infants cry a lot, some don't; some are easily soothed, some aren't; some quickly develop regular eating and sleeping patterns, whereas others are difficult to train to any schedule; some have powerful, intense emotional reactions, whereas others are calm and easygoing. Children are born with these differences. Every individual enters the world with his or her own particular constitution and reaction patterns, at least some of which can be traced to his or her genes. These are the inborn, biologically determined differences among all individuals that set the stage for the differences in personality.

THE FOUR HUMORS

The ancient Greeks believed that nature consisted of four elements: air, earth, fire, and water. Each of these cosmic elements was represented in the human body by a corresponding humor, or bodily fluid: blood, black bile, yellow bile, and phlegm. Based on these humors, Hippocrates, considered the father of Western medicine, formulated the first scientific typology of personality in the fifth century B.C. He postulated four temperament types, each of which corresponded to a predominance of one humor: sanguine (hopeful, enthusiastic, optimistic, energetic), melancholic (sad, moody, withdrawn), choleric (irascible, irritable, impulsive), and phlegmatic (apathetic, slow). Every person's personality could be classified into one of the four categories, which also predicted everyone's vulnerability to mental and physical disease.

This is a simple, scientific classification that anticipated modern understandings of temperament and personality in many ways. "The ancient Greeks had an uncanny knack for intuiting the nature of things thousands of years before the available instrumentation could confirm and refine their hypotheses," psychiatrist Allen J. Frances and psychologist Thomas Widiger have noted. "Their concept that behavior arises at least in part from the state of the body chemistries is as impressive a biological intuition as was the inspired physical intuition that matter consists of atoms."

Even though it strikes us today as naive, the "humorists" recognized simple, fundamental dimensions along which all human behavior can be measured. Hippocrates and his followers recognized also that these dimensions of personality are biologically determined. We know today that inborn biological style strongly shapes an individual's ultimate personality style.

THE THREE TEMPERAMENTS

Some twenty-five hundred years after Hippocrates, in 1956 husband and wife psychiatrists Alexander Thomas and Stella Chess began an ongoing study, following 133 individuals from their infancy onward. In their decades of research, they identified nine categories of inborn temperamental variables and three broad, basic, normal temperament styles into which the majority of infants seem to fit. Their work was the first in recent history to show scientifically that temperament and behavior by the age of three powerfully predict personality in adulthood.

THE VARIABLES OF TEMPERAMENT

1. *Activity level.* Every infant has a characteristic activity level, from slow to speedy.

2. *Regularity.* Some are regular in their eating, sleeping, and other biological functions, others unpredictable.

3. *Approach/withdrawal.* When presented with a new toy, food, person, or other stimulus, does the baby respond positively and with interest (approach) or negatively and fearfully (withdrawal)?

4. *Adaptability.* Does the child learn and adjust to new situations and tasks easily, or does he or she have difficulty adjusting to change?

5. *Threshold of responsiveness.* What does it usually take to get a "rise" out of the baby—a strong sensory stimulation such as a loud noise, or a mild one such as a soft voice? Does the child become overstimulated easily by sensory experiences?

6. *Reaction intensity.* Some react loudly to everything, whereas others typically are less intense in their positive and negative reactions.

7. *Mood.* Even babies have characteristic mood patterns, varying from predominantly cheerful to frequently unhappy.

8. *Distractibility.* Does the child tend to focus on tasks at hand, or is he or she easily distracted?

9. *Attention span and persistence.* How long does the baby typically stick with an activity, and will he or she persist despite difficulties?

About 40 percent of all children fit into what Thomas and Chess called the Easy Child category. These children adapt easily, are regular in their habits, are quick to adapt to new situations, are happy much or most of the time, and are usually quiet. Overall, they are easy to deal with.

Fifteen percent of children fall into the so-called Slow-to-Warm-Up group. They don't find new situations or people easy and they react in a mildly negative manner, but they take to them eventually, in their own time. They are not intense in their reactions and are fairly happy most of the time, after they get used to new things.

Thomas and Chess identified the Difficult temperament among 10 percent of the children in their studies. These kids are harder for parents to deal with because their reactions are intense and often negative, they don't adapt easily, and they don't adjust well to regular schedules. They are more demanding of parents, less easy to please.

While individual children display a wide variety of additional temperaments, according to Thomas and Chess these are three main categories into which most children seem to fall by reason of innate biology, regardless of culture. The temperaments represent normal styles of response with which children are born. Thomas and Chess have shown that the parents' attitudes and actions have little influence on their children's basic temperamental patterns.

INHIBITED AND UNINHIBITED TEMPERAMENTS

Harvard developmental psychologist Jerome Kagan represents the new breed of temperament investigators, seeking to identify the behavioral, emotional, and biological profiles of categories of temperament. Most of his work has focused on two temperamental opposites: inhibited and uninhibited children. Nearly half of all youngsters fall into one of these two categories. By age two, he has found, some 15 percent of children are clearly inhibited. By a small majority, most of them are girls. In response to unfamiliar people, objects, and situations, they retreat and become distressed. They're fearful, shy, timid, anxious. By contrast, about 30 percent of children, most of them boys, are bold, outgoing, spontaneous, and uninhibited. They become immediately interested in the unfamiliar and happily head right for it.

Not only do these children differ in reactions to novelty; Kagan's group has demonstrated that they are physiologically distinct as well. In response to stress, inhibited children's pupils dilate more, their hearts beat faster, and their blood pressure soars higher when compared with uninhibited children.

Kagan's experiments have demonstrated that these fundamental physiological differences can be observed in children by the time they are four months old. Others have shown that infants who are fearful and react poorly to challenge had high fetal heart rates in the womb.

Remarkably, the inhibited children even look different: they tend to have blue eyes and narrow faces. How could that be? "We interpret the fact that facial skeleton is a significant correlate of the two temperamental groups to imply the influence of a set of genes that affects features as diverse as the growth of facial bone, ease of arousal of infancy, smiling, and fear of the unfamiliar," responded Kagan and his colleague Doreen Arcus at an American Psychiatric Association symposium.

GENES FOR BEHAVIOR

Investigators are amassing strong evidence that at least some of the behaviors that characterize inborn temperament and later adult personality style are genetically determined. Current research in behavioral genetics suggests that from about a quarter to fully a half of all the variations among individuals results from inherited biology. Heredity appears to play a strong part in a person's tendency to be shy, to take command, to be impulsive, to be aggressive, to avoid harm, to react with obedience, to feel optimistic, and to worry and be easily upset, for example. Studies of adopted children show that their personalities tend to resemble those of their natural parents more than their adoptive parents. Similarly, studies of identical twins show them to be alike in personality and in looks whether they grow up together or apart. Individual animals of the same species demonstrate many of these same temperamental characteristics, which dog owners certainly know; some dogs are timid, some aggressive, some anxious and skittish, and so on. Studies of monkeys demonstrate that even if they are raised separately, those that are genetically related tend to react similarly to certain stressful situations.

BIOLOGICAL RESPONSE STYLES

Genes themselves don't cause a baby to respond to a new face with a rush of tears, an adult to go to pieces after a romantic breakup, or a monkey to cower in a corner when other monkeys enter the cage. What genes determine is the way an organism's brain develops and the range of its normal neurobiological and biochemical reactions that characterize its personal style of responding to the environment.

By focusing on people with personality disorders, who respond in an extreme way, neuroscientists have come up with tantalizing clues to some of the biologic underpinnings of personality dimensions. Antisocial personality disorder, for example, is characterized in part by extreme and dangerous risk taking and thrill seeking. Studies of individuals with this disorder suggest that their brains are relatively "underaroused" and that by seeking excessive stimulation they may in fact be compensating for inborn defects in their brain-arousal control mechanisms. Picture this need for arousal as rather like the desire to open the window for a blast of cold air to restore alertness while driving.

Antisocial, Sadistic, and Borderline people are prone to impulsive violence against others or against themselves. In numerous studies, low levels of the neurotransmitter serotonin have been found in individuals who are violent and aggressive, especially in those who are impulsively violent (see pp. 364–65 in chapter 16). Their relative levels of another neurotransmitter, noradrenaline (also known as norepinephrine) may make the difference between whether they turn that violence against themselves or toward others. Excessive noradrenaline is linked to overreactions to the environment. Combine high noradrenaline with low serotonin, and you have a formula for aggressive attacks on people and property. People with low noradrenaline levels, however, are more inhibited and would be more likely to turn that violence inward toward themselves, a formula for suicide.

Research with rhesus monkeys suggests that risk taking, too, is similarly linked with a serotonin deficit. In one study monkeys with low serotonin levels took longer and more dangerous leaps through the trees than did those with normal concentrations of the crucial neurotransmitter.

Biological investigations of Schizotypal people, who are very detached from others and communicate in an odd manner, yield similarly interesting findings. These individuals may have a subtle neurological dysfunction that shows up on a test of smooth pursuit eye movements (SPEM). Schizotypal people, together with schizophrenics and many of their family members, are unable to track a smooth moving target accurately. This inability seems to be an inherited trait that reflects some underlying problem in nervous-system functioning; perhaps it involves their inability to relate to other people or to think or communicate clearly. The brain's dopamine system, also implicated in schizophrenia, seems to account for many of the characteristics of Schizotypal personality disorder. Excessive levels of the neurotransmitter in certain parts of the brain may give rise to their eccentric thinking and speaking styles. Some Schizotypal individuals may suffer from *reduced* dopamine levels in other parts of the brain involved in relating to others and to the world in general.

We have mentioned these and other biological factors associated with personality disorders in the preceding chapters. Psychiatrist Robert Cloninger has proposed an intriguing comprehensive model of behavior based on specific genetic dimensions of temperament and related brain "neuromodulators" involved in each one. Dr. Cloninger suggests that it may be possible one day to understand each person's behavioral style according to his or her inherited mix of these brain chemicals. In time, similar investigative strategies may reveal the inborn response patterns that underlie normal, adaptive personality styles.

THE IMPACT OF LIFE . . .

Genes may present a range of possibilities, but it is experience that determines what will become of these possibilities. From birth, according to his or her temperamental style, an infant begins to learn from others, to adapt to his or her experiences within the family, and to develop styles of coping with the environment. But the interaction between heredity and environment goes two ways. Life shapes what will become of our genetic possibilities—but our inborn nature also affects what will happen to us.

. . . AND THE IMPACT OF TEMPERAMENT ON LIFE

Among the most significant findings of temperament research is that the newborn is not simply a passive victim of what life dishes out. From the beginning, a baby's temperament influences the kinds of experiences he or she is likely to have. How the parents react to their baby depends on the baby's temperament. And how the baby in turn deals with the parents' reactions, demands, and expectations depends on these same qualities of temperament. Psychiatrist Daniel Stern, using videotape studies of infants with their mothers, elegantly demonstrated many variations of mother-infant interactions, which he described in his book, *The Interpersonal World of the Infant.*

Dr. Stern and other investigators show that Easy babies make other people happy. These babies learn that their parents are easy to please and that the world can be a pretty fulfilling place. Cranky babies may irritate and frustrate their parents, some of whom may overreact and mistreat them. Difficult babies often bring out the worst in their parents, especially those who have personality difficulties. The fussier baby will have an even harder time dealing with negative parental reactions and will likely become even more difficult to manage.

EASY MELANIE AND DIFFICULT GUS

Take baby Melanie and little Gus. Melanie, an adorable two-year-old, is an Easy Child. "My baby was sleeping through the night within three weeks," brags Ruby, her mother. Melanie is easily soothed when she is upset, she smiles and giggles much of the time, she doesn't put up much of a fuss at bedtime, she takes readily to new people—Melanie is every parent's dream child. Her parents dote on her and reward her adaptability with love and attention. Because she is Easy, in other words, baby Melanie is having a nice, easy experience of other people.

On the other hand, Melanie's four-year-old brother, Gus, is a Difficult Child. He likes to stay up late, refuses to nap, and throws loud tantrums. In his first few weeks in nursery school he kept crying about wanting to go home. Then, once he settled in, he began to get wild and overexcited and would sometimes hit other children. At home, Ruby could never calm Gus when he got upset or overexcited. When Melanie turned out to be so different from Gus, both Ruby and her husband, Owen, breathed a sigh of relief. Owen had just gone back to work after a nearly yearlong layoff. Life was tough enough without Gus to deal with. They both openly prefer their little daughter. They shout at Gus when he cries, and when he won't stop they often send him to his room. "Why can't you be as good as your sister?" they ask him in exasperation.

As a result of his more complicated temperament, his parents' reactions to it, and their own life stresses, Gus is having a far different experience of life than is his little sister. He is learning that he is not as good as his sister—that's why his parents yell at him and criticize him so much, he thinks. His self-image is poor. He believes that he's bad and doesn't deserve his mommy and daddy's love. Lately he has become fearful and is afraid to go to sleep. He wakes his parents up late at night saying he's scared, but nothing they say to him comforts him. Owen thinks that they should be firm and tell him to stay in his room whether he's afraid or not.

There is nothing "wrong" with Gus's temperament. The 10 percent of children who share his Difficult temperament are well within the range of normal. But they are a handful, and Gus would be trying for any parent. His temperament, combined with his parents' lack of patience with his demanding nature, their tendency to fly off the handle, in addition to the stress that their financial uncertainty has put on their marriage, have begun to shape little Gus's experience and his developing personality pattern. Gus is becoming a very sad child. But lucky Melanie, because she is so adaptable and rewarding, and because she does not ask very much of her parents, is finding life a breeze.

THE GOODNESS OF FIT

Drs. Thomas and Chess found that the Difficult Child was the most likely of the temperament categories to develop behavior problems later in childhood. Behavior disorders in childhood often precede personality disorders in adulthood. As we saw with Gus and Melanie, children with Difficult temperaments end up with more problems than do their Easy siblings because their temperaments are stressful to their parents; they elicit more unpleasant responses, such as criticism or anger, to which in turn they are temperamentally more sensitive than other kids. These children may require more patience and understanding than many parents can give, especially if the parents are immature, inflexible, disordered, mentally ill, or overwhelmed by stress and conflict. When these kids try the patience of parents who lack internal controls, abuse often results.

For every developing child, the key to whether his or her inborn temperament will work well within the family or the larger environment is what temperament researchers call *goodness of fit*. Does the baby's individual temperament fit harmoniously into his or her family? Can the growing child, with his or her innate abilities, wants, and behaviors, and the family or social environment meet each other's needs and demands? When the parents, teachers, or culture repeatedly asks more of a child than he or she can give at a particular time, the stress on the child may begin to distort the way his or her personality develops.

DIFFICULT ADVANTAGES

Every temperament provides advantages and disadvantages, depending on the environment. If the fit is good, it can enhance strengths and help overcome vulnerabilities. Even the Difficult temperament has significant advantages, depending on what kind of family the Difficult Child is born into. For instance, it appears that children with Difficult temperaments tend to develop higher IQs than do Easy Children by age five *if* they come from middle- or upper-class families with excellent verbal skills. Difficult temperament is an advantage intellectually in these families because parents from higher educational and economic backgrounds tend to talk, communicate, and interact more with these demanding children in their efforts to get them to adapt better. This added stimulation promotes intellectual development.

An even more dramatic example of how a child's innate temperament can affect his or her destiny comes from the Masai tribe in East Africa. Dutch psychiatrist Marten deVries conducted a study among the Masai people in 1974 during a severe drought that resulted in high infant mortality. DeVries hypothesized that the risk of death would be higher among Difficult infants than among Easy ones. To his surprise, the reverse proved true. The Difficult infants tended to be survivors—perhaps because, as deVries discovered, in the Masai tribe feeding was on a demand basis: An infant was fed only when he or she fussed and insisted. Also, the Masai, a warrior tribe, admire aggressive behavior. The infant with a Difficult temperament tended to be more aggressive and demanding than the even-tempered, good-natured children and thus obtained more of what little food there was.

THE POORNESS OF FIT

Most children develop resilient personalities that carry them through even the worst stresses and abuses in childhood without developing psychiatric disorders then or later. Experience toughens them, but it doesn't distort them. While the Difficult Child is perhaps most at risk, any child can develop a behavior problem from the excessive stresses that result from poorness of fit. A very outgoing, adventurous family may repeatedly push and demand too much from a sweet, quiet, passive, stay-close-to-home child. A quiet, careful, stay-at-home family may unnecessarily restrict forward, adventurous behaviors in a very active, outgoing child. A sweet, happy, loving baby may be born to a very depressed mother who can't give the baby the rewarding feedback that healthy personality development requires. An easily distracted child may develop a problem if his or her parents insist that he or she concentrate for long periods without a break.

Although the parents of a child with problems may think the child's temperament is at fault, the difficulty lies in the nature of the match between family and child.

PROTECTIVE ENVIRONMENTS

Personality disorders likely result from a combination of inborn biological predispositions and external life stresses. A good fit may serve to protect a "genetically loaded" child from certain life experiences to which he or she may be inordinately susceptible. For example, children who go on to develop Borderline personality disorder may have inherited a biologic vulnerability to mood-regulation and/or impulse-control problems. In cases where they react with extremes of mood, especially depression, this tendency may make them oversensitive to real and imagined losses.

If the parents are nurturing and sensitive to the child's needs, they will take special care to help the child deal with separations and losses before the onset of troubled behavior. For example, the birth of a sibling can be stressful for most kids, but for intense, moody little Tara, age three, her baby sister's appearance on the scene spelled disaster. To Tara, her parents' attention to the new baby meant that they had abandoned her forever. Most children eventually weather this storm with few untoward effects on the course of their lives. Vulnerable kids like Tara, though, with each successive crisis may begin to develop a pattern of being unable to cope with disappointment and loss. Through intense clinging, sulking, and tantrums they may try to manipulate their parents and teachers into paying constant attention to them, so that they can avoid the devastating inner collapse that comes from feeling lost and rejected.

Fortunately for Tara, her grandmother and aunt perceived what a hard time she was having and pointed it out to Tara's preoccupied mother. Tara's parents both reached out to their firstborn and made sure to provide Tara with much continual love and reassurance.

In another case, a little boy named Justin was adopted at three months by a family who knew that Justin's biological mother suffered from schizophrenia. Children of schizophrenics appear to be at increased risk of either schizophrenia or Schizotypal personality disorder. Always rather timid, as Justin grew up he became increasingly shy. He began to avoid playing with other kids, preferring to stay by himself in his room, playing his flute. Seeing these patterns unfold, his adoptive parents made sure to prevent Justin's withdrawal. They gently kept him involved in nonstressful activities with other children. Justin is now in college. He's an interesting, unusual person with a love of the occult and a real talent for music—an Idiosyncratic type for sure, but not Schizotypal, thanks, perhaps, to the goodness of fit with his adoptive family.

TIPS FOR PARENTS

Do not try to treat all your children identically. Accept and respect each child's individuality. Recognize that his or her temperament is your child's fundamental inborn style and that he or she may have special

temperamental needs. Objectively identify the child's strengths and vulnerabilities, and support his or her positive qualities and individual
nature.

Do not blame your child or yourself if he or she does not meet your
expectations. Above all, do not fight your child's inborn temperamental
qualities and do not punish him or her for having difficulties. Keep in
mind that your child's temperamental difficulties do not in themselves
mean that he or she is destined for trouble later in life—unless you get
into a vicious cycle of negative reactions to each other.

A child with temperamental difficulties needs strong, loving management so that he or she can learn good coping skills. For a straightforward approach to dealing with a child with temperamental difficulties,
see *The Difficult Child,* by Stanley Turecki, M.D., with Leslie Tonner.
Turecki and Tonner point out that children with Difficult temperaments
can turn out to be highly creative, unusual, even exceptional people—
like Winston Churchill, for example.

THE SPECIAL IMPORTANCE OF THE FIRST FEW YEARS

A child's earliest life experiences are believed by many mental health
theorists and clinicians to exert the greatest determining influence on his
or her future personality style. Especially through our relationships
with our parents, we form our fundamental expectations of others and
of ourselves. We learn styles of relating to others and to the world in
general. These patterns persist through life within our personality
styles.

Controversy exists as to whether there are critical periods in personality development when certain experiences have more of an impact,
and if so, exactly when these periods occur. Certainly, classical theories
of development, such as those of Sigmund Freud, Erik Erikson, and
Margaret Mahler, would suggest that there are indeed critical phases.
Whether or not they hold with these theories, most mental health practitioners would probably agree that early adverse experiences can create
a vulnerability to personality problems and disorders in later years.
Probably a single traumatic experience is not so influential in shaping
someone's personality as clinicians used to think. Rather, long-term
patterns of adversity to which the developing child must continually
adjust exert a more damaging influence.

Drs. Thomas and Chess found that divorce or death of a parent did
not predict adult personality problems among their subjects, much to
the surprise of many child-development specialists. But conflict between
the parents did. If by the child's third year there was conflict and dis-

cord between the parents—in their attitudes toward each other as well as over how to handle the child—a troubled adulthood was indeed more likely to occur. Other investigators have expanded on this finding and determined that children at highest risk are those who in early life have to endure parents who do not agree with each other, who do not make their expectations clear, who lack firmness, and who are inconsistent in their demands. The nature of the personality problem the individual ends up with, from extremes of various styles to a personality disorder, may involve the impact of these early experiences on individual temperament and genetic vulnerability.

Although children are born hard-wired to respond to the environment in certain ways, that does not mean they are unalterably programmed to repeat set patterns throughout their lives. One can learn to direct or even overcome inherited tendencies (about which more in chapter 19). What else could account for the finding that identical twins reared apart are even *more* alike in personality than identical twins who grow up in the same home? Parents of twins so often try to teach them to go in separate directions and be different from each other. And Jerome Kagan's studies of inhibited and uninhibited children have shown that even though overly reactive physiology is inherited, more than a third of the children with this distinctive biological style are not extremely fearful by the time they're two. Kagan found that the parents' handling of the child influenced which of these reactive children would become inhibited. "A nurturing parent who consistently protected her high reactive infant from all minor stress made it more rather than less difficult for that child to control an initial urge to retreat from strangers and unfamiliar events. Equally accepting mothers who set firm limits for their children, making mundane age-appropriate demands for cleanliness or conformity, helped their high reactive infants overcome their fearfulness," reported Kagan and Arcus.

GENES, BIOLOGY, EXPERIENCE, AND PERSONALITY THROUGHOUT THE LIFE CYCLE

You are who you are by the time you exit your childhood—yet experience and biology continually mold and modify you, building on what has gone before and sometimes pointing you in new directions. Diseases and medical conditions (such as Alzheimer's, stroke, endocrine illnesses, brain tumors or injuries, drug abuse, or poisoning) can sometimes alter long-established personality patterns, usually in an unfortunate direction. But barring such illness or injury, physiologically the brain remains adaptable throughout the aging process, capable of reacting with the environment to form new connections among brain cells and to alter old ones. Indeed, according to neuroscientists, the potential ability of brain cells to adapt and to change may never deteriorate throughout your entire life cycle.

The process of aging may even modify your personality in a rather pleasant direction. Researchers have determined that the functioning of the tiny locus coeruleus, the brain's apparent "anxiety engine," begins to deteriorate after age forty—which is perhaps why most people seem naturally to mellow as they reach middle age.

Adaptation may come easily or with difficulty, but genetically one's pattern of responses carries with it always the built-in potential for expansion and change.

CHAPTER 19

Strategies for Change

FINDING THE RIGHT HELP

Sometimes life changes you. Many young men and women have gone to war and come back different, their values and attitudes rearranged for them the hard way. Sometimes education will provide the impetus for change. Many women began efforts to reshape their personalities as the Women's Movement taught them to question traditional views of women's roles. Rolling up your sleeves and getting to work on yourself with a psychotherapist is another way to change your personality.

Changes in personality do not come about overnight. For the Vietnam vets who were changed by their experience, for example, it took months of war horrors to set them on a changed life path. Women who are attempting to learn new roles and personality patterns must struggle with the attitudes and expectations that were set in motion when the doctor uttered, "It's a girl!" The work of psychotherapy may continue for months or years. Personality is an automatic pilot that guides us through our lives. To try to change it, one must learn the complex components of the system and learn to modify their arrangement—no small challenge.

FINE-TUNING THE SYSTEM

Your Personality Self-Portrait has given you a map of your own component styles, and the individual chapters have provided their descriptions and bases. This material, combined with the practical exercises, may be sufficient for you to make some adjustments in your personality system, or at least to smooth some of your rough edges. For example, if you know that you sometimes go too far out of your way for other people in your Self-Sacrificing manner, you can learn to catch yourself as you are about to offer too much. If your Self-Confident style sometimes makes you insensitive to other people's needs, you can practice paying more attention to them.

Having become aware of your style's characteristic trouble spots, you may now be able to learn better habits. Day-in, day-out habits are a big part of personality styles and, fortunately, with sufficient motivation habits can be changed. If you are Dramatically disorganized, for example, you might learn from a book how to get and stay organized. If you are a Leisurely procrastinator, you could sign up for a workshop on overcoming procrastination. Taking a yoga or meditation class may teach you techniques to lessen your Sensitive anxiety reactions. Assess your troublesome habits on a style-by-style basis and look for a practical way of dealing with them, as we have done in our exercises for making the most of each style.

TIME FOR AN OVERHAUL?

Changing the arrangement of styles in your overall pattern, from "deflating" some extreme styles to dealing with a potential personality disorder, will take more focused intervention. Before we consider the types of treatment you might choose, let's see whether your personality needs outside help.

LISTEN TO OTHERS

The Personality Self-Portrait does not diagnose personality disorders. How do you know if you have one? You may have identified with some or many of the personality disorders as you read about them—just as medical students are sure they have every disease described in their textbooks. Fulfilling some of the criteria for a personality disorder does not a diagnosis make. Establishing the correct personality disorder diagnosis is a serious and complicated undertaking even for a psychiatrist. Ironically, many of the individuals who suffer from a personality disorder are the last ones to realize it. They do not believe that they have any problem at all. They may think that if it weren't for the shabby or unreasonable way others treat them they'd be just fine, or that the problem is fate, or life, or the lousy human race. Blaming others, the environment, or "the system" for one's difficulties or experiences in life or failing to comprehend the nature or consequences of one's behavior may be signs of a disordered pattern. If people are always telling you they have problems with you or your behavior, try to open up to what they are saying. Consider whether you really do have some big troubles in your personality pattern that you could do something about.

USING YOUR PERSONALITY SELF-PORTRAIT TO ASSESS YOUR PROBLEMS

You can use your Personality Self-Portrait to assess the nature and the degree of the troubles you encounter in your life. Then, if you wish, consult a mental health professional and let him or her establish the correct diagnosis. Each style not only has minor wrinkles but also potential problem areas in one or more of the domains.

KEY DOMAINS

Look first at the key domains for your component styles and see how much trouble or unhappiness your style causes you. For example, if you are primarily Conscientious, do you work so much that you have no social life? At work, do you get so bogged down in the details that you never finish a project or are satisfied with the results? Is your marriage in trouble because you can't relax and stop worrying or let people do things their own way? With an Idiosyncratic style, do you find that you are always seeking and never finding in your spiritual life as well as in your relationships? How frustrating is it for you that people seem never to take seriously what's important to you and don't genuinely listen to what you have to say? Do you find yourself talking more to yourself than to other people? If you are Devoted, do you find that you simply can't make decisions or assert yourself and that you depend on others to bolster your poor self-image? If you are a primarily Self-Sacrificing person, do you get stuck in relationships in which you are repeatedly used and taken advantage of, and have you run into a dead end in your career? If Serious is among your top styles, are you unable to experience pleasure? Are you sure that nothing is ever going to work out for you in any area of your life? Do you work and work and work to no apparent avail? Do you see yourself as worthless and guilty?

LOVE AND WORK

After you have assessed your key domains, consider the effect your personality patterns have had on the two key domains of human life:

Love (Relationships) and Work. Are you continually frustrated, unhappy, unfulfilled, operating far below your potential, or unable to function at all in these essential areas? Are you sad and lonely? Frightened of asserting yourself? Unable to express or experience appropriate feelings? Are your creative powers trapped inside you, unable to come forth? Most important, do you find yourself repeating the same patterns time after time: the same old miseries in your love life, the same old problems at work? Have you tried to change some of these repetitive patterns yourself, to no avail?

THAT GRAY AREA

Even for clinicians, it is hard to pinpoint where style ends and disorder begins. If you find that your life pathway is more like a rut that you only dig deeper the harder you try to get out, or if you can't deal with stress or adjust to change and to new demands of each stage of life, psychotherapy may be of benefit whether you have a full-blown disorder or a problem associated with a personality style. Therapy can help you become more aware of self-defeating personality patterns and behaviors. It can open your eyes to the effect you have on others and why they respond to you as they do.

With the help of a professional, you may accomplish enormous changes in your personality—but even the smallest changes can have a large impact on the course or the quality of your life and your relationships. Hannah W. went into psychoanalysis when she was sixty-three. Although the process was only briefly under way when Hannah's husband retired and they decided to move away, Hannah's two children were amazed at how much easier she was to deal with. Hannah had always been fiercely manipulative, and her son and daughter had had to be on guard with her every minute. But after slightly more than a year in treatment, Hannah was able to communicate her needs more genuinely. For the first time in their lives, her children could actually *talk* to her. For her part, Hannah said she felt much more hopeful about moving into the last phase of her life. She wasn't so worried that her children were going to abandon her.

SYMPTOMS

Finally, consider whether you experience any specific symptoms of mental distress that may be associated with particular domains. Emotionally, do you feel extremely anxious, panicky, anguished, chronically unhappy, or seriously depressed? Do you find you can't experience pleasure—or any feelings at all? Do your moods shift frequently? Do you feel hopeless about your life? Do you think about killing yourself? Do you carry a burden of rage around inside you? Do you have a lot of trouble controlling your temper?

Many behaviors in addition to anger can be hard to control. Do you have real trouble controlling your impulses to eat (or to diet), to spend, to hurt people, to take dangerous risks, to gamble, to drink, to have sex, to abuse drugs?

In the Self and the Real World domains, do you sometimes think or feel that you don't really exist, that you have no identity, that you are utterly worthless, that you are a million miles away from everyone else, or that you are detached from your own body? Do you think people talk about you behind your back? Do you hear voices that no one else hears?

Whether they are associated with a crisis in your life or describe the way you often feel, each of these symptoms is sufficient in itself to warrant a consultation with a mental health professional, who will help you or refer you for the appropriate type of treatment.

TREATMENT

In the style chapters, we have already mentioned the most common treatment approaches for each personality disorder. Here we will provide a brief overview of what those treatments are, including the basic categories of psychotherapy practiced by psychiatrists and other mental health professionals. Although we discuss each of these categories of treatment separately, very often a therapist will combine many different approaches to achieve the optimal treatment for his or her patients.

MENTAL HEALTH PROFESSIONALS: WHO'S WHO

Psychiatrists are medical doctors who have completed four years of medical school and three or more years of psychiatric residency in a hospital setting. They are the only mental health professionals who are licensed to prescribe medication. Many psychiatrists prescribe medication and practice psychotherapy, although some (*psychopharmacologists*) specialize in medication only.

Clinical psychologists have earned a Ph.D., Psy.D., or Ed.D. in psychology or educational psychology, which usually takes about four years, after which they serve an internship year. During their training they learn to treat patients while being supervised closely by senior clinical psychologists. Clinical psychologists practice psychotherapy but do not prescribe medication.

Social workers have earned a master's (M.S.W.) or doctorate (D.S.W.) in a two- or four-year program at a graduate school of social work. Those who practice psychotherapy may have specialized in psychiatric social work. Their education consists of classwork and work in the field.

Other practitioners you might encounter include nurses (R.N.s) and pastoral or other types of counselors, some of whom may have master's degrees in psychology or education.

Psychoanalysts may be psychiatrists, psychologists, or social workers, who undergo rigorous training in the theories and techniques of this type of psychotherapy (see below) after they have completed their professional degrees. During the three to seven or more years they may spend training at a psychoanalytic institute, candidates must undergo their own psychoanalysis and be closely supervised as they treat their own patients.

Be aware that in many states, any untrained individual can practice psychotherapy and claim to be a mental health professional or psychotherapist. Be sure that the person you consult has appropriate credentials, is well trained, comes highly recommended, and has a license to practice, should your state require one.

Although psychiatrists are the only mental health professionals who can legally prescribe medication, all the foregoing professional categories can practice psychotherapy, regardless of what that therapy is. Some types of psychotherapy require specific training in addition to the individual's professional degree, however.

PSYCHODYNAMIC PSYCHOTHERAPIES

This broad category includes psychoanalysis and psychoanalytic psychotherapies, which are the traditional treatment of choice for working with longtime personality problems. Psychoanalysts and psychoanalytically oriented therapists hold that unconscious conflicts and beliefs influence our everyday behavior, and they work with patients to uncover these ideas and to reveal their influence on personality functioning. They explore the patient's childhood and show how conflicts from early relationships, some long forgotten, influence current behavior. They work with their patients to help replace immature patterns with adaptive, fulfilling, mature styles of functioning that will enable them to get more out of their lives.

In *psychoanalysis* the patient meets with the analyst three to five times a week for a period of years. The process is something like peeling an onion layer by layer, slowly bringing into focus the unconscious conflicts and assumptions hidden beneath. The patient lies on a couch facing away from the analyst, in order to minimize any distractions and make it easier to say whatever comes to mind (free association). The analyst does not direct the patient but instead makes interpretations of what the patient is saying, including dreams, in light of those underlying unconscious ideas as they begin to become clearer. Believing strongly that the past repeats itself in all present relationships, psychoanalysts emphasize the details of how the patient relates to and feels about the analyst, who all the while attempts to remain neutral and objective. Patients bring unconscious expectations and distortions to the relationship with the analyst, a phenomenon referred to as transference. The psychoanalytic relationship will mirror the conflicts the patient experienced with his or her parents, around which the patient's personality took shape. By gradually understanding these unconsciously distorted reactions to the analyst, the patient understands and works through those early conflicts, leading to improved human relationships and greater capacity for change.

The duration of psychoanalysis, the frequency of sessions, the expense (it's easier on the pocketbook at psychoanalytic training institutes), and its lack of directive structure make it a relatively uncommon form of treatment and not appropriate for everyone. While it can be an excellent approach for people who have relationship problems that result from their personality difficulties, in addition to time and money it requires strong motivation, a keen interest in one's own psychology, intelligence, and willingness to deal with powerful, often painful feelings and reactions.

Psychoanalysis aims to restructure personality and to change longtime patterns rather than to tackle individual problems, so it may be frustrating for individuals who want to see specific improvements quickly. It is usually not the treatment of choice for a person in crisis. Many psychoanalysts will work with patients using other techniques (sometimes including medication) until they are ready and willing to enter full-blown psychoanalysis. Many psychoanalysts also practice psychoanalytic psychotherapy.

Psychoanalytic psychotherapy is based on many of the same principles as psychoanalysis, but the therapist is generally more active, often offering a variety of techniques from support to medication (if the therapist is an M.D.), to crisis intervention and specific problem solving, depending on the needs of the patient. This is probably the most common category of psychotherapeutic treatment practiced in the United States today. The therapist need not be trained in psychoanalysis, although many are. Patient and therapist commonly meet one to three times a week individually and/or in a group setting with other patients, from a fixed period of months with a preset cut-off date (brief or time-limited psychotherapy) to an open-ended period of years. As in psychoanalysis, the best candidates for analytically oriented therapy are those who are capable of and interested in self-exploration and who can tolerate some unpleasant feelings that such "exploratory surgery" often brings up. The goals of treatment are determined by the patient and therapist together.

SUPPORTIVE THERAPY

The supportive psychotherapist is someone who is there to help you in a very immediate way—not to dig around in your psyche. These practitioners offer a kind ear, support, reassurance, advice, practical problem solving (such as learning social skills), and a safe place to unload some painful feelings. Supportive psychotherapy is sometimes carried out in conjunction with medication. This type of treatment is for people who are in crisis and who are not emotionally prepared to explore the issues more deeply, who are not psychologically minded, or for individuals whose personality structures may be too fragile to benefit from uncovering deeper conflicts. Some practitioners will provide supportive therapy as long as it is needed and then proceed to deeper work. Others are trained only to work in this way and may refer patients to other therapists for psychodynamic work.

BEHAVIOR THERAPY

Practitioners of this type of therapy train you how to change or control particular problem behaviors. They do not work with you to discover what may lie behind these behaviors. In weeks to months, they teach specific, directive techniques for overcoming anxiety, tension, phobias, stuttering, marital problems, eating disorders, sexual problems, compulsive gambling, drug abuse, smoking, and so on. Behavior therapy will not alter a personality pattern, but it can be a good way of dealing with some of the problems that can plague certain personality styles (and especially their concomitant disorders)—among them Mercurial food problems, Sensitive social anxiety, Adventurous/Mercurial/Idiosyncratic drug problems, and Conscientious/Vigilant tension. You have to follow orders in behavior therapy, since its techniques are very specific and require practice.

Behavior therapy is often practiced in conjunction with cognitive therapy, when it is called cognitive-behavior therapy.

COGNITIVE THERAPY

According to cognitive therapists, what you think determines how you feel and act. For example, if you think that you are worthless and are going to fail, you will feel depressed, and you won't try very hard to succeed. Developed originally as a short-term treatment for depression, cognitive therapy has now been extended to many other conditions, including personality disorders. Cognitive therapists conceptualize personality disorders as a characteristic set of behaviors, beliefs, feelings, and attitudes. During therapy sessions they teach patients to identify dysfunctional thinking patterns and the behaviors and emotions that ensue. For example, since Dependent people think that they can't survive on their own, they become completely reliant on others. Cognitive therapists then proceed to teach patients how to replace these basic, life-distorting assumptions with more realistic ones that will lead to better, more flexible functioning. Patients also learn techniques for dealing with symptoms, such as depression, and self-defeating behaviors, such as binge eating.

Like behavior therapy, with which it is often combined (cognitive-behavior therapy), cognitive therapy does not dwell on the past, and it requires a lot of homework and practice.

FAMILY, MARITAL, AND GROUP THERAPY

In family and marital therapy, practitioners treat the troubled family unit rather than just an individual member. Family therapists believe that the family is an interdependent system and that emotional problems or symptoms in any individual develop within the context of the whole family. Family and marital therapy provide an opportunity to observe and to change the way family members interact with one another.

In group therapy, people share their problems with a number of others and benefit from the kind of mutual problem solving that can be done only in a group. Very often the relationship problems for which individuals have come for help will manifest themselves in the group, giving patients the opportunity to get feedback as to how they relate to and affect others. There are many approaches to group therapy, corresponding to the categories of treatment we have discussed thus far. There are also many self-help groups such as Alcoholics Anonymous and other Twelve Step organizations, which have helped millions of people worldwide to get control of their lives.

EXPERIENTIAL THERAPIES

Hundreds of approaches constitute this very broad category of treatments, group encounters, and workshops that have proliferated since the 1950s. They emphasize emotional release, learning mind control, expanding consciousness, taking responsibility for actions and behaviors, becoming aware of psychological and physiological needs, perhaps even investigating "past lives." Generally their goals are the achievement of personal growth, self-actualization, and/or spiritual fulfillment.

These myriad approaches tend to reject intellectual self-understanding, scientific method, and diagnostic categories. Frequently experiential therapies take place partially or entirely in a group setting. Many of the experiential therapies are associated with the New Age and/or the human potential movement.

These unorthodox therapies may seem at odds with the more traditional therapeutic approaches; indeed, they developed in part out of the existentialist disillusionment with the alienating science and technology of our times. Nonetheless, experiential techniques, including meditation, role playing, massage, and encounter groups, may be used or recommended by clinicians from more orthodox backgrounds in their eclectic practices of psychotherapy.

While some of these experiential approaches achieve great popularity and then fade from view, they may nonetheless be emotionally freeing, stimulating, moving, or at least enjoyable experiences for many people. Dramatic, Mercurial, and Idiosyncratic individuals may find themselves emotionally suited to some of these workshops and seminars. Seriously troubled people, however, are best served by well-trained clinicians using techniques derived from an established body of research and accumulated clinical knowledge.

PHARMACOTHERAPY

Pills for personality? It makes sense, considering that at least some personality disorders may develop from inherited disturbances in biological functioning that result in painful, disruptive symptoms.

In contemporary psychiatric practice, medication is an important part of treating the devastating mental anguish of Axis I disorders (chapter 2) and their symptoms, to which many individuals with various personality disorders may be highly vulnerable—including major depression, manic-depression, severe anxiety and panic, obsessive-compulsive disorder, bulimia, and psychotic episodes. Modern medications are highly effective in treating many of these biologically driven disorders, with far fewer side effects than used to be true of psychoactive medications. Moreover, many psychiatrists are becoming increasingly expert in the creative use of such medications.

While medication is no "cure" for a personality disorder (see our discussion of the *Listening to Prozac* controversy in chapter 17, on p. 383), properly prescribed and supervised, it can substantially relieve or eliminate some of the severe neurologically based disturbances in functioning that torment many sufferers. Once these individuals regain their balance, they will be able to work on the personality patterns that have developed from or along with their painful inner experiences.

Although any medical doctor can prescribe psychiatric medication, psychiatrists are specifically trained in their use. Some psychiatrists will refer patients with complicated medication requirements to psychopharmacologists (psychiatrists who specialize in drug treatment).

THEN AGAIN, MAYBE YOU'RE FINE THE WAY YOU ARE

So many people want to change themselves. Before you consider psychiatric or psychological intervention to alter the essential shape of your personality pattern, you might ask yourself your reasons for wanting to change it.

Take a look at your Personality Self-Portrait. Compare it with those of others in your life. The Personality Self-Portrait shows you that you resemble other people in fundamental human ways and differ from them along the same dimensions. Notice that in overall shape, each Self-Portrait you observe is different. The intensity and configuration of the fourteen personality styles in your Self-Portrait are yours alone.

Throughout these pages we have recommended ways you can make many changes in your personality in order to make the most of yourself. We have also said that individual personality is a kind of fate. Changes or no changes, you are fated to be yourself—short of the ideal, full of your own peculiarities and blemishes, not the perfect companion or parent or leader or helper. Not the worst, either. You do things the way you do them. He does things the way he does them. She does them still another way. Most of the time, that's just fine.

Your brain cells and your psyche are at all times capable of learning to accept and appreciate yourself and others for the differences in the ways we all think, feel, and behave. For some of you, that may be the single greatest adjustment your personality really needs.

Two Self-Portraits

GRAPH INTERPRETATIONS

Although the fourteen personality styles are universal and are represented in every person to a greater or lesser degree, every human being is unique in overall personality pattern. To recognize this individuality when interpreting any Personality Self-Portrait graph, it is important to take into account not only which styles dominate but also how they influence one another. The following two graphs and their interpretations illustrate how the expression of each style is shaped by others in the pattern—and how they all work together to create a unique person.

LEONARD F.

Leonard F., Ph.D., at 43 has become the chairman of the biology department at a medium-sized Midwestern university. With the Conscientious style exerting the strongest influence on his personality, he finds his greatest meaning in life through his work, at which he is known for his typically Conscientious thoroughness. Although highly Conscientious individuals can be tedious grinds who get so bogged down in details that they lose sight of what they are trying to accomplish in their careers, Leonard's personality is almost as strong in the ambitious, competitive, I-deserve-success Self-Confident style. His strength in Aggressive style, which is noted for its determination to achieve power, further insures Leonard's political success and position of command.

Indeed, he's been the department star since his first years there. Just out of graduate school, his research and publications garnered him a small reputation and gave a hint of great things to come. Combined

PERSONALITY SELF-PORTRAIT GRAPH

A	B	C	D	E	F	G	H	I	J	K	L	M	N
14	14	18	16	18	16	18	14	16	16	14	16	16	14
13	13	17	15	17	15	17	13	15	15	13	15	15	13
12	12	16	14	16	14	16	12	14	14	12	14	14	12
		15	13	15	13	15		13	(13)		13	13	
11	11	14		14		14	11		12	11	12	12	11
		13	12	13	12	(13)		12					
10	10		11		11	12	10	11	11	10	11	11	10
		12		12		11							
9	9	11	10	11	10		9	10	10	9	10	10	9
		10	9	10	9	10	8	9	9	8	9	9	8
8	8												
7	7	9	8	9	8	9	7	8	8	(7)	(8)	(8)	7
6	6	8	7	8	(7)	8	6	7	7	6	7	7	6
		7		7	6	7		6	6		6	6	
(5)	5		(6)	6		(5)				5			5
		(6)	5		6		4	5	5		5	5	
4	(4)	5		(5)	5	5				4	4	4	4
		4	4	4	4	4	3	4	4				3
3	3	3	3	3	3			(3)	3	3	3	3	(2)
2	2	2	2	2	2	2	2	2	2	2	2	2	
1	1	1	1	1	1	1	1	1	1	1	1	1	1
0	0	0	0	0	0	0	0	0	0	0	0	0	0
VIGILANT	SOLITARY	IDIOSYNCRATIC	ADVENTUROUS	MERCURIAL	DRAMATIC	SELF-CONFIDENT	SENSITIVE	DEVOTED	CONSCIENTIOUS	LEISURELY	AGGRESSIVE	SELF-SACRIFICING	SERIOUS
A	B	C	D	E	F	G	H	I	J	K	L	M	N

Leonard F., 43, college professor

with his apparent potential and his obvious ambition, his extroverted, charismatic Self-Confident personality made him a force to be reckoned with. Leonard's belief in himself as well as his comfort and assurance when all eyes are on him are typically Self-Confident traits that have worked well in this academic setting. His office, his laboratory, his classes—everywhere he goes he is pursued by students and colleagues who wish a word with the Great Professor.

His immense Self-Confident appeal to others extends equally into his personal life—indeed, it may go too far, his wife, Gwen, believes, when she is honest with herself about his numerous affairs. Married for twenty-one years and the father of two teenage sons, Leonard has not been the model husband, especially for the last ten years. Although he Conscientiously provides very well for his family and, equally typical of the Conscientious style, feels guilty for having affairs, he is so strong in the Self-Confident style that he understands his own needs and feelings far better than anyone else's, including Gwen's. His Leisurely and Aggressive tendencies further underscore his need to be in charge of his own life and his reluctance, even outright refusal, to compromise in matters that are important to him. The Leisurely style in Leonard's pattern modifies the usual Conscientious tendency to work hard at everything. Leisurely people can be hard workers, but they tend to avoid chores that they don't consider their responsibility, which means that Leonard has never been one to help with the housework or, when the kids were young, the childcare.

Especially in the early years of their marriage, Leonard appreciated Gwen's typically Devoted–Self-Sacrificing skill at taking care of him, the house, and their children. But he long ago grew bored with her lack of self-direction—which at the same time he Aggressively had never encouraged her to express. Still, strongly Conscientious as he is, deep down he thinks it's "wrong" to divorce, that he "should" be a better husband; and even deeper down he loves his wife, which (like very Conscientious people in general, who have difficulty expressing their feelings for others) he has never been able to tell her.

Although his virility has always been a matter of great pride to Leonard (typically for those with strong Self-Confident and Aggressive styles), Leonard has always found it difficult to enjoy sex with his wife. At present they almost never sleep together. Gwen has always been reluctant to ask for attention—sexual or otherwise. Much of what drew them together as a couple was her worshipful attention to her brilliant young husband. Their lives have always centered around him and his career, with her in the supportive role. Ironically, had she been more assertive sexually she would probably have kept his interest—after the "conquest," intensely Self-Confident people often need to be reminded that the other person still exists.

Yet in certain situations Leonard will put others' needs on an equal footing to his own. His personality has a relatively strong Self-Sacrificing trend. Although the Self-Confident style modifies this Self-Sacrificing tendency, toward his sons in particular Leonard has been able to express his helping, giving, and accepting side. The boys are both bright scientists-to-be, which makes it easy for Leonard to go out of his way for them. He Conscientiously managed his limited academic salary so well that he was able to put away sufficient funds to ensure their educations. Altruism is highly associated with Self-Sacrificing style, and over the years Leonard has given money and worked on many scientific committees on behalf of people with AIDS.

Self-Sacrificing style also helps to explain a mystery in Leonard's career. Leonard has always wanted to be affiliated with a more prestigious university, and his work has often bordered on brilliance. With Leonard's Conscientious ability for tireless work, and his Self-Confident ambition and Aggressive drive for power—why has he remained at a second-rate college for his entire career? The answer is that he has never pushed himself to publish enough to gain the nationwide recognition he would need to move on. While he clearly possesses great ability, he also has a Self-Sacrificing reluctance to advance as high as he might go.

It is a time of challenge for Leonard, however. His younger son is soon to leave home, which is likely to trigger a marital crisis for him and Gwen. Alone with her for the first time in nineteen years, and facing middle and older age, he will probably not be able to avoid the question of what he and Gwen mean to each other. Despite his apparent independence and self-assurance, it is characteristic of Conscientious, Self-Confident, and even Aggressive people to need and depend on their mates. Leonard cares deeply about what Gwen thinks of him, feelings a crisis could well bring to the surface. He does not understand that he has these feelings or that he has a Self-Confident tendency to flee from intimacy. But soon he may be forced to resolve these conflicts and make choices to stay with and strengthen the marriage, eliminating the affairs, or to give up on one another. Should Gwen decide to leave him —which, typical of Self-Confident types, it has not occurred to Leonard that she might do—he would take it very hard indeed. As Conscientious, Self-Confident, and Aggressive as he is, Leonard needs to feel that he is controlling his destiny.

Similarly, a career crisis is waiting in the wings. Leonard is approaching the age when people begin to realize their greatest career successes.

It is work especially through which he seeks his meaning, and unless he wants to live out the rest of his life feeling that he failed to meet his own high standards, he will have to face the fact that his reluctance to publish has kept him back.

Leonard, in other words, is ripe for a mid-life crisis. As for so many others at his time of life, turmoil and disruption are what he needs to jar him out of the ruts he has dug for himself and to challenge the resilience inherent in his personality. Given that three of his leading styles—Conscientious, Self-Confident, and Aggressive—are known for their determination, and Conscientious types can't resist a problem to be solved once they acknowledge it—it is likely that Leonard will have the strength to meet these challenges.

CASSIE R.

Thirty-two-year-old Cassie is fat—but only at first appearance. She's always been overweight—now close to forty pounds above what her five-foot-four-inch frame might be expected to carry. But as soon as people get to know her, they don't notice it anymore. Cassie's beautiful. The way she carries herself, dresses, and projects a fiery sensuality has much to do with the dominance of the passionate, flamboyant Dramatic style in her personality. She's thoroughly at home in her body, very desirable, and like most powerfully Dramatic people, she is very aware of her effect on other people, delighted to cast a spell over new admirers.

Her lack of self-consciousness about her weight—rare in a thin-is-beautiful culture—has also to do with the complete absence of the Sensitive style in her personality. Sensitive style imparts a reticence around others, particularly at first meeting—but Cassie has never worried about what others might think, either about how she looks or the way she leads her life. Indeed, other people make her life worth living.

Cassie writes scripts for daytime soap operas—a job well-suited to her personality pattern. Dramatic is a romantic style, with a gift for emotional fantasy; and Mercurial brings with it a yearning for intense romantic attachment as well as an ability unmatched by other styles to throw oneself into other identities and ways of being. All this adds up to Cassie's gift for creating authentic characters and embroiling them in the melodramatic love triangles that are the delight of daytime soap opera audiences.

Much money can be made writing for the soaps by those who are good and also ambitious. Cassie's very good; with her moderate degree

PERSONALITY SELF-PORTRAIT GRAPH

Col	Trait	Score
A	VIGILANT	3
B	SOLITARY	3
C	IDIOSYNCRATIC	8
D	ADVENTUROUS	8
E	MERCURIAL	11
F	DRAMATIC	12
G	SELF-CONFIDENT	6
H	SENSITIVE	1
I	DEVOTED	5
J	CONSCIENTIOUS	7
K	LEISURELY	9
L	AGGRESSIVE	2
M	SELF-SACRIFICING	3
N	SERIOUS	4

Cassie R., 32, scriptwriter

of Conscientious style to temper the Dramatic disorganization, she can work hard and create a finished product. But rich and wildly successful on her own behalf she's not (her husband is)—largely because of the strong Leisurely influence on her pattern. Although the producers have offered her lucrative contracts, Cassie refuses to "spoil the quality of my life by working too hard." She does one script a month rather than the one a week that those on the "fast track" are expected to deliver. What is most important to strongly Leisurely people is that they be free to pursue their fundamental pleasures in life. Leisurely types like Cassie live by society's rules—she wants to work (although she procrastinates often for days on end before finally getting down to it), but she doesn't want, by her definition, to overwork. Also, like many strongly Dramatic people, Cassie is not determinedly goal-directed. Without much of the ambitious, single-minded personality styles in her pattern—such as the Self-Confident and the Aggressive—Cassie's quite content to do her own thing.

In addition, two unconventional styles, the Idiosyncratic and the Adventurous, influence Cassie to make her own rules. She possesses an Adventurous wanderlust, and between her marriages and before the birth of her daughter she would often just pick up and go when the spirit moved her—throw a bunch of clothes in a suitcase and head for the airport. Having a child has helped tame this side of her. Previously Cassie was far more willing to take risks, not only to travel on a whim but also to experiment with drugs. Dramatic, Mercurial, and Adventurous styles are all characterized by spontaneity and appetite. When they are all strongly represented in one individual, as with Cassie, problems with self-control are difficult to avoid. In the past, many of Cassie's problems have involved her tendency to overdo. Drugs, motorcycles, calories, sexual partners. . . .

What saved her from the potential consequences of going to extremes, even before she became a mother, was the streak of Conscientious style lurking within her personality pattern. Conscientious is a "head" style, bringing with it a powerful conscience and skill at self-control. While Cassie's much-stronger Dramatic and Mercurial tendencies lead her first to follow her heart and her urges, when she finally becomes aware that she is risking great harm (as when she first learned of AIDS and its relationship to multiple sexual partners), she is able to put on the brakes. Once Cassie became pregnant, her Conscientious side was strong enough for her to rule out endangering the health and safety of her child. Cassie has not smoked, taken drugs, or ridden her motorcycle since the day she discovered she was pregnant, now nearly three years ago.

In another important way Conscientious style saved her from the impulsive side of herself. Her second husband, Robert, a TV producer, is highly Conscientious—steady, responsible, serious, good with the necessary dry details of life (like paying the bills). It's a wonder that she ever became attracted to him—but she helps him let down his hair when he leans too far in the direction of restraint, and he enables her to remain steady and focused. Characteristic of Dramatic-Mercurial types, Cassie has a tendency to be moody, sometimes depressed, which Robert can deal with without succumbing to hopelessness himself. He accepts, respects, adores, and is excited by her, which is what her Dramatic and Mercurial sides urgently need, even though in her darker Mercurial moods she's sure he doesn't love her, since he is not as open with his feelings as she is.

Her first husband was much more like her in personality, which spelled doom. Clearly Adventurous, self-restraint was not his strong point either. He was nineteen, she eighteen, when they were married. Cassie, with her Dramatic-Mercurial mix, was focused entirely on finding love. They were both smitten with intense love and insisted on being married immediately. Neither of them had the ability to look ahead and plan. Her young husband got heavily into cocaine, was quickly out of a job and spending her waitressing money on his drug habit.

When Cassie realized the depths to which her life was sinking, she possessed the strength to bail out, although she became severely depressed afterward. She was successfully treated with medication and psychotherapy. She went back to school and continued in psychotherapy for five more years, through which she learned to channel her intense and creative personality more productively, such as into her work, rather than focusing all her energies on her love life.

Cassie and Robert's life is glittery by most people's standards—a Beverly Hills mansion, parties for the rich and famous. It all suits her flamboyant personality. Robert helps keep her on an even keel and with him she is able to experience what married love really is. Her work provides her a fulfilling outlet for her talents and emotions. Being a mother fosters her inherent Conscientious responsibility and encourages her to recognize the importance of planning for the future.

Future Dramatic-Mercurial-Adventurous risks for Cassie could be severe depression should she and Robert ever split. She may have difficulty encouraging her baby to separate from her and become independent and teaching the child the importance of limits. But age is on Cassie's side. Intense personality styles like Cassie's tend to mellow through the thirties and forties, and quite possibly her personality spent its excesses in youth. So what if she's heavy? Packing in the calories may be a risk to her health one day, but already it's begun to occur to her that she should get more exercise. "I've taken up running," she says, "—to the refrigerator!"

Chapter Notes

Introduction

page 1 This classification system: *Diagnostic and Statistical Manual of Mental Disorders, 4th edition* (Washington, D.C.: American Psychiatric Association, 1994).

page 4 In fact, as psychologist Thomas Widiger: "Deletion of Self-Defeating and Sadistic Personality Disorder Diagnoses," in W. J. Livesley, ed., *The DSM-IV Personality Disorders* (New York: The Guilford Press, in press).

page 5 I participated in: Loranger, Armand W., Virginia Lehman Susman, John M. Oldham, and Mark Russakoff, *Personality Disorder Examination (PDE): A Structured Interview for DSM-III-R Personality Disorders* (White Plains, New York: The New York Hospital–Cornell Medical Center, Westchester Division, 1985).

Chapter 2

pages 19–20 "General Diagnostic Criteria": DSM-IV, page 633.

page 20 According to the few studies: Weissman, Myrna M. "The Epidemiology of Personality Disorders: A 1990 Update." *Journal of Personality Disorders* 7 Supplement (Spring 1993), p. 6.

page 21 "Only when *personality traits*": p. 630.

page 24 "When an individual displays": Millon, Theodore, *Disorders of Personality DSM-III: Axis II* (New York: John Wiley & Sons, 1981), p. 9.

Chapter 4

page 62 Conscientious traits: Friedman, Howard S., Joan S. Tucker, Carol Tomlinson-Keasy, et al., "Does Childhood Personality Predict Longevity?" *Journal of Personality and Social Psychology* 65:1 (1993), pp. 176–85.

page 68 there is some . . . evidence: Smokler, I. A., and H. Shevrin, "Cerebral Lateralization and Personality Style." *Archives of General Psychiatry* 36 (1979), pp. 949–954.

pages 77–78 Diagnostic Criteria: DSM-IV, pp. 668–69.

page 78 Or, to cite an example: p. 669.

page 80 "the tyranny of the should": Horney, Karen, *Neurosis and Human Growth* (New York: W. W. Norton, 1950).

page 81 To cite another example: p. 670.

page 81 As the DSM-IV points out: p. 670.

page 82 In 1908: Freud, Sigmund, "Character and Anal Eroticism," in *The Standard Edition of the Complete Psychological Works,* James Strachey, ed. and trans. (London: Hogarth Press, 1957).

page 82 "To make a mistake" and "I must be perfectly in control": Beck, Aaron T., and Arthur Freeman, *Cognitive Therapy of Personality Disorders* (New York: The Guilford Press, 1990), p. 315.

page 83 Another Obsessive-Compulsive personality characteristic: Jorgensen, R. S., and B. K. Houston, "Family History of Hypertension, Personality Patterns and Cardiovascular Reactivity to Stress," *Psychosomatic Medicine* 48 (1968), pp. 102–17.

page 83 Obsessive-Compulsive persons are also: Skodol, Andrew E., and John M. Oldham, "Comorbidity of DSM-III-R Anxiety Disorders and Personality Disorders." Presented in a symposium at the Third International Congress on the Disorders of Personality, Cambridge, Massachusetts, 1993.

page 84 It is a common . . . twice as often among men: DSM-IV, p. 671.

Chapter 5

pages 98–99 Diagnostic Criteria: p. 662.

page 100 Psychiatrist Michael H. Stone: *Abnormalities of Personality* (New York: W. W. Norton, 1993), p. 268.

page 102 "Alternative beliefs": Beck, Aaron T., and Arthur Freeman, *Cognitive Therapy of Personality Disorders* (New York: The Guilford Press, 1990), p. 249.

page 103 "On the principle that": Lasch, Christopher, *The Culture of Narcissism* (New York: W. W. Norton, 1978), p. 82. He believed that: p. 101.

page 103 Regarding the influence: Kernberg, Otto F., "Narcissistic Personality Disorder," in *Psychiatry,* vol. 1, ed. Jesse O. Cavenar (Philadelphia: J. B. Lippincott Co., 1987), p. 3.

Chapter 6

pages 127–28 Diagnostic Criteria: pp. 668–69.

page 129 Notes psychiatrist Michael H. Stone: *Abnormalities of Personality* (New York: W. W. Norton, 1993), p. 343.

page 129 Cognitive treatments tackle: Beck, Aaron T., and Arthur Freeman, *Cognitive Therapy of Personality Disorders* (New York: The Guilford Press, 1990), p. 291.

page 130 The disorder is: DSM-IV, p. 667.

Chapter 7

page 148   Diagnostic Criteria: pp. 657–58.

page 150   Also, as the DSM-IV points out: p. 656.

page 150   Moreover, as the DSM-IV mentions: p. 656.

page 151   Cognitive therapy challenges: Beck, Aaron T., and Arthur Freeman, *Cognitive Therapy of Personality Disorders* (New York: The Guilford Press, 1990), p. 218.

page 152   Psychiatrists Michael Liebowitz, M.D., and Donald Klein, M.D.: Liebowitz, Michael R., and Donald F. Klein, "Hysteroid Dysphoria," *Psychiatric Clinics of North America* 2 (1979), pp. 555–75.

page 152   Many authorities believe: Beck and Freeman, p. 212.

page 152   Nevertheless, in at least one study: Lilienfeld, Scott O., Charles VanValkenburg, et al., "The Relationship of Histrionic Personality Disorder to Antisocial Personality and Somatization Disorders," *American Journal of Psychiatry* 143 (June 1986), pp. 718–22.

page 153   Thus, the DSM-IV suggests: p. 656.

Chapter 8

pages 169–70   Richard Harris: "Richard Harris," *The New Yorker* (September 21, 1987), p. 120.

pages 174–75   Diagnostic Criteria: p. 339.

page 176   "To live with a paranoid person": *Abnormalities of Personality* (New York: W. W. Norton, 1993), p. 203.

page 177   According to the DSM-IV: p. 635.

page 177   Drs. Beck and Freeman: *Cognitive Therapy of Personality Disorders* (New York: The Guilford Press, 1990), p. 48.

page 178   "Such patients often try": *Abnormalities of Personality* (New York: W. W. Norton, 1993), pp. 208–9.

page 178   The familial relationship with delusional disorder: Bernstein, David P., David Useda, and Larry J. Siever, "Paranoid Personality Disorder: Review of the Literature and Recommendations for DSM-IV," *Journal of Personality Disorders* 7:1 (1993), p. 57.

page 179   A study of five hundred: Barefoot, J. C., I. C. Siegler, et al., "Suspiciousness, Health, and Mortality: A Follow-up Study of 500 Older Adults," *Psychosomatic Medicine* 49 (1987), pp. 450–57.

Chapter 9

pages 196–97   Diagnostic Criteria: pp. 664–65.

page 198   In one study: Zimbardi, P. G., P. A. Pilkonis, and R. M. Norwood, *The Silent Prison of Shyness* (ONR Tech. Rep. Z-17), (Stanford: Stanford University, 1974). See Pilkonis, Paul A., "Avoidant and Schizoid Personality Disorders," in

Comprehensive Handbook of Psychopathology, editors, H. E. Adams and P. B. Sutker (New York: Plenum Press, 1984).

page 199 The condition, once thought rare: Kessler, Ronald C., Katherine A. McGonagle, Shanyang Zhao, et al., "Lifetime and 12-Month Prevalence of *DSM-III-R* Psychiatric Disorders in the United States: Results from the National Comorbidity Survey." *Archives of General Psychiatry* 52:1 (January 1994), pp. 8-19.

page 200 One study: Turner, S. M., D. C. Beidel, J. W. Borden, et al., "Social Phobia, Axis I and II Correlates," *Journal of Abnormal Psychology* 100 (1991), pp. 102–6.

page 200 (The social phobia contingent: Holt, C. S., R. G. Heimberg, D. A. Hope, "Avoidant Personality and the Generalized Subtype of Social Phobia," *Journal of Abnormal Psychology* 101 (1992), pp. 318–25.

page 200 Avoidant personality disorder, to which: DSM-IV, p. 663.

page 200 Rosenbaum, Jerrold F., Joseph Biederman, Elizabeth A. Bolduc-Murphy, et al., "Behavioral Inhibition in Childhood: A Risk Factor for Anxiety Disorders." *Harvard Review of Psychiatry* 1:1 (May-June 1993), pp. 2–15.

—————————————— **Chapter 10** ——————————————

pages 222–23 Diagnostic Criteria: pp. 734–35.

page 223 When the therapist advised: Liebowitz, Michael R., Michael H. Stone, and Ira Daniel Turkat, "Treatment of Personality Disorders," in *Psychiatry Update* vol. 5, American Psychiatric Association Annual Review (Washingon, D.C.: American Psychiatric Press, 1986), p. 384.

page 224 In one long-term study: Perry, J. Christopher, and Mark E. O'Connell, "Dynamic Conflicts in Course of Axis II Disorders." Paper presented at American Psychiatric Association, Chicago, May 1987.

page 225 "Being direct with people": Beck, Aaron T., and Arthur Freeman, *Cognitive Therapy of Personality Disorders* (New York: The Guilford Press, 1990), p. 338.

—————————————— **Chapter 11** ——————————————

pages 245–46 Diagnostic Criteria: pp. 649–50.

page 246 Antisocial personality disorder is among: Côté, G., and S. Hodgins, "Co-occurring Mental Disorders Among Criminal Offenders," *Bulletin of the American Academy of Psychiatric Law* 18 (1990), pp. 271–81.

page 247 As the DSM-IV notes: p. 647.

page 248 "Concerns have been raised": p. 647.

page 248 "The risk": p. 648.

page 249 Some studies . . . learn from experience: Siever, Larry J., Bonnie J. Steinberg, Robert L. Trestman, Joanne Intrator, "Biological Markers in Personality Disorders," in *Review of Psychiatry,* Vol. 13, John M. Oldham and

Michelle B. Riba, eds. (Washington, D.C.: American Psychiatric Press, 1994), p. 268.

page 249 Now neuroscientists are finding: Siever, Larry J., "The Relationship Between Impulsivity and Compulsivity," in *Impulsivity and Compulsivity,* John M. Oldham, Eric Hollander, Andrew E. Skodol, eds. (Washington, D.C.: American Psychiatric Press, in press).

page 249 One recent study: Luntz, Barbara K., and Cathy Spatz Widom, "Antisocial Personality Disorder in Abused and Neglected Children Grown Up," *American Journal of Psychiatry* 151 (1994), pp. 670–74.

page 249 Extreme poverty: Crowell, Judith A., Everett Waters, Ann Kring, and Lawrence P. Riso, "The Psychosocial Etiologies of Personality Disorders: What Is the Answer Like?" *Journal of Personality Disorders* 7 Supplement (Spring 1993), pp. 118–28.

page 250 Canadian psychologist Richard Tremblay: Tremblay, Richard E., Robert O. Pihl, Frank Vitaro, Patricia L. Dobkin, "Predicting Early Onset of Male Antisocial Behavior from Preschool Behavior," *Archives of General Psychiatry* 51 (September 1994), pp. 732–39.

page 250 ADHD is a risk factor: DSM-IV, p. 647.

page 250 "They do not seek help for their bad character": *Abnormalities of Personality* (New York: W. W. Norton, 1993), p. 298.

page 251 "My thoughts and feelings": Beck, Aaron T., and Arthur Freeman, *Cognitive Therapy of Personality Disorders* (New York: The Guilford Press, 1990), p. 154.

Chapter 12

page 257 "just another typical eccentric": Iyer, Pico, "Of Weirdos and Eccentrics," *Time* (January 18, 1988), p. 76.

pages 259–60 "It becomes apparent": Adapted from "Back in the High Life," by Ron Rosenbaum. This article originally was published in *Vanity Fair* (April 1988), pp. 133–44.

page 269 Diagnostic Criteria: p. 645.

pages 270–72 "The Case of Harry the Turtle": Perry, Samuel, Allen J. Frances, and John Clarkin, *A DSM-III Casebook of Differential Therapeutics* (New York: Brunner/Mazel, 1985), pp. 293–97. Copyright © by Samuel Perry, Allen J. Frances, and John Clarkin. Used by permission.

page 272 Drs. Beck and Freeman: *Cognitive Therapy of Personality Disorders* (New York: The Guilford Press, 1990), p. 141.

page 272 There is some suggestion: McGlashan, Thomas H., and Karen K. Bardenstein, "Schizotypal Personality Disorder: Gender Differences." *Journal of Personality Disorders* 2:3 (1988), pp. 221–27.

page 273 "According to one study": See Gunderson, John G., "Personality Disorders," in *The New Harvard Guide to Psychiatry,* ed. Armand M. Nicholi (Cambridge, Massachusetts, and London: The Belknap Press of Harvard University Press, 1988), p. 343.

Chapter 13

page 280 A 1987 study: Shaffer, J. W., et al., "Clustering of Personality Traits in Youth and the Subsequent Development of Cancer Among Physicians," *Journal of Behavioral Medicine* 10 (1987): pp. 441–47.

page 284 It is said that: Harris, William H., and Judith S. Levey, eds., *The New Columbia Encyclopedia* (New York: Columbia University Press, 1975), p. 760.

pages 289–90 Diagnostic Criteria: p. 641.

page 290 A study of personality disorders: Nestadt, Gerald, William R. Breakey, et al., "Personality Disorder in Baltimore's Homeless," new research presented at the American Psychiatric Association Annual Meeting, Montreal, May 12, 1988.

Chapter 14

page 312 Diagnostic Criteria: p. 654.

page 315 Increasingly, researchers in the biology of personality: Paris, Joel, *Borderline Personality Disorder, A Multidimensional Approach* (Washington, D.C.: American Psychiatric Press, 1994). Skodol, Andrew E., and John M. Oldham, "Differential Diagnosis of the Impulsive/Compulsive Spectrum of Disorders," in *Impulsivity and Compulsivity,* Oldham, John M., Eric Hollander, and Andrew E. Skodol, eds. (Washington, D.C.: American Psychiatric Press, in press).

page 315 Deficits in serotonin: Siever, Larry J., "The Relationship Between Impulsivity and Compulsivity," in *Impulsivity and Compulsivity,* John M. Oldham, Eric Hollander, Andrew E. Skodol, eds.

page 316 Studies have found: Paris, Joel, *Borderline Personality Disorder, A Multidimensional Approach,* p. 51.

page 316 Other research: "Borderline Personality—Part II," *The Harvard Mental Health Letter* 10:12 (June 1994).

page 316 Dr. Michael H. Stone: *Abnormalities of Personality* (New York: W. W. Norton, 1993), p. 226.

page 317 "For example": *Cognitive Therapy of Personality Disorders* (New York: The Guilford Press, 1990), p. 204.

page 317 Psychologist Marsha Linehan: Linehan, Marsha M., "Behavior Therapy, Dialectics, and the Treatment of Borderline Personality Disorder," in *Handbook of Borderline Disorders,* D. Silver and M. Rosenbluth, eds. (Madison, CT: International University Press, 1992), pp. 425–34.

Chapter 15

pages 340–41 Diagnostic Criteria: p. 374. Reprinted by permission of the *Diagnostic and Statistical Manual of Mental Disorders,* 3rd edition, revised. Copyright © 1987 American Psychiatric Association.

page 341 In 1916: Freud, Sigmund, "Some Character Types Met with in Psycho-Analytic Work," in *The Standard Edition of the Complete Psychological Works,* vol. 14, pp. 309–33, James Strachey, ed. and trans. (London: Hogarth Press, 1957).

pages 343–44   In any case: DSM-III-R, p. 375.

page 344   "A diagnosis that has the potential": Ross, Ruth, Allen Frances, Thomas A. Widiger, "Gender Issues in DSM-IV," in *Review of Psychiatry,* vol. 14, Oldham, John M., and Michelle Riba, eds. (Washington, D.C.: American Psychiatric Press, 1995), pp. 205–26.

page 344   Because studies: Skodol, Andrew E., John M. Oldham, Peggy E. Galler and Sophia Bezirganian, "Validity of Self-Defeating Personality Disorder," *American Journal of Psychiatry* 151:4 (April 1994), pp. 560–67.

page 344   Even so: Heisler, Lora K., Michael J. Lyons, John W. Goethe, "Self-Defeating Personality Disorder: A Cross-National Study of Clinical Utility." New research presented at the American Psychiatric Association Annual Meeting, Philadelphia, May 1994.

Chapter 16

pages 362–63   Diagnostic Criteria: p. 371.

pages 364–65   Researchers measured serotonin levels: Raleigh, Michael J., Michael T. McGuire, et al., "Social and Environmental Influences on Blood Serotonin Concentrations in Monkeys," *Archives of General Psychiatry* 41 (April 1984), pp. 405–10.

Chapter 17

page 369   Richard Harris: "Richard Harris," *The New Yorker* (September 21, 1987), p. 120.

page 375   Health psychologist: Friedman, Howard S., Joan S. Tucker, Carol Tomlinson-Keasy, et al., "Does Childhood Personality Predict Longevity?" *Journal of Personality and Social Psychology* 65:1 (1993), pp. 176–85.

pages 379–80   Diagnostic Criteria: p. 733.

page 382   "This recommendation reflects": Phillips, Katharine A., Robert M. A. Hirschfeld, M. Tracie Shea, John G. Gunderson, "Depressive Personality Disorder: Perspectives for DSM-IV," *Journal of Personality Disorders* 7:1 (1993), pp. 30–42.

page 382   In fact, some researchers: Akiskal, Hagop, "Proposal for a Depressive Personality (Temperament)," in Tyrer, Peter, and George Stein, eds., *Personality Disorder Reviewed* (London: Gaskell, 1993), pp. 165–80.

page 382   "It remains controversial": DSM-IV, p. 733.

page 383   "In an era": Kramer, Peter, *Listening to Prozac* (New York: Viking, 1993), p. 182.

Chapter 18

page 386   In the words of: Maziade, Michel, Robert Côté, Pierrette Boufik, et al., "Temperament and Intellectual Development: A Longitudinal Study from Infancy to Four Years," *American Journal of Psychiatry* 144 (February 1981), pp. 144–50.

page 386 "The ancient Greeks": Frances, Allen J., and Thomas Widiger, "The Classification of Personality Disorders: An Overview of Problems and Solutions," in *Psychiatry Update,* vol. 5, American Psychiatric Association Annual Review, Allen J. Frances and Robert F. Hales, eds. (Washington, D.C.: American Psychiatric Press, 1986), p. 241.

page 387 The Variables of Temperament: Thomas, Alexander, and Stella Chess, "Genesis and Evolution of Behavioral Disorders: From Infancy to Early Adult Life," *American Journal of Psychiatry* 141 (January 1984), pp. 1–9.

pages 388–389 Harvard developmental psychologist Jerome Kagan: Kagan, Jerome, and Doreen Arcus, "The Neurodevelopmental Origins of Behavioral Inhibition," presented at the American Psychiatric Association Annual Meeting, Philadelphia, May 25, 1994.

page 389 Others have shown: Kagan and Arcus mention the work of Nancy Snidman.

page 390 Their relative levels: Siever, Larry J., "The Relationship Between Impulsivity and Compulsivity," in *Impulsivity and Compulsivity,* John M. Oldham, Eric Hollander, and Andrew E. Skodol, eds. (Washington, D.C.: American Psychiatric Press, in press).

page 390 Research with rhesus monkeys: Mehlman, P. T., J. D. Higley, I. Faucher, A. A. Lily, et al., "Low CSF 5-HIAA Concentrations and Severe Aggression and Impaired Impulse Control in Nonhuman Primates," *American Journal of Psychiatry* 151:10 (October 1994), pp. 1485–91.

pages 390–91 Some Schizotypal individuals: Siever, Larry J., Bonnie J. Steinberg, Robert L. Trestman, Joanne Intrator, "Biological Markers in Personality Disorders," in *Review of Psychiatry,* vol. 13, eds., John M. Oldham and Michelle B. Riba (Washington, D.C.: American Psychiatric Press, 1994), p. 262.

page 391 Psychiatrist Robert Cloninger: Cloninger, C. Robert, Dragon M. Svrakic, Thomas R. Przybeck, "Physiological Model of Temperament and Character," *Archives of General Psychiatry* 50 (December 1993), pp. 975-90.

page 391 Psychiatrist Daniel Stern: Stern, Daniel N., *The Interpersonal World of the Infant* (New York: Basic Books, 1985).

page 393 For instance, it appears: Maziade, Michel, Robert Côté, Pierrette Boufik, et al.

page 394 Dutch psychiatrist Marten deVries: deVries, Marten W., "Temperament and Infant Mortality Among the Masai of East Africa," *American Journal of Psychiatry* 141 (October 1984), pp. 1189–94.

page 396 For a straightforward approach: Turecki, Stanley, and Leslie Tonner, *The Difficult Child* (New York: Bantam, 1985, 1989).

page 397 What else could account: Farber, S., *Identical Twins Reared Apart* (New York: Basic Books, 1981).

page 398 Researchers have determined: Roose, Steven P., and Herbert Pardes, "Biological Considerations in the Middle Years," in *The Middle Years: New Psychoanalytic Perspectives,* John M. Oldham and R. S. Liebert, eds. (New Haven: Yale University Press, 1989).

Bibliography

Adams, H. E., and P. B. Sutker, eds. *Comprehensive Handbook of Psychopathology*. New York: Plenum Press, 1984.

Akiskal, Hagop. "Proposal for a Depressive Personality (Temperament)." In *Personality Disorder Reviewed*. *See* Peter Tyrer and George Stein, eds.

American Psychiatric Association. *Diagnostic and Statistical Manual of Mental Disorders,* 3rd ed. rev. Washington, D.C., 1987.

———. *Diagnostic and Statistical Manual of Mental Disorders,* 4th ed. Washington, D.C., 1994.

Ames-Frankel, J., M. Devlin, B. Timothy Walsh, T. J. Strasser, C. Sadik, John M. Oldham, and Steven P. Roose. "Personality Disorder Diagnoses in Patients with Bulimia Nervosa: Clinical Correlates and Changes with Treatment." *Journal of Clinical Psychiatry* 53 (1992), pp. 90–96.

Asch, Stuart S. "The Masochistic Personality." In *Psychiatry*, vol. 1. *See* Cavenar, ed.

Beck, Aaron T., and Arthur Freeman. *Cognitive Therapy of Personality Disorders*. New York: The Guilford Press, 1990.

Bernstein, David P., David Useda, and Larry J. Siever. "Paranoid Personality Disorder: Review of the Literature and Recommendations for DSM-IV." *Journal of Personality Disorders* 7:1 (1993), pp. 53–62.

"Borderline Personality—Part I." *The Harvard Mental Health Letter* 10:11 (May 1994).

"Borderline Personality—Part II." *The Harvard Mental Health Letter* 10:12 (June 1994).

Bowlby, John. "Developmental Psychiatry Comes of Age." *American Journal of Psychiatry* 145 (January 1988).

Brown, Gerald L., Michael H. Ebert, et al. "Aggression, Suicide, and Serotonin: Relationships to CSF Amine Metabolites." *American Journal of Psychiatry* 139 (June 1982), pp. 741–46.

Cadoret, Remi. "Antisocial Personality." In *The Medical Basis of Psychiatry*. *See* Winokur and Clayton, eds.

Caplan, Paula J. "The Psychiatric Association's Failure to Meet Its Own Standards: The Dangers of Self-Defeating Personality Disorder as a Category." *Journal of Personality Disorders* 1 (Summer 1987), pp. 178–82.

Cavenar, Jesse O., ed. *Psychiatry,* vol 1. New York: Basic Books; Philadelphia: J. B. Lippincott Co., 1987.

Cloninger, C. Robert. "A Systematic Method for Clinical Description and Classification of Personality Variants." *Archives of General Psychiatry* 44 (July 1987), pp. 573–88.

Cloninger, C. Robert, Dragon M. Svrakic, Thomas R. Przybeck. "Physiological Model of Temperament and Character." *Archives of General Psychiatry* 50 (December 1993), pp. 975–90.

Coccaro, Emil F. "Psychopharmacologic Studies in Patients with Personality Disorders: Review and Perspective." *Journal of Personality Disorders* 7 Supplement (Spring 1993), pp. 181–92.

Coccaro, Emil F., Larry J. Siever, Richard Kavoussi, et al. "Serotonergic Correlates of Personality Disorder." Paper presented at the annual meeting of the American Psychiatric Association, Montreal, May 1988.

Coccaro, Emil F., Larry J. Siever, Howard M. Klar, Gail Maurer, et al. "Serotonergic Studies in Patients with Affective and Personality Disorders." *Archives of General Psychiatry* 46 (July 1989), pp. 587–99.

Coccaro, Emil F., Jeremy M. Silverman, Howard M. Klar, Thomas B. Horvath, Larry J. Siever. "Familial Correlates of Reduced Central Serotonergic System Function in Patients with Personality Disorders." *Archives of General Psychiatry* 51 (April 1994), pp. 318–24.

Cooper, Arnold M. "Histrionic, Narcissistic, and Compulsive Personality Disorders." In *Psychiatry: A Critical Appraisal of DSM-III,* Gary Tischler, ed. New York: Cambridge University Press, 1987.

Côté, G., and S. Hodgins. "Co-occurring Mental Disorders Among Criminal Offenders." *Bulletin of the American Academy of Psychiatric Law* 18 (1990), pp. 271–81.

Crowell, Judith A., Everett Waters, Ann Kring, Lawrence P. Riso. "The Psychosocial Etiologies of Personality Disorders: What Is the Answer Like?" *Journal of Personality Disorders* 7 Supplement (Spring 1993), pp. 118–28.

"Depression, Violent Suicide Tied to Low Metabolite Level." *Journal of the American Medical Association* 250 (December 16, 1983), p. 3141.

Depue, R. A., and M. R. Spoont. "Conceptualizing a Serotonin Trait: A Behavioral Dimension of Constraint." *Annals of the New York Academy of Sciences* 487 (1986), pp. 47–62.

deVries, Marten W. "Temperament and Infant Mortality Among the Masai of East Africa." *American Journal of Psychiatry* 141 (October 1984), pp. 1189–94.

Dubro, Alan F., and Scott Wetzler. "A Comparison of Three Tests for Self-Report Diagnosis." Paper delivered at the annual meeting of the American Psychiatric Association, Chicago, Illinois, May 1987.

Epstein, Seymour. "The Stability of Behavior: I. On Predicting Most of the People Much of the Time." *Journal of Personality and Social Psychology* 37 (July 1979), pp. 1097–1126.

Escalona, Sibylle K., and Grace Heider. *Prediction and Outcome.* New York: Basic Books, 1959.

Esman, Aaron H. "Dependent and Passive-Aggressive Personality Disorders." In *Psychiatry,* vol. 1. *See* Cavenar, ed.

Extein, Irl, and Mark S. Gold, eds. *Medical Mimics of Psychiatric Disorders.* Washington, D.C.: American Psychiatric Press, 1986.

Eysenck, Hans J., and Michael W. Eysenck. *Personality and Individual Differences: A Natural Science Approach.* New York and London: Plenum Press, 1985.

Farber, S. *Identical Twins Reared Apart.* New York: Basic Books, 1981.

Frances, Allen J., John Clarkin, and Samuel Perry. *Differential Therapeutics in Psychiatry: The Art and Science of Treatment Selection.* New York: Brunner/Mazel, 1984.

Frances, Allen J., and Robert F. Hales, eds. *Psychiatry Update,* vol. 5. American Psychiatric Association Annual Review. Washington, D.C.: American Psychiatric Press, 1986.

Frances, Allen J., and Thomas Widiger. "The Classification of Personality Disorders: An Overview of Problems and Solutions." In *Psychiatry Update,* vol. 5. *See* Frances and Hales, eds.

Freud, Sigmund. *The Standard Edition of the Complete Psychological Works.* Ed. and trans. James Strachey. London: Hogarth Press, 1957.

Friedman, Howard S., Joan S. Tucker, Carol Tomlinson-Keasy, et al. "Does Childhood Personality Predict Longevity?" *Journal of Personality and Social Psychology* 65:1 (1993), pp. 176–85.

Friedman, M., and R. H. Rosenman. *Type A Personality and Your Heart.* New York: Knopf, 1974.

Frosch, James P., ed. *Current Perspectives on Personality Disorders.* Washington, D.C.: American Psychiatric Press, 1983.

Gallagher, Winifred. "How We Become What We Are." *The Atlantic Monthly,* September 1994, pp. 39–55.

Gallahorn, George E. "Borderline Personality Disorders." In *Personality Disorders/ Diagnosis and Management.*

Gold, Mark S., and Lois B. Morris. *The Good News About Depression.* New York: Bantam Books, 1995.

Greenberg, R. P., and R. F. Bornstein. "The Dependent Personality: I. Risk for Physical Disorders." *Journal of Personality Disorders* 2 (1988), pp. 126–35.

———. "The Dependent Personality: II. Risk for Psychological Disorders." *Journal of Personality Disorders* 2:2 (1988), pp. 136–43.

Gunderson, John G. "Personality Disorders." In *The New Harvard Guide to Psychiatry. See* Nicholi, ed.

Haier, Richard J. "Biologic Response Styles and the Average Evoked Response: Personality, Vulnerability, and Topography." In *Biologic Response Styles: Clinical Implications. See* Klar and Siever, eds.

Heatherton, Todd F., and Joel L. Weinberger, eds. *Can Personality Change?* Washington, D.C.: American Psychological Association, 1994.

Heisler, Lora K., Michael J. Lyons, John W. Goethe. "Self-Defeating Personality

Disorder: A Cross-National Study of Clinical Utility." New research presented at the American Psychiatric Association Annual Meeting, Philadelphia, May 1994.

Hirschfeld, Robert M. A. Foreword to section 3, "Personality Disorders." In *Psychiatry Update,* vol. 5. *See* Frances and Hales, eds.

Hollander, Eric, Dan J. Stein, C. M. DeCaria, L. Cohen, et al. "Serotonergic Sensitivity in Borderline Personality Disorder: Preliminary Findings." *American Journal of Psychiatry* 151 (1994), pp. 277–80.

Holt, C. S., R. G. Heimberg, D. A. Hope. "Avoidant Personality and the Generalized Subtype of Social Phobia." *Journal of Abnormal Psychology* 101 (1992), pp. 318–25.

Horney, Karen. *Neurosis and Human Growth.* New York: W. W. Norton, 1950.

Horowitz, Mardi, Charles Marmar, Janice Krupnick, et al. *Personality Styles and Brief Psychotherapy.* New York: Basic Books, 1984.

Iyer, Pico. "Of Weirdos and Eccentrics." *Time* (January 18, 1988), p. 76.

Jorgensen, R. S., and B. K. Houston. "Family History of Hypertension, Personality Patterns and Cardiovascular Reactivity to Stress." *Psychosomatic Medicine* 48 (1986), pp. 102–17.

Kagan, Jerome, and Doreen Arcus. "The Neurodevelopmental Origins of Behavioral Inhibition." Paper presented at the annual meeting of the American Psychiatric Association, Philadelphia, May 25, 1994.

Kandel, Eric R. "From Metapsychology to Molecular Biology: Explorations into the Nature of Anxiety." *American Journal of Psychiatry* (15)140 (October 1983), pp. 1277–93.

———. "Psychotherapy and the Single Synapse." *The New England Journal of Medicine* 301, vol. 19 (November 8, 1979), pp. 1028–37.

Kass, Frederic I. "Self-Defeating Personality Disorder: An Empirical Study." *Journal of Personality Disorders* 1 (1987), pp. 43–47.

Kass, Frederic I., Roger A. MacKinnon, and Robert L. Spitzer. "Masochistic Personality: An Empirical Study." *American Journal of Psychiatry* 143 (February 1986), pp. 216–18.

Kass, Frederic I., John M. Oldham, and Herbert Pardes, eds. *The Columbia University College of Physicians and Surgeons Complete Home Guide to Mental Health.* Ed. dir., Lois B. Morris. New York: Henry Holt, 1992.

Kayser, Allen, Donald S. Robinson, et al. "Response to Phenelzine Among Depressed Patients with Features of Hysteroid Dysphoria." *American Journal of Psychiatry* 142 (April 1985), pp. 486–88.

Kernberg, Otto F. "Narcissistic Personality Disorder." In *Psychiatry,* vol. 1. See Cavenar, ed.

———. "Hysterical and Histrionic Personality Disorders." In *Psychiatry,* vol. 1. *See* Cavenar, ed.

Kessler, Ronald C., Katherine A. McGonagle, Shanyang Zhao, et al. "Lifetime and 12-Month Prevalence of *DSM-III-R* Psychiatric Disorders in the United States: Results from the National Comorbidity Survey." *Archives of General Psychiatry* 52 (January 1994), pp. 8–19.

Klar, Howard, and Larry J. Siever, eds. *Biologic Response Styles: Clinical Implications*. Washington, D.C.: American Psychiatric Press, 1985.

Klein, Marjorie, David J. Kupfer, M. Tracie Shea, eds. *Personality and Depression*. New York: The Guilford Press, 1993.

Korenblum, M., P. Marton, et al. "Personality Dysfunction in Adolescence: Continuities and Discontinuities." Paper presented at the annual meeting of the American Psychiatric Association, Montreal, May 1988.

Kramer, Peter. *Listening to Prozac*. New York: Viking, 1993.

Lasch, Christopher. *The Culture of Narcissism*. New York: W. W. Norton, 1978.

Liebowitz, Michael R. "Commentary on the Criteria for Self-Defeating Personality Disorder." *Journal of Personality Disorders* 1 (Summer 1987), pp. 196–99.

Liebowitz, Michael R., and Donald F. Klein. "Hysteroid Dysphoria." *Psychiatric Clinics of North America* 2 (1979), pp. 555–75.

Liebowitz, Michael R., Michael H. Stone, and Ira Daniel Turkat. "Treatment of Personality Disorders." In *Psychiatry Update*, vol. 5. *See* Frances and Hales, eds.

Lilienfeld, Scott O., Charles VanValkenburg, et al. "The Relationship of Histrionic Personality Disorder to Antisocial Personality and Somatization Disorders." *American Journal of Psychiatry* 143 (June 1986), pp. 718–22.

Linehan, Marsha M. "Dialectical Behavioral Therapy: A Cognitive Behavioral Approach to Parasuicide." *Journal of Personality Disorders* 1 (Winter 1987), pp. 328–33.

————. "Behavior Therapy, Dialectics, and the Treatment of Borderline Personality Disorder." In *Handbook of Borderline Disorders*, D. Silver and M. Rosenbluth, eds. Madison, CT: International University Press, 1992.

Linnoila, M., M. Virkkunen, et al. "Low Cerebrospinal Fluid 5-Hydroxyindoleacetic Acid Concentration Differentiates Impulsive from Nonimpulsive Violent Behavior." *Life Sciences* 33 (1983), pp. 2609–14.

Linscott, Robert N., ed. *Selected Poems and Letters of Emily Dickinson*. Garden City, New York: Doubleday Anchor Books, Doubleday & Co., 1959.

Livesley, W. John. "Trait and Behavioral Prototypes of Personality Disorder." *American Journal of Psychiatry* 143 (June 1986), pp. 728–32.

————, ed. *The DSM-IV Personality Disorders*. New York: The Guilford Press, in press.

Livesley, W. John, Malcolm West, and Arlene Tanney. "Historical Comment on DSM-III Schizoid and Avoidant Personality Disorders." *American Journal of Psychiatry* 142 (November 1985), pp. 1344–47.

Loranger, Armand W., John M. Oldham, and Elaine H. Tulis. "Familial Transmission of DSM-III Borderline Personality Disorder." *Archives of General Psychiatry* 39 (July 1982), pp. 795-99.

Loranger, Armand W., Virginia Lehmann Susman, John M. Oldham, and L. Mark Russakoff. *Personality Disorder Examination (PDE): A Structured Interview for DSM-III-R Personality Disorders*. White Plains, New York: The New York Hospital-Cornell Medical Center, Westchester Division, 1985.

————. "The Personality Disorder Examination: A Preliminary Report." *Journal of Personality Disorders* 1:1 (1987), pp. 1–13.

Loranger, Armand W., Norman Sartorius, Antoni Andreoli, Peter Berger, et al. "The International Personality Disorder Examination: The World Health Organization/Alcohol, Drug Abuse, and Mental Health Administration International Pilot Study of Personality Disorders." *Archives of General Psychiatry* 51 (March 1994), pp. 215–24.

Luntz, Barbara K., and Cathy Spatz Widom. "Antisocial Personality Disorder in Abused and Neglected Children Grown Up." *American Journal of Psychiatry* 151 (1994), pp. 670–74.

Lykken, David T. "Genes and the Mind." *The Harvard Medical School Mental Health Letter* 4 (August 1987), p. 437.

Magid, Ken, and Carole McKelvey. *High Risk: Children Without a Conscience.* New York: Bantam, 1988.

Maziade, Michel, Robert Côté, Pierret Boutin, et al. "Temperament and Intellectual Development: A Longitudinal Study from Infancy to Four Years." *American Journal of Psychiatry* 144 (February 1981), pp. 144–50.

Maziade, Michel, Philippe Caperaa, Bruno Laplante, et al. "Value of Difficult Temperament Among 7-Year-Olds in the General Population for Predicting Psychiatric Diagnosis at Age 12." *American Journal of Psychiatry* 142 (August 1985), pp. 943–46.

Maziade, Michel, Chantal Caron, Robert Côté, Pierret Boutin, Jacques Thivierge. "Extreme Temperament and Diagnosis." *Archives of General Psychiatry* 47 (May 1990), pp. 477–84.

McGlashan, Thomas H. *The Borderline: Current Empirical Research.* The Progress in Psychiatry Series. Washington, D.C.: American Psychiatric Press, 1985.

McGlashan, Thomas H., and Karen K. Bardenstein. "Schizotypal Personality Disorder: Gender Differences." *Journal of Personality Disorders* 2:3 (1988), pp. 221–27.

McGuffin, Peter, and Theodore Reich. "Psychopathology and Genetics." In *Comprehensive Handbook of Psychopathology. See* Adams and Sutker, eds.

Mehlman, P. T., J. D. Higley, I. Faucher, A. A. Lily, et al. "Low CSF 5-HIAA Concentrations and Severe Aggression and Impaired Impulse Control in Nonhuman Primates." *American Journal of Psychiatry* 151:10 (October 1994), pp. 1485–91.

Meissner, William W. "Psychotherapy and the Paranoid Personality." *The Harvard Medical School Mental Health Letter* 4 (December 1987), p. 436.

Millon, Theodore. "The Avoidant Personality." In *Psychiatry,* vol. 1. *See* Cavenar, ed.

———. *Disorders of Personality DSM-III: Axis II.* New York: John Wiley & Sons, 1981.

Morris, Lois B. "Social Anxiety." *American Health* 14:1 (January-February 1995), pp. 60–63.

Murphy, Lois Barclay, Grace M. Heider, and Colleen T. Small. "Individual Differences in Infants." In *Zero to Three,* Bulletin of the National Center for Clinical Infant Programs 7:2 (December 1986), p. 137.

Nestadt, Gerald, William R. Breakey, et al. "Personality Disorder in Baltimore's Homeless." New research presented at the annual meeting of the American Psychiatric Association, Montreal, May 1988.

Nestadt, Gerald, Alan J. Romanoski, et al. "Compulsive Personality Disorder in the Community." New research presented at the annual meeting of the American Psychiatric Association, Montreal, May 1988.

Nicholi, Armand M., Jr., ed. *The New Harvard Guide to Psychiatry*. Cambridge, Massachusetts, and London: The Belknap Press of Harvard University Press, 1988.

Oldham, John M. "Treating a Patient with Borderline Personality Disorder." *Journal of Personality Disorders* 1 (Summer 1987), pp. 207–10.

———. "DSM-III Personality Disorders: Assessment Problems." *Journal of Personality Disorders* 1 (Fall 1987), pp. 241–47.

———. "Brief Treatment of Narcissistic Personality Disorder." *Journal of Personality Disorders* 2 (1988), pp. 88–90.

———. "Current Perspectives on Personality Disorders." Grand Rounds presentation, UCLA, Department of Psychiatry, December 1988.

———. "Borderline Personality Disorder: An Introduction." *Hospital and Community Psychiatry* 42 (1991), p. 1014.

———, ed. *Personality Disorders: New Perspectives on Diagnostic Validity*. Washington, D.C.: American Psychiatric Press, 1991.

———. "Diagnosis and Treatment of Personality Disorders." *Psychiatric Quarterly* 63 (1992), pp. 413–24.

———. "Personality Disorders: Current Perspectives." *Journal of the American Medical Association* 272:22 (December 14, 1994), pp. 1770–76.

Oldham, John M., and S. Bone, eds. *Paranoia: New Psychoanalytic Perspectives*. Madison, Connecticut: International Universities Press, 1994.

Oldham, John M., and William Frosch. "Compulsive Personality Disorders." In *Psychiatry,* vol. 1. *See* Cavenar, ed.

Oldham, John M., Eric Hollander, and Andrew A. Skodol, eds., *Impulsivity and Compulsivity*. Washington, D.C.: American Psychiatric Press, in press.

Oldham, John M., and R. S. Liebert, eds. *The Middle Years: New Psychoanalytic Perspectives*. New Haven: Yale University Press, 1989.

Oldham, John M., and Michelle Riba, eds. *Review of Psychiatry,* vol. 13. Washington, D.C.: American Psychiatric Press, 1984.

———. *Review of Psychiatry,* vol. 14. Washington, D.C.: American Psychiatric Press, 1995.

Oldham, John M., and L. Mark Russakoff. *Dynamic Therapy in Brief Hospitalization*. Northvale, New Jersey, and London: Jason Aronson, 1987.

Oldham, John M., and Andrew Skodol. "Personality Disorders." In *The Columbia University College of Physicians and Surgeons Complete Home Guide to Mental Health. See* Kass, Oldham, and Pardes, eds.

———. "Personality Disorders in the Public Sector." *Hospital and Community Psychiatry* 42 (1991), pp. 481–87.

———. "Comorbidity of DSM-III-R Anxiety Disorders and Personality Disorders." Presented in a symposium at the Third International Congress on the Disorders of Personality, Cambridge, Massachusetts, 1993.

Pardes, Herbert. "Neuroscience and Psychiatry: Marriage or Coexistence?" *American Journal of Psychiatry* 143 (October 1986), pp. 1205–12.

Paris, Joel. "Personality Disorders: A Biopsychosocial Model." *Journal of Personality Disorders* 7:3 (1993), pp. 255–64.

Perry, J. Christopher, and Mark E. O'Connell. "Dynamic Conflicts in Course of Axis II Disorders." Paper presented at the annual meeting of the American Psychiatric Association, Chicago, May 1987.

Perry, Samuel, Allen J. Frances, and John Clarkin. *A DSM-III Casebook of Differential Therapeutics.* New York: Brunner/Mazel, 1985.

Pervin, Lawrence A., ed. *Handbook of Personality Theory and Research.* New York: The Guilford Press, 1990.

Phillips, Katharine A., Robert M. A. Hirschfeld, M. Tracie Shea, John G. Gunderson. "Depressive Personality Disorder: Perspectives for DSM-IV." *Journal of Personality Disorders* 7:1 (1993), pp. 30–42.

Pilkonis, Paul A. "Avoidant and Schizoid Personality Disorders." In *Comprehensive Handbook of Psychopathology. See* Adams and Sutker, eds.

Raleigh, Michael J., Michael T. McGuire, et al. "Social and Environmental Influences on Blood Serotonin Concentrations in Monkeys." *Archives of General Psychiatry* 41 (April 1984), pp. 405–10.

Ratey, John J., ed. *Neuropsychiatry of Personality Disorders.* Cambridge, MA: Blackwell Science, 1995.

"Richard Harris." *The New Yorker* (September 21, 1987), p. 120.

Roose, Steven P., and Pardes, Herbert. "Biological Considerations in the Middle Years." In *The Middle Years: New Psychoanalytic Perspectives. See* Oldham and Liebert, eds.

Rosenbaum, Jerrold F., Joseph Biederman, Elizabeth A. Bolduc-Murphy, et al. "Behavioral Inhibition in Childhood: A Risk Factor for Anxiety Disorders." *Harvard Review of Psychiatry* 1:1 (May-June 1993), pp. 2–15.

Rosenbaum, Jerrold F., Joseph Biederman, Rachel A. Pollack, Dina R. Hirshfeld. "The Etiology of Social Phobia." *The Journal of Clinical Psychiatry* 55:6 supplement (June 1994), pp. 10–16.

Rosenbaum, Ron. "Back in the High Life." *Vanity Fair* (April 1988), pp. 133–44.

Rosewater, Lynne Bravo. "A Criticial Analysis of the Proposed Self-Defeating Personality Disorder." *Journal of Personality Disorders* 1 (Summer 1987), pp. 190–95.

Ross, Ruth, Allen Frances, and Thomas A. Widiger. "Gender Issues in DSM-IV." *Review of Psychiatry*, vol. 14. *See* Oldham and Riba, eds.

Rutter, Michael. "Psychopathology and Development: II. Childhood Experiences and Personality Development." *Australian and New Zealand Journal of Psychiatry* 18 (1984), pp. 314–27.

———. "Meyerian Psychobiology, Personality Development, and the Role of Life Experiences." *American Journal of Psychiatry* 143 (September 1986), pp. 1077–87.

Salzman, Leon. *The Obsessive Personality.* New York: Science House, 1988.

"Schizotypal Personality." *The Harvard Medical School Mental Health Letter* 3 (May 1987), pp. 1–3.

Shader, Richard I., Edward L. Scharfman, and Daniel A. Dryfuss. "A Biological Model for Selected Personality Disorders." In *Psychiatry,* vol. 1. *See* Cavenar, ed.

Shaffer, J. W., et al. "Clustering of Personality Traits in Youth and the Subsequent Development of Cancer Among Physicians." *Journal of Behavioral Medicine* 10 (1987), pp. 441–47.

Shainess, Natalie. "Masochism—Or Self-Defeating Personality?" *Journal of Personality Disorders* 1 (Summer 1987), pp. 174–77.

Shapiro, David. *Neurotic Styles.* New York: Basic Books, 1965.

Siever, Larry J. "A Delicate Balance: Understanding the Biochemistry of Mental Illness." *The Mount Sinai Review* 7 (Spring 1988), p. 9.

———. "The Relationship Between Impulsivity and Compulsivity." In *Impulsivity and Compulsivity. See* Oldham, Hollander, and Skodol, eds.

Siever, Larry J., and Kenneth L. Davis. "A Psychobiological Perspective on the Personality Disorders." *American Journal of Psychiatry* 148:12 (December 1991), pp. 1647–58.

Siever, Larry J., Thomas R. Insel, and Thomas W. Uhde. "Biogenetic Factors in Personality." In *Current Perspectives on Personality Disorders. See* Frosch, ed.

Siever, Larry J., Howard Klar, and Emil Coccaro. "Psychobiologic Substrates of Personality." In *Biologic Response Styles: Clinical Implications. See* Klar and Siever, eds.

Siever, Larry J., Bonnie J. Steinberg, Robert L. Trestman, Joanne Intrator. "Biological Markers in Personality Disorders." In *Review of Psychiatry,* vol. 13. *See* Oldham and Riba, eds.

Simons, Richard C. "Self-Defeating and Sadistic Personality Disorders: Needed Additions to the Diagnostic Nomenclature." *Journal of Personality Disorders* 1 (Summer 1987), pp. 161–67.

Skodol, Andrew E., and John M. Oldham. "Differential Diagnosis of the Impulsive/Compulsive Spectrum of Disorders." Presented at the fourth annual New York State Office of Mental Health Research Conference, Albany, New York, 1991.

———. "Assessment and Diagnosis of Borderline Personality Disorder: Problems, Challenges, and Significance." In Special Section on Borderline Personality Disorder (J. M. Oldham, Guest Editor), *Hospital and Community Psychiatry* 42 (1991), pp. 1021–28.

———. "Personality Disorders and Mood Disorders." Presented at the annual meeting of the American Psychiatric Association, Washington, D.C., 1992.

———. "Comorbidity of DSM-III-R Anxiety Disorders and Personality Disorders." Presented in a symposium at the Third International Congress on the Disorders of Personality, Cambridge, Massachusetts, 1993.

Skodol, Andrew E., John M. Oldham, Steven E. Hyler, H. D. Kellerman, N. Doidge, and M. Davies. "Comorbidity of DSM-III-R Eating Disorders and Personality Disorders." *International Journal of Eating Disorders* 14 (1993), pp. 403–16.

Stern, Daniel N. *The Interpersonal World of the Infant.* New York: Basic Books, 1985.

Stone, Michael H. *Abnormalities of Personality*. New York: W. W. Norton, 1993, p. 268.

————. "Borderline Personality Disorder." In *Psychiatry,* vol. 1. *See* Cavenar, ed.

Suomi, Stephen J. "Response Styles in Monkeys: Experiential Effects." In *Biologic Response Styles: Clinical Implications. See* Klar and Siever, eds.

Thomas, Alexander, and Stella Chess. *Temperament and Development*. New York: Brunner/Mazel, 1977.

————. "Genesis and Evolution of Behavioral Disorders: From Infancy to Early Adult Life." *American Journal of Psychiatry* 141 (January 1984), p. 139.

Turecki, Stanley, and Leslie Tonner. *The Difficult Child*. New York: Bantam, 1985, 1989.

Turner, S. M., D. C. Beidel, J. W. Borden, et al. "Social Phobia, Axis I and II Correlates." *Journal of Abnormal Psychology* 100 (1991), pp. 102–6.

Tyrer, Peter, and George Stein, eds. *Personality Disorder Reviewed* (London: Gaskell, 1993).

Virkkunen, M., A. Nuutila, et al. "Cerebrospinal Fluid Monoamine Metabolite Levels in Male Arsonists." *Archives of General Psychiatry* 44 (March 1987), pp. 241–47.

Waldinger, Robert J. "Intensive Psychodynamic Therapy with Borderline Patients: An Overview." *American Journal of Psychiatry* 144 (March 1987), pp. 267–74.

Walker, Lenore E. A. "Inadequacies of the Masochistic Personality Disorder Diagnosis for Women." *Journal of Personality Disorders* 1 (Summer 1987), pp. 183–389.

Widiger, Thomas. "Deletion of Self-Defeating and Sadistic Personality Disorder Diagnoses." In *The DSM-IV Personality Disorders. See* Livesley, ed.

Winokur, George, and Paula Clayton, eds. *The Medical Basis of Psychiatry*. Philadelphia: Saunders, 1986.

Index

About the Authors

JOHN M. OLDHAM, M.D., Professor and Associate Chairman of the Department of Psychiatry at Columbia University College of Physicians and Surgeons, is Director of the New York State Psychiatric Institute and Chief Medical Officer for the New York State Office of Mental Health. He is a contributing editor of the *Journal of Personality Disorders* and has written and edited numerous books and articles on personality disorders and their assessment. A training and supervising psychoanalyst at the Columbia Psychoanalytic Center for Training and Research, Dr. Oldham is also in private practice. Born in Oklahoma and raised in New Mexico and Texas, Dr. Oldham lives in Westchester County, New York. He and his wife, Karen, have two children, Madeleine and Michael.

LOIS B. MORRIS has written six books on mental health and behavior, including *The Good News About Depression* with Mark S. Gold, M.D. She writes the "Mood News" column for *Allure* magazine, and her articles and advice appear frequently in magazines and newspapers. Born and raised in the Chicago area, she lives on Shelter Island, New York.

Dr. Oldham and Ms. Morris have collaborated as well on *The Columbia University College of Physicians and Surgeons Complete Home Guide to Mental Health,* which was named one of the outstanding reference books of 1992 by the New York Public Library.